LYNNE DUNCKLEY

Multimedia Databases

An object-relational approach

Addison-Wesley

An imprint of **Pearson Education**

London • Boston • Indianapolis • New York • Mexico City • Toronto
Sydney • Tokyo • Singapore • Hong Kong • Cape Town • New Delhi
Madrid • Paris • Amsterdam • Munich • Milan • Stockholm

PEARSON EDUCATION LIMITED

Head Office:
Edinburgh Gate
Harlow CM20 2JE
Tel: +44 (0)1279 623623
Fax: +44 (0)1279 431059

London Office:
128 Long Acre
London WC2E 9AN
Tel: +44 (0)20 7447 2000
Fax: +44 (0)20 7447 2170
Website: www.it-minds.com
         www.awprofessional.com

———————————————————

First published in Great Britain in 2003

ISBN 0 201 78899 3

British Library Cataloguing in Publication Data
A CIP catalogue record for this book can be obtained from the British Library

Library of Congress Cataloging in Publication Data
Applied for.

10 9 8 7 6 5 4 3 2 1

Typeset by Mathematical Composition Setters Ltd, Salisbury, Wiltshire.
Printed and bound in the UK by Biddles Ltd of Guildford and King's Lynn.

The Publishers' policy is to use paper manufactured from sustainable forests.

This book is dedicated to

Mat and Chris

Contents

Preface

This book is a comprehensive introduction to multimedia databases. It provides a solid understanding of multimedia data and database technology and explains why advances in both have come together to create the field of multimedia databases. The book as a whole is intended primarily as a textbook for those studying or professionally interested in the subject and working in either the multimedia or database areas. It will also be of interest to those learning about computing within a degree program. Readers may well come from a background of multimedia or databases and therefore a brief introduction to relational, object-oriented and object-relational databases is included at appropriate points in the text and in the appendices. Since SQL3 is a key development in the design and management of multimedia databases, this is covered in detail and illustrated with many examples.

The topic, multimedia databases, itself is interesting and poses a number of challenges for the database developer. The reader faces challenges that arise from integrating knowledge from a number of different fields such as multimedia, networks and communication systems, HCI and human sensory systems as well as database concepts. One of the motivations for writing this book came from the experience of needing to refer to numerous textbooks from different disciplines when developing multimedia databases.

Who Should Read this Book?

The primary audience for this book is those whose working life will be increasingly influenced by a need to know more about multimedia databases. This would include those working in web technology and e-commerce where many of the issues are now recognized to be database problems. Others may be involved in the growth of applications in this field, for example, media on demand, surveillance systems, GIS and medicine. Furthermore, it is likely that in the future most traditional commercial database systems will incorporate multimedia data types. For example, personnel systems will include images of employees, SOP systems will have images of products and videos of usage. Visualizations are also being incorporated into decision support systems derived from databases. Multimedia data include text so that the management of large document collections are also within the scope of this book.

This book could also be of interest and benefit to students of computing and information systems in the later stages of their degree programs. Since interest in multimedia is growing there are also students, now studying degree programs for multimedia information systems, who would find the text useful. This audience may have a good knowledge of relational databases but need an introduction to additional features such as large binary objects, methods and user-defined types available in SQL3. The object-relational approach can exploit features of PL/SQL (procedural SQL) to provide methods for the new multimedia object types.

The book can be followed within a second- or third-level course in advanced database technologies. It also includes examples and exercises to illustrate the principles and promote understanding. SQL code can be used in practical sessions and is supplied on the accompanying CDROM and the website, www.multimediadatabases.co.uk. The teaching approach is a blend of theory and practice. Wherever possible readers should be encouraged to try the examples within an appropriate database that supports multimedia data types. There are also examples of websites to illustrate techniques and applications. Two case studies are included in the text and there are further examples on the CDROM. SQL code is provided to implement simple multimedia databases for image, text and video data.

The production of multimedia systems themselves is not covered. For example, only the database aspects of development of application areas such as multimedia learning systems is mentioned. Details of the generation of the media by scanning or photographic systems are not included but the significance of different compression standards is discussed.

Multimedia databases are the result of the conjunction of developments in a number of areas. Advances in data capture and compression have allowed vast collections of multimedia data to be stored, while SQL3 provides a language that deals with large binary objects that can be used to store it. Object-oriented and object relational database design gives an insight into the effective realization of databases for this kind of data but up to now the expertise in this area has tended to rest in isolated research enclaves rather than to be generally available to database practitioners.

There had been a rapid development of the technology in databases and multimedia. In terms of databases the introduction of SQL3 in 1999 has corresponded with a number of vendors implementing features to store and manipulate large binary objects within object-relational databases. The development of technologies that provide content-based retrieval of media objects is highly significant. Early multimedia databases tended to be designed using object-oriented methods that were often application dependent and did not provide generic capabilities especially in terms of query languages.

How to Read this Book

The book overall is intended to be read in sequence but since readers may come from a background of either multimedia or databases they may skip appropriate sections in the earlier chapters. For example, readers with a background in multimedia will be familiar with much of the material in Chapter 2, while those from a database background will be familiar with much of Chapter 1 and the early sections of Chapter 4. There are separate chapters (10, 11, 12) dealing with database systems about text, image and real-time media (audio and video). These contain specialized information which the reader may chose to 'read over lightly' if it is an area that is not relevant to their interests. For example, Chapter 11 on image databases contains information derived from the disciplines of image processing and computer vision that is quite technical.

In the main text where examples of SQL statements are included SQL keywords are shown in upper case, although Oracle ignores upper and lower case except when testing for conditions involving character strings (such as department = 'Accounts'). Table, column and object names are generally in lower case, except where the column name is made up of several words such as numberOfFrames.

What is Included in the CD-ROM?

There is an accompanying CD-ROM on which is stored a series of exercises and solutions that relate to the various chapters and exercises of the book. The solutions to the exercises included consist of SQL and PL/SQL code for Oracle, MySQL and DB2 implementations of examples of multimedia databases. In addition, there are a number of case studies that provide additional practice in the implementation of MMDBMS.

The purpose of the CD-ROM is to provide examples that you can use to interact directly with the database management system. The CD-ROM is organized in chapters which contain the Oracle SQL*PLUS code referred to in the book text. There are separate exercise files for DB2 and MySQL.

The exercises usually involve the preparation and execution of SQL statements. The files contain a copy of most of the statements from the text in the book. You can simply type in the statements into an SQL editor or select and paste the SQL text. In the chapters some of the SQL statements are named. For example in Chapter 4

```
CREATE TABLE department
(department_number CHAR(4) CONSTRAINT prim_dept PRIMARY KEY,
  department_name       VARCHAR2(10 )
                                            prim_dept
```

The same name prim_dept is used in the corresponding exercise files so that you can locate the name of any particular query using a find without having to scroll through the whole text.

What Software is Used in this Book?

Most of the SQL examples used in the book are based on Oracle, versions *8i* and *9i*. The Oracle Corporation appears currently to be producing new versions and upgrades of their products at a rapid rate. However, for the majority of this book you do not need to worry about which version of Oracle you are using. Where these differ in terms of multimedia data this is made clear in the text. In addition, there are examples for DB2, mySQL and XML. In the case of DB2 this is a database management system with significant advantages and capabilities in the retrieval of multimedia data. However, since this text is also focused on SQL3 the procedural code examples are mainly written in Oracle's PL/SQL as this is closer to the SQL standard and development with DB2 tends to involve using a host language.

Acknowledgments

This book would not have been possible without the contribution of many people who were involved directly or indirectly in the production of the book.

First, I would like to thank my friend Osei Adjei for very thoroughly reviewing large sections of the manuscript, especially Chapters 5 and 12. Second, I benefited enormously from comments and discussions over several years with my former colleague Iain McClaren and the members of the Open University database team, Mike Newton, Hugh Robinson, Kevin Waugh, Steven Self and, of course, Hugh Darwen.

I would also like to thank Judith Sewell for patiently reviewing early drafts and raising many issues even though she would not consider herself a "database person".

I obtained considerable technical support with the various Oracle installations I used for the development of the practical exercises from my colleagues John Mullins and Frank Hines at the IT Center, Thames Valley University.

I should also like to thank and acknowledge Alex Murray, the Web Master at Berry Brothers & Rudd (www.bbr.com) for providing information and support in the development of the Fine Wine Shop case study and for providing such an interesting website.

The ideas for the protozoa database case study came from Dr David Roberts of the Natural History Museum and I would like to thank and acknowledge his help and support with the case study and for introducing me to the fascinating world of protozoa.

Finally, I am grateful to everyone at Addison-Wesley, especially Viki Williams my editor, and Tessa Fincham for all their encouragement and work.

chapter 1

Introduction to Multimedia Databases

Chapter aims

This chapter gives an introduction to a variety of issues relevant to the development and implementation of multimedia database systems. Through a study of this chapter the reader will develop a broad overview of the role of multimedia data within database development and some related application areas and should then be able to:

- understand why multimedia databases are being developed;
- appreciate database concepts in terms of multimedia;
- describe examples of multimedia data and the related metadata;
- understand the technological background;
- understand the problems of using context-based concepts.

1.1 Introduction

The growth in the importance of multimedia databases is the result of changes in technology and related changes in the social environment, particularly the way information is presented and used. In the past humans represented information through documents that combined the use of text and graphics to convey meaning. In the modern era this was largely replaced by the dominance of text and the consequent requirement for high literacy skills within the population. However, the human brain is much more efficient at processing and interpreting visual and audio information. In this century the nature of documents and information is changing. The last century witnessed unparalleled growth in the number, availability and importance of images in all walks of life. People now expect documents to incorporate not only graphics and text but possibly for web-based documents, sound and video images as well. These expanding user expectations and advances in technological capabilities are driving the development of multimedia databases. Facilities to catalog and index image data automatically, together with efficient storage and delivery mechanisms, have made multimedia database management systems (MMDBMSs) a practical possibility. Techniques that have been developed for text and image media are being extended for video and sound. However, developers of these databases claim that they are difficult and complex to develop because they are quite different from traditional databases, especially in terms of the data types, manipulation, storage and delivery. The nature and size of multimedia data and the high capacity required for the delivery of multimedia data streams cause problems that require different solutions.

In this book we will look at the multimedia data itself and then at the consequences this has for design and development of the databases that will contain this kind of data. In terms of this book multimedia data refers to a range of different types of media from text, usually in the form of documents, image, audio or video. The term multimedia database implies the ability to manage, store and retrieve all these different media. However, we will emphasize that beyond an understanding of the technical problems there is a need for a clear understanding of this kind of information and how this understanding is to be used effectively to manage the information and the development process. Whereas traditional database systems provide for data independence and multiuser support, multimedia databases do not provide the appropriate concepts and service for integrated modeling, management and interactive presentation of multimedia data in the same way. In dealing with multimedia information we are dealing with digital data representations and how these can be stored and manipulated to provide many more functions (such as rotation) than would be available in traditional forms of data. Most progress has been achieved, as we shall see later, in terms of text data, and therefore many of our practical examples will involve text.

1.1.1　The Need for Multimedia Databases

Early applications of MMDBMSs tended to use multimedia for presentational requirements only. For example, an employee database might include an image of each employee. A sales order processing system could include an online catalog that included a picture of the products offered. These systems could be implemented relatively simply by storing the image files externally to the database and storing a file reference in the database. The image would then be retrieved by an application process which referenced it through a traditional database record. However, this external data could not be manipulated by the DBMS. Multimedia applications are evolving because people want to exploit multimedia data in a "natural" way, interrogating, retrieving and manipulating the data. Complex applications are developing such as entertainment services (e.g. video on demand), multimedia sales for houses, goods and services, groupware, telepresence, surveillance and telemedicine. An essential requirement for these advanced multimedia databases is to search and manipulate the content of pictures, sound and video as easily as text data to retrieve the data needed. Later in this chapter we look at multimedia query styles and introduce some examples of multimedia applications.

1.2 What is Essential about Database Systems?

Before we look at multimedia databases, it is important to review what constitutes a database and what capabilities traditional databases should support. There are a number of competing views of what a database is. For example, it can be regarded as merely an electronic filing system for keeping records. Users of a database system expect to be able to manipulate the data to obtain useful output. This requires the ability to:

- insert new data;
- retrieve and change existing data;
- delete data.

Application programs use the database to retrieve and display the data required by the user. In terms of current commercial database systems we are normally talking about relational databases. Early database systems were based on different data models. The hierarchical model viewed the data and its connections like an upside-down tree, while the network model viewed the data as a graph. Both these models encouraged the user to visualize the data in the way it was stored. These pre-relational systems were data dependent. The way the database was physically represented in secondary storage and accessed was dictated by the application and knowledge of the physical representation and access techniques had to be built into the application code. To take an example, if two applications have product files including a data element called *cost*, in application A this is held as a binary number and in application B as a decimal. The database systems should be able to integrate the two data files by doing all the necessary conversions. Similarly, if changes are made to physical storage systems they should not require any changes to the application programs supported by the database systems. This is the objective of data independence.

In a relational database the data is presented to the user in tables. Every row represents the data stored about one entity (thing that exists in the real world). Every column represents a different property of the set of entities that the table holds information about. For example, a table holding product data could have columns representing part number, description, cost and quantity available. Every column is associated with a data type, so that all the data elements in the same column have the same data type, such as numbers, dates and characters. In Figure 1.1 we can see how the **part** table is set out in rows and columns.

A relation is a mathematical concept which is very useful as it represents a set of entities that all have the same attributes or properties. Entities are things that exist in the real world such as people, places and products that have attributes. A person would have an attribute **address** and a product a **cost** etc. A table in a database corresponds to a relation. Each attribute corresponds to a column in the relational table. The rows across the relation that hold the actual data are called tuples. The structure of the table is made up of columns of data types such as character, numeric, date and the actual values of those types (e.g. "Skirt", 15.0). These actual values are called occurrences. For each type there will be many occurrences which will change from time to time. The **part** table, in Figure 1.1, has the structure:

Column	Data type	Occurrence
partno	Character	101
descrip	Character	Skirt
cost	Decimal	15.00
qty	Integer	100

In Chapter 6 we will look at the relational model in much greater detail and discuss the way it has been developed to support an object-relational approach by utilizing large binary objects to include multimedia data.

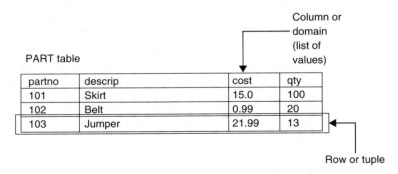

Figure 1.1 **part** table

A database system consists of four major components – data, hardware, software and users. Multimedia database systems require additional support for every one of these components. For example, database designers do not usually take into account the human information processing system and its requirements, but in the case of multimedia database systems the capacity and functions of the human sensory system can influence design decisions.

Let us look at each of these components in turn.

Data in a database is expected to be integrated. This means we would expect data to be stored in a way that minimized duplication and redundancy. Data should be able to be shared by every user, even though this may be for different purposes so that different types of users see different views of the data. It is expected that any given user would only see a small proportion of the database and consequently the database will be perceived differently by different users. As database systems have become more powerful huge amounts of data have been stored so that ways of summarizing and aggregating data to give an overview have become important features for some users. In addition, many users should be able to access the same data at the same time. When this happens it is known as a concurrent process and this adds to the difficulty of managing the database.

In a traditional database design the logical and physical aspects of the system are kept separate. The logical design is not concerned for example with the way the data is stored because these are considered to be "peculiar" to each database system. However, in the case of multimedia data, as we shall see later, we cannot entirely ignore the effect of different storage options on the design.

Database users include application developers, administrators and end-users. End-users may interact with the system through an application or through a query language processor. The query language should provide facilities such as to insert and to delete data as well as query it. In a relational database the data is normally retrieved using the SQL database query language which is covered in detail in Chapter 4.

The software system is essentially the database management system. Its responsibility is to look after the data. We expect certain important characteristics of data within a database:

- Data is persistent because once the data has been accepted into the database it can only be removed by some explicit operation of the database system.
- The data will be consistent with a data model in order to be accepted by the database system.

A data model is essential for organizing the data within a database. It is an abstract, logical definition of objects and operations that allows us to model the structure and behavior of the data. An implementation is a physical realization of the data model on a real machine. In principle there should be a clear distinction between the logical data model and the physical implementation. However, in practice even with traditional database systems this is often not the case. In multimedia database systems this distinction can be even more difficult to maintain.

To summarize, we would expect that any system claiming to be a database would have certain properties. The database approach should include the following concepts:

- Data can be shared.
- Redundancy can be reduced because data is integrated and redundancy controlled.
- Inconsistency can be avoided, i.e. not providing users with incorrect or contradictory data.
- Integrity is maintained by the use of integrity constraints – business rules that can be applied whenever any update is performed on the database.
- When a permanent change is made to a database it is called a transaction. It is a logical unit of work, typically involving several operations on the database.

EXERCISE 1.1

Give a brief explanation of the following terms:

(a) logical data independence;

(b) data model;

(c) tuple;

(d) domain;

(e) occurrence;

(f) transaction.

1.3 What is Different about Multimedia Data?

Conceptually it should be possible to treat multimedia data in the same way as data based on the data types (e.g. numbers, dates and characters) that we meet in traditional databases. For example, text data consists of groups of characters that obey certain syntactic rules, so that text could be used in structured processing. However, there are three challenges that arise from multimedia data that do not occur with other data types.

The first challenge is size. To get an idea of the size of media data objects, consider that the storage of a single good quality colored image could require 6 Mb. A video object which consists of a sequence of such images (called frames) will be very large. With 30 frames per second, a five-minute video clip would require 54 Gb. A typical sequence of audio will occupy 8 Kb for each second. Text media can range in size from a single page to a book with hundreds of pages. Data size will affect the storage, retrieval and transmission of multimedia. Therefore techniques that reduce the size of multimedia data without impacting on the information within the data are crucial.

The second challenge is time. Time cannot run backwards. The frames of the video must run in the correct sequence and at an acceptable rate, otherwise it becomes meaningless. The same is true of audio media, and therefore audio and video are regarded as continuous periodic media. This relationship with time will have significance for the way the media objects are stored, retrieved, transmitted and synchronized together. This effect of time is often referred to as the real-time nature of multimedia and we shall use this term frequently in the following chapters. A book does not communicate in real time because the reader cannot ask questions to which the author can respond immediately. A conversation is real time. It is this quality of multimedia involving the interaction of related components that creates a real-time dimension to the information conveyed, for example a video clip of an interview would include audio and image data that must be synchronized together. Real-time effects will be noticeable when we manipulate the data in the database.

The third challenge is that the semantic nature of multimedia is much more complex than for traditional data types. It makes it difficult to identify components within the media that could be used for retrieval or transaction processing. An apparently simple solution would be to add a description in words of the content of the image. It is an old adage that a picture tells a thousand words. However, when we want to find a way to retrieve a specific image we find that a picture often means different things to different people. For example, in Figure 1.2 we have an image of the product as well as a description in text. The context is important for interpreting the meaning of an image so that in database terms the application domain is even more significant than for traditional databases. In order to manage the semantic nature of the media, interpretations may need to be made based on certain features of the multimedia data and stored as metadata. Metadata is any data that is required to interpret other data as meaningful information and it is an extremely important aspect of multimedia databases since it is used for retrieving and manipulating the data. It can be based on the interpretation of information held within the media or, alternatively, it can be based on

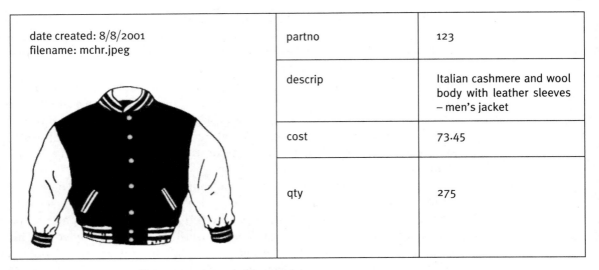

date created: 8/8/2001 filename: mchr.jpeg	partno	123
	descrip	Italian cashmere and wool body with leather sleeves – men's jacket
	cost	73.45
	qty	275

Figure 1.2   Image with metadata

the interpretation of multiple media and their relationships. In the case of multimedia, metadata deals with the content, structure and semantics of the data.

In Figure 1.2 we can see an image of a "men's jacket", but it would be very difficult to retrieve this particular image from a database unless we had some of the data alongside that identified it or the image itself. Note that some of the data refers to the product and some, like the date, is relevant only to the image. Most of the information in Figure 1.2 could be used as metadata for the image. The generation of metadata can be so laborious that it is necessary to use automatic or semi-automatic methods. One problem is that automatically generating metadata is difficult and the methods used often result in metadata that contains too little information to be useful while manually generated metadata is too costly to create and maintain for the large numbers of records in a database. We will find the topic of metadata will keep cropping up throughout this book because when we consider the storage of multimedia we will need to know how the metadata is stored. When we deal with retrieval it will also involve metadata.

Metadata generation is an important aspect of multimedia databases because directly querying the data can be extremely difficult. The traditional view of metadata is that it describes the structure of the database, the tables, indexes etc. However, in the case of MMDBMS metadata is used as well to describe individual occurrences. This means that every row in the body of a table could have metadata associated with it. Metadata can take the form of multimedia indexes and linguistic annotation added for specific attributes. The objective is to allow the media to be queried and manipulated by querying the metadata first and then retrieving the actual result set. This focuses some of the problems of MMDBMS on the structuring, representation, management and generation of metadata.

We could retrieve all the data about this product with a simple SQL query:

```
SELECT     partno, descrip, cost, qty
FROM       part
WHERE      descrip LIKE('%wool%')
```

The query would result in the details of the product in Figure 1.1 provided that the description included the character string "wool". The use of "%" enables any occurrence of wool in the **descrip** column of the relational table **part** to be matched and retrieved. This would only be effective if the user and the database developer used the same terms to describe the product.

To summarize, we have seen some of the problems related to the size of multimedia data that would arise in any large-scale database. There is a need to capture a large amount of information about the actual content of the data and the semantics of the application domain. Although text and image are regarded as time independent the sequence of letters, words and paragraphs within a text object is important for conveying information. In the same way the relative arrangement of features within an image is important for the meaning and coherence of the image. Another complication is that, in addition to operations traditionally required for databases, such as insert, update and delete, there will be a need for operations relating to the individual media. These would include, for video, operations such as play, pause, fast forward, reverse. Zoom and rotate are examples of operations for images.

1.3.1   How Will Users Query Multimedia Data?

Providing users with effective and, in terms of performance, efficient query languages is a critical requirement for multimedia databases. We will need to consider how a query is posed to an MMDBMS and then how the data is retrieved and subsequently presented. When relational databases were first proposed a number of different query languages were developed before SQL became the international standard. However, another early database language was based on "query by example", QBE. The idea was that, instead of using a nested syntax such as SQL, the user would be presented with a relational template that could be completed with sample elements to give examples of the tuples to be retrieved. An example of the style is shown in

Actress	Year	Film Title	Photograph
Natalie Portmann		P__	

Figure 1.3 QBE template for a database about films

Figure 1.3 for a request for films with a title beginning with "P", starring Natalie Portmann.

Often in a multimedia query, a text description of an image or audio clip could be provided. In querying multimedia databases the simple QBE style must be expanded, since the sample elements provided in the query may include image, video clip or audio. An alternative style would be to provide an image as an example or to sketch an image. For example, the user would sketch a sunflower as a basic outline (circular shape) and request images of paintings like it.

The solution to the problems of query design lies with an analysis of user's needs – such as why users seek images and what use is made of them. Evidence suggests that users need images to illustrate text and information reports particularly to convey information or emotions that are difficult to communicate in words. Other reasons are the need to record very detailed data for later analysis. The interrogation of multimedia data raises both opportunities and challenges not present in traditional database systems. For example, using visual information in queries results in different ways of constructing the queries and searching the data, as illustrated in Figure 1.4. This presents four combinations of different query and search modes that could be adopted by a multimedia retrieval system. For example, presenting a query in a linguistic mode such as "Find images of actresses in the film called *Phantom Menace*" but searching the database using visual attributes (visual mode). In Chapters 5 and 11 we will look in detail at the way visual

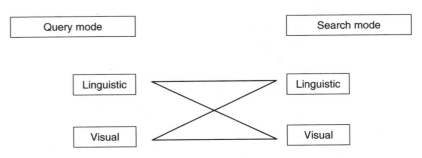

Figure 1.4 Query and search modes for multimedia databases

attributes can be used to search and index multimedia data. A visual attribute of an image is a numerical or logical attribute such as mean intensity or coarseness of texture.

The four combinations of modes can be described as follows.

Linguistic–linguistic (LL) mode operates on the basis of forming a query in linguistic terms as in standard query languages and then searching metadata which has been stored in the form of text in order to locate and retrieve the required multimedia information. However, it is clear that the attempt to solve all queries by matching a linguistic form against linguistic identifiers in the form of titles, keywords and captions offers limited retrieval possibilities.

Visual–visual (VV) mode is generally known as retrieval by content – for example the query is posed in the form of a sketch the user draws, with the underlying assumption – "I want something like this". One way to achieve this is to provide the user with a browser based on a small selection of images from the database to use as examples in a QBE style. These small images are referred to as polyphotos, icon browsers, index images or thumbnails. A more advanced approach would use a visual thesaurus. An example would be a plant leaf identification database. This is where the user manipulates a basic leaf shape with respect to a number of attributes, building up a visual match with a specimen leaf. Matching images are then returned in rank order of the attributes. For example, NASA developed one of the first visual thesauri to work alongside a text thesaurus for the space domain. Images from the thesaurus could be substituted for textual descriptions of the images in a retrieval system. QBIC, which was developed by IBM, is one example of a commercial VV system we will meet in the practical exercises and consider in theory later. However, most progress in using the VV approach has been in very specific application areas, e.g. facial recognition. In this case neural nets have been trained to learn facial feature extraction. Another example is databases of engineering drawings where edge detection software has been effective. Little has been achieved in generic content-based retrieval but we will review this in more detail in Chapter 11.

Visual–linguistic (VL) mode provides example images which are then retrieved by linguistic metadata. In this case images are specified by sets of pixels with specific values for color, morphological (shape) and geometric relations but indexed by name/title etc. Queries use a text thesaurus. The image is included in an QBE-style query which places limitations on the variety of information needs that can be expressed by the user.

In the linguistic–visual (LV) approach the images are indexed by visual attributes and possibly supplemented by a visual thesaurus. However, the user expresses the query in linguistic form using a standard query language.

Both the VL and LV modes involve the issue of how to create an index by mapping ideas about a subject expressed in different media. The whole topic of indexing using visual attributes is very complex and is considered in greater detail in Chapters 5 and 11.

EXERCISE 1.2

1. Use the website with URL www.hermitagemuseum.org. This is the site of the famous Imperial Museum in St Petersburg, Russia.

2. Use the Advance Search option in English.

3. Complete a query process to identify the name, artist and date of any paintings created in France between 1700 and 1900 on the topic of classical religion and mythology.

4. Identify the multimedia query–search mode used by this query based on Figure 1.4. Give reasons for your answer.

EXERCISE 1.3

1. Use both www.altavisata.com and www.gallery.yahoo.com to complete the following queries:
    (a) all images described by the terms "sunset" and "sea";
    (b) all images described by the terms "red" and "flower";
    (c) all video clips about "jazz";
    (d) all video clips about "battles".

2. How successful were the queries and how were the result sets presented to the user?

1.4   Multimedia Applications

Our society is becoming more visually conscious and many organizations currently maintain large collections of images and video objects that require flexible management in a database. To illustrate the application areas that are being developed Figure 1.5 provides various usage scenarios for a number of MMDBMS.

The different application areas that are emerging for MMDBMS have different requirements that effect the design of these systems. The key differences can be summarized as follows:

● The degree of integration of data required to support the application. Some applications can be supported with the minimum integration using external media files which are loosely coupled to the main database. This will only provide limited retrieval capabilities and no data manipulation.

● The pattern of usage – independent multiusers versus multiple simultaneous users, working together on multimedia data.

Entertainment systems – video on demand

The registered user of the system can request a video from the catalog. The videos may be available according to a previously advertised fixed schedule or available at any time, subject to a small delay. The user can select a video based on textual information of the cast, production team and a synopsis of the plot. Production information such as storyboards, screenplay and production notes can be included. Users can view the video contiguously or play randomly selected scenes. The video can be paused and resumed play as requested within constraints.

Public protection
In a number of countries police use visual information to identify people or to record the scenes of crime for evidence. These photographic records are a valuable archive. In the UK everyone arrested is photographed and their images are sampled and stored with their fingerprints. It is also planned to store sampled DNA profiles of suspects. Until a subject is convicted, access to photographic information is restricted. Interrogation of the database may be on the basis of automatic fingerprint recognition, DNA matching and face recognition. Video surveillance also needs to be linked to the facial recognition system.

Medical information systems
The medical and related health professionals use and store visual information in the form of X-ray, ultrasound and other scanned images for diagnosis and monitoring purposes. There are strict rules on confidentiality of such information. The images are kept with patients' records stored by unique identifier (e.g. national insurance number). Visual information, provided that it is rendered anonymous, may also be used for research purposes. Effective image processing such as edge detection and feature extraction can be important in assisting expert diagnosis of lesions, tumors and tracking their growth. Images may be the result of a single instrumental approach, e.g. X-ray, or the result of a combination of data from several different sources.

Figure 1.5 Multimedia applications usage scenarios

- The quality of the multimedia data and presentation – how much data loss can be tolerated by the users before the product becomes unusable.

We can summarize the complexity of the applications sketched in Figure 1.5 as follows.

The requirements of video-on-demand systems are relatively straight-forward, for example:

- This is a single media application.
- The user is not involved in capturing, editing or manipulating the media.
- Communication of the media data is unidirectional, for example only videos are retrieved and are then delivered unidirectionally to the client.
- Delivery may be simplified by scheduling requests and combining the delivery to several users at the same time.
- There is a high data volume that requires high performance storage and networking systems.
- There is a large number of users.
- Scalability is important.
- The users may accept some loss of quality.

For public protection information systems:

- the user is involved in capturing, editing or manipulating the media;
- bi-directional data flow;
- complex content modeling for complex correlated queries;
- diverse media – maps, images, audio, video;
- interactivity with media through simple matching queries.

For medical information systems:

- the user is involved in capturing, editing or manipulating the media;
- highest quality media data with little toleration of data loss;
- confidential security required;
- bi-directional data flow;
- complex content modeling for complex correlated queries;
- diverse media – maps, images, video;
- interactivity with media, could involve multiple simultaneous users in decision making.

The ultimate MMDBMS will have integrated media and will allow:

- arbitrary manipulation and presentation of multimedia data into compositions;

- the translation of media data into other forms.

However, as we shall see later, in terms of current systems these concepts are theoretical and idealistic. In practice MMDBMSs are more likely to be based on loosely coupled systems of media files that are external to a traditional database schema with correspondingly limited retrieval capabilities which are based not on the actual content but on the metadata descriptions of the content. However, things are changing and the technology is improving all the time.

EXERCISE 1.4

Consider the three application scenarios described in Figure 1.5. For each application evaluate the use that could be made of a visual query mode and give examples based on each scenario.

MULTIMEDIA CASE STUDY

At a number of points within the text, the theory will be illustrated with real-world examples or case studies. At this point we will just introduce the first case study application in detail without any attempt to identify requirements or specify solutions. This is an example where multimedia information, in the form of audio, image and text, is used to solve a commercial problem. In addition metadata plays a significant role.

Fine Wine Shop – Berry Bros & Rudd

The wine business was established in the early eighteenth century and has provided fine wines to customers since then. The objective of the company is to specialize in the buying and selling of the world's finest wines. As well as operating a number of retail shops selling wine and related products directly to its customers, the company offers a number of other services to its customers, both individual and corporate, including advice on selecting wines for laying down. The company provides secure temperature-controlled cellars for customers to store their wine if they choose not to store it in their own home. However, recently the company has embraced web technology enthusiastically in order to market its wines internationally and consequently is making extensive use of multimedia to attract and retain customers through its website.

Wines are priced from £4.00 to £4,000. A wine is from a region which may be a country like New Zealand or a region of a country like Bordeaux or in the case of port a group of geographically related regions. Wines are classified as red, white or rosé. The regions may be further subdivided into groups. For example, classic red Bordeaux wine is further divided into Médoc, Pomerol and St Emilion. Each of these has a set of well-known vineyards, usually referred to as chateaux, that supplies the wine. The company provides a brief note on the flavor and origin for many wines and this includes a recommendation of when the wine should be drunk. This information is provided to individual and corporate customers both through mailing paper-based catalogs and its website. In addition, the company offers a number of events to promote its wines through wine tastings, dinners and lectures.

The wines have a character such as "medium dry" and also the fine wines show information such as the origin of the vineyard and the blending of the grapes used. There may also be a description of their taste and bouquet. Most of the finest and most highly priced wine will come from a single vineyard. There is a database of producers. They are grouped by a mixture of regional styles or country, e.g. Champagne, Sherry or Argentina. For each producer there is a note about them – the family and the date they started producing; an image of a bottle showing the producer's label may be

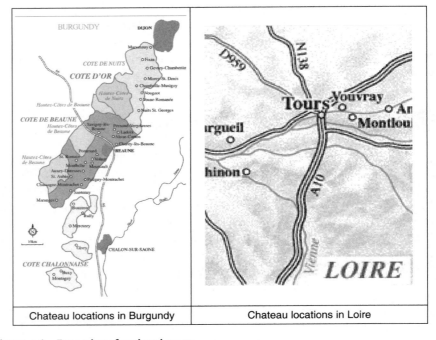

| Chateau locations in Burgundy | Chateau locations in Loire |

Figure 1.6   Examples of regional maps

included. Maps are provided showing the location of the vineyards for most regions as shown in Figure 1.6.

Wine is sold in bottles of a particular size and price. The sizes of bottles available are described as double magnums, magnums, liters, bottles, half-liters and half-bottles. Price is related to both the size of the bottle and the quality of the vintage. Discounts are available for buying cases of wine. The wine may have a vintage (given as the year) and there is also a table showing the quality of the vintage for the last 20 years. The quality of the wine is dependent on the type of wine and the vintage, e.g. 1970, 1982 and 1985 being particularly good years for red Bordeaux. Wines will be produced from grape varieties such as Chardonnay and will belong to a region such as Alsace or they may also be a blend of grape varieties. Information about the main grape varieties and examples of their images are also provided to customers as illustrated in Figure 1.7.

The website is used both for e-commerce and to promote interest and selection of wines. Some wines have a detailed description, a picture of a typical wine bottle and an audio file containing the correct pronunciation, particularly for French wines. The wines are stored in the company's ware-houses and can be delivered to customers anywhere in the UK or beyond. Alternatively, the customers can collect the wines from the shops. The wines are listed in the wine list which is available online. The online wine shop uses multimedia to create a similar ambience to the actual shops. For example, there is a list of recipes, grouped as type of food, each with a number of suggestions for wine to drink with different dishes. Video presentations are also provided to show the customer the shops and cellar facilities.

The wines are sold and delivered internationally. The price list quotes the bottle price (as illustrated in Table 1.1) but this will be subject to local

| Chardonnay | Zinfandel | Semillon |

Figure 1.7 Examples of grape varieties

Table 1.1   Examples from the wine list

Region	Wine	Vintage	Basic price (£)
Alsace	Gewurztraminer	1999	10.95
Australia	Goona Warra Pinot Noir	2000	11.45
Bordeaux	Ch. Des Antonins	1996	5.95
Beaujolais	Morgon	1999	6.95
Burgundy	Nuits St George	1997	26.45
Champagne	Theophile Roederer		18.75
Hungary	Tokaji Aszu		13.95
Germany	Erdener Treppchen	1997	10.95
Italy	Villa Geggiano Chianti	1997	8.95
New Zealand	Hawkesbridge Sauvignon	2001	7.95
North America	Peachy Canyon	1996	19.95
Rhône	Chateauneuf-du-Pape	1999	25.00
South Africa	Waterford Chardonnay	2000	9.95
South America	Errazuriz Wild Ferment	1999	9.95
Spain	Lagar de Cervera	2000	9.95
Vintage port	Smith Woodhouse	1994	30.00

taxes depending on the country where the wine is sold. Some wines are sold at a discount and a discount may be available on certain orders. Orders of over a threshold value are delivered free; otherwise there is a delivery charge.

Customers can search the wine information in a variety of ways to locate text, image, audio and video data. In later chapters of the book we will look at the way in which a multimedia database could be developed and used to provide the wine shop's requirements.

EXERCISE 1.5

(a) Describe the three challenges in dealing with multimedia data.

(b) Explain why there are four query search modes for multimedia databases.

1.5   What is in the Rest of the Book?

This book is concerned with the development and design of MMDBMS, the storage and transfer of multimedia data over distances and the organization of the data to meet various user needs. The text begins by looking at the nature of multimedia data and considers why it creates problems for database design. Later chapters look at the delivery, storage and consequent architecture of MMDBMS. It considers the limits on the rate at which multimedia data can be transferred efficiently, the issues of data loss and quality of service and the impact and unavoidability of errors. The increasing complexity of data processing power needs to be balanced against the cost of the extra processing power and the use of more powerful equipment. For example, in Chapter 5 the techniques being developed to query and manipulate multimedia data are introduced, particularly content-based searching and indexing. Chapter 6 looks briefly at design approaches to MMDBMS in the context of object-oriented and object-relational design.

Having completed this chapter you should be able to:

1. describe the challenges multimedia data pose to the development of databases;
2. describe why MMDBMS are being developed;
3. describe a range of applications and their complexity;
4. understand the different paradigms used to query multimedia data.

To design, implement and develop a multimedia database involves the integration of skills and knowledge based in many different disciplines such as database design, image processing, information retrieval, computer vision, human–computer interaction and multimedia networking. Indeed one of the motivations for writing the book was the experience of needing to refer to many different texts when faced with developing a MMDBMS. In order to restrain the size of the book to something manageable, material has had to be selected from these disciplines and the reader may feel that certain aspects of MMDBMS have not been covered. For example, there is little in the book about the design of the user interface but a great deal about the problems of data retrieval and query processing. This omission is not because user interfaces and multimedia devices are not important topics but because they have been covered in detail elsewhere.

The perspective taken has been based on trying to understand the challenges and the technology available both commercially and in research institutions. The material selected focuses on the diagnostic issues of MMDBMS rather than looking at the treatment level of how to deal with an already ailing database system. It poses the question how can we achieve the correct combinations of technology for a given application and what more must be done to achieve generic multimedia database systems. With this aim the contents of the individual chapters often include a description of the theory combined with a number of simple SQL examples of how to create and interrogate database objects.

Certain style conventions have been used throughout the book. For clarity all SQL keywords are in upper case (although this does not make any difference to the DBMS). The names of tables, columns, constraints, objects and procedure variables are all in lower case. Many of the SQL examples are accompanied with a name in bold in the right margin. These statements are stored with the demonstration tables and procedures on the electronic CD.

When reference is made to tables and other database objects in the text these are highlighted in bold.

SOLUTIONS TO EXERCISES

Exercise 1.1

All the definitions are in the Glossary.

Exercise 1.2

3. Three paintings should result – by Francoise Bucher (1740), Jean-Jaques Lagrenee (1795) and Narisse Diaz (1857).

4. This is a VV paradigm based on QBE. The results were presented with text and thumbnail images (polyphotos).

Exercise 1.3

These two search engines use different MMDBMS products to complete the search. You will find that some of the queries are unsuccessful. This could be because the database did not contain any matching images but also because the retrieval systems are inadequate. You may find by exploring the database further which of these is the case.

The result sets of images are presented using thumbnail images.

The video result sets are presented through a text and image synopsis giving the user the opportunity to view the whole clip.

Exercise 1.4

- *Video on demand.* Use of visual queries is limited. Users are unlikely to be able to submit a video clip. It is possible users could provide an image of an artist and then request a list of films including that artist.

- *Public protection.* Visual queries could be extensively used such as a user submitting a fingerprint image or a photograph and requesting video records of the suspect.

- *Medical information system.* Visual queries could be extensively used such as a user submitting an X-ray, magnetic resonance image or computerized tomography scanned image for comparison and diagnosis. Video queries are limited but could include video records of operations, patient interviews etc.

Exercise 1.5

(a) The three challenges are:
   - the gigantic size of media data
   - the semantic nature
   - the real-time nature

(b) Multimedia data could include text, image, video, audio or any combination of these. There are two query modes based on either linguistic queries or visual queries. We have used the general term visual to describe the presentation of queries for image, video and audio that involve a visualization of non-linguistic requirements. Thus visual queries range from a sketch of a picture, a musical theme to a video clip. There are also two search modes based on their linguistic or visual terms.

Recommended Reading

Connolly, T., Begg, C., Strachan, A. (1997) *Database Systems*, 2nd edition, Addison-Wesley, Reading, MA.

Date, C. J. (2000) *An Introduction to Database Systems*, 7th edition, Addison-Wesley, Reading, MA.

chapter 2
Multimedia Data

Chapter aims

This chapter reviews the nature and characteristics of the different kinds of multimedia data – text, audio, image and video. Through a study of this chapter the reader will develop a broad overview of the role of multimedia data within database development and should then be able to understand:

- the main features of multimedia data;
- the role played by techniques such as compression;
- the role and origin of metadata;
- the role of standards.

As we explained in Chapter 1, the special nature of media data causes problems for the design, implementation and maintenance of multimedia databases. These problems are the result of the sheer size, real-time character and semantic nature of the data. There is also the problem of timing and relationships between different media. In this chapter we will address all these problems and look forward to their possible solutions. For example, the way metadata is used in solving some of these problems is crucial. In the following sections we will look at the three problems in turn and introduce ways they could be addressed in databases.

2.1 Multimedia Data Size

The size of media data can make storage, processing, transmission and reception of this data very costly. It is easy to understand why this is the case with text data when the object may be a book but why does an image such as the Chardonnay grape shown in Figure 1.7 cause problems? One reason is the result of the stages multimedia data go through from their initial data capture until they are stored in the database and then transmitted to the user. Multimedia data almost always arises from the data capture of analog signals. In Chapter 1 we saw how applications involved scanning or sampling images such as photographs or X-rays. This means that the original information will be in the form of a wave signal, usually referred to as analog data, that must be converted into a digital form. For text and image media this data capture is often called scanning. We need to know, right at the beginning, how much of this raw signal data will be useful information for the end-user in particular application areas, otherwise we will be storing more data than we actually need. One approach is to do some statistics on the signal first to identify the amount of redundancy that it may be possible to remove, before the data is processed further. A source of redundancy might be repeated patterns in the data such as the repeated grape objects within the Chardonnay image.

However, this extra processing will cause some delay. In database applications where the data may not be needed immediately this may be manageable. When we reduce the size by removing the redundant data this may result in a loss of quality – small details may be lost. Therefore often what we are dealing with is a controlled loss of quality. The amount of redundancy that can be removed is very dependent on the task and the user. For a diagnostic medical application it may be essential to preserve all the details while an online shopping catalog can sacrifice details for speed of delivery.

2.1.1   Multimedia Data Acquisition

Figure 2.1 shows the stages involved in processing an analog media signal from its capture, usually as an analog signal, to its final display in digital form for the user. Note that Figure 2.1 does not show at what stage the data is stored in the database. This is because the stage at which the data is stored

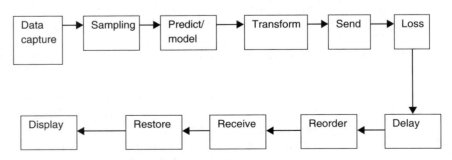

Figure 2.1   Stages in processing an analog signal to provide a digital display

in the database needs to be selected carefully so that the minimum quantity of data of the correct quality is stored.

In the first stage of Figure 2.1 multimedia data is captured. This can be achieved in many different ways, for example by exposing a photographic film. Data capture methods do not interest us but the way in which the data is subsequently processed is important. The second stage in Figure 2.1 involves sampling the analog signal and converting this to a digital value. The original data, whether it is a photograph, audio sample or video, needs to be sampled in this way so that the result is a digital representation of the original. When a continuous analog signal, such as music or image, is sampled it can be converted to a sequence of digital values, called samples. Figure 2.2 shows an analog signal's frequency changing with time. At regular time intervals the sampler records the frequency of the signal as a digital value. The accuracy of the digital representation depends on the rate at which the analog signal is sampled and the number of bits used to represent each sample. It has been shown theoretically (by Nyquist) that to accurately reproduce an analog signal of maximum frequency f with a digital signal the sampling rate should be equal to or greater than $2f$. Bandwidth is the difference between the minimum and maximum frequencies in the analog signal. Therefore the signal must be sampled at double the bandwidth.

The capabilities of the human visual and audio sensory systems, which are described in Chapter 3, need to be considered in deciding the requirements of multimedia systems. Often as in the case of voice we can reduce the rate of sampling without losing very much quality information. For example, for the human voice (frequency range 0–4 kHz) to be digitized accurately, we must sample at double the highest frequency (4 kHz) which would be 8 kHz. Human speech covers the frequency range from 100 to 7000 Hz but research has shown that the intelligible part of human speech

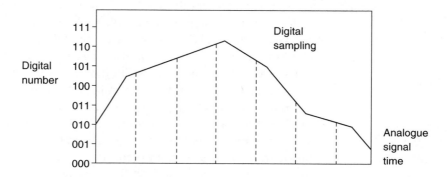

Figure 2.2   Digital sampling of an analog signal

is carried in the 300–3400 Hz range. This range, called the voice band, can use smaller bandwidth. An example where the quality could be reduced would be the telephone system where a modem will use the voice band frequency range in order to keep the bandwidth low enough for an efficient data transfer rate. In this case a digital voice sample would need to be taken every 125 μs. If the application involves music we may need a much higher sampling rate, increasing the data size of the media object. The audible range for humans is 20 kHz, doubling the bandwidth would require 40 kHz, corresponding to a sample being taken every 23 μs.

An image can be sampled in a similar fashion. However, with an image we sample fixed horizontal and vertical intervals, giving a two-dimensional (2D) digital image. When we sample an image such as a picture or a photograph the result will be a 2D array composed of m rows and n samples, where each digital sample is called a pixel. Each pixel contains information (usually intensity) about the image at that point in space. The quality of the image is determined by the number of pixels ($m \times n$), which directly affects its clarity and the amount of detail that can be shown. Once more, the accuracy is affected by the number of bits used to record each sample. The human eye perceives color as a combination of three so-called primary colors: red (435 nm), green (546 nm) and blue (700 nm). These primaries can be mixed to produce secondary colors – such as magenta, cyan and yellow. An image that uses 8 bits to represent each pixel is limited to 256 colors while a 24-bit image can represent over 16 million colors because each of the basic colors, RGB, can be represented by 8 bits. It is an important design decision when we choose the number of levels (8-bit or 24-bit color) of samples since for each pixel in the image it makes 1–3 bytes storage difference. This means even an average sized digital photographic image with 24-bit depth would require roughly 6 Mb of storage.

Size is even more significant for three-dimensional (3D) images. In the case of digital radiography the energy source is X-ray and its adsorption by tissues is measured as the sample. This results in a 2D image which is a projection of a 3D structure on a 2D plane. This can result in a very large image size, with 2000 × 2000 to 4000 × 4000 digital samples. Whereas the individual elements in 2D digital images are referred to as pixels (picture elements), in the case of 3D images the individual elements are known as voxels (volume picture elements). A number of biomedical imaging techniques generates 3D digital images. In conventional X-ray computerized tomography (CT) the scanner rotates through a full 360° while recording projections at fine angular increments during the rotation (0.5°–1°). All the projection information is considered to correspond to a single slab of tissue and multiple adjacent slices are acquired. Three-dimensional volume images are constructed from sequential adjacent CT sections so that a stack of slices can be effectively represented by a 3D array. Whereas the shape of a pixel is square in the plane of an image, most voxels that result from 2D slices are not cubic in shape as shown in Figure 2.3. In CT scanning the slice thickness varies from 1 mm to 10 mm. Images are usually reconstructed in a range from $512 \times 512 \times 1$ to $512 \times 512 \times 100$.

In spiral CT scanning the projection acquisition process traces a spiral trajectory rather than a sequence of parallel flat projections so that this results in a significant improvement in the time needed to capture 3D volume images of many structures in the human body. For example, spiral CT scanning can acquire image representation of 60 cm in 60 s but the resulting image size is immense.

2.1.2 Dealing with Media Object Size

There are basically two database approaches that have been used for coping with media data size:

- storing the data externally to the database;
- reducing the size of the media data so that it could be stored within the database.

In practice a combination of these strategies is used. Next we will consider how the captured digital media can be integrated within the database.

The relational model has been very successful at dealing with structured data types but less successful with media data. Object-relational databases offer a means of storing and processing multimedia data, based on SQL:1999. In fact there are a number of alternative approaches. SQL:1999 itself offers two new data types that can hold media data. The first of these is the "large object" or LOB data type. This has two variants, BLOB for "binary large object" and CLOB for "character large object". These can be

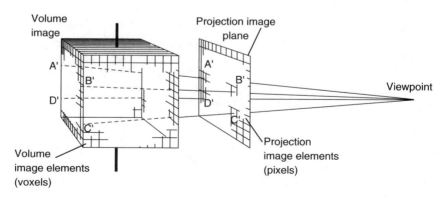

Figure 2.3   Concept of volume elements projected into pixels

combined to form user-defined types and classes with methods that provide the required multimedia functionality.

Both these data types are restricted in terms of many standard SQL operations. For example, they are restricted from primary and foreign key constraints and from use in comparisons other than pure equality tests. However, the standard provides for a number of BLOB operations including concatenation, substring, overlay and trim.

The way in which the new data types are implemented varies. For example, *Oracle9i* supports two types of large object types. Firstly, those which are stored in the database can have data types BLOB and CLOB. These are described as internal LOBs. However, it also supports another data type for media objects that are stored externally as operating system files (e.g. BFILE data type). These are called external LOBs although BFILE is not part of the SQL:1999 standard. In the Oracle implementation small LOBs can be stored within the database tablespace (see Chapter 8) while larger LOBs are stored externally within the operating system files. Manipulation of these data types can be achieved through a LOB locator. A locator is a unique binary value that acts as a surrogate for the actual binary object held in the database. It can be used to identify either a binary large object or a character large object.

In Table 2.1 we summarize the data types that were available in *Oracle9i* for the different kinds of media. Video data would usually be held as BFILE because of its gigantic size and limited interaction. However, if the video object has been segmented for indexing purposes then the individual segments could be held as BLOB data types. This is discussed later in this chapter. External LOBs could be located in another part of the network or on CDROMS or DVDs. However, the BFILE data type allows read-only access to these large files and they cannot participate in transactions.

Table 2.1   *Oracle9i* multimedia data types

Name	Data type	Size	Characteristics
BLOB	Binary	4 Kb in table space 4 Gb external table space	Random access Transaction support Needs locator
CLOB	Character	4 Gb	Random access Transaction support Needs locator
NCLOB	National character sets	4 Gb	Random access Transaction support Needs locator
BFILE	Binary		Read only External file

LOBs in *Oracle9i* have the advantage of being able to accommodate large size (up to 4 Gb) and to support random access. A LOB can also be broken down for processing into chunks. When a LOB data type is declared for a column in a table, the values stored are references, that is the LOB locators that specify the location of the large stored object. If the LOB is small (up to 4 Kb) it can be stored with its locator but otherwise it will be moved to a different physical location in the database.

We introduced the Fine Wine Shop system in Chapter 1. The database in this case needs to hold data about wines, grapes and vineyards that will help the customers select the wines they wish to purchase. This means the database will need to store images and videos of the wines, grapes and vineyards as well as other descriptive attributes. When this is implemented in *Oracle9i* a BFILE data type can be used to store the video or image data. An example of an SQL statement to set up a grape table would be:

```
CREATE TABLE grape
(grape_name          VARCHAR2(25) PRIMARY KEY,
picture              BFILE)
```

The table is created using the Oracle equivalent (VARCHAR2) of the SQL standard data type for character data and a column with BFILE data type. The locator is also important in *Oracle9i* since, before data can be added to the LOB, the locator must be non-NULL. This is done by initializing the locator of the BFILE column by using the BFILENAME() function. We noted that the BFILE data type was external to the database. Therefore to insert data into a BFILE data type we need to inform the database where the data will be located in the file system. In order to associate the BFILE objects with a directory we will need to create a DIRECTORY object. This is done by giving the subdirectory holding the video a logical name, using the statement

```
CREATE DIRECTORY "PHOTO_DIR" AS 'C:\PICTURES';
```

A directory object will be created to hold the external files, called "PHOTO_DIR". We must be connected as dba/system to do this and then grant the users access to the directory object.

```
GRANT READ ON DIRECTORY PHOTO_DIR TO scott
```

We can now use an SQL INSERT statement with a BFILENAME() function to add the data giving the location of the binary object in the named directory and its filename, as follows:

```
INSERT INTO grape (grape_name, picture)
VALUES
('chardonnay',
BFILENAME('PHOTO_DIR','chardonnay.jpeg'))
```

This shows how a multimedia database can be developed by creating tables including LOB data types and inserting data into these new data types. LOB data cannot be directly queried using SQL. Specific methods must be developed for dealing with the media data. This is considered in Chapter 4.

IBM follows a similar approach with their proprietary database *DB2*. *DB2* recognizes several types of LOB:

- CLOB;
- BLOB;
- DBCLOB (double-byte character large object).

Image, audio and video objects can be stored as LOBs in a *DB2* database. However, character LOBs are treated a little differently – CLOBs are character strings made up of single-byte characters with an associated code page. This data type is used for text objects that contain single-byte characters. DBCLOBs are character strings made up of double-byte characters with an associated code page. This data type is used for text objects where double-byte characters are used (such as some languages).

Each LOB can be up to 2 Gb in length; however, *DB2* allows many LOB columns per table so that it is possible to store up to 24 Gb of LOB space per row and up to 4 Tb of LOB space per table. In addition DB2 can use user-defined data types and object relational features to develop multimedia applications.

An alternative approach is based on SQL/MED (Management of External Data Standard) that does not involve storing large binary objects within the database itself. A database table can be defined containing the DATALINK type that can store a pointer to data on a remote machine. For example, once a URL has been entered into the database, the system can treat the media file as if it were actually stored in the database in terms of security, integrity and transaction consistency. SQL statements such as INSERT, UPDATE and DELETE that affect DATALINK columns can be processed to link and unlink files from the database. An example of SQL/MED to create a table is given next:

```
CREATE TABLE result
(download_result DATALINK,
      LINKTYPE URL
      FILE LINK CONTROL
....
File_name      VARCHAR(150) NOT NULL,
File_size_byte      INTEGER....)
```

The LINKTYPE URL indicates the values stored in the DATALINK column are specified using URL syntax so that the remote file, server host, directory structure and filename can be identified. The `FILE LINK CONTROL` parameter ensures that a check will be made on the existence of the file when the database is modified. A `DATALINK` value can be entered using an SQL INSERT statement, where the value takes the form:

```
http://host/filesystem/directory/filename
```

In addition an SQL Java standard is being developed (SQLJ) that provides a means of developing libraries of routines for inserting and updating LOB data types.

2.1.3   Reducing the Media Object's Size

Significant reduction in media object size can be achieved by data compression. In Figure 2.1 there are two stages described as "predict/model" and "transform". The purpose of these two stages is to allow the digital data to be compressed to reduce its size. There are hundreds of different ways of compressing images, called compression algorithms, which have been developed by computer scientists. The purpose of the "predict/model" stage is to estimate how much redundant data exists that could be removed in this way and select the best compression algorithm. Although there are many different ways in which this can be achieved the principles are the same – removing information that is duplicated and abbreviating information whenever possible. For example, one way of compressing an image is by abbreviating any repeated information in the image and eliminating information that is difficult for the human eye to see. When an image is restored this is called decompression. If it can be decompressed in such a way that none of the original information is lost this is known as **lossless** compression. However, if some information is lost by the process it is known as **lossy** compression. Even lossy compression can be applied to images of text documents without any significant loss and may result in a much smaller binary object. However, when the object cannot be restored to the original, lossy compression may not be appropriate for some applications such as medical imaging. Lossless compression techniques typically result in ratios of 2 : 1 or 3 : 1 in medical images. Lossy compression can accomplish 10 : 1 to 80 : 1 compression ratios. In the case of text, this could be achieved by building up a dictionary or look-up table where frequently used words were mapped to a symbol. The file would then be coded so that its size would be very much reduced. The dictionary method can also be applied to image and audio files. For example, a group of pixels with the same color values can be replaced by a single symbol as shown in Table 2.2 which demonstrates run-length encoding. Fortunately we will not be concerned with the details of how this is achieved. For image, audio and video there are devices that encode,

Table 2.2   Example of run-length encoding

Original pixels	Compressed pixels
2211333334333222 *(16 characters)*	22 21 53 14 33 32 (i.e. two 2s, two 1s, five 3s, etc.) *(12 characters)*

decode, compress and decompress all together, called *"codecs"* (coder/decoders). However, we will be concerned with the results of the process.

The amount of abbreviation can be significant; with voice coding a codec system can just send differences in adjacent speech samples, reducing the size by 50%. This can be very effective because, even if information has been lost, humans can interpolate speech to make gaps comprehensible. However, because musical input is much more varied than speech this can be more of a problem as significant loss of information can be very noticeable. Coding and compression are closely linked because the result will influence design decisions as we shall see in Chapters 8 and 9, such as buffer size and real-time delay. Highly compressed data objects would be smaller to store and transmit but may take longer to decompress when received at the target site. There is a trade-off between the costs and benefits of storage versus speed of processing. A slightly more complex compression method is Huffman coding (also called Limpel–Ziv). This technique searches for patterns in the data that can be represented by a smaller number of bits. These patterns are mapped to a number of representative bytes and sorted by probabilities. In biomedical image databases this can be very successful because smooth gradations can occur repeatedly in this kind of image. An example is shown in Table 2.3.

There are many different compression methods which all attempt in different ways to address the same objectives:

- reduced bandwidth and/or storage;
- decoded signal should be as close as possible to the original;
- lowest possible implementation strategy;
- application to as many signal types as possible;
- robustness;
- scalability;
- extensibility.

The raw media file consists only of the data itself. In order for the data to be of use in a computer system we need to know some characteristics of

Table 2.3   Example of Huffman coding

Original pixels	Map	Compressed data
12334123343212334 *(17 characters)*	12334 = A 32 = B	AABA *(4 characters)*

Table 2.4 Media data, their nature, data type and format standards

Media data	Common input format	Special nature	Oracle data types	Typical digital file formats
Text data	Printed text		CLOB	ASCII, RTF, HTML, SGML, XML
Audio data	Audio tapes, direct speech, CDs	Time dependence with digitized data size can affect quality	LOB/BFILE	WAV, AU, MPEG – MP3
Image data	Photographs, pictures, drawings	Results from pictures, drawings and photographs	LOB/BFILE	JPEG, GIF, TIFF, BMP, PNG
Video data	Video tape	Time-dependent sequence of video frames	BFILE	AVI, FLI, GIF, JPEG, MPEG

the data and the objects it represents. Multimedia data is available in a range of file formats, such as those shown in Table 2.4, that can appear confusing and unnecessarily complicated. When a multimedia designer specifies a file format, this often dictates the compression method that will be used as well. Therefore we will consider these in more detail. However, although this variety could appear confusing, this gives the designer great flexibility. We may select a format that would suit the application and also change the file format to meet the requirements of different users. Data can be stored in one format, compressed and transmitted to the user in another format.

In an image file we would need to know the size of the image in x and y dimensions and the number of bytes representing each pixel or voxel. The file header is the first part of the data file that provides a description of the image, typically height, width, color encoding. In the TIFF (tagged image format file) format this data is defined by a set of tags. The different file formats are associated with different compression processes. The effect of the different compression processes is illustrated in Figure 2.4 where a computer graphic image is transformed into different formats. The dictionary compression method can be used with the TIFF file format to give a lossless compression so that all the original data is preserved.

In an application we may want to store data in one compression format but transform the data into another compression format for transmission or presentation. This means that we need to store information about this. We can exploit the provision in SQL:1999 to create user defined data types to store these attributes. Both IBM's DB2 and Oracle allow for this by providing respectively DB2IMAGE and ORDIMAGE types so that, for example, we could change the definition of the grape table as follows:

```
CREATE TABLE grape
(grape_name          VARCHAR2(25) PRIMARY KEY,
 picture             ORDSYS.ORDIMAGE )
```

	This computer-generated graphic image can be stored in several different file formats.
	As a bit map the file size is 1088 Kb.
	As a JPEG file with lossy compression, the file size is 748 Kb. Note that JPEG is designed for photographs so it is not necessarily the best format for computer graphic files.
	As a GIF file with compression based on a dictionary compression method the file size is reduced to 109 Kb.

Figure 2.4   Size versus different compression formats for a computer-generated image

This would allow the inclusion of the following attributes:

- CompressionFormat – values such as JPEG, LZW, GIFLZW, HUFFMAN3;
- CompressionQuality – values such as LOWCOMP, MEDCOMP, HIGHCOMP;
- ContentFormat – values such as image type/pixel/data format 24BITRGB;
- Cut – x, y, z data of size;
- FileFormat – values such as BMP, JFIF, TIFF, PICT.

Another important file format relates to the JPEG standard which includes both lossless and lossy compression methods. This was designed specifically for photographic images containing thousands of colors or shades and can typically compress files from 10 : 1 to 20 : 1 with no visible loss of image quality. It is a standard of the ISO and can operate in four modes:

- sequential – the simplest and most frequently used where an image is encoded in a single left-to-right, top-to-bottom scan;
- progressive – where there are multiple scans so that the image is built up so the user can watch the image develop – this is useful for long transmission times across networks and display on web pages;
- lossless – this guarantees exact recovery for applications for medical/safety-critical use;
- hierarchical – this is an adaptable mode which can provide versions with different resolutions.

The hierarchical mode is particularly useful for data delivery since it enables the application to decode an appropriate version of the image. For example, if the system is operating on a congested network, packets containing the highest resolution data can be dropped so that the users get a degraded image but this may be preferable to a long delay. (These issues are covered in detail in Chapter 9.)

A number of different file formats are available for each kind of media since they are suitable for different kinds of applications because they are designed to support special features such as annotation or object representation. Table 2.5 lists common digital video formats, their application and features. Wavelet compression, featured in INDEO files, has become very popular in many areas of signal and image processing applications as a lossy compression technique. Wavelet compression exploits the fact that real-world images tend to have internal morphological consistency, locally similar luminance values, edge continuance and textures. (These features of images are described in detail in Chapter 11.) These features allow image signals to be distinguished from noise so that wavelets efficiently encode image structures. For biomedical images such as CT images wavelet compression can achieve 80 : 1 compression ratios.

Codecs are devices used for audio and video continuous data. Audio signals vary depending on the application. In the case of a voice signal as shown in Figure 2.5 there is much similarity in adjacent speech samples. Data files are typically compressed using simple schemes such as run-length encoding or Huffman codes. Audio signals are also often compressed using logarithmic encoding because this is closer to the way humans perceive audio, for example using either µ-law which predominates in the USA and Japan or A-law encoding which is widely used in Europe and the rest of the world. There is an increasing number of different audio standards, which now include those from mobile telephony such as SSM.

The fundamental standard for videoconferencing applications is G171 which defines pulse code modulation (PCM) and belongs to the International Telecommunications Union family of audio standards. In PCM a sample representing the instantaneous amplitude of the input wave

Table 2.5   Digital file formats, applications and features

Digital video format	Application	Features
MPEG	Multimedia	Key frame plus motion encoding
INDEO	Web pages	Wavelet progression
CINEPAK	Computer	Video efficient
SORENSON	Computer/videophone	Video efficient
QUICKTIME	Computer	Incorporates compression
AVI	Computer	Incorporates compression

Figure 2.5 Voice signal

is sampled regularly (usually 50 ppm). At this rate voice communication can be encoded acceptably. Samples are then stored as 8-bit data using logarithmic encoding based on either A-law or μ-law. (Most sound chips that originate outside Europe follow the μ-law.) Another important standard is G721 which describes adaptive differential pulse code modulation. An interesting alternative approach to coding speech is known as linear predictive coding. This will compress audio at 16 Kbps and the decoder will generate synthetic speech that is very similar to the original. The result is intelligent but robotic-sounding speech.

Although there are a number of alternative approaches to compress speech, music demands a higher quality. High quality compression is obtained by using the MPEG standards for digital audio and video of the Moving Picture Expert Group. The different features of the MPEG audio standards are set out in Table 2.6. In MP3 the different compression layers give increasing quality/compression ratios with increasing complexity and consequently increasing demands on processing power. Several new standards are being developed. Whereas MPEG-4 was concerned with how to

Table 2.6 MPEG multimedia standards

Standard	Features	Purpose
MPEG-1 (1992)	2 audio channels; specifies decoder but not encoder	Interactive CDROM Video CDROM Audio – MP3
MPEG-2 (1994)	5 audio channels plus low-frequency enhancement channel Three compression levels: audio I, II, III	Digital TV DVD Audio – Music
MPEG-3 (MPEG-1/2 Layer 3)	Higher quality encoding but was dropped because MPEG-2 at higher rate was of sufficient quality	HDTV
MPEG-4	Uses model-based image coding schemes (i.e. knowing what is in the picture)	Multimedia for fixed and mobile Web
MPEG-7	Descriptive elements for low-level signal features and structural information	Search video and audio content
MPEG-21	Work-in-progress to deal with digital rights management	Multimedia framework for interoperability

represent multimedia content, MPEG-7 is concerned with how to describe content and MPEG-21 has resulted from concerns about interoperability. (MPEG-4 is a special standard designed for low bandwidth applications and is based on a coding scheme which needs to know what is in the image and its purpose.)

2.1.4 How Large is a Video Object?

As we have seen, compression is essential for audio and image media. However, video media is potentially much larger. Most video devices capture an image in digital form although it may be converted to analog for storage. When the digital video is output it uses an area of memory called the frame buffer. By changing the frame buffer once per scan we get animation. Humans appear to be better at adjusting to poor visual information than poor audio – so that compression can make video data manageable without so much loss of quality. There are two potential methods for reducing the size of video objects:

- Use less space for each frame by sending less detail – spatial compression.
- Reduce the number of frames because little is moving – temporal and spatial compression.

There are two main compression standards for video, the ISO's Motion JPEG standard and the newer MPEG method. Both methods rely on the fact that much of the information will be the same in successive frames; for example, if people move through the same scene, much of the background will remain the same. Table 2.7 gives an idea of how much reduction in size can be achieved using these compression techniques for different video-screen dimensions.

Some video standards when uncompressed can have 25 frames per second. Therefore, slowing the frame rate down to 15 or even 2 frames per second by removing some frames will reduce the storage required. However, this kind of lossy compression is not acceptable to some classes of user, e.g.

Most common formats for digital video are related to the visible area for each of the different international television standards. PAL TV displays video at 625 lines – spatial resolution 833 × 625, frame rate 1/25 s; NTSC at 525 lines – resolution 700 × 525, frame rate 1/30 s.

Table 2.7 Reduction of video clip size by compression methods

Time	640 × 480	320 × 240	160 × 120	Compressed JPEG 25 : 1 640 × 480	Compressed MPEG 100 : 1 640 × 480
1 s	27 Mb	6.75 Mb	1.68 Mb	1.1 Mb	270 Kb
1 min	1.6 Gb	400 Mb	100 Mb	65 Mb	16 Mb
1 h	97 Gb	24 Gb	6 Gb	3.9 Gb	970 Mb
1000 h	97 Tb	24 Tb	6 Tb		

radiologists and air traffic controllers. The MPEG standards provide for several different qualities of video. The two most commonly used are MPEG I and MPEG II.

The MPEG standard for video compression takes advantage of the fact that adjacent frames in a continuous video steam are often similar. It categorizes three main types of frame:

- **I** frames are coded so that the decompression depends only on the information *inside* the frame.
- **P** frames are coded with reference to a *previous* I or P frame.
- **B** frames or *bidirectional* frames are coded with reference to a previous or subsequent *P* or *I* frame.

Sometimes P and B frames are referred to as D or delta compressed frames. In MPEG files 70–80% of frames will be delta frames. This is a variable compression process that is much more efficient than Motion JPEG which uses fixed compression. However, it has the disadvantage that the B frames that have the highest compression and smallest size cannot be used to support random access for reasons explained in Chapter 5. Note that this is also the reason that methods, such as those provided in Oracle *interMedia*, which change compression and file formats are very useful in multimedia databases.

Research and development work is going on into new compression techniques such as wavelet, vector and fractal compression methods that could deliver high quality in the future. In later chapters we shall find that MPEG compression frames have significant effects on the delivery and indexing of video objects. In a network situation media data can be lost in transit from one node to another and delayed so that some simply do not make the destination. The degradation of the signal received and then perceived by the user will be increased by compression. Lossy compression which reduces a signal to its bare essentials may remove so much redundancy that it also reduces the signal's tolerance to loss so that it cannot be adequately reconstructed. The designer has to choose a compression scheme to minimize the impact of loss. Multimedia packets are large so that the loss of even one is usually significant.

2.2   Real-time Nature of Multimedia

Video is a continuous media but for database storage and manipulation such as random access it is important to be able to deal with portions of the video object. The process of subdividing a video object is called **video**

segmentation. It could be done manually but this would be very costly. Much research has focused on segmenting video automatically by detecting the boundary between camera shots. A shot may be defined as a sequence of frames captured by a single camera in a single continuous action in time and space, for example two people having a conversation. It may consist of a number of close-up views of their faces interleaved to make the scene. **Shots** define the low level syntactic building blocks of a video sequence. A number of different boundaries can exist between shots which can affect the automatic detection methods. A cut is an abrupt transition between shots that occurs between two adjacent frames – this is easy to detect. A fade is the gradual change in brightness either starting or ending with a black frame. A dissolve is similar to fade except it occurs between two shots, so the frames of the first shot become dimmer and the images of the second shot become brighter until the second replaces the first – this is much more difficult to detect. Other changes can be wipes or morphing that are computer generated. These transitions will cause problems for indexing and retrieving video segments and we will consider this in detail in Chapter 12. It can be more meaningful to work with a scene rather than a shot. A scene is the logical grouping of shots into a semantic unit. A single **scene** focuses on a certain object or objects of interest but the shots included can be from different angles. The segmentation of a video into scenes is a lot more useful than segmentation into shots because end-users visualize a video as a sequence of scenes, not shots. Another term used for a digital video document is a clip but this is not clearly defined so it can last from a few seconds to several hours. A **clip** has two important properties that must be retained – it consists of a sequence and the sequence is made up of contiguous video frames. The term video segment is used for any contiguous portion of a clip. The consequence is that when a video object is transmitted across a network, transformed and delivered to the user we have to pay particular attention to the sequence of frames that were encoded and will be delivered.

2.3   Why is the Semantic Nature of Multimedia Data a Problem?

Unlike data in traditional databases, multimedia data, images, video and audio clips, instead of having an explicit nature, have an implicit semantic nature. Chapter 1 introduced the concept of metadata that is used to deal with the contents, structure and semantics of media data. In traditional database systems information that is of interest to the system itself such as schema definitions, indexes, users, integrity constraints, security constraints etc. is known as metadata and is held in a data dictionary or catalog.

However, in multimedia database management systems (MMDBMS) meta-data can refer to information about individual objects.

The semantic nature can only be made explicit by some kind of analysis and additional processing. Although metadata can take the form of text descriptions we can also use characteristics of the media data as metadata. For example, specific metadata for different types of raw data could include:

- texture for images;
- frequencies for audio;
- font size for text;
- motion direction and lighting for video;
- speech – keywords such as identification of the speakers, place, time;
- video clip – camera motion and lighting.

The use of keywords in creating an index to a traditional database is an example of metadata annotation that we have already met.

Consider the three images displayed in Figure 2.6 (Please turn to Inside Front Cover for Color version of Figure 2.6). We could annotate the set of images by adding a simple text description of each image. However, this will be time consuming for a large image database and also it can prove to be surprisingly difficult to describe an image precisely in text in such a way as to capture the user's association and impression of the image. A better method would be to exploit values of specific features in the image, which could be generated automatically, but these will usually be associated with the image's structure and syntax in terms of color or texture. For example, images can be both classified and manipulated by using their histograms. A histogram is a graph of image color values, typically RGB values, sometimes with luminance as well. In Figure 2.6 three images are displayed together with their corresponding histograms. The spectrum for a color component appears on the horizontal axis, and the vertical axis indicates the portion of the image's color that matches each point on the component's spectrum (a measure of the number of pixels with that color value). The luminance spectrum also appears, ranging from zero luminance (black) to full lumi-nance (white). The vertical axis in this case indicates the percentage of the source image that matches a point on the luminance spectrum. It can be seen that the image's histogram is almost a "fingerprint" of the image. The three images produce histograms that are very different and this difference can be exploited for indexing and searching for images within a database. The histograms of the individual frames in a video can be used in the same way. In Chapters 5, 11 and 12 this topic is covered in detail.

Chapter 5 considers the problems of searching complex and multime-dia database systems in detail, including retrieval and browsing of large data

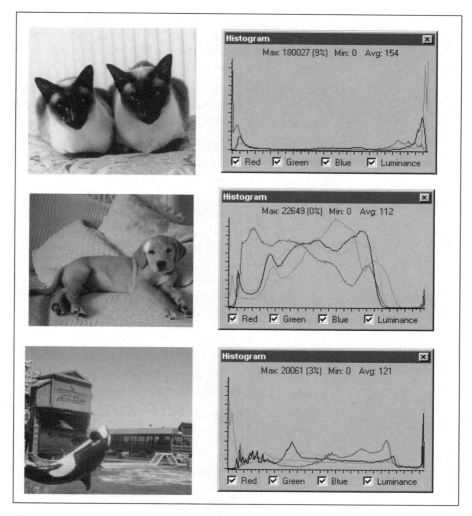

Figure 2.6 Three images and their corresponding histograms

sets. Query language design, specification and optimization issues for multimedia data and the particular role that metadata management fulfills, will be covered then. Other issues include what the metadata is and how it will be stored and organized.

The generation of metadata is costly and is usually carried out after the raw media has been stored. There are three classes of metadata:

- The manual generation of metadata could involve the recognition of the structure of a document in semi- or non-structured text, the extraction of features from images, the segmentation of audio by speakers, recognition of scene cuts in videos.

- Semi-automatic methods of generating metadata involve adding information that could not be extracted from features in the raw data. This will involve a knowledge of the application domain, the content of the data and the user's purpose.

- A third type of metadata can be generated automatically when the raw data itself is captured. This could be the time and place a photograph is taken together with its histogram.

Metadata needs to be updated when the raw data is changed. This can mean that, for example, if the color of an image changes we would want to be able to update only the values of color-related features but not other types of information such as spatial location of objects. This in turn requires explicit knowledge of the structure and semantics of the metadata. Metadata itself may need updating in isolation from the raw data if the semantic nature of the domain is changed. One example would be new medical findings which changed the diagnostic pattern in a medical application.

A new standard is emerging, MPEG-7 (see Table 2.6), which will have a major impact on the issue of metadata. It aims to set up a standard framework for multimedia content, including:

- low-level descriptions of each individual object in a scene, such as shape, size, color, position and movement;

- high-level abstract descriptions of the scene, the objects it contains and the events taking place;

- audio information such as key, mood and tempo.

An MPEG-7 description of a video clip might consist of a set of codes conveying information, for example, "Scenes of Paris by the Seine", but also metadata such as format, when and by whom it was recorded and copyright information. MPEG-7 codes could also be used to describe the content of still images so the potential benefits of the new standard are considerable. It should make the process of searching and retrieving an image or a video clip much easier.

EXERCISE 2.1

This exercise is designed to help your understanding of multimedia data definition and manipulation based on the text in Chapter 2 about the nature of multimedia data. You need to have studied Chapter 2, examples for the **grape** *table before you carry out this exercise. Start the activities in this question as user* **scott** *connected to the Oracle database – Application development – SQLPLUS but note that you are also required to work as user* **sys** *when this is indicated in the instructions.*

(a) In this exercise you will create a multimedia table by using an external BLOB. This is the simplest way of creating a multimedia database table. The BLOB value is stored in the operating system files outside the database. This will use the BFILE data type. Oracle SQL enables the definition of a BFILE object and its association with a corresponding external file. A BFILE column stores a BFILE locator which can be considered as a pointer to a file in the external system.

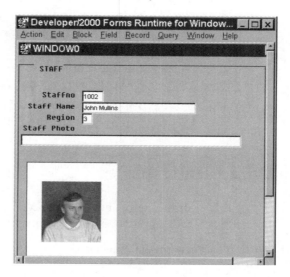

Create a table called **staff** in Oracle SQLPLUS with the specification in Table 2.8.

Table 2.8

Column name	Format	Width
staff_number	character	4, not null
staff_name	character	25, not null
region	character	1
image_file	character	80
picture	bfile	no restriction

(b) The following data in Table 2.9, which gives values for the traditional data types, is to be inserted into the **staff** table.

Table 2.9

Name	Data
staff_number	John Mullins
staff_name	1002
region	3
image_file	c:\pictures\john.jpg

Give INSERT statements for the row.

Populate the table **staff** *with the row given in part (b).*

(c) In order to associate the BFILE objects with a directory you will need to create a DIRECTORY object. You need to store the image files for this exercise in a directory on your system and then name this directory as a DIRECTORY object. Create a directory to hold the external files, called "Photo_dir". You must be connected as dba/system to do this.

(d) Insert a row into the staff table including a binary file using BFILENAME function for example BFILENAME ('PHOTO_DIR', 'john.jpeg')) in the INSERT statement.

Give INSERT statements for the row.

Populate the table **staff** *with the row given in part (b).*

(e) Update an existing row of the **staff** table to include a binary file. This can also be achieved by using the BFILENAME function.

2.4   Summary of Chapter

In this chapter we reviewed the special characteristics of multimedia data and the problems this poses for databases, that is:

- size of the media objects;
- real-time nature;
- semantic nature.

At the start of this chapter we have explored the reasons for the large size of multimedia objects and the different methods used to reduce their size. However, these methods may themselves introduce other problems.

Some solutions to these challenges were introduced. The size of media objects can be reduced by compression methods which can be lossless or lossy. The choice depends on the application area and the amount of detail that must be stored. Media data can be stored internally or externally with respect to the database. The multimedia data types (LOB, BLOB, CLOB and BFILE) were introduced and their different application was explained.

The real-time nature was also discussed in relation to compression of video objects. However, the impact of managing the real-time nature of the media will be more significant when we come to store the data and transmit it across networks to the users. These topics are covered in later chapters.

The semantic nature of media data was also considered together with the role of metadata. The use of color histograms to describe images and therefore video frames was introduced. Having completed this chapter you should now be able to:

1. describe the general characteristics of multimedia data;
2. describe the role of compression with an MMDBMS;
3. explain the purpose of metadata in MMDBM;
4. describe the main standards associated with multimedia data.

SOLUTIONS TO EXERCISES

Exercise 2.1

(a) Create a table called **staff** in Oracle SQLPLUS.

```
CREATE TABLE staff
( staff_number          CHAR(4) PRIMARY KEY,
  staff_name     VARCHAR2(25) NOT NULL,
region          CHAR(1),
image_file      VARCHAR2(80),
picture         BFILE)
```

(b)

```
INSERT INTO staff (staff_number, staff_name, region,
image_file)
VALUES ('1002', 'John Mullins','3',' c:\pictures\john.jpg'
```

(c) In order to associate the BFILE objects with a directory you will need to create a directory.

```
CREATE DIRECTORY "PHOTO_DIR" AS 'C:\PICTURES';
```

(d)

```
INSERT INTO staff VALUES
('1002', 'John Mullins','3','c:\pictures\john.jpg',
BFILENAME('PHOTO_DIR','john.jpg'))
```

(e) Update an existing row of the **staff** table to include a binary file. This can also be achieved by BFILENAME function.

```
UPDATE staff
SET picture =BFILENAME('PHOTO_DIR','john.jpg')
WHERE staff_name='John Mullins'
```

Recommended Reading

Crowcroft, J., Handley, M., Wakeman, I. (1999) *Internetworking Multimedia*, Morgan Kaufmann, San Francisco, CA.

Fluckiger, F. (1995) *Understanding Networked Multimedia*, Prentice Hall, London.

Subrahmanian, V. S. (1997) *Principles of Multimedia Database Management Systems*, Morgan Kaufmann, San Francisco, CA.

chapter 3

The Human Sensory System and Multimedia

Chapter aims

This chapter reviews some of the current knowledge about the way in which the human sensory system works, how the brain processes this information and how this is relevant to dealing with multimedia information. Through a study of this chapter the reader will develop a knowledge of the main features of the human sensory system in relation to the delivery of multimedia data and the way this can influence database development. At the end of the chapter the reader should be able to:

- appreciate the main features of the human sensory system;
- appreciate the way the brain processes multimedia information;
- understand the kind of multimedia applications where the way the human sensory system operates can influence requirements and design;
- understand how this influences the development of multimedia database systems.

There are several reasons for studying the rather technical information in this chapter. The chapter aims to provide a theoretical understanding of issues that are taken up in a number of later chapters. The problems of developing ways of retrieving multimedia data based on their content are discussed in Chapter 5 and later chapters also suggest that we need to know more about the ways and reasons users search for media objects in the information space. We need to understand the intentions and goals of the users as this will help to define the way metadata is structured. Later, when we study media retrieval we shall find one approach is based on storing a text description of the media objects in a database. This is achieved by means of a human being annotating the media to generate metadata – for example adding a note on the fragrance of an image of a flower or a wine. The effectiveness of this will depend on human cognition and perception of the different media by both the annotator and the user.

Another reason for studying this chapter is that many multimedia technologies we will learn about in later chapters attempt to mimic the way the human brain processes sensory information – for example the way humans learn to distinguish an object from its environment and from other objects. Great progress has been made in understanding how the human visual system works and in Chapter 11 we shall see how to use this knowledge to develop meaningful representations of a visual scene.

It is essential to be able to develop a user-centered approach to designing effective media retrieval systems. In contrast to the great progress in some areas, many aspects of user interfaces date from nineteenth century concepts such as the mechanical typewriter. Many components including the keyboard and the mouse were developed without taking human behavior sufficiently into account – how we sit at desks and hold devices in our hands. We still know relatively little about the long-term effects of using computer and communication technologies. It is clear that if multimedia, three-dimensional visualizations and virtual reality applications are to be successful in the future we will need to pay attention to vital aspects of human physiological and cognitive behavior.

The chapter is structured so that general concepts about human cognition are introduced first, with an emphasis on memory and processing. Theories of perception are introduced and related to the design of multimedia systems. This is followed by theories about the functions of the human brain and the senses – visual, acoustic and somatic. We are particularly concerned with the way the brain recognizes objects and deals with moving pictures. Our brains process visual information so easily that it is difficult to appreciate how difficult and complex object recognition and motion detection are. Some of the material is quite technical and there are parts the reader may wish to skip or return to when some of the more practical aspects are being dealt with in later chapters.

3.1   Introduction – Human Information Processing

During the 1960s and 1970s psychologists were so strongly influenced by the way computer systems had been developed that cognitive psychology characterized humans as information processors. Everything that is sensed (sight, hearing, touch, taste, smell) was considered to be information which

Figure 3.1   Human information processing stages

the mind processes. The basic theory then was that information enters and exits the mind through a series of ordered processing stages (Lindsay and Norman, 1977) as illustrated in Figure 3.1.

This idealized model was developed to provide a theoretical basis for describing cognitive processes and has been very influential in the design of user interfaces for information systems and for other computer artifacts. For example from this basic theory Norman developed a model of action which is now known as the "Seven stages of action" (Norman, 1986) and this is presented in Figure 3.2. Later from this theory came theories of the principles of design for interactive systems.

The simple information processing model shown in Figure 3.1 has been extended to deal with the concepts of attention and memory. In the extended model:

(a) information is perceived by the perceptual processors;

(b) information is attended to;

(c) information is processed and stored in memory.

A model of memory was also developed at the about the same time (Atkinson and Shiffrin, 1968) which suggested that there were the following memory stores:

- The sensory store (SS) is specific for a modality (vision, audio, etc.) and holds information briefly for a short period of time (a few tenths of a second). In the visual sensory memory the memory trace time is about 0.1 s. This means that separate picture frames will appear as a continuous flow if the time interval is short enough. If the time interval is too long the human subject will notice.

| 1 Form a goal |
| 2 Form an intention |
| 3 Specify the action sequence |
| 4 Execute the action |
| 5 Perceive the resultant state |
| 6 Interpret the resultant state |
| 7 Evaluate the outcome |

Figure 3.2   Norman's seven stages of action

- The short-term memory (STM) store can hold information for a few seconds. This area of memory is now usually referred to as working memory because it is thought to be a working area for holding information temporarily for another processing activity. The main characteristic of this working memory is that it is very limited in amount and time. Miller (1956) suggested on the basis of experimental results that the number of items (digits, letters, names) the average person can remember at any one time is about seven. This phenomenon is known as "the magic number 7 ± 2". Although we have this limitation, we can perform more than one thing at a time, for example drive a car, talk on the phone, but two similar tasks at the same time will create difficulties, for example remembering a 7-digit phone number and talking.

- The permanent long-term memory (LTM) store was considered to hold information indefinitely.

The evidence for these theories of cognition and memory was largely based on the study of human subjects with brain damage and a small number of controlled experiments. However, our knowledge of cognition has improved considerably with the advent of technologies such as magnetic resonance imaging (MRI) which enable scientists to study the brain while subjects are actually processing information.

We now know that STM is more complicated than implied by Atkinson and Shiffrin's model. Baddeley's theory (Baddeley,1999) suggests that our STM consists of a central executive with limited capacity but in overall control, along with two "slave" systems:

- phonological loop – focuses on sound not meaning of words;
- visuo-spatial sketch map – registers images.

The central executive allocates attention and directs the operation of the slave systems. The phonological loop consists of a memory store and a rehearsal system (you speak the words/numbers to yourself in your head). It acts like an inner voice and inner ear and is primarily concerned with our perception and production of speech. The visuo-spatial sketch pad is the inner eye. It is a bit like a visual Post-it note for remembering visual data such as where we have left something. A memory has approximately 18 s duration in STM.

It is assumed that the slave systems have limited capacity and therefore, if people are asked to perform two tasks at the same time that use the same slave system, their performance on one or both may be affected, for example to read information and perform a verbal reasoning task. If this is the case we need to consider this when we develop multimedia retrieval systems that require the user to actively participate in the stages of retrieval in a way that is not necessary in conventional databases (see Chapter 5).

Similarly, a number of different LTMs have been distinguished:

- episodic memory – memory of events (stored in the hippocampus of the brain) – this is fragile and easily lost;
- semantic memory – background knowledge of the world;
- procedural memory – for motor skills, the most durable;
- prospective memory – what you have to do in the future, most fragile, declines with age, males lose this earlier than females;
- state-dependent memory – associated with an environment where an event took place, for example what happened under the influence of alcohol (memory of a traumatic event is better than normal).

EXERCISE 3.1

Below there are a number of names randomly scattered across the page. In order to investigate Miller's magic number, show them to five friends for 20 s and get them to write down as many names as they can remember.

(a) Find the average score.

(b) Does it support Miller's theory?

(c) How would SS and LTM affect the results?

Spencer	Ursula	Joshua		Frederick
Timothy	Lionel	Alexis		
Tracy	Fatima	Jeremiah	Gertrude	Seth
Jean		Xerxes	Hilary	
Wolfgang	Bertrand	Marie	Eric	Pamela
Yolanta	Martha	Sebastian	Richard	
Georgina	Gandalf		Elizabeth	

For human users perception is fundamental for interacting with computers. The user must be able to perceive information in various ways in order to use a computer successfully. In early computer systems the interface designer was only concerned with the user's perception of visual information. With multimedia the designer must consider other perceptual modalities such as sound and even touch. For multimedia systems it is important to understand how theories of perception can influence not only the design of the user interface but also the underlying database system itself – how much information from the media object we need to store.

3.1.1 Theories of Perception

In the twentieth century there were two groups of theories of perception that are relevant to our study:

- constructivist theories that were based on the assumption that the process of seeing is an active one in which our view of the world is constructed both from information in the environment and from previously stored knowledge;

- ecological theories that believe perception involves the process of picking up information cues from the environment and does not require any processes of construction or elaboration.

Both these theories claim that humans are active perceivers but, whereas constructivists suggest that we perceive by embellishing and elaborating retinal images, the ecologists propose that we perceive by actively exploring the objects in our environment by seeing, smelling, listening and touching. The main assumption of the constructivist approach is that perception involves the intervention of representations and memories. What we see is not a replica of a real-world image such as a camera would produce but rather a construction of the visual system – a model created by transforming, enhancing, distorting and discarding information. According to this theory our ability to see objects on the computer screen is the result of our prior knowledge and expectations as to what should appear and the actual images that fall on the retina of the eye. Another aspect of the constructivist theories is that the process involves decomposing or partitioning images into separate entities that can be easily recognized. The object (the figure) is distinguished from the rest of the information (the background).

In a further development the Gestalt group of psychologists theorized that our ability to interpret meaning from scenes and objects was based on us having innate laws of organization. According to this theory the organizing principles that enable us to see patterns as meaningful wholes are defined as:

(a) proximity – the entities appear as groups rather than as a random cluster;

(b) similarity – there is a tendency for elements of the same shape or color to be seen as belonging together;

(c) closure – missing parts of a figure are filled in to complete it so that it appears as a whole;

(d) continuity – the stimulus appears to be made of continuous lines rather than dots;

(e) symmetry – regions bounded by symmetrical borders tend to be perceived as coherent figures.

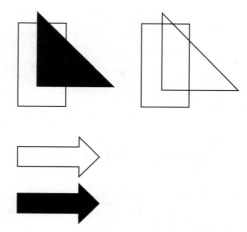

Figure 3.3   Gestalt principles illustrated

The application of this theory to information design is illustrated in Figure 3.3, where a contrast boundary is better than a line boundary for making a shape stand out.

We can devise computer processes that mimic the constructivist and Gestalt theories and apply these to help a computer system deal with the semantic nature of media information. For example, we can apply the same organizing principle to break down a complex image or video sequence into smaller components.

The ecological approach in contrast argues that perception is a process in which information is directly detected rather than constructed. This approach is concerned with how we deal with continuous events over a period of time, rather than how we make sense of a single scene. It asks what we need to know about our environment to carry out a task and how this might be known. A central concept of this approach is "affordance". This is an aspect of an object that makes it obvious how the object is to be used in its environment. This concept has been used extensively in design, including the design of user interface objects, as illustrated by the scroll bars and command button in Figure 3.4. The shape, color and the texture of a figure with respect to its background give cues when the behavior of the object is observed. The affordance of the scroll bars is achieved because the arrows afford the property of being clicked by the mouse and the scroll bar itself invites being moved with the mouse. The exit button invites clicking with the mouse.

The theory of affordance has been very influential in the development of user interface design which uses the direct manipulation paradigm. We can see this particularly in windowing systems and the web. In this way

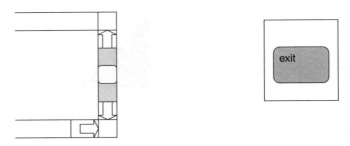

Figure 3.4   The affordance of objects

interfaces are constructed from objects that have an appearance and behavior that enable the user to perceive how to use the objects and navigate through the interface.

EXERCISE 3.2

Assign an organizing principle based on the Gestalt theory for each of the following:

(a)

(b)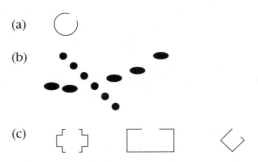

(c)

Current theories of human information processing are derived from the much clearer picture that is starting to emerge from studies of the human brain. These tend to support the constructivist theories that what we perceive is constructed by the brain and also that different parts of the brain are specialized to process different types of information. A number of different areas of the brain are significant in sensory perception.

3.2   Human Brain and Multimedia Information

The adult human brain weighs about 3 lb. The forebrain contains the temporal lobe which controls our ability to smell and hear. Also in the forebrain are the occipital lobe which controls vision and the parietal lobe which controls our speech, reading and taste. The forebrain also includes the cerebral cortex consisting of two identical-looking halves or hemispheres:

- left hemisphere associated with language, logic, scheming;
- right hemisphere associated with color, rhythm, imagination.

The two cerebral hemispheres are not functionally equivalent, particularly with respect to:

- *Language.* Over 95% of humans are right handed; the left hemisphere is dominant for language. In left-handed people right hemisphere dominance is still rare, with left or bilateral language capabilities more common.
- *Visuo-spatial abilities* are more highly developed in the right hemisphere.
- *Attention.* From studies of brain-damaged humans it appears that there is a difference in attentional mechanisms so that when the left side is damaged the right side is slow to respond.

In addition there are areas of the brain associated with particular functions such as:

- Cerebral cortex is the site of perception and intelligence.
- Hippocampus (sea-horse shape) is essential for memory processing.
- Hypothalmus is connected with arousal.
- Amygdala is linked with emotions, for example anger, anxiety and fear.

Different areas of the brain are specialized to process particular information received from the senses. For example, vision is processed at the part of the brain at the back of the head, the visual cortex, and takes up roughly 30% of the cortex while 8% is used for "touch" and 3% for hearing. When brain damage occurs, e.g. in stroke, then part of the information may not be processed. Since different cells process different bits of information some process must go on in the brain to put all the pieces of information together and make sense of the result. This is why when this is not completely successful we can experience visual and audio illusions.

The brain is built up of cells called neurons which are all unique cells capable of signaling and communicating to perform different functions. Neurons are cells specialized for processing information that have specialized projections called dendrites and axons. Dendrites bring information into the cell while axons take information away. Information flows from one neuron to another across the synapse which is a small gap between two neurons as shown in Figure 3.5. Neurons need lots of energy to keep in

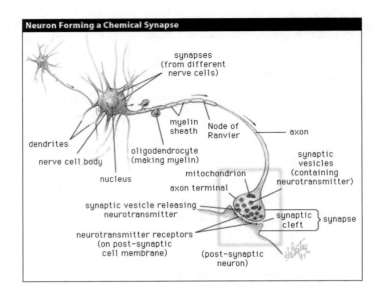

Figure 3.5   Neuron and synapse

balance. The axon is a long wire-like structure which relays an action potential that allows the neurons to communicate with one another. The neurons are often linked in tightly folded sheets and arrays. For example, the neocortex is a folded sheet of neural tissue that covers much of the brain. It has an area of about 200 000 mm^2. It is thought that folding reduces the amount of connections needed to link different parts of the sheet. Neurons can communicate with other neurons up to a meter away. Neurons carry out the many operations that extract meaningful information from a sensory receptor. Arrays of neurons at the organism's periphery translate these into action, imagery and memory.

Memories are stored in the forebrain. We now know that synapse formation and modification in the forebrain occur throughout life. Even LTMs are not truly fixed.

Originally, the role of neurons was assumed to be a simple means of integrating synaptic inputs until a threshold was reached, initiating an output pulse. This concept has now evolved into recognizing neurons as much more sophisticated processors with mixed analog–digital logic and highly adaptive synaptic elements. We now recognize the importance of neurotransmitters (such as serotonin), molecules that can diffuse across the synapse with the result that the neurons' behavior is changed. Changes in the local concentration of neurotransmitters affect the likelihood that a neuron will or will not fire under the influence of a stimulus.

3.3 The Senses

Within the cerebral cortex there are a number of primary sensory areas which we will introduce in turn. There are the visual cortex, the auditory cortex and the somatosensory cortex.

3.3.1 Visual Perception

The visual system in humans is extremely complex. It can distinguish objects with a wide range of brightness and color. It can also perceive and follow rapidly moving objects and rapidly decaying events such as a lightning strike. Vision is a creation of the brain. Color, edges, movement and angles are processed by different sets of cells in the visual cortex.

The retina is a light-sensitive surface at the rear of the eye. It consists of about ten layers of cells, with the eighth layer consisting of cone and rod photoreceptor cells. These have the ability to turn light into electrical signals which are transmitted to the brain. It takes the photoreceptor cells about 25 ms to perform this transformation. This means that a very rapidly moving object will have moved a distance of meters before it has been perceived. This is one reason why fast serves at tennis are a problem.

The central area of the retina is mainly populated with cones while rods dominate at the periphery. Although image resolution is poor at the periphery of the retina, anything that moves in the periphery is very noticeable. Rods are concentrated here and are about 300 times more sensitive than cones. Cones can distinguish about 8 million colors. Rods do not process color but can detect brightness. In a dark room rods can increase in sensitivity by a factor of 75 000. The amount of detail the eye can see is known as its resolution. Color sensations arise because there are three types of color receptors that are sensitive to three significantly overlapping portions of the visual spectrum. The "blue" cones peak at 445 nm, "green" cones at 535 nm and "red" at 570 nm (Figure 3.6). The sampling action of the cones is interpreted by the brain as various color hues. Relatively late in the evolutionary process primates developed the trichromate (three-color) vision system.

We are able to focus on an object though an automatic feedback mechanism. The lens of the eye is very flexible and adaptable and it has been found that the lens is permanently oscillating slightly. This gives the visual system the ability to keep a part of a scene in clear focus while the rest of the scene is blurred. This allows us to focus on a specific zone in our field of vision (FOV).

The photoreceptor cells react to pulses of light. The rod receptor potential reaches a peak in about 25 ms while cones react about four times faster. This combined action results in persistence of vision that is fundamental for multimedia display. Our ability to integrate discrete images into a visual

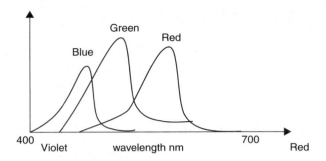

Figure 3.6   Relative sensitivity of cone receptors in the human eye

continuum takes effect at the critical fusion frequency which can be as low as 20 Hz but it depends on both image size and brightness. In the cinema the frame rate is 24 frames per second which is interrupted by a three-bladed shutter to increase the rate to 72 images per second. Television is refreshed (60 Hz in USA, 50 Hz in UK) but as the eye's sensitivity to flicker is proportional to scene brightness it is possible to reduce the refresh cycle for certain scenes, for example dusk and dark, without affecting the viewer. Sensitivity to flicker also depends on where it appears in our FOV. A display screen that can appear stable in the center of our FOV can appear to flicker when seen "out of the corner of our eye".

The retina can process about 100 Mb of information per second. However, the information is passed on to the optic nerve, which can only handle a fraction of this information. This is achieved by cutting out data that can be predicted once the overall pattern has been understood. However, this early processing makes optical illusions possible. At the back of the eye, the retinal photoreceptors connect to a series of neurons within the retina itself before connecting via the optic nerve to the brain. One of the oldest brain features is the representation of the retina on the roof of the midbrain (known as the optic tectum). The retina of each eye sends its axons to terminate in topographical maps in the optic tectum on the opposite side of the brain.

We now understand that the output from the retina has already separated different types of information into different bundles (e.g. shape, orientation, motion and color). These functions are then processed in distinct regions of the visual cortex.

3.3.2   Detailed Visual Processes

This and the next section contain fairly detailed information about human visual object recognition for readers who want to know more.

The effectiveness of the visual system depends on the cooperation of a number of different subsystems within the brain. The visual system has evolved two distinct functional streams, one sensitive to motion and small differences in contrast and the other responsive to shape and form of visual objects. Like other primates our visual field is focused directly in front with less peripheral vision and with highly developed visuo-motor coordination. Primates fixate on an object mainly by eye movements rather than by head movements. One of the key issues for an effective visual system is a mechanism for stabilizing the retinal image so that the image will not be blurred by movement. Retinal stability is achieved through the vestibular system which senses head movements and sends signals to the hindbrain. The hindbrain rapidly relays signals to the extraocular eye muscles to move the eye in all three planes in the opposite direction to compensate for head movement. In addition, signals sent by the cerebellum to the eye muscles precisely calibrate so as not to move the eye too rapidly or too slowly. (The cerebellum literally means little brain and is found at the back of the cerebral cortex. It regulates balance, posture and movement.) It also compares the eye velocity with the head velocity and adjusts the signal through the eye muscles.

Much more of the visual cortex is devoted to the representation of the central part of the retina than to the periphery. The central part has much higher acuity and is our most important means of probing our environment for information. There are many cortical visual areas, each with its own map of the visual field. For example, Tootell *et al.* (1996) have used functional MRI to map more than 25 different areas. Sensory information from the olfactory, visual, auditory and somatosensory system is combined. Information is received from the tectum and the site where these information streams converge is known as the telecephalon.

The main input comes from a layer of neurons in the thalamus. This is topographically organized and is responsible for different sensory maps. There is considerable plasticity in these cortical areas. Yet the basic topographical pattern is relatively constant in individuals of the same species. Beneath the topographic map of the retina in the roof of the midbrain there are inputs from the other senses and thus the midbrain is an important center for the integration of spatial information from the different senses not just in humans but in all vertebrates.

Much analysis of the visual scene involves comparison between topographically adjacent features that differ in shape or color. Primates have extremely well-developed visual capacities and a large number of cortical maps devoted to visual perception and memory. There is also support for the ecological theory from recent progress in neurology. The parts of these maps contained in the cortex that are used the most have the largest representations. The cortical circuitry is highly plastic in that it can change the functional organization in response to experience and this is crucial for memory and information storage. The price of this plasticity is the risk of widely uncontrolled oscillations in neural activity that occur in epilepsy. Functional imaging experiments have demonstrated that the mappings of the cortex depend on experience, i.e. training and learning.

The representation of the hand, for example, expands as a result of performing complex finger movements and is the most notable in Braille readers and in musicians of stringed instruments. The finer the degree of control and use of the muscle, the larger the representation in the cortex.

3.3.3 How Does the Brain Recognize Objects?

Understanding how the brain recognizes objects would be of great advantage to both biologists and computer scientists. We know our brain is very good at picking out faces of our friends or even people we have only seen on one occasion. How does it work? The visual system is able to generalize across huge variations of an object such as a face even though the viewpoint is changed, the illumination is different and another object is in the way.

An object can also be recognized at different levels of specificity. A dog can be recognized as "my dog" at an individual level, or "a dog", "a mammal", etc. There are two tasks involved – identification and categorization. There are differences here between human beings and computer systems. Human beings are very good at categorization but computer systems find this difficult. Identification is simpler for computer systems when it is a question of accessing information about a person and checking whether the face matches.

Evidence from psychophysical and psychological experiments supports theories of object recognition based on the brain synthesizing different views. The process is complex. Neurons can be very specialized. Some are sensitive to particular line orientations such as straight lines and edges. The detection of line edges and curvature forms the basis for the visual analysis of complex objects. The selectivity of the cortical neurons is a computationally ideal system for analyzing images of natural scenes (see Chapter 11).

Some neurons are very sensitive to direction of movement. It has been suggested that these neurons are organized in vertical columns. Neurons in adjacent columns are specialized in sensitivity to movement in the opposite direction. The columns of neurons respond only to one direction and are inhibited by movement in the other direction. The columns are joined so that activity in one direction suppresses activity in the neurons of the adjacent column. This can lead to optical illusions such as the waterfall effect. If you watch a waterfall for a minute or two, then gaze at nearby rocks, the rocks appear to move upwards – opposite to the falling water. The explanation is that the movement has continued for long enough to exhaust the neurons detecting the down movement and so there is no longer a balance between the antagonistic columns.

It appears that within the primary visual cortex (V1) there are arrays of neurons that specialize in different features of the image. In addition an area called the inferotemporal cortex (IT) is very significant. Neurons in V1 respond to simple stimuli while neurons in IT show large receptive fields and respond to complex stimuli. Some neurons in IT were tightly shape-tuned to training objects. The majority of neurons respond only to a single view of an object with a much smaller number responding to a single object-invariant viewpoint. Studies of neurons in IT that respond to faces (face neurons) suggest there is a distributed representation of the object so that the identity of the face is jointly encoded by the activation pattern over a group of face neurons. The evidence for this is from functional MRI studies. Information from IT is provided to the prefrontal cortex for the control of complex behavior. There are many different theories of how this could work. The main difference is whether the models use feedforward models of processing or favor feedback control. Electroencephalogram studies show that the human visual system can solve an object recognition task within 150 ms. This speed of processing is compatible with a class of view-based processing theories that rely only on feedforward processing but it suggests feedback mechanisms would just be too slow.

The analysis of images requires the tracking and identification of moving objects. While the midbrain handles fixation on interesting objects, the forebrain has evolved two distinct systems for seeing motion and the form of objects in the visual scene. The detection of motion requires the fast conduction of information to parts of the brain that plan the movement of the eyes and hands.

3.4.4 Hearing

As soon as you begin to speak muscles in the ear operate to damp down the incoming low frequencies, otherwise you would not be able to talk and listen to people at the same time. The loudness of sound is measured in decibels, 30 dB for a whisper, 60 dB for normal conversation, 90 dB for a shout. If you hum when a loud noise is expected this will reduce the incoming sound to 20 dB. When hearing cells are damaged they can never be replaced. The brain processes the information to map precisely where a sound is coming from to create a three-dimensional (3D) map based on the incoming frequency of the sound.

Sound is a compression wave propagated through a medium such as air or water. The range of frequencies relevant to hearing is 20 Hz–20 kHz. Although the effect is small the action of listening to something modifies the perceived sound because our bodies interact with the pressure wavefronts. Sound is the brain's interpretation of the pressure wave that impinges on the ear. When vibrations enter the part of the ear known as the cochlea they generate electrical signals. It is widely believed that there is a time lag between sound paths to the two ears and the difference in amplitude in the signals is used by the brain to localize the source of the sound. Assuming a distance of about 20 cm between our ears the time delay is about 0.6 ms if one ear is turned towards the sound.

When we listen to a stereo sound through a pair of loudspeakers it generates what is known as a sound stage that has both depth and breadth. The sound stage appears to be between the two speakers but this depends on the type of speakers and their position in relation to the walls of the room. When we listen to a stereo recording through headphones the left and right ears hear the sounds from the individual transducers; this is called binaural hearing. Some sound transmission occurs through the skull from one ear to the other. In the case of headphones the sound stage appears to be located somewhere within the listener's head. Research by Shaw (1974) showed that part of the ear called the pinna has a significant effect on shaping the spectral envelope of the incident sound. This depends on the spatial location of the sound source. Thus the brain learns to extract spatial information from the unique "earprint" the pinnae impress on the incoming pressure waves. This shaping of the sound by the pinnae is responsible for creating an external rather than an internal sound stage. Since headphones, especially those that fit into the inner ear, ignore or destroy the action of the pinna on the perceived sound stage is inside the head. This effect may be corrected by the use of head-related transfer functions (HRTFs) but these need to take into account the head, shoulders and body. This was done in the NASA AMES 3D Auditory Display Project.

Binaural audio has opened a range of new applications. It is now possible to simulate how multiple sound sources are influenced by reflective objects. Technology can support stationary and moving sound sources, non-uniform emitters and Doppler effects that can be experienced by the user independent of their head orientation.

3.3.5 Somatic Senses

Somatic senses collect data from our own body and tell us about its state and relationships with its surroundings. Somatic sensations are associated with how we sense a surface, vibrations, movements against the skin, position, pressure, pain and temperature. The brain's somatic sensory cortex translates signals received from receptors distributed over the body's surface and within deep tissue into a rich variety of sensory feelings. Somatic senses have a wide range of receptors that monitor the body's position and response to touch.

The parts of the body are represented in the brain by mappings in the somatic sensory cortex. Different parts of the body have different size maps, with the lips consuming the largest part. The sensations of touch, pressure and vibration are all detected by the same types of sensors.

The tactile receptors include:

- free nerve endings – these can fire in response to small surface changes;
- Meissner's corpuscles – responsible for fingertip touch sensations, adapt very quickly to any stimulus and detect small changes in pressure;
- Iggo dome receptors – respond to strong signals and continue to fire and adapt slowly to stimuli used to help us locate the position of a stimulus and therefore the nature of the surface being touched;
- Pacinian corpuscles – these have a very fast response and are used to respond to vibrations.

Somatic senses can be exploited in multimedia and virtual reality systems. Since there is a wide range of sensors there is great potential for haptic devices. A simple touch response can be generated by a low-frequency electromagnetic transducer. In applications such as surgical simulation or molecular modeling there is a requirement to track and feed back forces relating to the orientation of a handle or probe.

3.3.6 Equilibrium

The body's mechanism for maintaining equilibrium is the vestibular system. This is located on both sides of the head, very close to the inner ear, and is the organ that registers the head's state of equilibrium. It consists of a system of membranes that monitor the direction of gravity, head orientation, linear acceleration, head rotation and static equilibrium. The vestibular system is responsible for detecting both linear and angular head movements. The system consists of two separate parts oriented at right angles to each other to detect rotational movement. Apart from sensing head equilibrium the vestibular system is closely linked to the visual system. This ensures that when the head is rapidly rotated the retinas continue to record a reasonably stationary image. Otherwise we would have to be stationary before we could see an image.

In addition to the normal functioning of the vestibular system, a sense of balance requires input from the visual system and the vestibulospinal systems. When there is a disruption to the calibration or balance between the two peripheral vestibular systems and any of the other systems the result will be a loss of balance, a sensation of vertigo. Even if a user is sitting at a computer and there is conflict between visual and vestibular information a feeling of nausea can be induced. In some cases this has been so severe that symptoms such as sweating, pallor, vertigo and disorientation occur. In a virtual reality (VR) simulator a visual effect can suggest to the user motion cues such as flying upside down while the sense of equilibrium tells the user that the head is vertical and the position senses that the body is stationary. The brain is tricked into believing it is in motion and would expect the vestibular senses to provide information to support this. When this does not happen an area of the brain called the chemoreceptor trigger zone is excited to induce the vomiting response. It is a zone normally linked to impulses from the gastrointestinal tract but can also be triggered by rapid changes in motion. One interpretation is that this is a warning to the body to stop what it is doing.

Another aspect of simulator sickness is concerned with accurate synchronization of motion cues and visual cues. When this does not occur conflicting sensory signals are generated. This link accounts for the eyestrain and dizziness associated with simulator sickness. It appears that the brain concludes that a mismatch is a consequence of the stomach being poisoned and elicits a vomiting response. This mismatch is most likely to occur when a large screen image is displayed that takes up a considerable portion of the user's FOV. In a virtual head-mounted display there can be additional cause for conflict owing to the time lag involved in a head movement and its representation on the screen. When systems take 200 ms to repaint the screen this is sufficient for sensory conflict to arise. Studies have shown that latency (speed of update of image in response to movement) is more important to the user's feelings of presence in a VR environment than high resolution imaging. Time lags are also caused by 3D trackers. If more than one 3D tracker is used this will also slow the system down unless parallel processing is used.

3.4 Converting Data into Sensory Perception

Most multimedia applications involve the presentation of data to human beings so the data needs to be converted into a form that can be discerned and interpreted by human beings. This often involves some form of visualization even when the data represents sound waves. This will involve numeric data being converted into a sensation-provoking signal such as light, sound, touch or any combination. The image display exploits the following properties of the human visual system:

- high bandwidth;
- rapid ability to recognize patterns;
- interpolation of missing data;
- ability to discriminate dimensionality.

Humans can detect 1 000 000 colors and differentiate 20 000. However, when colors are used to encode abstract information more than 20–30 colors produce confusion rather than enhancing interpretation. For example, X-ray images have been found to be more easily interpreted by radiologists when presented as gray-scale images than when color coded.

As well as the problems described above, it has been suggested that multimedia applications, and VR particularly, can cause psychological effects including addiction, hallucinations, dissociation and retreat from reality. However, there have been few systematic studies of these effects, which are listed in Table 3.1 (Kolansinski, 1995).

It can be argued that these applications can also have a lot of health and safety benefits that are often overlooked. VR can help operators learn to avoid accidents and react correctly in a crisis.

Although multimedia input devises are not covered in this text, we are concerned with the eventual presentation of data if it is likely to affect database design. Therefore in the following sections we look at the different information requirements to support two-dimensional (2D) and 3D displays.

Table 3.1 Potential factors associated with simulator sickness in VR

Individual factors	Application (VR) factors	Task factors
Age	Binocular viewing	Altitude above a terrain
Concentration level	Calibration	Degree of control
Experience with real-world task	Interocular distance	Global visual flow
Adaptation	Contrast	Head movements
Flicker fusion frequency	FOV	Luminance level
Gender	Flicker	Unusual maneuvers
Illness	Motion platform	Method of movement
Mental rotational ability	Position-tracking error	Self-movement speed
Perceptual style	Phosphor lag	Sitting versus standing
Postural ability	Refresh rate	
	Scene content	
	Frame rate	
	Time lag (transport delay)	

3.4.1 Two-dimensional Displays

Workstations are described as bit mapped when a 2D display is broken down into individually addressed pixels. The value of each pixel is stored in a memory address on a graphics card. The display screen is scanned, resulting in the repainting of all pixels many times (30–60) per second. Each scan refreshes all the pixels and is known as progressive scanning. With television screens, half the pixels are refreshed during each scan, interlacing odd lines between even lines at about 1/30 s. Interlacing is better for displaying moving images.

Color coding using 8-bit color values allows 256 colors out of a total palette of 16 million colors to be displayed at once on the screen. Some multimedia applications will require the display of more than 256 colors. In these cases the display will run out of colors. This is most noticeable in regions containing color gradients over large areas, resulting in a "banding" effect. Another problem arises when an application uses a number of graphic windows on the same screen. When the system uses separate color maps in each window and applies the maps based on the location of the cursor, this can result in "flashing". The result is that the window in which the cursor resides will display the correct colors but the other windows will be displayed with uncorrected colors. Banding and flashing are overcome when 24-bit displays are used since these systems are capable of displaying 16 million colors simultaneously but this also triples the amount of memory needed to store the image.

The number of pixels that can be displayed at any one time varies from 640 × 480 up to 1600 × 1200. However, if a higher resolution is used without a corresponding increase in the dimensions of the screen on which the display is presented then the image, text and windows become smaller, as illustrated in Table 3.2. Higher screen resolutions are required for biomedical image displays.

Table 3.2 Screen resolution and image size

Screen resolution	Size of 256 × 256 image
800 × 600	5.12 in
1024 × 768	4.0 in
1280 × 1024	3.2 in
1600 × 1200	2.56 in

3.4.2 Three-dimensional Displays

Devices called 3D graphic accelerators include, in hardware, part or all of the rendering algorithms required to display 3D surface images. These facilities provide simple mathematical descriptions of the 3D objects along with information about the viewpoint (the 2D window that will hold the final image) and lighting parameters in the graphic space. Special graphic constructs called texture maps can be injected into the rendered scene to paint the surfaces of the graphical objects. Using these elements the accelerator computes the appearance of each object as seen in the viewpoint and presents the results to the display screen, exploiting these 3D graphic accelerators by converting 3D image data into geometric objects.

However, the simplest way of generating 3D image displays is to present a pair of appropriately offset 2D images, one for each eye. Some images are also designed to be viewed by the users "crossing their eyes" while viewing the image. This 3D effect is achieved by providing each eye with a separate view of a 3D object separated by a viewpoint difference of between 6° and 10°. This corresponds to the angular separation of the eyes at a viewing distance of 12–24 in. By "crossing one's eyes" the picture will fuse into a single perceived image in the center of the separate images. The fused image has all the 3D cues used to perceive depth of scene, such as objects appearing closer or further in front or relative to each other. However, "crossing one's eyes" is not a viable requirement for long-term use so we need a system that will produce the equivalent effect. The presentation of the two stereoscopic images can be rapidly alternated so that by exploiting the persistence effect of the visual system the user will perceive a blend of the separate images into a single 3D image. These views can be produced easily with monitors which have double-buffered graphics systems that can store both complete images. Each buffer holds one of the stereoscopic images and no flicker is perceived by the user. This would mean for a 3D image database that we may need to store both images in a linked way.

An alternative approach is to view the images through special glasses with the lens of one eyepiece formed by a liquid crystal display that can be switched to synchronize with the switching images on the screen. A small infrared sensor in the glasses receives a switching signal from the computer.

To illustrate how these various human factors can impact on an application we will look at the following scenario.

3.4.3   Surgery planning and rehearsal

Neurosurgery has benefited from and in turn contributed to the development of image-guided and computer-assisted surgery. Neurosurgery involves an extended knowledge and understanding of relationships between normal anatomy and pathology. Patients with brain tumors undergo multimodal image scanning prior to surgery to help the neurosurgeon understand the patient's anatomy. Different scans can be coregistered in order to produce a single visualization which provides complementary information. Image registration is the term used to describe the way separate images of the same object acquired in different ways can be combined. In biomedical applications scanning with computerized tomography (CT), MRI, etc. will result in separate images. To be of use in practical surgery these images need to be combined in the same spatial alignment. When accurately registered each separate image will represent the same physical volume as the corresponding voxel in another image. The term fusion is used to mean the actual combining of separate registered images into a single image. The technical aspects of registration and its implication for databases are discussed in later chapters on multimedia retrieval.

Specific anatomical objects may then be identified and segmented. The surgeon can then use this information to carefully plan the surgical approach. In a typical scenario CT scans used to reconstruct the skull surface are combined with MRI scans used to reconstruct the cortical brain surface and a single-photon-emission computerized tomography is used to image the region of activation produced by the injection of the radioscope. All the images are registered together and the surgical plan can be developed from sequences of visualizations of the registered data. These visualizations enable more precise and expedient navigation to the target site and provide more accurate ways of distinguishing the border of the offending tissue from the margins of adjacent functional tissue. These procedures can also provide online, updated information to accommodate any shifts in the brain position during operational procedures.

This application of multimedia can result in a number of benefits – increased physician performance, reduced operating procedure times, increased patient throughput and reduced healthcare costs. Behind the surgical user interface there must be an effective database that can retrieve and reformat the data as required.

Analyzing complex images as required in the application described above can involve other senses, particularly hearing and touch. Hearing is stereophonic and can be used combined with sight. Other senses can be stimulated via devices that use pixel values from digital images. One example is a stereophonically synthesized heartbeat to assist spatial orientation and intervention timing in an immersive environment while the surgeon is exploring organs within the body. Haptic devices produce touch sensations that can be driven by images whose voxels are parametric to force or pressure in a given direction so that a person can feel virtual objects in 3D space. There is such a system for simulating arthroscopic knee surgery based on volumetric object models derived from 3D MR images. The system provides feedback to the user via real-time volume rendering and force feedback to enable haptic exploration.

3.5 SUMMARY OF CHAPTER

In this chapter we reviewed the human information processing system in relation to multimedia data. We introduced a simple model of information processing which led to the seven stages of action and concepts such as affordance that influenced design.

Processing multimedia data also involves memory and the senses. The visual system is vitally important but we also learned how different parts of the brain work together in complex ways to enable the interpretation of information from the senses. The concept of equilibrium is very important in more complex multimedia applications and virtual environments.

Having completed this chapter you should now be able to:

- describe theories of cognition;
- describe theories of perception in relation to the presentation of media objects;
- appreciate the way the brain processes multimedia information and recognizes objects;
- appreciate the different systems in the cortex that govern the senses and understand how these need to be kept in balance.

SOLUTIONS TO EXERCISES

Exercise 3.1

(a), (b) You should find that most people remember between five and nine names. The most frequently remembered names are likely to be the unusual ones such as Xerxes and Gandalf.

(c) Note that we have suggested 20 s for the display which is slightly longer than the 18 s quoted for STM residence time. LTM should not be significant in this time span in terms of the number of items but it may affect their selection. It is easier to learn a name that is associated with the reader. Another factor is that the names are all associated with Western culture. Readers from Asia or Africa may find the names more difficult to remember because of cultural differences.

Exercise 3.2

(a) Closure – missing parts are filled in.

(b) Continuity – stimulus appears as two continuous lines rather than random set of dots.

(c) Symmetry – regions bounded by symmetrical borders tend to be perceived as coherent figures.

Recommended Reading

Baddeley, A. D. (1999) *Essentials of Human Memory*, Psychological Press, Hove.

Hoffman, D. D. (1998) *Visual Intelligence*, Norton, New York.

Preece, J., Rogers, Y., Sharp, H. (2002) *Interaction Design*, Wiley, New York.

Robb, R. A. (2000) *Biomedical Imaging, Visualization and Analysis*, Wiley-Liss, New York.

Smith, A.(1997) *Human Computer Factors*, McGraw-Hill, Maidenhead.

Vince, J. (1995) *Virtual Reality Systems*. ACM SIGGRAPH, Addison-Wesley, Reading, MA.

Brain map movies can be found at http://cogsci.ucsd.edu/~sereno/movies. html.

chapter 4

An Introduction to SQL and Multimedia

Chapter aims

This chapter reviews the role of SQL and the way the language has been developed to provide support for multimedia data. Through a study of this chapter the reader will develop a knowledge of the main features of SQL data types in relation to multimedia data and within relational database development. Examples will contrast the SQL standard with implementations using Oracle and DB2 to create multimedia relational databases and the reader should then be able to understand:

- the role of standards;
- the main features of SQL data types in relation to multimedia data;
- how stored procedures can be used to create methods to manipulate large binary objects.

The purpose of the chapter is to understand what can be achieved in terms of the storage and manipulation of multimedia data using system-defined data types provided by SQL3 and following a relational approach. The application of object-relational features is postponed until Chapter 6. First we shall find out how to create tables using SQL and then go on to study the means to manipulate data stored in tables. After reviewing the essential features of SQL required to create relational tables and integrity constraints we will learn how to incorporate multimedia data types into a relational table. Multimedia data cannot be manipulated by SQL *built-in* functions so we need to understand how to create SQL routines (functions and procedures) to carry this out. Therefore we continue our study of SQL with a basic review of PL/SQL provided by Oracle DBMS in order to define functions and procedures and then look at the way PL/SQL can be used to manipulate multimedia data. In many cases we will use text examples to show the principles because the results will be easily visible without needing to use an application to render the media data but we note that these same principles can be applied to other media types including audio, image and video data. Examples using these media are given later in this chapter, while more complex issues of multimedia queries and data retrieval will be dealt with in Chapter 5, and in later chapters special issues involving the different media data are studied.

4.1   Introduction to SQL

As an introduction, we will look in detail at the development of SQL and in the process briefly revise some of the main concepts of the language. In most cases we will focus on those aspects of SQL that are particularly relevant to multimedia data. A more comprehensive account of the SQL language can be found elsewhere. Those readers who are already familiar with SQL can skip the basic sections of this chapter.

SQL is the standard language for dealing with relational databases. Although E. F. Codd published his paper setting out the relational model for databases in 1970, the first ANSI standard was not ratified until 1986, followed by the international standard for SQL published in 1987. It is formally referred to as SQL:1987. SQL had been developed from an earlier Structured English Query Language, SEQUEL, developed by IBM in the 1970s. During the 1980s and 1990s over a hundred database products were developed that supported some dialect of SQL as it had already become the *de facto* standard of the database world.

The main aim in developing this initial standard was to ensure application program portability, so that the resulting specification of SQL provided a basic core of SQL which was common to many SQL implementations at that time. It also had the advantage of making the training of database management system (DBMS) staff simpler. However, as SQL:1987 was a basic core, there were many DBMS issues that were not included, such as how to deal with interoperability among the different SQL implementations. Probably the most important capability it lacked was some of the features to support relational theory, especially primary key and foreign key constraints. These are very important means of ensuring the integrity and consistency of relational databases.

Consequently, a revision of the SQL standard was published in 1989, entitled *Database Language SQL with Integrity Enhancement*. This version became known as **SQL:1989**, specified the constraint definitions that could be used, but otherwise it did not provide any additional capabilities for defining or accessing data. Most SQL implementations now support these constraints. The introduction of constraints still left gaps in the 1989 version of the SQL standard which the standard bodies, ISO and ANSI, continued to work on, resulting in many additional capabilities being specified in the version known as **SQL2**. ISO published this version as an international standard in 1992. **SQL2** is more formally referred to as **SQL:1992**. Since 1992 there have been further developments of SQL. In 1999, **SQL3** or **SQL:1999** became the standard, replacing SQL:1992 and commercial systems are currently being developed to support the new standard.

When SQL was originally developed it had been intended as a language that would be used interactively in immediate mode but, as databases developed, application programs became an important means of users communicating with databases. The standard therefore needed to address the issue of the portability of application programs, resulting in an important development of SQL, agreed in 1996 with the incorporation of Persistent Stored Modules (PSMs) within the standard. This allowed developers to create complete applications in SQL without needing a so-called host language to support the limited computational power that SQL possessed.

For this text, a significant development in SQL3 is that the users are permitted to create their own data types and are no longer limited to the *built-in* (system-defined) data types. This version of the standard provides a range of new facilities, but in particular it extends relational concepts to include "object" capabilities, which are covered in Chapter 6. This gives a great deal of flexibility when dealing with multimedia data which as we have seen in Chapter 2 can exist in a wide range of different formats and compression levels. SQL3 also enables new media standards to be incorporated in an application when necessary. Thus there is not one SQL standard but many. It is not envisaged that an SQL implementation would support all SQL3 capabilities, but a number of packages are proposed for particular purposes, such as providing enhanced integrity management or object support.

A database should be self-describing and a data dictionary is one way in which this can be achieved. The SQL standard includes the specification for a catalog (data dictionary) called the **information schema**. An SQL schema in the standard refers to the descriptors of the part of the database that belongs to a particular user. A catalog will have one *information schema* and many SQL schema. The *information schema* includes views, tables, columns, privileges, constraints, key column usage and assertions. The information stored in the catalog is often called metadata. However, this kind of metadata refers to tables and users whereas the metadata we will deal with in Chapter 7 to describe multimedia data includes in addition data about individual objects and values within tables.

Another useful part of the SQL standard is the Call Level Interface (SQL CLI). The objective of SQL/CLI is to allow an application that has been written in a host language (such as C, C# or JAVA) to manipulate data in a relational database. This is achieved by the host language issuing requests expressed in SQL and special CLI routines. The various SQL database vendors provide their own CLI routines. Later we will see how some of these work. SQL CLI, ODBC and dynamic SQL allow applications to be written for situations where the exact SQL statement is not known at run time. However, SQL CLI has an advantage that applications can be database independent to some extent and generic applications can be developed.

Relational terminology sometimes causes confusion because there are precise terms that are derived from relational theory's origins in discrete mathematics and other more informal terms that are in general use. Table 4.1 gives some important examples of this. Note that in this text we will avoid using the term record to refer to a row in a relational table. At the moment the term domain is tending to be replaced by the term **type**. In formal relational theory a domain is a special kind of set – the source set of a function or relation. The term "type" is also used for a set of values. These values can be drawn from the traditional system defined data types such as INTEGER, CHARACTER, etc. or in SQL3 they can be user-defined types, such as a set of weights or the size of bottles in our wine shop. A user-defined type is one created by the designer of the database. This concept of type has an advantage that only certain operations can be allowed, that is are valid, for a given type. For example, arithmetic operations will only be valid for a numeric data type; finding the time intervals between two dates can only apply to date data types. When user-defined types are created in SQL3, the user can also specify the operations (methods) that can be applied to them. This facility has given the SQL user the ability to introduce the concepts of object-oriented development into databases, giving the basis for the development of object-relational databases which are discussed in Chapter 6.

Table 4.1   Relational concepts in practice

Formal relational term	Informal equivalent
Relation	Table
Tuple	Row or record
Cardinality	Number of rows
Attribute	Column or field
Degree or arity	Number of columns
Primary key	Unique identifier
Domain	Pool of legal values
Project	Select columns
Restrict	Select rows
Join	Combine tables

There is no restriction in the relational model on the kinds of things that can be defined as types, but this theoretical ability has only been available in practice since the development of SQL3. However, now we can have types made up of maps, images and videos by using user-defined types. But the values of a type must only be manipulated by the operators defined on that domain. Date (2000) defines two kinds of types: scalar and non-scalar. According to Date, non-scalar types are defined so they have user-visible components while scalar types have no user-visible components. Scalar types are often described as atomic or encapsulated. Date gets round the problem that scalar types such as dates appear to have components such as day, month and year by arguing that scalar types can have representations that have components. In SQL3 the data type DATE defines a single value but the special date functions YEAR, MONTH and DAY can access the different parts of a DATE value and manipulate them.

EXERCISE 4.1

Give one sentence to describe the following terms:

(a) information schema;

(b) project in SQL;

(c) host language;

(d) type in SQL3.

4.1.1 SQL – Creating Tables and Constraints

All the data values within the same column of a relational table must all be of the same data type. The main categories of traditional data types are character string, numeric, bit string and date–time. Standard SQL3 data types are given in Table 4.2 but these may be implemented in slightly different ways by different DBMS vendors as illustrated by the columns giving the DB2 and Oracle equivalents. In Oracle VARCHAR data types should always be specified as VARCHAR2.

MMDB applications frequently need to represent and manipulate dates and times. The date–time data types include the separate data types DATE, TIME and TIMESTAMP that are given in Table 4.2. TIMESTAMP is a data type that includes all the fields for both date and time and is often an important attribute for multimedia data such as photographs and video. A good review of these data types is included in Darwen and Date (2000). Date–time data types are different from other SQL data types, in that they have components called date–time fields. Fields in date–time data can be manipulated

Table 4.2   SQL standard data types with corresponding implementations in Oracle and DB2

SQL standard	Description	DB2 specification	Oracle specification	Purpose
CHAR(n) or CHARACTER(n)	Fixed length character strings of length n	CHARACTER(n)	CHAR(n) where n is the length in bytes.	Used when exact length of data is known, such as codes
CHAR VARYING(n) or CHARACTER VARYING(n)	Character, varying length where n is the maximum length in bytes	VARCHAR(n): the size is limited for example up to 4000 bytes.	VARCHAR2(n): the size is limited for example up to 4000 bytes.	Used when data length varies, such as names and addresses
INTEGER, SMALLINT or INT	Integer numbers	INTEGER or SMALLINT	NUMBER	Used when integer operations are required
NUMERIC (p, scale)	Decimal numbers of precision exactly p, with scale digits after the decimal point	DECIMAL	NUMBER(p, s), numbers of precision exactly p, with scale digits after the decimal point	Used when numeric operations are required
FLOAT	Floating-point numbers of precision p	REAL		
DATE	Date–time data	DATE	DATE	Used when date/ interval operations are required
TIME(p)	Clock time of precision p	TIME	TIME	
TIMESTAMP(p)	Date and time of precision p	TIMESTAMP		
Interval	Time interval			
BLOB	Binary	BLOB	BLOB	Used when random access and transaction support required; needs locator
CLOB	Character	CLOB/DBCLOB	CLOB	
NCLOB	National character sets		NCLOB	
BFILE	Binary	GRAPHIC	BFILE	Read only External file
			RAW/LONG RAW	Binary data; used for import and export

individually so that we can deal separately with years, months, etc. In the SQL standard, date–time fields are ordered from most significant, YEAR, to least significant, SECOND. Each field has a fixed number of "positions" that are independent of the way they are implemented by any particular DBMS such as Oracle and DB2. For example, the length of a DATE value in the SQL standard is 10 positions, based on the international date format YYYY-MM-DD. In Oracle a date is stored as a 7-byte number together with the time in hours, minutes and seconds, but dates are displayed by default as "dd-mmm-yy", for example 18-Mar-02. The year field of the date is stored as a four-digit year where the first two digits are defaulted to the current date. The date format is designed to preserve the century digits even when entered as a two-character year. However, it is wise to use four-digit years in the format "dd-mmm-yyyy" as much as possible. As we shall find later, date and time are important in multimedia data.

We have noted in Chapter 1 that multimedia data requires data types with very large size. A multimedia database can be created in SQL3 in a number of different ways, for example using:

- binary large objects (BLOBs) stored within the local database that could contain text documents, audio, video or image data;
- separate files of large objects stored as BFILEs, stored within the operating system file system;
- streaming audio or video data stored on specialized media servers;
- URLs containing audio, image or video data stored on any HTTP server – There are many examples of HTTP servers, such as Microsoft Internet Information Server, Apache HTTPD server and Oracle Application Server.

In the last three cases a pointer is stored in the database and the media data is stored externally. This is a convenient way of storing large media repositories. This media data can be imported into a BLOB within the database when needed for database transactions. Table 4.2 gives details of the different data types, fields and range values according to the SQL standard and illustrates the variations that occur when the standard is implemented by different vendors, in this case Oracle and DB2.

Note that BLOBs, CLOBs and BFILEs are all examples of LOBs – large binary objects. In this text, when we use the term LOB the principle we are describing applies to all three types, otherwise the principle only applies to the specific data type described. We could describe the term LOB as the generic term and BLOB, CLOB and BFILE as specializations that have different characteristics and methods associated with them. The idea that data types are associated with a limited number of operations that could be used to manipulate the data is nothing new. However, because these operations were associated with system-defined data types listed in Table 4.2 the user was not conscious of them. Now when we define a new user-defined data type we need to think about the methods that are needed, for example we may need a method that changes the way an image is compressed.

4.1.2 Creating Relational Tables

The relational model is based on a number of essential concepts that include:

- Structure – the user perceives the data as existing in tables.

- Integrity – the tables must satisfy certain integrity constraints.
- Manipulation – the operations performed on the tables result in deriving tables from tables. There are three important operations: restrict, project and join.

In this chapter we are focusing on relational databases. The tables are based on the concept of a relation and all relations have the following essential properties:

- There are no duplicate tuples.
- Tuples are unordered, top to bottom.
- Each tuple contains exactly one value for each attribute.

We will see how SQL can be used to ensure that these properties hold for all the tables in the database.

In order to set up a relational table we must first create the structure of the table and then populate the table with data by using an INSERT statement. In SQL, a table is defined using the **CREATE TABLE** statement. The format of this statement for a simple table is:

```
CREATE TABLE <table name>
        (<column definition list>,
        PRIMARY KEY (<column name>))
```

The SQL schema for the **part** table, which was introduced in Chapter 1, with the primary key **part_number** would be as follows:

```
CREATE TABLE part
(part_number      CHAR(4),
descrip           VARCHAR2(120),
part_name         VARCHAR2(25),
cost              NUMBER(6,2),
PRIMARY KEY (part_number))
```

The primary key clause is optional, but if one were not defined it would permit a table to have duplicate rows and this would violate the relational model. Note that we have opted to specify the **part_number** column as a CHAR rather than a number. This is because every type includes a set of operations. We do not want to carry out any arithmetic on the **part_number** as it is just a code. Therefore it is more appropriate to specify it as a CHAR. As a code it also has a fixed width and format so we should not specify it as a VARCHAR. A CREATE TABLE statement has to be executed by a DBMS in the same way as any other kind of SQL statement. During the processing of such a statement, the table definition is first checked to make sure that it is syntactically correct, the defined properties are then stored in the database schema and an empty table is constructed ready to hold new data.

In the case of the **part** table we specified the primary key as a table constraint, adding it after the list of columns. Constraints can also be specified for a single column as column constraints as in the following example:

```
CREATE TABLE department
(department_number    CHAR(4) CONSTRAINT prim_dept PRIMARY KEY,
department_name       VARCHAR2(10)           ]              prim_dept
```

In this example the definition of the primary key, which is known as a primary key constraint, is given a name **prim_dept** which must be unique in the information schema. Giving the constraint a meaningful name is optional but good practice. Once a table has been created its structure can be changed by defining additional columns and constraints or changing existing definitions. For example, if we had created another table

```
CREATE TABLE employee
(employee_number    CHAR(4),
employee_name       VARCHAR2(30),
salary              NUMBER(6,2),
start_date          DATE)                              emp_table
```

SQL will allow us to create this table even though it would not have a primary key constraint which would violate one of the rules of relational theory and mean that such a table would not really be a *relational* table. However, we can add a constraint once a table has been created by using the ALTER TABLE statement. The general format of this statement is

ALTER TABLE <table name> <alter action>

For example, the next statement would be used to define a primary key for an existing table:

```
ALTER TABLE table_name
      ADD (CONSTRAINT constraint_name
      PRIMARY KEY(column_names))
```

We can use this to add a primary key to the employee table:

```
ALTER TABLE employee
      ADD (CONSTRAINT prim_emp PRIMARY KEY(employee_number))
                                                          prim_emp
```

To summarize, we can apply constraints to the whole table or to individual columns. Users frequently become confused about which type of constraint to use. All constraints can be added as table constraints but you cannot add a column constraint to a column when the constraint involves more than one column. Many tables can only achieve the "no duplicates" rule by having composite primary keys that consist of several columns. (Check constraints that are described below frequently involve more than one column. These have to be specified as table constraints.)

- *Table constraints*. These may reference one or more columns and are defined separately from the definitions of the columns in the table.
- *Column constraints*. These reference a single column and are defined within the specification for the owning column.

Table constraints are placed in the CREATE TABLE command after all the columns are declared and therefore start with a comma. Column constraints are added after the column definition before the comma. Primary key constraints cannot include columns with LOB data types.

Each constraint should be assigned a name. The keyword CONSTRAINT allows you to name a new constraint yourself; it is easier if you supply one yourself so that it may be easily referenced later, but if not then a name is automatically generated by the DBMS.

We can create the basic structure of the database in this way but we need to use additional constraints to ensure the integrity of the data. This is because in a relational database the entire information content of the database is represented explicitly by values in columns in rows in tables. There is no connection between the rows of the employee table and the rows of the department table so we do not know which employees belong to which departments. We can solve this problem by adding a column to the employee table to hold the department number of the department that the employee currently belongs to. It will be important to ensure that the column holds a valid department number. We may also want to ensure that every employee has a department number.

We can use the ALTER TABLE statement to add the **department_ number** to the **employee** table.

```
ALTER TABLE employee
    ADD (department_number CHAR(4))                    add_column
```

A foreign key is a column, or columns, in one table (the "referencing" table), which contain values that match those in the primary key of another table (the "referenced" table). We can ensure that the **department_number** in the **employee** table will match a value in the department table by making it a foreign key. This can be expressed either as a column constraint

```
department_number CHAR(4) NOT NULL REFERENCES department
```

or as a table constraint

```
FOREIGN KEY (department_number) REFERENCES department
```

In both of these foreign key definitions, it is implicit that **department_ number** is referencing the primary key of the department table, that is **department_number**. It is possible to have a foreign key referencing a column or columns, defined as an alternate key with a unique constraint rather than a primary key. For example, the foreign key definition for **department_number** is added as follows:

```
ALTER TABLE employee
ADD (CONSTRAINT emp_dep_fkey FOREIGN KEY(department_number)
REFERENCES
department(department_number))
```

add_referential

These constraints are therefore called referential integrity constraints. Foreign keys can also be removed with the ALTER TABLE statement. A primary key can also be enabled or disabled in Oracle to allow data to be loaded in bulk which is important for multimedia data because of its huge size. This would be done with the statement

```
ALTER TABLE table_name
        DISABLE constraint_name
```

Alternatively, it could also be removed altogether but note we need to know the constraint name:

```
ALTER TABLE table_name
            DROP constraint_name
```

When we add data to a table we have to take into account the referential integrity constraints. For example, we could add the data to the employee table with a simple insert statement:

```
INSERT INTO employee
(employee_number, employee_name, salary, start_date,
department_number)
VALUES ('7902', 'FORD', 175.66, '12-May-1991', '3010')
```

Before the data can be inserted into the table employee, the DBMS must check the referential constraint to ensure that the department number "3010" is valid and exists already in the department table. Foreign keys provide referential integrity rules either within a table or between tables. A foreign key is used in a relationship with either a primary or a unique key elsewhere in the database. It could be used, for example, to prevent deletion of a department in **department** if employees exist with the same depart- ment number in **employee**. As with primary keys, we can specify a foreign key as either a table or column constraint: table constraint syntax,

```
,[CONSTRAINT constraint_name]FOREIGN KEY (column, column, ...)

REFERENCES table (column, column, ...)
```

column constraint syntax,

```
[CONSTRAINT constraint_name] REFERENCES table (column,
column, ....)
```

ON DELETE CASCADE Option

Before we leave this topic it is important to note another feature provided to manage referential integrity. As a result of the above constraints, a department could not be deleted if rows exist in **employee** with the same **department_number** value. We can ensure that corresponding employees are deleted automatically if the parent department in **department** is deleted by adding the clause ON DELETE CASCADE:

```
CONSTRAINT fk_deptno FOREIGN KEY (department_number)
REFERENCES department(department_number)ON DELETE CASCADE
```

EXERCISE 4.2

Write an SQL statement to:

(a) add a column to the **employee** table to hold a photograph of each employee using an appropriate data type;

(b) create a table called grape to hold information about the grapes used to produce the wines – there must be a column to hold text information about the grape and also a column to hold a photograph.

Columns that are specified as LOB data types cannot be used in the definition of primary or foreign keys. We could regard the employee's picture as unique but we still cannot use it as a primary key. We could, however, use columns that contained metadata about the media objects in constraint definitions.

In addition to primary key constraints there are several other types of key that can be defined and add to the integrity of the database.

Constraint Types

We may define the following constraint types:

- NULL/NOT NULL   to prevent missing values

- UNIQUE   for candidate keys
- PRIMARY KEY   ensures no duplicate tuples
- FOREIGN KEY   ensures referential integrity
- CHECK   for data verification

UNIQUE Constraints

This designates a column or combination of columns as a unique key. This is the way to declare a candidate key that would be an alternative key to the primary key. The unique constraint means that no two rows in the table can have the same value for this key. The primary keys are always unique so it would not be appropriate to add this constraint to a primary key. The constraint is intended as a way of creating alternate keys that will be unique but may be null – have missing values in some rows of the table. NULLs are allowed if the unique key is based on a single column.

The table constraint syntax is

```
,[CONSTRAINT constraint_name] UNIQUE (Column, Column, ...)
```

The column constraint syntax is

```
[CONSTRAINT constraint_name] UNIQUE
```

The CHECK Constraint

The CHECK constraint explicitly defines a condition that each row must satisfy (or make unknown owing to a NULL). In Oracle the check condition may use the same constructs as those in a query restriction, with the following exceptions:

- subqueries are not allowed;
- references to pseudo-columns such as SYSDATE are not allowed.

The syntax is

```
[CONSTRAINT constraint_name] CHECK (condition)
```

Using these features of SQL we can now create a relational table for the **Fine Wine Shop** we introduced in Chapter 1. We want a table to hold wine list data using LOBS. In addition to the requirements for normal business processing, the table we create needs to fulfil the following multimedia requirements:

- the ability to store a large amount of text about the origin and history of the wine;
- the ability to store an audio clip of the correct French pronunciation of the wine name;

● a picture related to the wine which could be of a bottle or the vineyard.

We can write the following schema for the wine shop database in Oracle:

```
CREATE TABLE wine_list
(       wine_code    CHAR(6),
        wine_name    VARCHAR2(30) NOT NULL,
        region       VARCHAR2(20) NOT NULL,
        year         NUMBER(4),
        category     VARCHAR2(20),
        grape        VARCHAR2(20),
        price        NUMBER(5,2),
        bottle_size  NUMBER(4),
        character    VARCHAR2(50),
        note         CLOB DEFAULT EMPTY_CLOB(),
        pronunciation    BLOB DEFAULT EMPTY_BLOB(),
        picture          BFILE,
        CONSTRAINT prim_wine PRIMARY KEY (wine_code))
```

Although we could assume that the name of the wines will be unique and should not be null, this may not always be the case and therefore this is not an appropriate column to make the primary key; therefore it is preferable to create a unique **wine_code**. Region is also important and has been constrained as not null. The character column will hold a small amount of text that users may want to search to make their wine selection. The main text will be held in the note column and defined as a CLOB data type. The audio clips of the pronunciation will be stored in the pronunciation column as a BLOB data type. The picture could have been defined as a BLOB or as a BFILE data type. When we use BFILE the media data will be stored externally to the database. Oracle stores a BLOB locator in the database with the other column attributes. The BLOB itself is stored within the database but in other tablespaces (see Chapter 8). This has the advantage that a table can be created with multiple BLOBs. For example the **wine_list** table could be extended to hold a short video clip, an audio recording describing the contents of the clip and a map of the location of a vineyard. The disadvantage of using BFILEs is that they are not under total control of the database and users could delete the files or change their location in the file system without updating the database. This would cause an inconsistency with the BFILE locator. This also means that we will not be able to use a BFILE in database queries and transactions. However, we can create a temporary BLOB when we need to do this and transfer the BFILE data into it when required.

To summarize we use a temporary LOB when:

● the data is stored in the user's temporary workspace;

● the temporary LOB is not stored permanently in the database

However, note that

● all temporary LOBs are deleted at the end of the session in which they were created;

● a temporary LOB cannot be used with EMPTY_LOB functions.

Implementations of SQL3 vary so the same table would be specified in DB2 as follows:

```
CREATE TABLE wine_list
(      wine_code     CHAR(6) NOT NULL,
       wine_name     VARCHAR(30) NOT NULL,
       region        VARCHAR(20) NOT NULL,
       year          NUM(4),
       category      VARCHAR(20),
       grape         VARCHAR(20),
       price         DECIMAL(5,2),
       bottle_size   NUM(4),
       character     VARCHAR(50),
       note          CLOB(5123),
       picture       BLOB(10 240),
   CONSTRAINT prim_wine PRIMARY KEY (wine_code) )
```

In this case there are slight differences. The data type for character varying is VARCHAR. The primary key column, **wine_code**, must be declared NOT NULL before being identified in the primary key constraint as a table constraint. In addition the LOB data types must be constrained by values.

The structure of the **wine_list** table illustrates a simple way to create a relational table to hold multimedia data. For many applications this may be the most appropriate development. However, it has the disadvantage of not providing a way of storing the metadata about the media data instances together with the data and not participating fully in integrity constraints. It may seem possible to simply add additional columns to the tables to hold metadata attributes, for example, the date a photograph was created and the name of the photographer. This would create what is termed a functional dependency between the media column, which cannot be a primary key, and the metadata columns that would be inconsistent with relational theory – i.e. such a table would not conform with Third Normal Form – for an outline of normalization see Appendix A. This situation could lead to problems in maintaining the consistency of the database when updates occur. We learned in Chapter 1 how important metadata is for multimedia and in later chapters we will see how it is used for multimedia queries.

EXERCISE 4.3

Write an SQL statement to:

(a) add a foreign key to the **wine_list** table to ensure that all the grape values already exist in the **grape** table;

(b) add a check constraint to the **wine_list** table to ensure that when the wine is from a French region there is a pronunciation available.

4.1.3 Manipulating Data Using SQL

Consider the following data for rows for the **wine_list** table:

WINE_CODE	43107B	NOTE
WINE_NAME	Ch.Haut-Rian	*From the glorious 2000 vintage Haut-Rian Sec*
REGION	Bordeaux	*is a blend of 70% Sémillon and 30%*
YEAR	2000	*Sauvignon Blanc. It is pure and aromatically*
CATEGORY	France Red	*fresh on the nose leading on to a crisp palate*
GRAPE	Sauv-Blanc/Sémillon	*with hints of citrus fruits and gooseberries.*
		Ideal as an aperitif but would also go well
		with fish dishes.
		PRONUNCIATION
PRICE	5.75	PICTURE
BOTTLE_SIZE	75	
CHARACTER	Light-medium bodied dry ready but will keep	

We defined the **note** column as a CLOB. Unlike the other LOBS, the CLOB data type can be manipulated with SQL to a limited extent. For example, we can insert the structured data with the following statement:

```
INSERT INTO wine_list (wine_code, wine_name, region, year,
category, grape, price, bottle_size, character)
VALUES ('43107B', 'Ch.Haut-Rian', ' Bordeaux',2000,' France
red','
```

```
Sauv-Blanc/Sémillon',5.75,75,
' Light-Medium Bodied, Dry, Ready, but will keep')
```

wine_clob1

After the insert we can add the CLOB data with an update statement provided we have initialized the CLOB with the EMPTY_CLOB() function. The text data is then added to the LOB locator:

```
UPDATE wine_list
SET note = 'Ideal as an aperitif but would also go well with
fish dishes'
WHERE wine_name ='Ch.Haut-Rian'
```

update_wine_clob1

The next two rows would contain

WINE_CODE	40484B	NOTE	
WINE_NAME	Reisling Trimbach	*One of the greatest dry Rieslings in the world, the excellent 1996 vintage of this stylish bone-dry wine, with its honeyed citrus nose and taut minerally lime fruit would benefit greatly from another year or two in the cellar.*	
REGION	Alsace		
YEAR	1996		
CATEGORY	White		
GRAPE	Reisling		
		PRONUNCIATION	
PRICE	22.50	PICTURE	
BOTTLE_SIZE	75		
CHARACTER	Medium bodied dry ready but will improve		

WINE_CODE	41482B	NOTE
WINE_NAME	Chablis Billaud-Simon	*This wine has an appealing youthful*
REGION	Burgundy	*freshness of ripe green apples and citrus*
YEAR	1999	*fruits with steely and mineral qualities*
CATEGORY	France white	*which are the hallmarks of good Chablis.*
GRAPE	Chardonnay	*Drinking very well now, this would be*
		perfect with any cold white meats.
PRICE	9.45	PRONUNCIATION
		PICTURE
BOTTLE_SIZE	75	
CHARACTER	Light-medium bodied dry ready but will improve	

The CLOB value can also be changed using an SQL statement so that the previous text is replaced as follows.

```
UPDATE wine_list
SET note = ' From the glorious 2000 vintage Haut-Rian Sec is a
blend of 70% Sémillon and 30% Sauvignon Blanc.'
WHERE wine_name ='Ch.Haut-Rian'
```

The INSERT statement is used to insert new rows into a table. In the example we have always used the optional column list. This is good practice as it will make the database more maintainable but also it is important to use this form with multimedia data as we may need to add the LOB data separately using specific methods.

EXERCISE 4.4

Write an SQL statement to insert statements for the structured data for the two rows of the wine list table given above. (Do not try to insert into the columns with LOB data types.)

4.2 Methods Using PL/SQL Stored Procedures

Functions and procedures are facilities common to many computer languages, to such an extent that some languages are characterized as procedural. There are considerable differences in the way these facilities are supported by different DBMSs, even though there is now a standard specification given by what are known as – SQL PSMs, which was published as an international standard in 1996. When the facility was introduced into the SQL standard in 1996, it added a number of advantages to the SQL language. Since stored procedures only require the calling parameters the transmission of whole results sets or intermediate tables required for SQL statements is avoided and network traffic can be reduced. Stored procedures are executed in compiled format which greatly reduces code execution times. Stored procedures are also a way of controlling development and are an essential part of object-relational development. Firstly we will look at how functions and procedures are developed in PL/SQL and then in Chapter 6 we will look at the way PL/SQL procedures can be used as members of object types.

In this section we will use Oracle's version of PL/SQL to illustrate the use of functions and procedures and to describe those available for manipulating multimedia data. PL/SQL stored procedures access data stored in tables and combine this with variables created to hold data for processing within the procedure. PL/SQL variables can have a wide range of data types, such as:

- scalar;
- composite (user-defined types, see Chapter 6);
- reference to database structures, e.g. %type;
- LOBs;
- Non PL/SQL – from host languages.

As well as SQL built-in data types, PL/SQL allows variables to have additional data types:

- PLS_INTEGER, signed integers that require less storage than NUMBER;
- BOOLEAN, which can hold the values TRUE, FALSE or NULL.

For example, we can declare a BOOLEAN variable, set to true as follows:

```
v_valid BOOLEAN NOT NULL := TRUE;
```

Referencing nonPL/SQL variables is achieved through using the colon prefix as for **quantity**:

```
Total :=:quantity*price;
```

4.2.1 Functions

A function is a mapping from an input set, the source, to a specific output set, the target, as illustrated in Figure 4.1. When we give a function a valid argument from its input set, it will return a single value from the output set. However, *built-in* SQL functions are slightly different from those met in most programming languages because they will operate on a set of values, from the rows of a table, to map each one to the output set of values. For example, the SUBSTR function will extract a string from a column which has a character data type:

```
SELECT      wine_code, SUBSTR(wine_name,1,5)
FROM        wine_list
```

The PL/SQL functions we are now considering have the same properties as *built-in* functions but are likely to operate on single values or rows rather than on sets of values. They are defined by a user for a specific task that is likely to be applicable to just one database. Thus they are often referred to as user-defined functions.

To define these functions, SQL includes facilities comparable with most programming languages, which can be used for any data, and not just those related to tables. For example, we can define a function, using Oracle's PL/SQL, that returns as the result the sum of two integer numbers, which would look like this:

```
CREATE OR REPLACE FUNCTION fun_sum (first INTEGER, second INTEGER)
RETURN NUMBER(2)
AS
      result NUMBER;
BEGIN
  result := first+second;
RETURN result;
END;
/
```

The data type of the value returned is specified in the RETURN clause.

The definition of a function consists of two main parts. In the first part, a function is defined by giving it a unique name and a list of parameters; each parameter must have a distinct name and a data type, followed by the keyword RETURN with the data type of the result of the function. In this way the input and output sets of the function are specified. When the function is called the arguments must be members of these valid input sets. The inclusion of the keyword IS or AS is essential, since the declaration of variables needed by the stored procedure is placed between the words AS and BEGIN. The second part, between BEGIN and END, forms the **body** of the

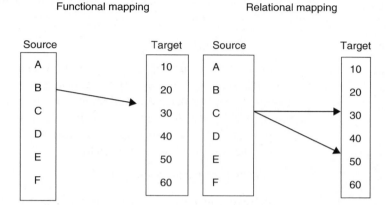

Figure 4.1 Functions and relations

function in the form of a **compound statement** that expresses step by step how the function processes the data. Although the compound statement may consist of a number of SQL statements separated by semicolons, it is essential that the definition of the body of the function is treated as a complete unit, and not as a series of individual SQL statements.

In our first example the name of the function is **fun_sum**, there are two parameters, **first** and **second**, both have integer data types, and the result returned is an integer. The following statement defines another example of a function, called **wine_price**:

```
CREATE OR REPLACE FUNCTION wine_price (my_wine IN VARCHAR2)
RETURN NUMBER
AS
my_price NUMBER(5,2);
BEGIN
SELECT price INTO my_price
FROM wine_list
WHERE wine_name = my_wine;
RETURN my_price;
END;
/                                                        fun_wine_price
```

According to the function definition it accepts the name of a wine (**my_wine**) as an argument and returns a decimal number that is the price of the wine. In this function there is a SELECT statement which selects a single value from a table and places it INTO the variable **my_price**. The value held by the variable **my_price** is returned by the function. Functions are written in PL/SQL, saved into the database and compiled so that they can then be used in an SQL query; for example, **wine_price** could be used:

```
SELECT wine_price('Haut Brion')
FROM wine_list
```

In the previous example the user would be able to give the name of a wine as an input argument and the function would return the price. The function body processes the SELECT statement to retrieve a single value that is returned by the function. Note that there must be a FROM clause in any valid SQL query and sometimes if a function does not need data from a table then we use a dual table. For example,

```
SELECT SYSDATE from DUAL
```

will give the current date. We can use the dummy table with function **fun_sum** as well:

```
SELECT sum(2,9) from DUAL
```

4.2.2   Procedures

In many ways procedures are very similar to functions: they are both routines that can accept arguments, with a body containing a compound statement, so let us consider the differences. A procedure does not return a value like a function does, so it does not have a RETURN clause, nor does the body include a RETURN statement to provide a value. A procedure may carry out some internal data processing but may not return any value. Thus a procedure cannot be used within queries and other SQL statements, but it can be invoked. In standard PSM/SQL a procedure is invoked in a CALL statement such as:

```
CALL<procedure name>(<argument list>)
```

A procedure argument can be used the same way as a function argument, to provide a value to be used in the processing, but additionally it can be used to return a value. In Oracle a procedure can be called by using its name or executed in SQL*PLUS as follows:

```
EXECUTE<procedure name>(<argument list>)
```

or in Oracle SQL*PLUS

```
<procedure name>(<argument list>)
```

Since there are two potential uses of an argument, the definition of a procedure needs to specify for each parameter whether the parameter is expected to provide data or return data or both. (The key words IN, OUT and INOUT are used for this purpose; see below.)

As an example, the following procedure has the same purpose as the function **wine_price**:

```
CREATE OR REPLACE PROCEDURE proc_price
(my_wine IN VARCHAR,
 my_price OUT NUMBER)
AS
BEGIN
 SELECT price
 INTO my_price
 FROM wine_list
 WHERE wine_name = my_wine;
END;
```
                                                                    create_proc_price

The query statement in this procedure is exactly the same as that in the function **wine_price**. The differences are that in the procedure **my_price** is a parameter rather than a variable and the procedure does not explicitly return a value for the result as a function does. Also note that the parameter **my_wine** is qualified by IN, which specifies that it provides a value to be used by the procedure but this value must not be changed by the procedure. In contrast, **my_price** is qualified by OUT, which specifies that it does not provide a value to be used by the procedure but is to be used to return a value. We can use the **wine_price** procedure to obtain the same data as that in the example of the function **wine_price** by invoking the procedure in Oracle as follows:

```
EXECUTE proc_price ('Reisling Trimbach', : new_price)
```

The value "Reisling Trimbach" is provided as the IN parameter **my_wine**. However, what is **new_price**? In Oracle it is possible to use two kinds of parameters in PL/SQL: **actual** parameters that are fed into the stored procedure and **formal** parameters that are part of the procedure declaration. It is good practice to use different names for the actual and formal parameters. The second formal parameter, **my_price**, is specified as OUT, and when the procedure is executed a value is assigned to **my_price** through the INTO clause. Thus wherever the procedure is executed there must be a variable for the second argument, to receive the value assigned to the formal parameter **my_price** by the execution of the procedure. **new_price** is the actual parameter.

Parameter Data Types

A procedure is defined with a list of parameters, and we now examine further details of how these parameters are specified and used because there are some important issues that will affect the development of methods for dealing with multimedia data. Each parameter for a procedure must have a name that is unique for that procedure, a data type and a mode of use. As well as the IN and OUT modes we have already seen, there is an INOUT mode. Below the purpose of the three modes of parameter and the way parameters of the different modes can be used are listed:

IN   provides an input value; an argument for this kind of parameter can be a literal (i.e. an actual value), a variable or an expression. It cannot be assigned a different value by the procedure and so cannot be placed on the left-hand side of an assignment statement or receive data through either a SELECT ... INTO statement or a FETCH statement.

INOUT   can either provide an input value or return an output value; an argument for this kind of parameter must be a variable so that its value can be changed by the procedure.

OUT   returns an output value; an argument for this kind of parameter must be a variable.

If a mode is not specified for a parameter, it is assumed to be an IN parameter. An IN parameter for a procedure can never be changed within the procedure. It must have the same value after an invocation call as before it.

An OUT or INOUT parameter does not have these restrictions and can be used much more freely in a procedure. You should note, however, that an OUT parameter does not have an initial value (and an INOUT parameter may not have one) so initialization is required if it is used to provide a value. In the following example a procedure to process a customer's wine order is defined with the formal parameters. The formal parameters **customer_no** and **quantity** may be constants or variables but because they are IN parameters you cannot assign a value to them. We can, however, use **total** in expressions and assign values to it.

```
CREATE OR REPLACE order_proc (customer_no IN CHAR, quantity IN
INTEGER,total OUT NUMBER)
```

When parameters are passed to Oracle procedures, this can be achieved by virtue of position or by name. For example, to use the position the parameters appear in the evocation we would write as follows:

```
order_proc (new_ customer_no, 32, quantity);
```

The named method involves specifying the formal parameter and the actual value assigned to it, as follows:

```
order_proc (customer_no=> new_ customer_no, quantity=> 32);
```

We cannot execute a function or a procedure if there are compilation errors. In SQL*PLUS the command SHOW ERRORS will display a list of compilation problems.

EXERCISE 4.5

This is a practical exercise for developing familiarity with PL/SQL. In the following exercises, you may either create your PL/SQL block in the SQL buffer by typing the code directly and later SAVE it to a file or alternatively create a file directly using a text editor such as Notepad and input your block using the host editor.

PL/SQL is designed to be used with application programs so that when we use it in SQL*PLUS it can be difficult to observe the results of the processing, particularly for multimedia data. In many of the exercises, we will need to record general results in a table; the general-purpose table MESSAGES may be used for this and you should create it as follows:

Table MESSAGES

Column	Description
NUMCOL1	NUMBER (9, 2)
NUMCOL2	NUMBER (9, 2)
CHARCOL1	VARCHAR2 (60)
CHARCOL2	VARCHAR2 (60)
DATECOL2	DATE

For some simple practice of PL/SQL expressions, create a block which declares four variables:

V_BOOL1	Boolean
V_BOOL2	Boolean
V_CHAR	Character (variable length)
V_NUM	Number

Then assign values to these variables as follows:

Variable	Value
V_CHAR	The literal "42 is the answer"
V_NUM	The first two characters from V_CHAR
V_BOOL1	TRUE or FALSE – depending on whether V_NUM is less than 100
V_BOOL2	The opposite of V_BOOL1

Note that a formal parameter cannot be constrained to NOT NULL although variables declared within program blocks can be. However, in Oracle we can constrain a formal parameter to the data types of an actual table or column. The %TYPE attribute casts a parameter to a column defined in a table. For example, the following declaration constrains the parameter

v_name to the type of the column **wine_name** in the **wine_list** table:

```
v_name IN wine_list.wine_name%TYPE
```

Similarly, the %ROWTYPE attribute creates a PL/SQL record that contains all the columns in the specified table:

```
v_row OUT wine_list%ROWTYPE
```

This is mainly used when a complete table row is required as the OUT parameter, for example,

```
CREATE OR REPLACE PROCEDURE get_wine_detail
(wine_name IN wine_list.wine_name%TYPE,
 wine_row OUT wine_list%ROWTYPE)
 AS
 BEGIN
  SELECT*INTO wine_row
  FROM wine_list
  WHERE wine_name = wine_name;
END;
```

This is very useful for maintenance because if the table definitions are changed our procedures will still be consistent and will not need to be altered.

Now we will look at a more complex procedure in more detail. The following example checks whether a wine is in stock in the inventory and if it is, then reduces the stock level by 1; if the wine is out of stock it sends a message instead to the purchase table.

```
CREATE OR REPLACE PROCEDURE example2_proc (
    qty_on_hand OUT NUMBER);
AS
BEGIN
    SELECT quantity INTO qty_on_hand
    FROM wine_inventory    WHERE wine_code='44010' ;
    IF qty_on_hand >0 THEN UPDATE wine_inventory
        SET quantity = quantity - 1
        WHERE wine_code ='44010' ;
    ELSE
        INSERT INTO wine_purchase VALUES
        ('Out of product 44010', SYSDATE) ;
    END IF;
    COMMIT;
EXCEPTION
    WHEN no_data_found THEN
```

```
        INSET INTO errortable
        VALUES ('wine_code 44010 NOT FOUND ');
    END;
```

This procedure **example_proc** contains a procedure declaration with parameter definitions and an exception section. When a procedure is being developed it is important to check the success or failure of the individual SQL statements. EXCEPTION is an important section which is executed whenever an error occurs based on a group of predefined PL/SQL errors. Using the EXCEPTION clause which is an optional part of the COMPOUND statement is a way of clearly separating error processing from normal processing statements. A database exception statement is raised whenever a PL/SQL statement violates a processing rule. Predefined internal exceptions that Oracle provides are shown in Table 4.3. To understand how these work consider the clause

```
    SELECT quantity INTO
```

This creates an implicit cursor that must only return one row. When the SELECT ... INTO ... FROM ... statement returns no rows the Oracle exception NO_DATA_FOUND is raised. The overall syntax is

```
    EXCEPTION WHEN exception_name THEN
          exception block;
    WHEN exception_name | OTHERS THEN
          exception block;
    END;
```

We also used a COMMIT statement after the INSERT statement. This is necessary in PL/SQL in order to explicitly store data into a table from a procedure.

Stored procedures can be important ways of improving database performance and constraining and trapping processing errors.

Table 4.3 Oracle exceptions

Commonly used predefined exceptions	Purpose
NO_DATA_FOUND	SQL query retrieves no rows
TOO_MANY_ROWS	Implicit cursor returns more than one row
ZERO_DIVIDE	Attempt to divide by zero
INVALID_NUMBER	Attempt to insert or update a column with a numeric data type using a variable that cannot be converted to a numeric data type

4.3 Manipulating Large Objects

As we have seen, it is difficult to manipulate LOBs in SQL because the standard functions do not exist and often SQL editors cannot cope with the display of multimedia data. However, there are often reasons why using SQL to update LOBs or extract segments of data without necessarily displaying the data to the user would be an advantage. There are three approaches to manipulating a LOB in Oracle:

- using Oracle API;
- using DBMS_LOB package;
- using Oracle Call Interface (OCI).

In the following examples we will use the **grape** table which is a very simple table that contains two LOBs to illustrate the different ways in which LOB manipulation can take place. The **grape** table could be defined using a BLOB or BFILE column to hold the photographic data, for example,

```
CREATE TABLE grape
(     grape_name  VARCHAR2(30),
      grape_text  CLOB DEFAULT EMPTY_CLOB(),
      picture     BLOB DEFAULT EMPTY_BLOB(),
      CONSTRAINT prim_grape PRIMARY KEY (grape_name))
```

The grape table should contain the data set out in Figure 4.2.

In the first example we will manipulate CLOB data from the grape table created in Exercise 4.2. In general we need to use PL/SQL functions and

Grape_name	Chardonnay
grape text	Picture
The Big Daddy of white wine grapes and one of the most widely planted in the world. It is suited to a wide variety of soils, though it excels in soils with a high limestone content as found in *Champagne*, *Chablis*, and the Côte D'Or. *Burgundy* is Chardonnay's spiritual home and the best White Burgundies are dry, rich, honeyed wines with marvellous poise, elegance and balance. They are unquestionably the finest dry white wines in the world. Chardonnay plays a crucial role in the Champagne blend, providing structure and finesse, and is the sole grape in Blanc de Blancs.	

Figure 4.2 Data from the grape table

procedures to manipulate LOBs since there are few SQL built-in functions available for multimedia data. We must retrieve its locator value before we can process a LOB. In this example we shall write a simple procedure to retrieve a LOB locator.

```
CREATE OR REPLACE retrieve_lob IS
      Grape_pic      BLOB;
BEGIN
      SELECT         picture
      INTO   grape_pic
      FROM   grape
      WHERE          grape_name = 'Chardonnay';
END;
```

CLOB data is often easier to deal with. We can get rid of the data in the CLOB by using the statement

```
UPDATE grape
SET grape_text = EMPTY_CLOB()
WHERE grape_name = 'Chardonnay'
```

If instead the table is defined using a BFILE data type there will be a number of ways in which the photographic data can be added to the database.

```
CREATE TABLE grape
(     grape_name  VARCHAR2(30),
      grape_text  CLOB,
      picture     BFILE,
      CONSTRAINT prim_grape PRIMARY KEY (grape_name)
```

As stated before, BFILEs are externally stored in the file system which could be CD-ROM, network drive, etc. Before we can use a BFILE in a procedure or within a table we must create a directory object that will be used as an alias for the physical operating system directory that will contain the actual BFILE. The Oracle DBA must create the directory and grant access to it as shown in the following example (for WindowsNT):

```
CREATE DIRECTORY "PHOTO_DIR" AS 'C:\Images';

GRANT READ ON DIRECTORY "PHOTO_DIR" TO scott;
```

We can now use INSERT and UPDATE statements using the BFILENAME function.

```
INSERT INTO grape (grape_name, picture)
VALUES
('chardonnay', BFILENAME('PHOTO_DIR', 'chardonnay.jpg'))
```

We can use the same function to change the data:

```
UPDATE grape
SET picture = BFILENAME('PHOTO_DIR', 'chardonnay.jpg');
```

It is likely that we will want to create different directories for different kinds of media data as follows:

```
CREATE DIRECTORY "AUDIO_DIR" AS 'C:\Audio';
CREATE DIRECTORY "FRAME_DIR" AS 'C:\Images';
```

4.3.1 Using the DBMS_LOB Package

In Oracle we can use a special package DBMS_LOB provided for manipulating LOBs. The DBMS_LOB package also processes BFILEs. DBMS_LOB is a package which is based on working with LOB locators. It consists of a number of routines for manipulating LOBs. Most of these are listed in Table 4.4, together with a brief note on their purpose and an example of their use. Before users can access the package, the SYS user must either execute both **dbmslob.sql** and **prvtlob.plb** scripts or execute the **catproc.sql** script. Then users can be granted privileges to use the package.

The DBMS_LOB package routines would normally be used within a PL/SQL procedure but some of the DBMS_LOB functions that deal with CLOBs can be used directly in SQL*PLUS, for example to find the size of a LOB:

```
SELECT grape_name, DBMS_LOB.GETLENGTH(grape_text),
DBMS_LOB.SUBSTR(grape_text, 10,10)
FROM grape
```

The next procedure is an example of how to incorporate the DBMS_LOB routines within a PL/SQL procedure that changes the photograph in the grape table. It opens, reads and then closes the existing BFILE using the routines listed in Table 4.4.

```
CREATE OR REPLACE PROCEDURE wine_read_bfile
IS
     Lob_loc    BFILE := BFILENAME('PHOTO_DIR',
'chardonnay.jpg');
     Amount     INTEGER := 32767;
     Position   INTEGER := 1;
     Buffer     RAW(32767);
BEGIN
     /* Open the BFILE: */
     DBMS_LOB.OPEN(Lob_loc, DBMS_LOB.LOB_READONLY);
```

Table 4.4 Routines provided by DBMS_LOB package

DBMS_LOB routines	Purpose	Example of use
DBMS_LOB.OPEN	Open the BFILE	DBMS_LOB.OPEN(lob_loc, DBMS_LOB.LOB_READONLY);
DBMS_LOB.READ	Read data from a LOB starting at a specified offset	DBMS_LOB.READ(lob_loc, amount, position, buffer);
DBMS_LOB.WRITE	Write data to a LOB from a specified offset	DBMS_LOB.WRITE (locator, amount, offset, text)
DBMS_LOB.WRITEAPPEND	Writes data to the end of a LOB	DBMS_LOB.WRITEAPPEND(lob_loc, amount, text)
DBMS_LOB.SUBSTR	Return part of a LOB value starting at a specified offset	SELECT DBMS_LOB.SUBSTR(note, 5, 12)
DBMS_LOB.INSTR	Return the numerical position of part of a LOB value	SELECT DBMS_LOB.INSTR(note, 'Rian')
DBMS_LOB.GETLENGTH	Gets the length of a LOB	SELECT DBMS_LOB.GETLENGTH(note)
DBMS_LOB.TRIM	Trims a LOB value to the specified shorter length	DBMS_LOB.TRIM(lob_loc, no_bytes)
DBMS_LOB.CREATETEMPORARY	Creates a temporary LOB that exists for a session and is useful if a LOB is being changed and then stored again	
DBMS_LOB.COPY	Copies part or the whole of a LOB to another LOB	DBMS_LOB.COPY(to_lob, from_lob, no_bytes, from_offset, to_offset)
DBMS_LOB.APPEND	Appends the content of a LOB to another LOB	DBMS_LOB.APPEND(to_lob, from_lob)
DBMS_LOB.COMPARE	Compares two similar LOB types	DBMS_LOB.COMPARE(lob_1, lob_2, no_bytes, offset1,offset2)
DBMS_LOB.ERASE	Erases part or the whole of a LOB, starting at a specified offset	DBMS_LOB.ERASE (lob_loc, no_bytes, offset)
DBMS_LOB.LOADFROMFILE	Loads BFILE data into an internal LOB	DBMS_LOB.LOADFROMFILE(from_lob, to_lob, no_bytes, from_offset, to_offset)
DBMS_LOB.CLOSE	Close the BFILE	DBMS_LOB.CLOSE(lob_loc);

```
        /* Read data: */
        DBMS_LOB.READ(Lob_loc, Amount, Position, Buffer);
        /* Close the BFILE: */
        DBMS_LOB.CLOSE(Lob_loc);
   END;
```

The BFILE is manipulated through the LOB locator which is retrieved by the BFILENAME function. The PL/SQL variables **amount** and **buffer** are set at the maximum size. Binary data is read from the file starting at position 1. The following version shows how to select the BFILE to locate the LOB locator:

```
CREATE OR REPLACE PROCEDURE wine_read_bfile
IS
     Lob_loc      BFILE;
     Amount       INTEGER := 32 767;
     Position     INTEGER := 1;
     Buffer       RAW(32767);
BEGIN
     /* Select the LOB: */
     SELECT picture INTO Lob_loc FROM grape
       WHERE grape_name = 'Chardonnay';
     /* Open the BFILE: */
     DBMS_LOB.OPEN(Lob_loc, DBMS_LOB.LOB_READONLY);
     /* Read data: */
     DBMS_LOB.READ(Lob_loc, Amount, Position, Buffer);
     /* Close the BFILE: */
     DBMS_LOB.CLOSE(Lob_loc);
END;
```

BFILEs need to be closed after use since there is a constraint on the number of BFILEs that can be open at any one time. This constraint is set by the SESSION_MAX_OPEN_FILES parameter in the INIT.ORA file. The default value of this is 10 but it can be changed as follows:

```
SESSION_MAX_OPEN_FILES=20
```

This is another example of a procedure to change the value of the **grape_text** column for the grape called "Chardonnay":

```
CREATE OR REPLACE PROCEDURE grape_cloba IS
    lob_loc CLOB; -- TO HOLD LOB LOCATOR
    newtext VARCHAR2(32767)   := ' It is the mainstay of white
wine
production in California and Australia, is widely planted in
Chile and
South Africa, and is now the most widely planted grape in New
Zealand.';
    amount    NUMBER;
    offset    INTEGER;
BEGIN
```

```
        SELECT grape_text
        INTO lob_loc
        FROM grape
        WHERE grape_name = 'Chardonnay' FOR UPDATE;
        OFFSET := DBMS_LOB.GETLENGTH(lob_loc)+2;
        AMOUNT := LENGTH(newtext);
        DBMS_LOB.WRITE(lob_loc,amount,offset,newtext);
    /* Read data: */
    /* */
      INSERT INTO MESSAGES (numcol1, numcol2,charcol1)
VALUES (amount,offset,'CLOB data');
COMMIT;
EXCEPTION
    WHEN NO_DATA_FOUND
    THEN DBMS_OUTPUT.PUT_LINE('COPY operation has some
problems');
END;
```

The purpose of this procedure is to change the value of the **grape_text** column in the grape table by adding data at the end of the existing CLOB. There is no formal parameter list because the procedure itself contains the text to be added as the variable **newtext**. Three other variables are declared (**lob_loc**, **amount** and **offset**) which will be needed as parameters for the part of the DBMS_LOB package we shall use. With CLOBs offset and amount parameters are always in characters whereas, with BLOBs, the offset and amount parameters are always in bytes. In this procedure the variable **lob_loc** is used to hold a LOB locator. **lob_loc** acts as a variable to hold the location of the CLOB note in the table **grape**. The amount variable will hold the length of the text we want to add but is limited to 32 Kb because this is the size of the PL/SQL buffer.

A very important line is

```
        SELECT grape_text
        INTO lob_loc
        FROM grape
        WHERE grape_name = 'Chardonnay' FOR UPDATE;
```

This statement searches for the CLOB that matches the condition in the WHERE clause; it then stores the value of the LOB locator for the row into the variable **lob_loc**. It is essential that the statement only returns a single value in the result set. It also locks the row because of the expression FOR UPDATE. We use the SQL built-in function LENGTH to evaluate the length of **newtext** but to check the size of the CLOB we need to use another DBMS_LOB function. The DBMS_LOB package writes new data into the

CLOB at the place specified by the offset. In this case the value of the offset is controlled by the length of the existing CLOB. If we run the procedure a second time we should find the same text added to the previous text. Note also the variable **newtext** is declared also as VARCHAR2(32767) while the other variables are unconstrained. This is because 32 767 is the size limit for the data type VARCHAR2 and when we deal with text media we may be dealing with very large objects. This is why it is often necessary to bulk load LOB data into the database with utilities like SQL*LOADER.

The procedure would be stored in the database under the name **grape_cloba**. When it has been saved and complied, we can execute the procedure in SQL*PLUS with the command

```
EXECUTE wine_clob2a
```

It is possible to check its effects by looking at the messages table. As well as seeing the changes to the grape table, this procedure places data into the messages table when executed. This is used to record the parameters used by the DBMS_LOB.WRITE function.

An alternative would be to use the WRITEAPPEND routine, as follows:

```
CREATE OR REPLACE PROCEDURE grape_clobb IS
    lob_loc CLOB; -- TO HOLD LOB LOCATOR
    newtext VARCHAR2(32767) := ' In warm climates Chardonnay has
a tendency to develop very high sugar levels during the final
stages of ripening and this can occur at the expense of
acidity. Late picking is a common problem and can result in
blousey and flabby wines that lack structure and definition.
Recently in the New World, we have seen a move towards more
elegant, better-balanced and less oak-driven Chardonnays, and
this is to be welcomed.';

    amount    NUMBER;
    offset    INTEGER;
BEGIN
    SELECT grape_text
    INTO Lob_loc
    FROM grape
    WHERE grape_name = 'Chardonnay' FOR UPDATE;
    AMOUNT := LENGTH(newtext);
    DBMS_LOB.WRITEAPPEND(lob_loc,amount,newtext);
/* Read data: */
/* */
    INSERT INTO MESSAGES (numcol1, numcol2,charcol1)
    VALUES (amount,offset,'CLOB data');
```

```
      COMMIT;
      EXCEPTION
         WHEN NO_DATA_FOUND
         THEN DBMS_OUTPUT.PUT_LINE('write operation has some
problems');
      END;
```

When this procedure is compiled and executed it will add more data to the **grape_text** CLOB previously selected. When we use WRITEAPPEND there is no need to measure an offset value because the routine adds data to the end of the existing CLOB.

PL/SQL procedures can be used to manipulate both BLOBs that are permanently held in the database system and temporary BLOBs. Temporary BLOBs are useful for holding media data that are stored in external BFILEs. This is because the only operation that can be performed on a BFILE is read whereas when the data is transferred to a BLOB data type it can be changed and then written back to the BFILE.

Another issue to note is that, in using DBMS_LOB.LOADFROMFILE, the amount parameter must not be larger than the size of the BFILE. When using the amount parameter it must be smaller than the size of the buffer which is restricted to 32 Kb in PL/SQL.

4.4   Summary of Chapter

In this chapter you have learned:

- the different SQL standards and how they can contribute to the development of multimedia DBMS (MMDBMS);
- the role of BLOBs in relation to multimedia data storage;
- basic SQL statements for creating tables and updating both structured and multimedia data;
- PL/SQL to create functions and procedures to manipulate structured and multimedia data and to use the DBMS_LOB package.

In this chapter we have looked at the relational approach to developing MMDBMSs using simple data types and stored procedures. In the following chapters we look at many other issues including the object-relational approach to developing MMDBMS. Later chapters cover other issues such as the architecture of MMDBMS, delivery and performance issues. The rich semantic nature of multimedia data creates difficulties for information retrieval that require the application of advanced techniques. Although queries can be carried out based on attributes and text annotation the goal is to achieve content-based retrieval, which is introduced in the next chapter. In fact several of the following chapters are about the problems of retrieving useful information from MMDBMSs and delivering it to the user in an acceptable and meaningful way.

SOLUTIONS TO EXERCISES

Exercise 4.1

(a) The *information schema* is part of the SQL standard and includes views, tables, columns, privileges, constraints, key column usage and assertions.

(b) The project operation in SQL selects specified columns from a table.

(c) Application programs use what are termed host languages, so called because the SQL is embedded within the code.

(d) Types in SQL3 can be system-defined data types such as INTEGER, CHARACTER, etc. or they can be user-defined types that represent a set of values with operations to access them.

Exercise 4.2

(a) Any of the following would be acceptable:

```
ALTER TABLE employee
    ADD (employee_picture    BLOB)
ALTER TABLE employee
    ADD (employee_picture    BLOB DEFAULT EMPTY_BLOB())
ALTER TABLE employee
    ADD (employee_picture    BFILE)
```

(b)

```
CREATE TABLE grape
(    grape_name    VARCHAR2(30),
     grape_text    CLOB,
     picture       BLOB,
     CONSTRAINT prim_grape PRIMARY KEY (grape_name))
```

or

```
CREATE TABLE grape
(    grape_name    VARCHAR2(30),
     grape_text    CLOB,
```

```
picture        BFILE,
CONSTRAINT prim_grape PRIMARY KEY (grape_name))
```

Exercise 4.3

(a)

```
ALTER TABLE wine_list ADD (CONSTRAINT wine_grape_fkey FOREIGN
KEY(grape) REFERENCES
grape (grape_name))
```

(b)

```
ALTER TABLE wine_list ADD (CONSTRAINT check_pronun) CHECK
(region='France' AND pronunciation NOT NULL)
```

Exercise 4.4

```
INSERT INTO wine_list (wine_code, wine_name, region, year,
category, grape, price, bottle_size, character)
VALUES ('41482B', 'Chablis Billaud-Simon', 'Burgundy', 1999,
'France white', 'Chardonnay', 9.45, 75, 'Light-medium bodied
dry ready but will improve')
/
INSERT INTO wine_list (wine_code, wine_name, region, year,
category, grape, price, bottle_size, character)
VALUES ('40484', 'Reisling Trimbach', 'Alsace', 1996,
'white', 'Reisling', 22.50, 75, 'Medium bodied dry ready but
will improve')
/
```

Exercise 4.5

```
CREATE OR REPLACE PROCEDURE exercise45_proc
AS
 v_bool1         BOOLEAN;
 v_bool2         BOOLEAN;
 v_char          VARCHAR2 (20) : = '42 is the answer';
 v_num           NUMBER;
BEGIN
 v_num              := TO_NUMBER(SUBSTR(v_char,1,2));
  IF v_num < 100 THEN
     v_bool1:= TRUE;
     v_bool2:= FALSE;
```

```
        ELSE
            v_bool1:= FALSE;
            v_bool2:= TRUE;
        END IF;
        INSERT INTO messages (CHARCOL1, NUMCOL1)
        VALUES (v_char, v_num)
    END;
```

We can then compile and execute the procedure in SQL*PLUS by typing

```
    exercise45_proc
```

since it has no input parameters.

Recommended Reading

Date, C. J. (2000) *An Introduction to Database Systems*, 7th edition, Addison-Wesley.

Date, C. J., with Darwen, H. (1997) *A Guide to the SQL Standard*, 4th edition, Addison-Wesley.

Querying Multimedia Data

Chapter aims

This chapter introduces the ways in which different kinds of multimedia data – text, audio, image and video – can be retrieved from database systems. In this chapter we will firstly identify the problems in querying multimedia data and secondly study general approaches adopted for dealing with multimedia data. In Chapters 1 and 2 we noted the characteristics of media data related to size, real-time and semantic nature. These properties generate special problems when dealing with the different media. In the case of text, size is the main issue, although we should not ignore the fact that increasingly some text is stored in graphic formats, fonts can cause problems and many languages require Unicode to represent them adding to the problems for multimedia processing. With image data it is mainly the semantic nature that is the problem, while video and audio present difficulties in terms of their real-time nature as well. All forms of media cause problems with regard to the gigantic size of the data objects. Therefore later chapters will look at specialized approaches that relate to text (Chapter 10), image (Chapter 11) and video and audio (Chapter 12). Through a study of this chapter the reader will develop an understanding of the problems associated with multimedia retrieval in general and look at some of the solutions currently available.

At the end of the chapter the reader will know:

- the main problems with manipulating multimedia data, particularly in relation to querying, indexing and summarizing;
- the different kinds of solutions currently available;
- the part played by metadata and ontologies;
- the role of feature selection and extraction;
- examples of retrieval for different applications and media.

5.1   Introduction

The ability to retrieve and manipulate information from a multimedia database is of course the essential objective. Humans are very good at understanding multimedia information, recalling audio and visual images and linking complex information together. The way in which the human visual system in the brain is able to do this is not well understood although relevant concepts were introduced in Chapter 3. Clearly this involves a number of transformations to the data in the brain received by the sensory systems. In contrast this way of processing information is very difficult to achieve with current computer systems. As we shall see, progress in querying multimedia database management systems (MMDBMSs) has only been achieved in a few key areas using computationally intensive algorithms. We shall look at the different approaches taken to this problem and introduce the requirements of different application areas. For example, the requirements of some multimedia applications such as video on demand can be limited to simple queries, whereas users in other application areas, such as medicine, need to be able to browse and navigate their way through large collections of multimedia objects such as digital images. In yet other applications, such as multimedia Group Decision Support Systems (GDSS) and learning systems, users may wish to work collaboratively on multimedia documents so that multimedia updating and record locking become key issues.

In the past MMDBMSs have been developed for specific application areas or even specific applications in such a way that, although successful for a single application area, the processing cannot subsequently be adapted to lead to generic multimedia retrieval capability. Advances in technology such as computer vision and image processing have provided ways to collect and organize visual information. Computer vision is the ability to recognize patterns in the data to promote image understanding by recognizing certain features present in the image. In contrast image processing is about effectively processing and analyzing images in order to faithfully extract the information they hold and to accurately quantify and interpret this information. A key step in the future will be turning computer vision technologies that were developed to deal with a sequence of images one at a time into algorithms that can deal with a large repository.

The reduction in hardware cost and the increase in hardware performance has enabled the assembly of large heterogeneous collections of raw image and video data. Initially applications have been driving the development almost entirely so that although an application "works" its functionality is not transferable to any other domain. Examples of this type of development are interactive games and WWW encyclopedias where often content is supplied through a single WWW link. The approach adopted has often been based on extracting index information and attaching it to objects rather than on the organization of the information itself. It is clear that, without an adequate underlying representation of the data, generic content-based image retrieval will not be possible. This depends on conceptual information as much as it does on techniques such as image analysis.

Manipulating multimedia involves some operations that would never arise in traditional DBMS. Table 5.1 shows a typical range of operations associated with the different media that a multimedia database system would be expected to support. Those shown in italics are still poorly understood, and you may note that fundamental database operations, *indexing* and *searching*, feature frequently. Indexing mechanisms are also needed to sort the multimedia data according to the features of interest to the users. Developing ways of effectively indexing the various multimedia data types will be important and this is discussed in detail later in this section.

Most of these operations can be summarized as being concerned with:

- manipulation (editing and modifying data);
- presentation;
- analysis (indexing and searching).

Table 5.1   Range of operations supported by different media types in digital form

Operations	Text	Audio	Graphic	Image	Animation	Video
Manipulation	Character manipulation	Sample manipulation	Primitive editing	Geometric manipulation	Primitive editing	Frame manipulation
	String manipulation	Waveform manipulation	Structural editing	Pixel operations	Structural editing	Pixel operations
	Editing	Audio editing	Shading	Filtering		
Presentation	Formatting	Synchronization	Mapping	Compositing	Synchronization	Synchronization
	Encryption	Compression	Compression	Compression	Compression	Compression
			Lighting			Video effects
			Rendering		Rendering	Mixing
	Sorting	Conversion	Viewing	Conversion		Conversion
Analysis	Indexing	Indexing	Indexing	*Indexing*	Indexing	*Indexing*
	Searching	*Searching*	Searching	*Searching*	Searching	*Searching*

5.1.1 Query Statements in SQL

The basic relational operations needed to support a database, include restrict, project and join (see Chapter 1). All these operate at the set level. SQL is sometimes referred to as non-procedural in the sense that the users of the language specify what they want, not how the data is to be retrieved. Let us look at two examples. In Chapter 1 we found that data can be retrieved from a database using SQL in a query statement as follows:

```
SELECT *
FROM wine_list
```

This is equivalent to requesting the database to retrieve all the data from the table called **wine_list**. The table **wine_list** must already exist in the database for the query to succeed; otherwise we would say the statement was invalid for that database. Recall that the * symbol is the wild card that returns every column in the table. This query will not succeed with the **wine_list** table created in Chapter 4 because we cannot display the data held in LOB columns in the standard way.

We can carry out the restrict operation by simply adding another clause, the WHERE clause, to the SQL query to specify a search condition that restricts the number of rows to those that match the condition specified. We can carry out the project operation by simply specifying the SELECT clause in detail so that it lists the columns required so that only the data in the columns specified is returned by the database, for example,

```
SELECT     wine_name, price
FROM       wine_list
WHERE      region = 'France'
```

where_France

This query will return the details (wine_name, price) of the wines from the **wine_list** table that exactly match the condition in the WHERE clause, i.e. have the value "France" and only "France" in the column **region**.

It is important to note that the project and restrict operations cannot be used in this way with multimedia data types and user-defined types will need new methods to be specified for these operations. For example, we can use the methods available in the DBMS_LOB package introduced in Chapter 4:

```
SELECT wine_name, price,
DBMS_LOB.SUBSTR(note,10,20) AS smallstring
FROM wine_list
WHERE DBMS_LOB.INSTR (note, 'poise, elegance and balance')<>0
```

where_poise

(These queries use a brief name to substitute for the long functional expression so that, for example, when the data is displayed it is listed under "smallstring'.) This will display the details of wines, including a small string from the CLOB note column where the wine is described by the words "poise, elegance and balance". In traditional relational databases data is manipulated in several ways for the purpose of reporting. It is frequently summarized by grouping similar data together and aggregating the results from groups of rows. The SQL statements for creating this kind of report follow the pattern

SELECT	⟨select list⟩
FROM	⟨table list⟩
WHERE	⟨search condition⟩
GROUP BY	⟨grouping column list⟩
HAVING	⟨search condition⟩

The **GROUP BY** clause is used to organize rows into groups, such as grouping wines by regions, and the **HAVING** clause is a way to apply a search criterion to every group. For example, the following query will list the average price and maximum price for each category for each year, in the Bordeaux region for years from 1995 until 1998:

```
SELECT category, year, AVG(price)AS average_price,
       MAX(price) highest
FROM       wine_list
WHERE region = 'Bordeaux'
GROUP BY   category, year
HAVING     year BETWEEN 1995 AND 1998
ORDER BY category, year
```

The result table shown in Table 5.2 illustrates how this kind of report is generated. The BETWEEN operator restricts the year to those equal to and greater than 1995 and less than and equal to 1998. The column names listed in the GROUP BY clause are allowed to appear in the SELECT clause as they both relate to the whole group. The groups are also ordered by the grouping columns. Two aggregate functions, AVERAGE and MAX, apply to the groups

Table 5.2   Result set summarizing structured data

Category	Year	Average price	Highest
Medoc and Pessac-Léognan	1995	55.45	250.00
Medoc and Pessac-Léognan	1996	45.70	285.00
Medoc and Pessac-Léognan	1997	34.50	230.00
Medoc and Pessac-Léognan	1998	20.50	175.00
Pomerol and St Emilion	1995	65.00	800.00
Pomerol and St Emilion	1996	55.00	590.00
Pomerol and St Emilion	1997	65.00	430.00
Pomerol and St Emilion	1998	86.00	1150.00

so that for each group of rows the average price is returned together with the maximum value in the group. Other columns not involved in the GROUP BY clause or the aggregate functions cannot be included in the SELECT clause. This report is typical of the output from traditional databases and could be used in a catalog for customers or for management purposes.

There are good reasons why users might want to gather media objects into logical groups, for example grouping images by topic, color or textual characteristics. A key issue is whether we would be able to generate any comparable reports from a multimedia database and whether similar aggregate functions can be identified. Also, will we be able to place a set of multimedia objects in a meaningful order? How would a result set including audio clips be presented?

5.2   Manipulating Multimedia Data

Interacting with multimedia data is a relatively new possibility. Therefore it is an area where little is known about users' requirements such as in what way users would wish to manipulate and change multimedia objects. Design applications, learning applications and journalists' application are the most likely candidates for needing to manipulate the actual content of media data but others are rapidly developing.

As a general rule we want constraints on interactivity to be kept to a minimum, for example multiple users should be able to edit shared data simultaneously along the lines shown in Figure 5.1. Any lock should be imposed on as small a part of the data as possible because, in addition to the problem of concurrency, multimedia has the problem of real-time synchronization.

Manipulating different kinds of media can be very computationally intensive and time consuming, for example – in the case of a video search the result could be a series of video clips that need to be presented and ranked in order.

	Single media	Multimedia
Single user	Simple query, using other attributes or metadata	Composition using several different media combining images, may need synchronization; journalist or medical applications
Multiuser	Concurrent use of same data – real-time, broadcasting, e.g. video on demand	Users can edit shared object simultaneously, e.g. Computer Supported Cooperative Work (CSCW)

Figure 5.1   Manipulating multimedia and constraints

5.2.1 Presenting Results

Graphical user interfaces (GUIs) are difficult to design for multimedia and suffer from high costs. Furthermore, development teams may be organized in functional lines with responsibility for screen layout, dialog and application software separately. The main issues that must be addressed are:

- media composition of the result set;
- result set will consist of items that are similar to the target rather than exactly matching;
- way the result set will be ranked in presentation.

Figure 5.2 presents one way of modeling the process of GUI design, by considering it as a set of levels:

1. The lexical level deals with the lowest level and includes:
   - The presentation model describes the constructs which will appear on the end-user's display and the dependences between them.
   - The interaction model specifies the set of possible low level interactions between the user and the system environment. This will be determined by the underlying toolkit technology which was used to implement the interface. It is concerned with the efficiency of the interaction and should be modeled in a way which is independent of the dialog model.

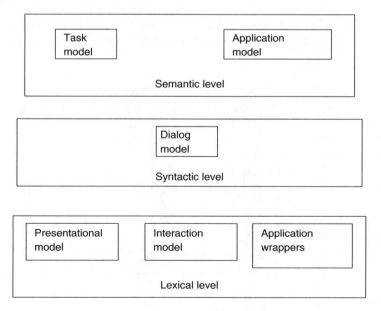

Figure 5.2   Levels of presentational design in databases

- The application wrapper represents the interaction between the higher levels and the application functionality and includes method signatures and data item declaration.

2. The syntactic level deals with the dialog model which describes the low level input activities that may be performed by the end-user when using the interface.

3. The semantic level deals with the context – the user's task model and the application model itself.

Unlike traditional databases a key issue is how to present the results of the multimedia query to the user. The result set could vary from a single relational table to a picture gallery or a summary of a number of documents. Many queries will return a set of similar items rather than an exact match so there is the question of how to rank the results of a multimedia query. One solution is to apply methods to estimate the distance of each item in the set from the desired criteria. At the same time it is essential that querying the database does not involve unacceptable response times due to the enormous data volumes. With our online wine shop we may want to answer the query

"show a picture of the vineyard Grand-Puy-Lacoste and a map of its location"

The query interface needs to support both the presentation of multimedia data and the nature of the interaction that takes place during the presentation. A typical presentation is shown in Figure 5.3 where one user interface will hold separate areas for the presentation of the different types of media that are related together. Unlike a traditional database system the

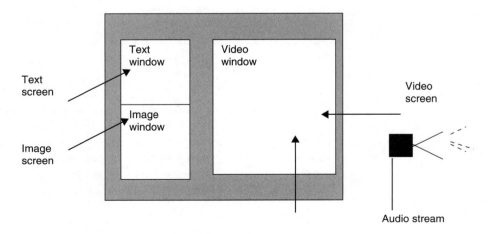

Figure 5.3   User view of multimedia database

presentation of the result of a multimedia query can be challenging and involve consideration of the human visual processing system.

Multimedia data introduces different kinds of relationships between data. For example, the relationships between the data items may be both spatial and temporal. Temporal relationships describe:

- when an object should be presented;
- how long an object is presented for;
- how one object presentation relates to others (audio with video).

For example, to retrieve the required data the user will need to be able to:

- query the content of a media object;
- query by example ("get me a video clip of this song");
- time-indexed queries ("show me a clip 30 minutes after the start of the movie");
- spatial queries ("show me a video clip where John is standing behind Paul");
- application-specific queries ("show me where a cell becomes cancerous").

5.2.2 Querying Multimedia Databases

In order to solve some of these problems with image data we need information about how the human visual system works and how to use this information to develop meaningful ways of extracting low and intermediate level features and so build representations of the visual scene. We need a still deeper understanding of video information. Progress has been made on object recognition and detection but a general query like "what is this scene?" is well beyond the capabilities of today's MMDBMSs. One solution is to constrain the domain in various ways by only considering a limited number of cases, for example rigid objects, fixed positions, precise models, specific queries. Instead of the exact match expected with traditional database queries it is more likely that the query will take the form "Does the model match the given model within a certain tolerance?" The system may then return a label and a confidence level that represents how likely the label is to be correct. Later in the chapter we will look at how multimedia data objects can be labeled.

Previously the focus in database development has been on addressing problems where both the data and the type of questions we ask were restricted. The objective now is to create systems which require fewer and fewer assumptions to be made and have fewer and fewer constraints on the domain. By describing the world one piece at a time we could have the ability to answer more and more complex queries.

However, for each medium there are different properties that could be used as a basis for comparison. For example, images can be compared on the basis of color, shape or texture, while audio segments can be compared by frequency, tempo and rhythm. When a user asks for similar objects the initial problem is that the appropriate types of similarity may need to be indicated. Another problem is that the properties that a human would use to compare objects are rather different from those a computer system would need to use.

The process of querying multimedia data is complex and we can approach this in two ways:

- what information can be retrieved;
- how the information can be retrieved.

There are three levels of complexity associated with the "what":

- *Level 1.* Retrieval of primitive features such as color, shape, texture, spatial location and object movement. The query is posed in terms of features such as

  "find clips of objects flying from top-right to bottom-left of screen"

- *Level 2.* Retrieval of logical features related to the identity of the object within the media – query example would be

  "find a clip of an aeroplane taking off"

- *Level 3.* Retrieval of abstract attributes associated with an understanding of the nature or purpose of the object:

  "find a picture of nutritional disasters"

Levels 2 and 3 are regarded as **semantic media retrieval**. However, success in answering multimedia queries is largely limited to level 1. The difference between simple queries at level 1 and those at levels 2 and 3 has been called the semantic gap. At present relatively little has been achieved at level 3 and most of this is still at the research stage. There has been an attempt to use the subjective connotations of color (such as whether a color is perceived to be warm or cold, or whether two colors go well with each other) to allow retrieval of images evoking a particular mood (Kato and Kurita, 1992; Corridoni *et al.*, 1998). We still do not know how to solve either the technical problems of retrieving the data from large data sets or the usability issues to enable the user to express this kind or query effectively.

The "how" can also be classified on the basis of whether the information is retrieved by:

- attribute-based systems;

- text-based systems;
- content-based systems.

These three retrieval approaches use different indexing and searching methods. We shall start by looking at the ways all three approaches can be used in queries, their advantages and disadvantages, and how the results of queries can be presented. Then we will look at indexing and searching methods and the role of metadata. Finally we will look at the problems of manipulating multimedia data.

Attribute-based Retrieval

Attribute-based retrieval (ABR) is a method that uses a set of structured attributes in the same way as traditional DBMSs. When this method is applied to multimedia data it uses essentially the same principles, except that these must be able to cope with gigantic media objects such as video clips. This method can be particularly effective with text data. However, the method does not make use of the rich content of images to retrieve information so that it is essentially limited to level 1 queries. (An implementation could be achieved by using Oracle *interMedia* as described in Chapter 6 to create user-defined types that stored the attributes with the media objects.)

   The following example specifies a table definition for an ABR system based on SQL3 standard data types:

```
CREATE TABLE song
(      cdref          CHAR(6),
       songid         CHAR(6),
       artist         VARCHAR2(30),
       title          VARCHAR2(30),
       script         CLOB,
       writer         VARCHAR2(30),
       duration       INTEGER,
       audio_source      BLOB,
       PRIMARY KEY(cdref, songid))
```

Text-based Retrieval

Text-based retrieval (TBR) methods work by adding annotations, usually brief descriptions combined with some structured data. One example of a system with this capability was the Kodak Picture Exchange. The disadvantage of text-based systems is that they are very difficult in practice. The following example gives the definition of a table to include audio media:

```
CREATE TABLE audio_example
(      id                 CHAR(8) PRIMARY KEY,
       description        VARCHAR2(4000),
```

```
audio_data          BLOB,
format              VARCHAR2(31),
comments            CLOB,
encoding            VARCHAR2(256),
no_of_channels      NUMBER,
sampling_rate       NUMBER,
sampling_size       NUMBER,
compressiontype     VARCHAR2(4000),
audioDuration       NUMBER)
```

The annotations have to be added manually in such a way that a typical user would be able to come up with the same description of the **audio_example** in the table above. This is a resource-intensive process that is difficult and costly to achieve. Some images, such as abstract art and computer graphics, are very difficult to describe in text. For successful retrieval the user who searches this material must be able to use the same descriptive terms as the annotator. However, people may give quite different descriptions of the same image. In addition, if large amounts of descriptive text are involved the retrieval methods become more complicated.

Content-based Retrieval

Content-based retrieval (CBR) methods, which we will look at in detail later in the section, have been developed to try to overcome some of the difficulties of TBR. The idea is that the important details can be extracted from the media by automatic methods which will be more efficient for data capture and more reliable for retrieval. Retrieval of images by manually assigned keywords is definitely not CBR. Another more fundamental difference in the three methods is that ABR can be used to address level 1 queries, while the TBR and CBR address levels 2 and 3 – the semantic gap. CBR implies the ability to search based on the user's association and impression of an image, for example sunset at sea. In order for this to be possible a method must exist that defines the semantic quality and similarity of images. This could mean setting up a mapping from the user's ideas and concepts to both the raw image data and the image characteristics.

All three methods summarized in Figure 5.4 involve the use of metadata but the nature of the metadata and its source changes with each method. Often the process of retrieval will be based on searching the metadata using standard SQL and using these results to locate the required data. Most simple queries are expected to focus on a single media, where the media type of query is usually the same as the target, for example providing a medical image from a patient and requesting a display of similar images. The kind of questions the system should be able to answer includes

"How does my patient's tumor look compared to other similar cases?"

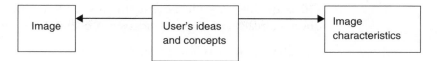

Nature of retrieval	Techniques employed
Attribute based	Fixed set of structured attributes, with indexing based on B+ trees and inverted files
Text based	Text descriptions and structured fields Indexing by full text – scanning, inversion files, signature file methods
Content based	Content features automatically extracted

Figure 5.4   Retrieval strategies and the techniques employed

The result of the query would be a collection of images that have similar spatial characteristics. A more complex query would be

"What is the normal growth rate of this kind of tumor?"

The answer to the above query will involve the rate of change of the tumor. Therefore, the MMDBMS must accommodate not only spatial images but also some time reference to be able to estimate the growth rate.

In these situations Boolean queries are often combined with query-by-example (QBE) methods to provide feedback to narrow the search after the initial Boolean query. In order to carry out a QBE there must be a way to

- describe (to capture spatial, temporal and semantic patterns);
- specify (intuitive and visual metaphors that interact with multimedia);
- depict (visual metaphors to identify matching patterns).

Queries can be *ad hoc* or persistent. The set of sample data items may also need to be supplemented with examples from the semantics of the domain of interest. This is the most challenging type of query because it involves locating the relevant domain concept within the media. For example, the user may be interested in video clips showing trucks crossing bridges. The result of all these difficulties is that systems have been built to address specific tasks which impose constraints on the data that is being analyzed, for example,

Given a street scene, count the number of people.

Given a set of objects such as cars – classify these into a fixed number of classes from the existing classification model.

Video queries provide potentially the widest scope. In addition to the queries already mentioned, videos can be queried by using:

- spatial features as for images;
- temporal features;
- spatio-temporal features;
- frame based;
- clip based;
- scene based;
- complete video object.

Because of this range query languages have been specifically designed for video. Examples are OVID which provides VIDEOSQL and video query algebra.

In the next sections of this text we will look at the three retrieval methods outlined above in more detail and introduce the role that metadata and ontology play in them. Ontology is used to help understand the meaning of the user's query and also to match the search conditions in the data set. Metadata is used by all three approaches. Next we will look at ontologies. Both these topics are complex so that Chapter 7 is devoted to them. Finally we look at the ways of generating metadata and how it is used.

EXERCISE 5.1

Explain the difference between the terms semantic media retrieval and content-based retrieval.

What is an Ontology and How is it Used?

We have seen that there needs to be an understanding between the user and the objects in the database. Why is this so important for multimedia queries? Consider again the three images displayed with their histograms in Chapter 2 – Figure 2.6. Their histograms are sufficiently different to distinguish between them but if they were used in a query such as "find some more images like this" it would be much easier if the system already knew that two of the images were of employees. One way to capture this understanding is through an **ontology** that provides a shared understanding of the application domain that can be communicated between people and computers and incorporated in the database as part of the metadata. This means that key information about the kinds of objects in the database can be captured and reused many times for many different queries with any kind of media data. The word ontology originated in philosophy where it was used to describe the existence of beings in the world but it was borrowed by researchers in artificial intelligence to describe what could be represented by a computer about the world within a program. Ontology is a set of semantic concepts of knowledge interconnected by patterns of association that are consistent with a set of knowledge representation rules. The ontology must contain:

- a list of special terms used in the domain with their definitions;
- information about the sorts of objects included;
- the relationships between the objects and concepts.

An ontology is a semantic network of the concepts, conceptual relationships and conceptual patterns characteristic of the field of discourse. A definition that we could work with might be that an ontology is a formal, explicit specification of a shared conceptualization. A domain ontology is an ontology encoding the semantics of a specific logical application area. This means that the ontology can be formally specified and very clearly defined and, because it is shared, it is the view of a group and not just an individual. It may therefore be important to develop ontology collaboratively to uncover the knowledge required, i.e.:

- What is the domain ontology of the end-users?
- What is the association between the domain and the media?

For example, we might start to create an ontology about wines for our wine shop. We could define these wines as products we wanted to sell. We could create subclasses such as sparkling wines. We would then list a series of assertions (any statements that are true) about our ontology, such as "any kind of red wine" would be in our ontology. We can also add details such as the classes that can have slots which describe characteristics such as vintage. At the moment we will not consider how an ontology is specified. What is important is how it is used and where it should be stored in the database.

How is Metadata Used in Query Processing?

Before we consider the role of metadata for separate media, it is helpful, particularly when considering design options, to classify metadata and relate this to the three types of information retrieval, as:

- content independent (i.e. associated with media, for example photographer's name), so used in ABR;
- content descriptive – used in TBR;
- content dependent (for example features of faces from photographs or video operations in a clip), used in CBR.

Table 5.3   Metadata classes

Metadata class	Example	Usage
● Content independent	Associated with media, e.g. photographer's name	ABR
● Content descriptive	The speakers and topic discussed	TBR
● Content dependent	Features of faces from photographs or video operations in a clip	CBR

In Table 5.3 we give examples of the classes for the different media to clarify the way content-dependent, content-descriptive and content-independent features are used. In addition to these classes we should recognize that content-descriptive metadata can be further subdivided into:

● domain-independent metadata which is independent of the application or subject topic – file formats, compression;

● domain-dependent metadata which is specific to the application area.

Recently, as metadata has become increasingly important, a number of international standards have been developed which are covered in more detail in a later chapter. The role and development of both metadata and ontologies are studied in more depth in Chapter 7 linked to the design and implementation of the databases so that we are only gaining an overview in this chapter.

Table 5.4   Summary of metadata classes for different media

Media	Content independent	Content descriptive	Content dependent
Text	Status Date of update Components Location	Keywords Categories Format Language	Subtopic boundary Word image spotting
Speech	Start, end time Location Confidence of word recognition	Speakers	Speech recognition Speaker recognition Prosodic cues Change of meaning
Image	Creator Title Date	Format Keywords	Feature selection Image characteristics, e.g. histogram, image segmentation
Video	Product title Date Distributor	Camera shot distance, e.g. close-up etc. Shot angle Action Description	Shot boundary Frame characteristics, e.g. histogram Camera motion, height, lighting level

In Chapters 10, 11 and 12 we will look at content-dependent metadata (see Table 5.4) in detail for text, image and audio/video data respectively.

The management and generation of content descriptive metadata are currently most well developed for text media. There are several document information models that have been developed such as SGML and HyTime (hypermedia-timebased structuring language) that produce structured metadata. Metadata of this type can be used for internal representations of documents including storage models and indexing as well as supporting query processing.

In this section we have introduced a number of concepts:

- ontology;
- metadata classes;
- complexity levels of queries;
- classes of retrieval systems (ABR, TBR, CBR).

Now we have enough information to consider how these concepts can be integrated in a retrieval system. At the physical level the media data may be stored separately or together but the media will need to be processed separately by systems called media processors to extract the features required to support CBR. This will result in media-dependent metadata being generated that will also require storage. When it is necessary to interrogate more than one kind of media in a query the metadata can be combined through a meta correlation which may involve applying rules and concepts stored in the domain ontology to generate the required data.

The most demanding queries are those where we have a database that contains a number of different media types where the user can ask complex semantic queries at level 3. This would require the data to be stored and organized with its metadata in the way presented in Figure 5.5, although not available in current commercial systems. This is distinct from the process referred to as "registration" described earlier (Chapter 3) where the actual media data is correlated so that images from different sources of the same object can be combined together. In meta correlation it is the metadata from the different media that are correlated for the purpose of retrieving the required data object.

Figure 5.5 sets out an overview of the role of metadata in query processing. It shows how the physical storage view relates to the conceptual data view that we will look at in more detail in Chapter 8. The physical multimedia data goes through a media processor to automatically generate the metadata we have already discussed. For example, with image media the media processors would generate histograms and object edge detection data. The term meta correlation describes the situation that can arise when metadata about different kinds of media data has to be correlated to provide a

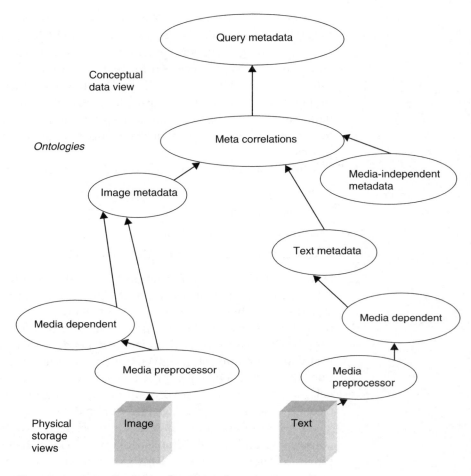

Figure 5.5 Example of role of metadata in query processing

unified picture of the multimedia database. The way these techniques fit together is shown in Figure 5.5. This unified picture is actually the query metadata. For example, a geographical information system may get the query

"Give the images of vineyards that are over 2,000 square meters, showing at least two people processing wine."

The result of this query needs to be obtained by combining information from text (the areas of the vineyards) with images. In addition the content of the images must be used to locate images showing at least two people. In addition there then needs to be a correlation between the areas of the vineyards and their available images. Referring to Figure 5.5, text and image preprocessors generate media-dependent metadata. In addition, media-independent data is retrieved from the database. The media ontologies add information about concepts and relationships from the domain to the media metadata. This allows a meta correlation to be carried out to provide the query metadata that can be used to retrieve the result of the query. The way in which the ontologies link the physical storage view of the media data to the conceptual data view through the generation and processing of metadata is shown in Figure 5.5. The process involves:

- The information about the names and areas of the vineyards will need to be found using the text media processor.
- The information about the areas is media dependent because it will be found within the text document.
- The image media-dependent metadata can be used to retrieve images showing at least two people.
- The image media-independent metadata retrieved from the database would also include the names of the vineyards.
- The data from the text and image sources can be combined together and cross-checked.
- The two metadata sources are then correlated to give the query metadata which is used in the presentation of the results to the user.

Whether we are using ABR, TBR or CBR the query presented to the database is more likely to be to be based on a QBE, looking for similar items to the example rather than for an exact match. In order to locate the similar items we need to be able to separate the data into groups of similar items and then decide which group is nearest to the example we provided.

5.3 What is the Classification Problem?

Humans are very good at classifying objects, events and phenomena. Without any theory of classification humans were able to study their environment and develop classification of plant and animals species, tools and weather conditions. However, with technological advances providing very large data sets it is now important to have automatic machine-based methods for classification, for example the classification of human faces for facial recognition purposes. The general process of automatic classification is shown in Figure 5.6.

The feature extraction stage is used to derive unique features from the raw media data, for example the input image. At this stage the size of the features may also be reduced. The pattern classifier accepts an input pattern with certain features and outputs the correct class. The classification decision is based on the feature characteristics of the input image. One

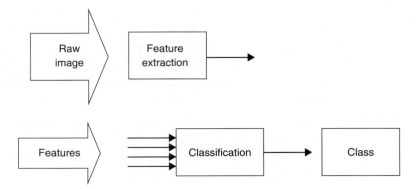

Figure 5.6   Recognition and classification

problem is that sometimes classes can overlap, causing an ambiguous classification.

A good classifier needs the following characteristics:

- There must be features (measurements or tests) by which the patterns can be characterized.
- There must be a specification for the classification function.
- There must be a method for determining what the classification function is from sample patterns.
- If the number of classes is known then there must be a classification method for every group.

Database tables are characteristically composed of a set of columns, which can be regarded as features, some of which are quantitative measures (e.g. price, quantity in stock), some are qualitative descriptions and some Boolean. When we chose a method to classify our data we will also need to consider some practical problems:

- How time consuming is the procedure?
- Is there any bias in the classes produced?
- How consistent are the estimated classes?

A number of commercially available DBMSs are now including CBR methods. Before we look at the application of some of these we will look at the underlying techniques. The reason for trying to understand the way the multimedia data is being processed is that there is an element of subjectivity involved in the automatic processing of multimedia data of which the user is not always aware. When the user makes decisions based on the presentation of multimedia data it would be wise also to know the degree of certainty associated with the presentation. Is the result set really related to the target? How reliable is the result?

In CBR we cannot usually work with the raw data but have to process the media to extract features of interest. There is a very large number of techniques that could be applied. In this book we will look at just three techniques that have a potential to be of interest in text, image and video data. These techniques are:

- data clustering;
- principal components;
- latent semantic indexing.

5.3.1 Data Clustering

Cluster analysis is an important means of processing multimedia data. It is basically the organization of a collection of patterns into clusters of similar objects. Patterns within valid clusters are more similar to each other than they are to a pattern in a different cluster.

Figure 5.7 shows the input data set transformed into a set of clusters with data points in the same group given the same label (1, 2 or 3). Clustering is often referred to as unsupervised classification. It is a different process from a related technique known as discriminant analysis which is also known as supervised classification, because in that case we start with a set of labels already and the system learns what the labels are.

In MMDBMSs we usually start with unlabeled data points and we need to discover how to cluster these into groups. Clustering is also an important technique in data mining where it is usually used with structured data but we are going to be interested in using it for text and image retrieval. It is a particularly useful method because we do not need to make any assumptions about the nature of the data and we can use it to uncover any structure in the data that we will be able to exploit to query the data.

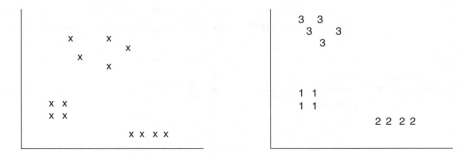

Figure 5.7 Data clustering – input data followed by labeled output groups

Clustering can allow us to carry out the following activities that can help in query processing:

- representing patterns in the data so that we can reduce the size of the media;
- defining a way of measuring the proximity of different patterns in the data so we can find the instances that match our example (in Figure 5.7, is cluster 1 nearer to 2 or 3?);
- clustering or grouping the data in preparation for matching;
- data abstraction, particularly of features that we can store as metadata;
- assessing the output by estimating how good the selection is.

Representing the patterns in data involves identifying the number of classes, the number of available patterns and the number, type and scale of features available. We can perform a number of transformations on the original data to produce new features that are more expressive than the original data and are therefore much more powerful for classifying the data. Thus we can address two of the problems that continually face us with media data – size and semantic nature. Feature extraction is the use of one or more transformations of the input features to produce more expressive features. Feature selection is the process of identifying the most effective subset of the original features to use in clustering. The stages of clustering are presented in Figure 5.8.

We noted that because we will usually retrieve a number of items that are similar to the sample target there needs to be a way of ordering the result set. Therefore we need a means of measuring the similarity of the items to the target. Pattern proximity is measured by applying a special distance function to pairs of patterns. We can decide whether the grouping step will be hard – an item may only belong to one group – or fuzzy where each pattern has a variable degree of membership in each cluster.

The process of extracting simple and compact representations of the data set is called data abstraction. By simplicity we mean the ability for the machine to perform the process efficiently or from the human perspective that the representation should be easy to understand and intuitive. A typical data abstraction from the clustering process should be a compact description

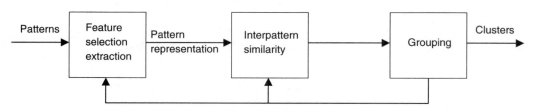

Figure 5.8   Stages in clustering

of each cluster. There are many different clustering algorithms available. How can we judge that the clustering process has produced a "good" set of clusters? Looking back at Figure 5.7 was this the best set of clusters? Note that data that does not contain clusters should not go through this process. The assessment of the clustering process is the clustering validity and usually the criteria are somewhat subjective. We can compare a cluster output with our expectations, check whether the process was appropriate for the data set and compare two different outputs to measure their relative merit. There are still a number of unanswered questions that we should be aware of when we deal with the output of clustering:

- How should the data set be normalized?
- What is the best similarity measure for the data?
- How should domain knowledge be used?
- How can we process very large data sets?

Humans are quite good at clustering data in two dimensions. For example, humans would outperform machines for a task such as Figure 5.7 presents. However, we are not capable of clustering data with many dimensions. Domain data is also very important. When we deal with clustering processes it is useful to work with a set of definitions:

- A pattern is a single data item used by a clustering algorithm that represents a vector of measurements.
- The individual scalar components of a pattern are called features or attributes.
- Hard clustering attaches a label to each pattern, identifying its class.
- Fuzzy clustering procedures assign each input pattern a fractional degree of membership to each output cluster.
- A distance measure is a metric for quantifying the similarity of patterns.

Selecting the correct features on which to base the cluster process is vital. For example the pattern shown in Figure 5.9 would be split into three clusters by many processes but one cluster if polar coordinates were used. As humans we would notice the pattern formed by this data but the clustering process can easily be misled.

This form of data analysis can deal with a wide range of patterns, for example from a chair on one hand to a style of writing. The features used to analyze the pattern can be:

- quantitative, e.g. weights, counts, intervals (duration of events);
- qualitative, e.g. color, ordinal;
- structured, e.g. trees.

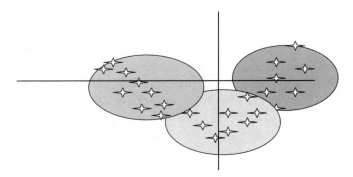

Figure 5.9   A pattern that would give ambiguous clusters

Structured data can be trees with parent nodes and child nodes. For example, a parent node *vehicle* can have child nodes *cars, buses, trucks, cycles*; the child *cars* can have another set of child nodes – *Ford, Toyota, Renault, Morgan*. Selecting features is a process of isolating the most descriptive and discriminatory features in the input set and using those in subsequent steps. Feature extraction is the process of generating new features from the original set. This can improve both computation efficiency and classification. This can involve a trial-and-error process where various subsets of features are selected, the resultant patterns clustered, the output evaluated. Principal components analysis (PCA) is one way of reducing the number of features and extracting new ones, discussed later.

Clustering Methods

There are a large number of different clustering methods available. In selecting a clustering technique for a particular set of data, the following issues need to be taken into account:

- *Agglomerative versus divisive*. An agglomerative approach begins with a pattern with each cluster having only one member. The algorithm merges clusters together until a stop criterion is reached. In contrast a divisive method begins with all patterns in a single cluster and performs a splitting procedure until the stopping criterion is met.

- *Polythetic versus monothetic*. Most algorithms are polythetic, i.e. they use the whole feature set together. Monothetic procedures consider one feature at a time; however, this tends to produce far too large a number of patterns to be useful for database queries where a very large number of features can be involved.

- *Hard versus fuzzy*. Hard algorithms allocate each pattern to a single cluster.

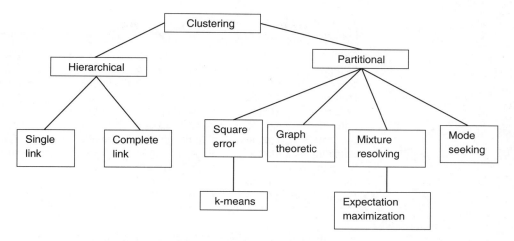

Figure 5.10   **Classes of clustering methods from Jain and Dubes (1988)**

There are some issues that are about performance with large databases:

- *Incremental versus non-incremental*. This is an issue when there are constraints on execution time and memory space because of large data sets.

- *Deterministic versus stochastic*. This is whether the process tries to optimize the allocation or uses essentially random search techniques.

Data mining has triggered the development of more efficient clustering algorithms that minimize the number of scans of the whole data set required. We do not need to know the details of the equations or algorithms because they are readily available, but it is important to look at the effects of using the different methods.

Partitional algorithms are preferred with large data sets where a function is used as the stop criterion because the process of selection is faster. The most important cluster method used for QBE systems is called **k-means**. It is the most popular algorithm and works well with compact and isolated clusters. It starts with a random partition of the data and keeps reassigning the patterns to clusters until there is no reassignment or the squared error ceases to decrease significantly. The procedure allows k-samples with the smallest measured distance between clusters to be selected.

Let us start by clustering some structured data. We will look at an example using a small database of economic data of European Countries shown in Table 5.5. (Note this is not real data.) We will cluster the data using a hierarchical and a partitional method to contrast the results. There must be some means of measuring the similarity of the different clusters so that we can put them in order for the user. Measuring similarity is a fundamental issue in clustering because of the variation in the feature types and scales.

Table 5.5 Data to be clustered

Country	Area	GDP	Cars	Population	Births	Deaths
Germany	357.00	826.00	25 346	77 854.00	584.00	696.10
Greece	132.00	42.80	1 156	9 897.80	123.00	88.40
Spain	504.00	216.20	8 879	38 345.00	456.00	289.00
France	544.00	674.80	20 800	54 678.00	768.00	543.00
Ireland	68.90	24.10	719	3 543.00	67.00	32.30
Italy	301.00	473.60	20 888	57 009.70	547.00	532.00
Denmark	92.00	28.90	657	100 987.00	64.00	97.20
Belgium	34.00	25.60	567	1 435.00	38.00	56.70
Sweden	246.00	256.70	17 213	5 678.00	142.00	97.80
UK	244.00	612.34	25 678	56 789.40	729.00	644.00
Netherlands	144.00	378.80	1 854	12 455.00	132.00	115.00

Therefore the way the distance is measured must be carefully chosen. Euclidean distance is the most popular metric. It has an intuitive appeal because it is used to measure the distance between two points in three-dimensional space. It works well when a data set has compact or isolated clusters. The problem with this measure is that there is a tendency of the largest-scale feature to dominate the others. When a feature is a continuous variable this can be solved by normalizing the data. (This means adjusting all the data to a standard distribution.) The Mahalanobis distance is a variant of Euclidean distance that compensates for its shortcomings. There are also some distance measures that take into account the effect of the surrounding or neighboring points, which are termed the context. One metric which is defined on the context is the mutual neighbor distance. An area of particular difficulty is where some of the feature data is not continuous since the different types of features are not comparable. Some algorithms therefore work on the set of distance values rather than the raw data.

Table 5.6 k-mean clusters with the distance between members

Cluster membership			
Case number	Country	Cluster	Distance
1	Germany	1	10 726.159
2	Greece	2	4 390.210
3	Spain	2	26 730.440
4	France	1	14 942.173
5	Ireland	2	9 415.027
6	Italy	1	12 649.358
7	Denmark	1	36 318.158
8	Belgium	2	11 386.099
9	Sweden	2	13 645.999
10	UK	1	14 483.198
11	Netherlands	2	3 267.532

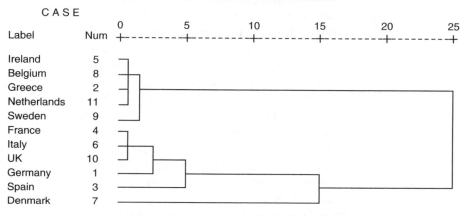

Figure 5.11   Dendrogram presentation of clusters of European countries

If we use k-means with the European database we obtain the set of clusters with a Mahalanobis distance measure for each country shown in Table 5.6. The first cluster consists of Germany, France, Italy, UK and Denmark while the second cluster is made up of Greece, Spain, Ireland, Belgium, Netherlands and Sweden.

Now we can also cluster this small data set using hierarchical clustering analysis (HCA) with a single link and the result can be displayed in a dendrogram as shown in Figure 5.11. A dendrogram is a diagram that shows how the nested clusters are related. It looks like a tree on its side.

This HCA process has created two main clusters – Ireland, Belgium, Greece, Netherlands and Sweden form one cluster while France, Italy, UK, Germany, Spain and Denmark form the second cluster. We can see the second cluster also has a subcluster of France, Italy and the UK.

EXERCISE 5.2

Study the dendrogram presented in Figure 5.11. Summarize the semantic meaning of the clusters of countries formed by the technique. Present a brief interpretation for the meaning of the clusters.

These techniques can be used to support QBE style queries of the kind "I sell my cars in a country like this – find similar countries". From the two different methods we have got slightly different results. This means that the result set will need interpretation by the user or the incorporation of domain knowledge. When we design the presentation system we need to create a user interface which allows for this.

Neural networks can also be used for classification and clustering but can only apply to quantitative features. Neural networks may learn adaptively. Well-known examples for clustering include Kohonen self-organizing feature maps (KSOFM), although initially these methods did not scale up well for database requirements they are now being used with large data sets by using distributed computation.

As a task, clustering is subjective. The same data set can be partitioned in a number of different ways for different purposes as we have seen. Subjectivity is incorporated into the clustering criterion by including domain knowledge in one or more stages of the clustering. Every clustering algorithm uses some type of knowledge either implicitly or explicitly. Implicit knowledge plays a role in selecting a pattern representation scheme using prior experience to select and encode features – selecting a similarity measure, selecting a grouping scheme. Domain knowledge is also used implicitly in neural networks to select learning parameter values that affect the performance of these algorithms.

It is also possible to use domain knowledge explicitly to constrain and guide the clustering process. Domain concepts can be incorporated as one of the features. Domain concepts can be used to confirm or veto a decision arrived at by a traditional cluster algorithm. Any implementation that includes domain knowledge explicitly in a clustering technique has to address:

- representation, availability and the completeness of the domain concepts;
- construction of inferences using knowledge;
- accommodation of changing or dynamic knowledge.

In some domains, knowledge is complete but in others it is difficult to extract as in the case of MMDBMSs. In these cases learning by example can be used. It is, however, difficult to verify soundness and completeness of data sets because such knowledge cannot be represented by prepositional logic. Knowledge and data may change over time. The most difficult problem is to deal with very large knowledge bases for clustering in data mining, image segmentation and data retrieval. For example, to segment an image with 500×500 pixels requires 250 000 pixels to be clustered. In text information retrieval there may be 100 dimensions to cluster. Some other well-known approaches are based on techniques such as genetic algorithms, tabu search and simulated annealing but cannot be used with large data sets. The emerging discipline of data mining has spurred on the development of new algorithms for clustering large data sets using the following strategies:

- Divide and conquer. Subsets of the data, too large to cluster in main memory, are clustered independently and then combined later.

- The data is stored in secondary storage and transferred one at a time to main memory for one at a time clustering.
- Clustering algorithm may be implemented using distributed computation.

In Chapter 11 we shall see that image segmentation is fundamental to many MMDBMS applications. Image segmentation is the partition of an image into regions each of which is considered to be homogeneous with respect to some property of interest. The segmentation of the image presented by the query is critically dependent on the scene, the image geometry, configuration and sensor used. The applicability of the clustering methods to image segmentation problem was recognized for over 30 years. Three different types of techniques are:

- region based;
- edge based;
- cluster based.

These are dealt with in more detail in Chapter 11.

5.3.2 Principal Components Analysis

The second important technique we mentioned earlier was PCA. This can reduce significantly the amount of features we need to use. For example, if we apply a standard PCA treatment to the European database we will obtain one principal component that accounts for 76% of the variation in the data set. The value of this component is shown together with the original data set in Table 5.7.

The principal component is a new artificially created attribute that is related to all the original attributes and represents something important about the total information system of attributes. In a way we can look at the

Table 5.7 Data set with PCA values added

Country	Area	GDP	Cars	Population	Births	Deaths	PCA F1
Germany	357.00	826.00	25 346	77 854.00	584.00	696.10	1.396 86
Greece	132.00	42.80	1 156	9 897.80	123.00	88.40	−0.921 24
Spain	504.00	216.20	8 879	38 345.00	456.00	289.00	0.235 97
France	544.00	674.80	20 800	54 678.00	768.00	543.00	1.316 17
Ireland	68.90	24.10	719	3 543.00	67.00	32.30	−1.117 25
Italy	301.00	473.60	20 888	57 009.70	547.00	532.00	0.770 85
Denmark	92.00	28.90	657	10 098.70	64.00	97.20	−0.663 84
Belgium	34.00	25.60	567	1 435.00	38.00	56.70	−1.163 87
Sweden	246.00	256.70	17 213	5 678.00	142.00	97.80	−0.352 22
UK	244.00	612.34	25 678	56 789.40	729.00	644.00	1.122 79
Netherlands	144.00	378.80	1 854	12 455.00	132.00	115.00	−0.624 22

process as discovering something important about the database table and summarizing the information in it. Usually several components are identified but in this case, with a small set of data, the process has only identified one. The values of the principal component for every row can be evaluated as shown in Table 5.7.

The principal component is related to varying degrees to all the original attributes. This information is available in the correlation matrix shown in Table 5.8. This gives the correlation coefficients between the new component which has been identified by the algorithm and the original attributes. If there were a perfect correlation this coefficient would have the value of +1, whereas zero would indicate no relationship. An inverse relationship is indicated by −1. Therefore in correlation measures the coefficients can range from +1, perfectly aligned, to −1 inversely aligned.

Now we have reduced the data set to a single column of data we can cluster this instead of using the original data. This time we get a slightly different cluster again as shown in Figure 5.12. Our two main groups – Ireland, Belgium, Greece, Netherlands, Sweden and Denmark – form one cluster while France, Italy, UK, Germany and Spain form the second cluster. We can see the second cluster also has a nested cluster of France, Germany and the UK. Users may not always be aware of the differences small changes in options during processing can make to the resulting clusters. We should also note that in our example we have a very small data set to look at.

PCA is very useful because, in computer vision applications, images can be described by a very large number of features. Examples are given in Chapter 11 for color, texture and shape. Any means that can reduce the number of features will therefore bring great advantages in database retrieval. As we have seen above, PCA provides a means of reducing six features to a single value that can then be used in classification. PCA exploits the statistical variation and regularities of the input data by extracting and compressing the information. (*Note that in computer vision and pattern recognition research PCA is also known as the Karhunen–Loeve transform.*)

In PCA we have a method that will take *n* dimensions of original data and map these to a new reduced number of *m* dimensions that retains most

Table 5.8 Correlation matrix of attributes and PCA factor 1

Variables	Correlation	Interpretation
Area	0.795	Less strongly related
GDP	0.930	Strongly related
Cars	0.925	Strongly related
Population	0.606	Least strongly correlated
Births	0.966	Strongly related
Deaths	0.972	Most strongly positively correlated

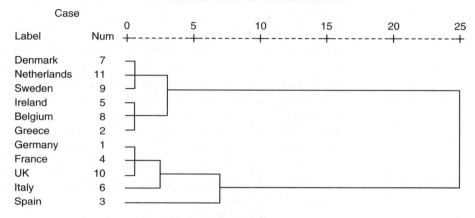

Figure 5.12 Dendrogram of PCA output

of the intrinsic information in the original data. The application of PCA results in the transformation of huge amounts of data into a set of statistically independent features (or components) usually ordered according to decreasing information content. Since PCA can itself be computationally expensive due to large sizes of images, some innovative computational methods may be required, particularly, using neural computation and distributed processing. Although we will lose some information and the process is not reversible (we will not be able to reconstruct the original data from the components) this will be acceptable from the database point of view as long as the features extracted provide the uniqueness property. Furthermore, we can use SQL directly with the new PCA features, for example

```
SELECT    country
FROM      Europe
WHERE     pcaf1 BETWEEN 0.1 AND 0.9
```

5.3.3 Latent Semantic Indexing

This is a very different approach to the two previous methods, although we will be familiar with some of the techniques it uses. It was originally developed for text databases but has recently been applied to images and has a lot of potential uses in multimedia.

Latent semantic indexing (LSI) relies on the terms (words and phrases) already present in a media object such as a document to suggest the document's semantic content. However, the LSI model views the terms in a document as somewhat unreliable indicators of the concepts contained in the document. It assumes that the variability of word choice partially obscures the semantic structure of the document. By reducing the dimensionality of the term–document space, the underlying, semantic relationships between documents are revealed, and much of the "noise" (differences in word usage, terms that do not help distinguish documents, etc.) is eliminated. LSI statistically analyzes the patterns of word usage across the entire document collection, placing documents with similar word usage patterns near each other in the term–document space and allowing semantically related documents to be near each other even though they may not share terms. LSI explicitly represents terms and documents in a rich, high-dimensional space, allowing the underlying latent, semantic relationships between terms and documents to be exploited during searching. LSI is able to represent and manipulate large data sets, making it viable for real-world applications.

The LSI process involves:

(a) Reduce the query to its essential terms.

(b) Take each media object such as text document and remove the stop words. Stop words are those that are so common they have no relevance and so are ignored, e.g. "the", "in addition", "however", "and", "but", and "only".

(c) Reduce the object to a list of unique terms (words or phrases) and note the number of times the term occurs in each document.

(d) Generate a matrix where each row represents a unique term in the whole collection of objects and the columns represent each object. The individual cells represent the weight of the term in the object (see Figure 5.13). Since the number of terms in a given object is much less than the total number of terms in the whole set this will result in a very sparse matrix. The cell value could be the number of occurrences but it is usually more complex. For example, it is possible to apply local weights to particular documents and global weightings, across the whole lot.

(e) Apply a distance measure (cf. data clustering) to estimate the distance of each object from the query and rank the object accordingly. Several different similarity measures such as Euclidean distance can be applied to compare the queries and the terms so that it is found that different similarly measures emphasize different latent properties of the object set.

(f) Use relevance feedback. Relevance feedback involves allowing documents as well as terms to form the query and using the terms in those documents to supplement the query, increases the length and precision

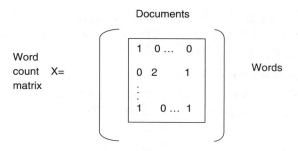

Figure 5.13   Latent semantic analysis – sparse matrix

of the query, helping the user more accurately to specify what he or she desires from the search.

The LSI information retrieval model builds on prior research in information retrieval, using what is known as singular value decomposition to reduce the dimensions of the term–document space. In Chapter 10 we will take a step-by-step look at this process in the analysis of text databases.

The three techniques we have looked at for feature extraction have a number of common aspects:

- They all aim to reduce the size of the media objects.
- They aim to be able to classify, group and rank the media objects.
- They aim to uncover and summarize the semantic nature of the media objects.

The processes involve intense computation and result in findings that are much more subjective that we are accustomed to when dealing with Boolean queries in SQL statements. Small changes in the parameters of the feature extraction process can result in different groupings. The user needs to be involved in and have an understanding of the sources of uncertainty in a way not required for results of Boolean queries.

5.4   Summary of Chapter

The rich semantic nature of multimedia data creates difficulties for information retrieval that require the application of advanced techniques. Although queries can be carried out on the basis of attributes and text annotation the goal is to achieve CBR. In this chapter we introduced several techniques that can be used to support multimedia queries.

In this chapter you have learned:

- three levels of information retrieval for multimedia data;

- three approaches to retrieval (attribute, text and content based);
- the role of domain ontologies in multimedia retrieval;
- standards for metadata;
- feature selection and extraction;
- specific techniques for generating metadata for every kind of media – cluster analysis (HCA and k-means), PCA and LSI.

SOLUTIONS TO EXERCISES

Exercise 5.1

Semantic media retrieval is about the level of information retrieved whereas CBR is one kind of implementation.

Exercise 5.2

The clusters represent some feature of the data which tends to group the countries together. The first cluster may represent countries that are geographically dispersed from the central area of the EU and have more in common than those countries grouped in the center of the EU. The subcluster with France, Italy and the UK is interesting in that when we speculate what these have in common it may be a strong historical connection dating back into our cultural heritage that influences economic performance. The important thing to note is that we have summarized the data and also discovered something about the data by this process.

Recommended Reading

Chatfield, C., Collins, A. J. (1995) Multivariate distributions. In *Introduction to Multivariate Analysis*, Chapman and Hall, London, pp. 19–33.

Cichoki, A., Unbenhauen, R. (1993) *Neural Networks for Optimisation and Signal Processing*, Wiley, New York.

Modeling Multimedia Databases

Chapter aims

This chapter starts by reviewing the different kinds of conceptual models available to represent multimedia in databases. We review the reasons for the development of object-oriented databases and object-relational databases. Using the examples of Oracle and DB2 we look at the ways in which object-relational databases could be implemented in terms of user-defined types, objects and methods. Through a study of this chapter the reader will develop a broad overview of the role of multimedia data models within database development and should then be able to:

- understand the issues of designing multimedia database management systems;

- appreciate the role of semantic data modeling;

- understand the reasons for adopting an object-oriented design;

- understand the reasons for adopting an object-relational design;

- appreciate the implementation of user-defined types in Oracle and DB2.

6.1 Issues of Designing Multimedia Database Management Systems

The first multimedia databases developed were designed to fulfil the requirements of specific applications, for example web-based encyclopedia. One of the consequences of the way these multimedia databases were developed was that the designs could not evolve to provide generic multimedia database management systems (MMDBMSs). A key issue to consider is how and to what extent present database models can successfully meet the challenges posed by multimedia data. One of the main problems with modeling multimedia database systems is the need to deal with the temporal characteristics of much of the data. This means capturing relationships that involve:

- time;
- duration;
- synchronization.

In this chapter the semantic modeling of multimedia and its representation by complex data types is explored. Both object-oriented and object-relational approaches are contrasted through the study of detailed examples.

Modeling the different media for multimedia database design can often mean using already existing media data that has been created without any specific model in mind. This is unlike the situation in a traditional database where a data model is created before the data and the relations or objects are then deliberately populated with data of the correct specification. A creative object such as a photographic image or a film will not have been created with a pre-existing data model in mind. However, superimposing a data model on a collection of media objects can certainly assist data indexing and retrieval.

One of the most challenging media to model is video. A suitable model could include references to:

- physical objects (people, buildings, vehicles);
- video segments;
- video features;
- video shots;
- whole video object.

This range implies a hierarchy which is discussed in more detail in Chapter 12 and that could be used to provide a data model, as shown in Figure 6.1.

Figure 6.1 shows the relationship between a video object and a set of video clips, scenes and shots. The relationship between them is both spatial and temporal. The spatial relationships are represented by two- and three-dimensional coordinate systems. The relationship between two temporally related video segments can be described by one of the following: before, meets, overlaps, during, starts, finishes, equals. This is a complex set of relationships to capture in a database model.

Figure 6.1   Hierarchy of video objects

The problem of design at the heart of relational database systems is that the meaning of the data is not encapsulated within the data itself which is held as sets of values. As Date says, "the database systems typically have only limited understanding of what the database means" (Date, 2000). For example, a wine order has no meaning in a relational database and the order itself does not exist but will be represented by a number of relational tables.

Thus databases behave in a way that is not "intelligent". The role of SQL is limited to checking the data types of the values and comparing them using Boolean logic (predicate calculus). This is not to say that there are not semantic elements within the relational model. Integrity constraints, candidate keys and foreign keys represent meaning within the relational model. However, as database systems developed at the end of the last century there was a recognition that it was essential to capture information about the "business rules" of an application and to find some way to incorporate these within the data model. This attempt to capture the meaning of the data itself is described by the general term **semantic data modeling**. However, we should recognize that attempts with any of today's data models to actually be "semantic" has had very limited results. We will now discuss the objectives of semantic data modeling and then look at the way object-oriented models and object-relational models attempt to address this semantic gap.

6.1.1   Semantic Data Modeling

Several attempts were made to extend the relational model and link it to conceptual data models such as the entity–relationship model. The relational model was formally specified by Codd in 1970, so it pre-dates the entity–relationship model The entity–relationship model was the conceptual model of choice for database design for about 30 years. It was widely accepted and had the benefit of limited rules resulting in simple schema so that it was relatively straightforward to learn although more complex to actually put into practice. It works well with simple transactional systems. However, whereas the relational model provides only one semantic element – the relation – to model a real-world situation, the entity-relational model still only provides two/three elements so that adopting either of these models results in a severe reduction of expressiveness.

Date (2000) makes the point that Codd must have had informal ideas about entities in his mind when he developed the formal relational model. The overall approach to the development of a database model can be described as:

1. Identify useful semantic concepts.
2. Devise formal objects.

3. Devise formal integrity rules.

4. Devise formal operators.

This approach needs to be followed with both the entity-relational model and the relational model. Note that the first step is informal while the others are formal.

In semantic analysis we attempt to describe the real world by making simple declarative propositions about it. A proposition is a sentence that describes a state of affairs, therefore capturing something meaningful about the system. The sense of an expression is its indispensable hard core of meaning. In understanding the meaning of the real world the context is crucial. For example the table

```
CREATE TABLE employee
(employee_number  CHAR(4),
employee_name     VARCHAR2(30),
salary            NUMBER(6,2),
start_date        DATE,
department_number CHAR(4) CONSTRAINT emp_dep_fkey NOT NULL
REFERENCES department,
CONSTRAINT prim_emp PRIMARY KEY(employee_number))
```

must be understood in the context of an organization in which employees belong to one and only one department at a time.

Date (2000) suggests that we do not need to use an entity-relational model to derive a relational model for a database system. His preferred approach would be to write down the predicates that describe the enterprise and then map those predicates straightforwardly into a database model.

Other database experts have criticized the process of normalization which is essential for a good relational database design (see Appendix A) that is intended to reduce redundancy of the attributes of the data because it has the consequence of proliferating the number of keys. The process of normalization has the effect of destroying the natural structure of the data which is replaced by multiple relational joins which most users find difficult to understand. The integrity of the database rests on the maintenance of the foreign and primary key values so that changing a key value is a troublesome process. The relationships between entities in the system are never explicitly represented in the relational model. They may be represented by the posting of a foreign key within a table such as **employee** or by the creation of a distinct relation. For example, the employee table is linked to a department table which we specified as

```
CREATE TABLE department
(department_number     CHAR(4) CONSTRAINT prim_dept PRIMARY
KEY,
department_name   VARCHAR2(10))
```

Our employees can only belong to one department but in the course of time are likely to change to another department. We can use an insert to add an employee to the marketing department

```
INSERT INTO employee
(employee_number, employee_name, salary, start_date,
department_number)
VALUES ('7902', 'FORD', 1756,'03-May-1991',1234);
```

We can also update an employee's row to record their move to Marketing by changing the value of the foreign key from "1234" for Accounts to "3010" for Marketing

```
UPDATE employee
SET department_number = '3010'
WHERE employee_number = '7902'
```

However, organizations have a tendency to change and reorganize themselves so that the department called "Accounts" may have a new number such as "2010" and be renamed "Finance" this means as well as changing the primary key data all the foreign keys have to be changed. The statement

```
UPDATE department
SET department_number  = '2010'
WHERE department_number ='1234'
```

will fail to execute in Oracle, giving a message about the integrity constraint **scott.emp_dep_fkey** being violated because of a "child record found".

This is why Oracle allows foreign keys to be temporarily disabled because otherwise we would need to create the new department, change all the employee rows to the new department and then remove the old department row. This is why some database developers would prefer to model the employee and department relationship as explicitly represented in another table **dep_emp**.

The relational table like **employee** also consists of columns representing scalar attributes. In designing the database it would be much more efficient to be able to use composite attributes to represent data such as an address that is only meaningful if the elements are kept together. It is also difficult in the relational model to show that some entities have common characteristics. Both the employees and the customers of the wine shop have a number of common attributes that we are interested in. Although this can be represented in the entity–relationship model as supertype–subtype it cannot be easily mapped into the relational model.

Consequently, semantic data modeling remains a goal which has not been realized by traditional database models.

6.1.2 Object-oriented Design

Object-oriented database management systems (ODBMSs) were developed because designers of complex systems believed the relational model and SQL were too limited. Technically there is no official standard for object databases. The Object Database Standard ODMG-V2.0 describes the industry-accepted *de facto* standard. One of the first attempts at defining a standard for object-oriented design was based on the formation of the Object Management Group (OMG) in 1989. The OMG is an international software industry consortium with two primary aims:

- promotion of the object-oriented approach to software engineering in general;
- development of models and a common interface for large-scale distributed applications using object-oriented methodology.

The OMG proposed a core object model and a specified set of components appropriate for a given domain. In object-oriented design we talk about an object model rather than a data model because the object represents more about the real-world object than merely the data. It is based on a small number of concepts:

- objects;
- operations;
- types;
- subtyping.

An object is a representation of any kind of entity – a person, a machine, a document, a department or an object on a user interface such as a button. The object must have a distinct identity that cannot be changed and persists as long as the object exists. The object's identity is independent of the object's attributes or behavior. Each object has a unique identity that is distinct from and independent of any of its characteristics. Attribute values can vary over time but the identity of the object is constant. In the OMG object model the object identifier is called the OID. The OMG core model has nothing to tell us about what the internal structure or format of the OID should be. In the core object model OIDs denote the same concept as object references in CORBA – the Common Object Request Broker Architecture which was standardized by the OMG in 1997 to provide a component-based approach to object systems. Operations can be applied to an object's behavior. For example, we may want to perform the operation **get_date_of_birth** on an employee object. In order to deal with objects in a database we do not define each object individually. Instead we gather objects that have the same attributes and behavior together and we define a type. The OMG defines a type as a set of attributes and operations that characterize the behavior of its objects. Objects are created as instances of their types which is the same as saying that an object is of some type. Each operation of a type has a signature which is a name, a set of parameters and a set of results. The set of operation signatures constitutes the interface of the type. The term parameter is used when referring to the signature of an operation while the term argument is used when referring to the invocation of an operation. The consequences of invoking an operation may be:

- an immediate set of results;
- a change of state.

In the core model subtyping is a relationship between the types based on their interfaces. Inheritance is a notational mechanism for defining a type S in terms of another type T. The definition of S inherits all the operations of T and may provide other operations. Inheritance is a mechanism for reuse.

A type's interface defines the externally visible state and behavior of instances of that type; for example, an image would be defined as

```
type Image
operations:
get_width
get_length
set_width
scale (i: Image, by FACTOR)
rotate(i: Image, by DEGREES)
```

In a pure object system such as the *Smalltalk* language all values are associated with objects but the core object model recognizes things that are not objects and distinguishes between these and objects. In CORBA there are non-object types representing the traditional data types.

An object-oriented approach may appear "natural" for a multimedia database, particularly as it can encapsulate code and data together in one object. One of the main advantages claimed is that it is possible to present a class hierarchy for multimedia objects, for example:

- media
  - variables – OID, window dimensions, presentation, duration
  - methods – start presentation, stop presentation
    - text
      - variables – text format, font type, page size
      - methods – present text
    - video
      - variables – compression format, frames per second
      - methods – present video

The advantage of this approach is that image, audio and video objects can be modeled as binary objects (BLOBs) as part of user-defined data types and methods. In addition inheritance can be used, for example where a slide show can involve audio and image classes. However, one of the problems that arose with object databases for multimedia was that the structure of the data tends to be characteristic of the application so that reuse may be limited. Although the object-oriented approach was one of the earliest used for specific multimedia applications it has been difficult to develop general-purpose multimedia databases in this way.

As well as these advantages there are a number of disadvantages to the pure object-oriented approach, which are outlined next:

- Multimedia applications often need to group diverse objects together and access them in a collective manner; while object-oriented programming languages tend to work with individual objects, multimedia databases need set-oriented access that requires the ability to use characteristics that relate to a set of objects.

- Metadata can be difficult to accommodate within the object-oriented paradigm because it may need to be added or modified dynamically. This could also mean that class hierarchy and database schema may change.

- Pure object-oriented approaches may not allow some operations which are required. For example, edit operations in a multimedia database may need to involve new objects that are composed of a portion of an existing object.

Video Object Models

Although object-oriented approaches are popular there are specific problems with this approach when it is applied to video data. This is because:

- The data consists of media data and metadata that are often created independently.

- Object-oriented design requires a full specification of objects and their attributes at the time of creation. In this sense the object-oriented model is too static for video data.

- The attributes associated with semantic content tend to be discovered and added gradually to the media data.

- Descriptions of video data are user and application dependent.

- Object-oriented models support class-based inheritance but many video objects such as segments and scenes can overlap so that these relationships need to be modeled through inclusion inheritance to enable video objects to share descriptive metadata.

One attempt to address these problems is through OVID. The OVID database was an example of an object-oriented multimedia database system.

It stands for Object Video Information Database. In this schema a video object consists of a set of frames and their contents can be described in a dynamic and incremental way. The video database schema does not really exist and the class hierarchy is not assumed to be the database schema. The inheritance of object attributes is based on interval inclusion relationships. An interval is represented as a starting frame number, an ending frame number and a continuous sequence of frames. An OVID object can be composed of a multiple of intervals. In OVID a video object would have a definition consisting of:

- an OID;
- a set of intervals.

To summarize, for multimedia database systems the features frequently required which are additional to traditional object-oriented approaches are:

- set-oriented access;
- class hierarchy independent of the database schema;
- media-specific features.

6.2   Using UML

In the last few years, object-oriented design and UML (Unified Modeling Language) have become increasingly important. UML (version 1.3) was adopted as a standard by the OMG in June 1999. Object-oriented programming methods are in widespread use, while at the same time object-relational databases are now available to the extent that object-oriented design may achieve a dominant role in this area not achieved by pure object-oriented databases.

Object-oriented design has been particularly significant for software development of the underlying technical system. However, the application and integration of UML in database design has been much less significant, perhaps because it is a relatively recent standard and because historically there is a strong attachment to entity–relationship modeling. A number of the texts referenced at the end of this chapter that deal with object-oriented database design make no mention of UML even though UML includes a number of models described in Table 6.1 that are important to the database designer following this approach.

Adopting an approach based on UML shifts the design emphases for the database designer because, instead of treating the database as the backbone of the system around which everything else revolves, it recognizes that the database must exist together with the rest of the organization in which the

Table 6.1   Descriptions of the UML diagrams

Diagram	Description
Use case	A model of the system's intended functions and its environment that supports the business processes.
Interaction	These can be either sequence or collaboration diagrams. They show the interaction of objects within the system. They can be used to understand queries that will affect the database and help build indexes.
Activity	These show the flow of process. They can show a high level view of the business and how it operates. They also provide insight into conceptual data for the database designer.
Statechart	These capture the dynamic behavior of objects within the system.
Class	Logical models that show the basic structure of the system.
Database	The database diagram depicts the structure of the database, including tables, columns, constraints.
Component	These show the physical storage of the database, tablespaces and partitions.
Deployment	This shows the hardware configuration that is used for the database and applications.

different components – the applications, transactions and user processes – coexist.

The important information of the organization exists within the database but there are many other things that make up the company and its information so the database is just part of the picture. With structured methods there has been a tendency to fragment and specialize development so that different teams specialize in requirements, application development and database design and also use different techniques and diagram standards. This makes communication between teams more difficult and creates the potential for misunderstanding.

One of the main reasons for using UML is to promote communication between different groups of software engineers so that requirements engineers, application developers and database designers can use the same notations to minimize the risk of misunderstanding. This is especially important when requirements change. The stages of UML modeling as shown in Figure 6.2.

The use case model describes the requirements of the system from the users' point of view. This is intended to be a user-oriented approach and uses the terms actor and use case. An actor is a user of the system in a particular role and could be an external system as long as it interacts or makes demands on the system. A use case is a task which an actor needs to perform with the help of the system and it is essential that the use case provides something of value to the actor. An instance of an actor class can exist only

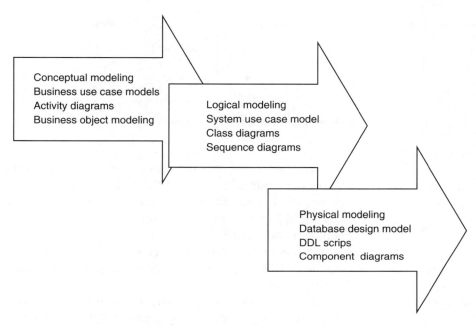

Figure 6.2   Stages of modeling using UML constructs

when a user does something to the system. The same users could therefore act as instances of several different actors.

The use case concept was introduced by Ivar Jacobsen in 1987 as a development of scenarios. His original concept was a model that would describe the system, its environment and how it and its environment are related, providing a black-box view of the system so that taken together the system's use cases represent everything the user can do with the system. Actors are fulfilling a role in a use case so that it does not necessarily mean that they are involved in carrying out a task; rather, they are beneficiaries involved throughout its development. In fact an extreme view would be that only actors who are beneficiaries should be shown, not other users needed for the task execution. An actor may play different roles in different use cases, the role referring to one specific collaboration, and an actor can be regarded as a coherent set of roles.

A scenario, in UML, is an instance of a use case, analogous to object and classes. A scenario is a possible interaction with the system. The scenarios in the use case are all attempts to carry out essentially the same task.

The use case diagram presented in Figure 6.3 specifies the actor in the role of customer. The use case itself is named "Order wine" and the name should be brief and start with an active verb. The rectangle around the use case can show the boundary of the system. Lines of communication connect

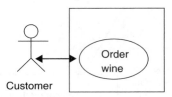

Figure 6.3   Use case – Order wine

the actor to the use case showing the exchange of information between the actor, the external entity and the system. Use cases are useful in database design for showing the interaction between external systems.

An object in UML is something in the problem domain that has state, behavior and identity. The fact that an object has state implies that it acts as a container of data. An object has properties that are represented as its attributes. A class is a description of a set of objects that share the same attributes, and operations.

In Figure 6.4 we represent an object as an instance of a class of employee. The object has an identifier, "7902", and a set of attributes and values. The identity is a label, "7092", given to an object so that it may be distinguished from all other objects of that class. (Sometimes the object's name is omitted but the class name is then preceded by a colon and underlined to distinguish it as an object.) All the attributes are named in lowercase letters. Although an object is a collection of related data with the processes that act on it, the object's representation does not include any information about the methods that act upon it. The class itself is shown in Figure 6.5.

In UML the class is not a collection of objects, it is a definition of the object's data and operations. In Figure 6.5 the attributes of the class are listed and the operations are in the bottom rectangle. This structure is always shown even if no operations are shown.

Generalization/specialization refer to the logical relationship between classes. Inheritance describes the mechanism for implementation. This is

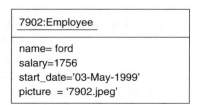

Figure 6.4   Employee object

Figure 6.5 Employee class, with attributes and operations

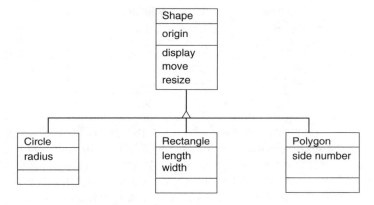

Figure 6.6 Superclass with subclasses

often shown in texts by using a graphical illustration. The structure in Figure 6.6 shows that there is a class definition for Shape, the superclass. A number of other classes, Rectangle, Circle and Polygon, have an "is-a-kind-of" relationship with Shape. The arrowhead always points to the superclass. The subclasses have all the attributes of the superclass and some of their own. Operations are also inherited.

EXERCISE 6.1

(a) What do all instances of a class have in common?

(b) What is the difference between a class and an object?

(c) What is the difference between an instance and an object?

(d) What is the difference between a class and a type?

Table 6.2 Nouns from Fine Wine Shop case study – Berry Bros & Rudd

The wine business	New Zealand	Origin
Fine wines	Bordeaux	Individual and corporate customers
Customers	Port	Catalogs
The company	Médoc	Events
Retail shops	Pomerol	Wine tastings
Other services	St Emilion	Dinners
Cellars	Vineyards	Lectures
Vineyard	Date started producing	Cases of wine
Blending details	Image of a bottle	Year
Taste	Label	Table
Bouquet	Bottles	Quality of the vintage
Producers	Size	Grape varieties
Categories	Price	Chardonnay
Champagne	Double Magnums	Alsace
Argentina	Vintage	Blend of wines
Family	Discounts	Cases of wine
Website	Chateau	Regional maps
Region	Brief note	Character
Country	Flavor	History

This is not a systematic way to develop the user requirement specification of a multimedia database as there are many techniques that would be employed to elicit and specify the requirements. It is, however, a quick way to start to think about the classes in the problem domain.

One of the issues that is important is how we recognize classes when a design is being developed. Initially we can examine the names of things in the problem domain. This can be based on the description of the problem in the use case model. Since we cannot cover the development of the use case model in this text we will follow a quick method. We will now try to look again at the **Fine Wine Shop** case study description to identify candidate classes. Listing the nouns in the order they appear in the problem description in the case study gives us the list in Table 6.2.

This list of candidate classes can be pruned by removing any that are:

- redundant – where the same thing is given more than one name, e.g. blend of wines, blending details;

- vague – it is not clear what the noun represents, e.g. other services;

- event or an operation – these may belong to a class;

- proper names, as these are more likely to be instances of classes, e.g. Médoc, St Emilion;

- attribute – where we recognize that the noun is an attribute of another, e.g. origin of wine.

By following these guidelines we can produce a set of candidate classes as in Table 6.3. These can be examined to determine whether we should definitely accept them as classes and for what reasons, definitely reject or

Table 6.3   List of candidate classes and decisions

Candidate class	Accept/reject/investigate	Reason
Fine wine	Accept	Has attributes, price etc.
Individual and corporate customer	Accept	Has attributes but could have subclasses
Vineyard	Accept	Has attributes, name
Retail shop	Reject	This may be outside the domain
Table	Reject	There is only one
Cellar	Reject	This may be outside the domain
Brief note	Reject	Attribute of fine wine
Label	Reject	Attribute of bottle image
Bottle	Accept	Has attributes
Producer	Accept	Has attributes, history etc.
Category	Reject	Attribute of fine wine
Vintage	Reject	Attribute of fine wine
Discount	Reject	No attribute
Family	Reject	Attribute of producer
Website	Reject	Only one
Region	Accept	Has attributes
Country	Accept	Has attributes
Catalog	Investigate	Are there more than one?
Events	Accept	May be a superclass
Wine tasting	Accept	Is a kind of event
Dinner	Accept	Is a kind of event
Lecture	Accept	Is a kind of event
Case of wine	Accept	Has attributes
Year	Reject	Attribute of wine
Grape variety	Investigate	Is a kind of grape?
Regional map	Investigate	Attribute of region?

perhaps investigate further. A key reason for accepting a class is that we have already recognized some attributes. When we carry this exercise out with the whole list of nouns we will already have identified some class attributes as well as the classes themselves. It must be emphasized that this is an informal subjective process. Different designers would probably arrive at slightly different set of classes.

This leaves us with a small set of potential classes:

Potential classes	
Region	Events
Fine wine	Wine tasting
Individual and corporate customer	Dinner
Catalogs	Lectures
Vineyard	Case of wine
Bottles	Grape varieties
Producers	Country

We start to add details to some of the classes by assigning attributes at this stage:

Fine wines
name
vintage
year
note
character
image
price
size

Region
name
location
map

Producer
name
family
history
address

Country
name
location

EXERCISE 6.2

Create a superclass diagram for the set of classes Event, Wine Tastings, Dinner, Lecture based on the example for Shape. Add some plausible attributes.

How do we recognize operations of a class? Every class will have a constructor method for creating instances of the class as part of its definition. One way of recognizing other methods would be to look at the attributes and decide how they would change. For example, for Customer:

Customer
name
address
date of birth
credit details
corporate

Methods are likely to be involved in the change of attribute values. When we look at these attributes we may decide **date_of_birth** will not change but all the other attributes might so we need to be able to update these. Pure object-oriented approaches would define a set of "set" and "get" operations for attributes.

The class diagram represents relationships between classes. We need to represent logical connections between instances of classes. In UML, the multiplicity or cardinality of a relationship (whether it is one to many or many to many) is represented by numeric notations placed along the line of association joining the classes. For example

This represents the proposition that a producer in the wine shop system will produce at least one wine and may be many. It also states that a wine is made by only one producer. It also implies that we will not have information about any producers whose wines are not sold by the wine shop.

Notation examples	Meaning
*	From 0 up to any number
4..6	From 4 to 6 inclusive
3..*	From 3 up to any number
1	Exactly 1

The other kind of relationship we would be concerned to represent is aggregation, particularly compositional aggregation, which in basic English means that, in the relationship between A and B, A is a part of B; in our case we may decide that a Region is part of a Country:

The filled diamond is immediately next to the containing class. The representation includes multiplicity. The relationship can be stated as "a country consists of at least one or more regions".

Multimedia applications are frequently cited as reasons for adopting an object-oriented approach. This was true before SQL3 when there were no real means of handling the huge data objects other than on the basis of a record at a time processing. This is no longer the case; as we have seen, we are able to create relational tables for multimedia just using BLOBs. One of the key issues in multimedia design is where the metadata will go. The next chapter discusses the various metadata standards. One option suggested would be that metadata should be stored in a separate object-oriented database while the media data is stored in relational tables as BLOBs and there are a number of examples where this is done later in the book. The two databases are controlled and linked by application code. In the next section we look at the way Oracle has implemented objects and the way the object-relational approach could enable metadata to be stored with the media data in complex objects.

6.2.1   Transforming to Database Design

In their book on UML and database design Naiburg and Maksimchuk (2001) suggest two approaches to transforming the UML models into a relational design including the issue of mapping classes to tables. Note that their emphasis is on arriving at a relational and not an object-relational design:

- Change the logical design to become the object/class diagram that will represent the application directly and then map that part of the model directly to the data model.
- Use the logical design to two separate models – the application design model and the database design model.

Mapping Classes to Tables

Reasons for mapping include performance, security, ease of querying, **dba** requirements, corporate standards and DBMS requirements.

Many-to-many associations (Figure 6.7) must be broken down into one-to-many relationships by creating an association table. It is good practice to have additional columns that provide information about the association in addition to the foreign keys of the parent tables. If there are no additional columns the relationship should be reinvestigated to check whether it is actually one to many.

Mapping Subtype Classes to Tables

1. Map each class to a separate table.
2. Map each concrete class to a table, rolling down the supertype table to its subtypes. The attributes of the superclass become columns in the table that map to the subtype classes.
3. Map one table per hierarchy, rolling up the subtypes to the supertypes as illustrated in Figure 6.8. The attributes of the subtype classes are mapped to columns in the single table that maps to both the subtype and the supertype. New columns or multiple columns may be required.

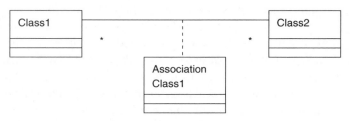

Figure 6.7   Many-to-many associations

Logical design   class Hierarchy

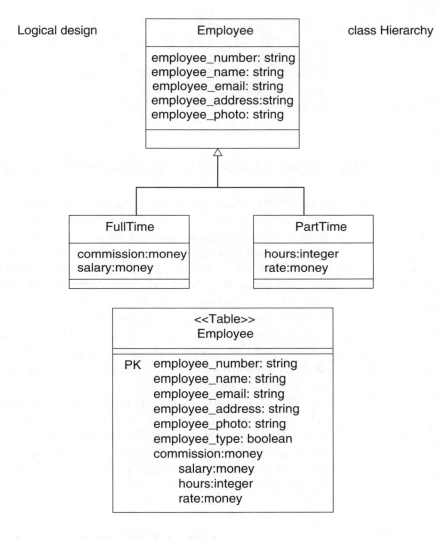

Figure 6.8   **Mapping to a relational design**

This design will result in a table with many nulls and the addition of a column **employee_type** which is not in the logical model but is there to be able to query the table to identify the different subtypes and also to provide a column that could be used in a check constraint.

Mapping Attributes to Columns

Decisions may be based on integrity, performance and security. In a pure relational design some attributes may map to multiple columns, for example address may become separate columns for number, road, city, state, post code. In terms of security requirements these cannot be assigned to a single column but only to a whole table. However, views can be used to achieve some security. Foreign keys will not exist in the logical analysis model but are created to represent relationships in the database design.

6.3 Object Implementation in Oracle

User-defined data types make it easier for applications developers to work with complex data such as images, audio and video. With an object-relational database management system (ORDBMS) it is possible to create **object types** that are more complex than the simple data types in SQL. This means that we would be able to create object types with more complex structures that could hold both media data and the related metadata. These object types can then be used in a number of ways. In Oracle an object type is equivalent in concept to a class in UML – it can have three kinds of components. It must have a *name* that uniquely identifies it within the database schema. It can have *attributes* that are either *built-in* types or user-defined types and *methods* that describe the operations that can be applied to the object type (Figure 6.9).

These methods can be functions or procedures written in PL/SQL or written in an external language such as C++ or Java and stored externally to the database. Firstly we will look at some simple objects without multi-media data. For example, we could create an object type **person**. We can then use the object as a column in a relational table by specifying it in the normal way. An example of a full specification of object and attributes

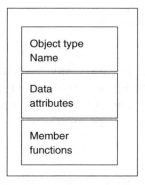

Figure 6.9 An object type's components

would be

```
CREATE TYPE person_t AS OBJECT
( first_name CHAR(20),
  second_name CHAR(20),
  d_o_b       DATE);
```
                                                              person_t

We can also introduce multimedia data types into object definitions and use objects in definitions of other objects, for example we can define an employee object as a specialization of **person_t**:

```
CREATE TYPE employee_t AS OBJECT
(employee_number  CHAR(4),
employee_detail    person_t,
salary    NUMBER(6,2),
start_date  DATE,
skills CLOB,
picture BLOB);
```
                                                              employee_t

This object type, just like a class, can be used to specify the structure of the data and the ways of operating on it. An instance of data that is structured according to the object type and stored in the database is an object. Since an object type is a concept or a template, when it is defined in the database it does not result in any allocation of storage. Since Oracle is following an object-relational paradigm instead of storing the objects in the database we can create an object table that is defined for the purpose of holding object instances of a particular type. We can think of an object type as a template that specifies a set of elements that makes up a more complex unit of data like a sales order.

We can now deal with a more complex example. In our fine wine shop the customers can order wine on the web, as shown in Figure 6.10. The customer's wine order contains data about the customer and the actual wines ordered. The wine order can be seen as consisting of several parts. There is the order header which includes information about the whole order, who the customer is, the date and overall total value, tax, etc. This is followed by a number of orderlines that have a repeated structure. The number of orderlines would vary from order to order. Another problem is that applications often need status information that is calculated dynamically such as the current total value of the order items. The orderlines are part of the order. In UML we would represent this relationship as compositional aggregation as follows:

Creating a relational model of a complex object like an order involves splitting it into separate components because we need to represent it as a simple set of tables where each cell in the table has only one value. In a relational database normalized tables cannot include any repeating groups and a real-world object like an order would be separated into tables, **order** and **orderline** linked by referential constraints (primary and foreign keys). Although the relational design is a very efficient way of organizing data, it can be difficult for users to understand, particularly the importance of primary and foreign keys and the concept of referential integrity. Using the object type is a way of getting round this problem because we can create a composite object type that represents the relationship as an object with attributes and methods as follows:

```
CREATE TYPE wine_order AS OBJECT
(    order_id        CHAR(6),
     customer        person_t,
     orderline       lineitem_list,
     order_total     NUMBER(6,2),
     MEMBER FUNCTION
     Get_total   RETURN NUMBER);
```

We can see that this definition of the wine order includes a number of user-defined types and a function. Some of the attributes are themselves complex. The **customer** attribute has a **person_t** data type and the **orderline** attribute is specified with **lineitem_list** data type. This data type, as we shall see later, can contain a variable number of items because it is a nested table. We can also specify methods associated with the type that reflected a real-world user requirement. Therefore for the wine order we could have a method that calculated the total value. We could also store the customers' wine orders in object tables where each row of the object table corresponds to a single order and the columns of the table are the attributes of the order. Another advantage is that for client–server systems object schemas can be transmitted as whole objects so that when a client-side application requests information about an order all the relevant data will be transmitted in a single transmission.

We are now going to go through the process of arriving at complex objects like the wine order step by step before we look at some multimedia objects. In this example, Figure 6.10, there is an orderline for a bottle of Chateaux Haut-Rian, showing the item name, price and the quantity ordered. An object type **line_t** can be specified using simple SQL system data types as follows:

```
CREATE TYPE line_t AS OBJECT
(wine_code       CHAR(6),
 quantity        number(2))                              line_type
```

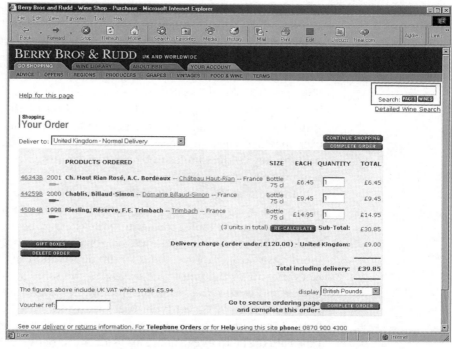

Figure 6.10   Example of a wine order

In Oracle, object tables will not be listed in the system table called tab and cannot be shown by the query SELECT * FROM TAB but we can use DESCRIBE to look at the structure of objects and object tables.

It should not hold the price data as this is already available in the **wine_list** table and we can access the information from the **wine_code**. We can use this user-defined type in two ways: to specify an attribute in a relational table or to generate an object table of this type. An object table is a special kind of table that holds objects and provides a relational view of the attributes of those objects. This is an example of how to define an object table:

```
CREATE TABLE line_table OF line_t;                    line_table
```

When an object table is formed each object forms a complete row of the object table. Objects that appear in object tables are called **row objects**. Every row object in an object table has an associated OID. The purpose of the OID is to uniquely identify the object in an object table in order to construct object references to row objects that are an alternative to foreign keys. The OID allows object types and relational tables to refer to the row objects in the object table. Oracle automatically assigns a unique system-generated identifier called the OID for each row object. Oracle provides no documentation of, or access to, the internal structure of the object identifiers. This is a hidden column with a structure that can change at any time. Object references are used to fetch and navigate objects. We can regard the use of the OID as a compromise as it conflicts with relational theory and it is not very meaningful in an object-relational database. Oracle manages this object access by creating and maintaining an index of the OID column of the object table. This can be an advantage in distributed and replicated database environments because the objects are unambiguously identified. However, Oracle also provides the option of specifying a primary key value of a row object as the object identifier of a row object. Primary-key-based identifiers have the advantage of more efficient loading of the object table because system generated object identifiers need to be remapped by the DBMS using user-specified keys. In the **wine_order** type the **order_id** could serve as a primary key. Object tables can have constraints associated with them in the same way as relational tables.

In the relational model database integrity is maintained because tables are linked by primary and foreign keys. In a one-to-many relationship the primary key of the table representing the *one* may be included as a foreign key in the table representing the *many*. For example, in Chapter 4, the department has many employees and so the department number may be included in every row of the employee table and the same system would be used for **order** and **orderline**. In object-relational systems we can represent **order** and **orderline** by object types that are implemented as object tables. When both sides of the relationship are row objects, Oracle provides a *built-in* data type called REF to encapsulate an association between two row objects.

Object-oriented design is considered to result in a more natural representation of real-world objects. We have also seen how data and methods can be encapsulated together. However, objects do not have the same referentially integrity that can be incorporated into relational tables. Objects need an alternative mechanism for referring to each other. This is achieved by a referencing method that uses a special REF structure. The REF structure allows an object type to directly refer to its row objects in the object table because the object table contains pointers or references to an external table that contains the row object's data.

Let us look first at a simple example. Suppose we wanted to add a table to our Fine Wine database that recorded data about the wines customers have reserved and remain stored in the wine shop's cellar. We can utilize the **person_t** type to hold data about the customers in an object table and refer to this with a REF:

```
CREATE TABLE person_table OF person_t
```

For example, the following statement creates a reference from the **customer_id** attribute of **wine_reserved_t** object type to the **person** object table using the **person_t** object type:

```
CREATE TABLE wine_reserved
(wine_code      CHAR(6),
 customer_id    REF person_t)
```

The **customer_id** column will reference data that is stored elsewhere. The REF first points to the **person_t** data type which in turn points to the object table for the **person_t** type. Both an object and a column type can be declared a REF. It is possible to constrain this reference to reference a specified object table. In this case the REF is called a scoped REF and has the advantage of requiring less storage, providing faster access and more efficient processing.

There are three ways in which the REF referencing can be achieved and we can think of these as REF constraints. We will demonstrate this with three type definitions:

- The simplest way is through the **rowid**. The REF is declared with a **rowid** so that the **rowid** is stored in the column that includes the REF. For example we would write

    ```
    (customer_id REF WITH ROWID person_t,
    ```

- Alternatively we can use unscoped REFs that do not contain a reference to a specific object table but instead must contain the object table's metadata to enable the referencing as follows:

    ```
    customer_id REF person_t,
    ```

    We would be able to insert the data as follows

    ```
    INSERT INTO wine_reserved
    SELECT '40484B',
    REF(P)
    FROM person_table P
    WHERE SECOND_NAME = 'FORD'
    ```

- The way to achieve fastest access to the reference is, however, to use a scoped REF. This merely references the object table and allows the REF to be smaller since it does not use **rowid** or metadata to achieve the reference. This is written as

    ```
    SCOPE FOR customer_id IS person_table
    ```

This is probably a good place to digress into the issue of Oracle **rowid**. In a relational table there is no order to the rows. However, Oracle has always assigned a **rowid** to the rows of its tables. This represents the physical address of the row in the database. The format of the **rowid** can be remembered by the mnemonic BARF – block, address, record, fileID. In other words, it links the logical table to the internal physical schema.

In the object-relational world this has been extended to support table partitions, index partitions and clusters. The new extended **rowid** includes all the previous information (BARF) and the data object number. The data object number is an identification number that the server assigns the schema objects in the database. This information can be displayed by a statement such as

```
SELECT rowid FROM employee
```

We can use REF to link the objects in a compositional aggregation such as our design for **order** and **orderline** but there is an alternative approach provided by Oracle. These are called collection types and are designed to replace the single value we expect to find in every cell of a relational table with multiple values. There are two complex data types called collection types that can be used in the development of object-relational databases. These are:

- VARRAYs;
- NESTED TABLEs.

Collection types provide a way of dealing with multiple instances of the same data element or object type. You will recall that multiple occurrences are not permitted in relational tables in first normal form. In a relational design multiple occurrences are separated into another relational table, linked by foreign keys. For example, suppose a person has multiple phone numbers, one for their home, one for work and a mobile number:

```
home_number      VARCHAR2(15)
work_number      VARCHAR2(15)
mobile_number    VARCHAR2(15)
```

All these attributes have the same data type and have essentially the same purpose – to hold the person's contact numbers. In a relational design we would create a separate table:

Person_id	home_number	work_number	mobile_number
3421	01639 637689	01908 653427	07891234

A collection type provides an alternative design. The first method uses a VARRAY type. This is similar to an array but is stored in a column of a table. We can use a VARRAY as:

- a data type in a table;
- an attribute in an object table;
- a PL/SQL variable (see Chapter 4).

In Oracle columns with a VARRAY data type can be stored in the same table-space as the rest of the row, provided that the size is not greater than 4000 bytes – beyond that size the column values are treated in the same way as LOBs. However, we cannot create VARRAY types that include LOB data types. Each VARRAY is defined with a fixed number of array elements. The elements may be null. Oracle gives all the data elements in the VARRAY an index corresponding to the element's position in the array. The syntax would be

```
CREATE TYPE tname AS VARRAY(number)  OF data type
```

For example, for the person's phone numbers we need an array with three elements for the phone numbers and we would write

```
CREATE TYPE contact_t AS VARRAY(3)  OF VARCHAR2(15)
```

As an alternative to the key word VARRAY we could use VARYING ARRAY. We can also create a VARRAY of object types. In an object-relational representation of the **wine_order** we could have an **order** object that contained a number of order items. One design approach would be to use a VARRAY of objects to describe the order items in the definition of the **order** object. We would have to use an upper bound to limit the number of lines per order. We can use the **line_t** type we created earlier with 12 as the limit:

```
CREATE TYPE line_items AS VARRAY(12)  OF line_t
```

When we specified the **wine_list** table we had an attribute size for the different wine bottles which was defined as a number. The size available are called magnum, bottle, half-bottle, liter and half-liter. Since the wine can be provided in a number of different sizes and corresponding prices, we can create a **wine_size** object as follows:

```
CREATE TYPE wine_size AS OBJECT (
        bottle_type       VARCHAR2(15),
        price             NUMBER(5,2) )
```

This new type can be used to refine the specification of the **wine_list** table to include an array of **size_price**:

```
CREATE TYPE sizes AS VARRAY(5) OF  wine_size
```

We can use this and all the other types we have created in relational tables as user-defined types.

A nested table type is another collection type that is very similar to a VARRAY data type but the main difference is that the elements can be unordered and unbounded. As implied by the name a nested table can exist within another table. There can be multiple rows in the nested table for each row in the main table. A nested table in Oracle may contain a LOB (but not an NCLOB). Nested table types are limited to contain only one attribute which has a data type that is either an object type or a single *built-in* data type. If we want to nest a structure such as the **orderline** with more than one attribute we would have to define an object type first. We cannot create a nested table that contains another nested table. These collection types can be specified as

```
CREATE TYPE type_name AS TABLE OF data type
```

We could use a nested table type as:

- a data type in a table column;
- an object type attribute;
- a PL/SQL variable (see Chapter 4).

We should use a nested table in a design when:

- The order of the data elements is not important.
- There is a requirement to index the column specified as a collection.
- The number of elements in the collection is not known.
- The elements need to be queried.

To create a nested table type we would enter

```
CREATE TYPE nest_t AS TABLE OF nest_data_type
```

The nest_data_type will then be the basis of the nested table. The data of the nested table is not stored "in_line" with the rest of the main table's data. Instead it is stored in a separate table called a storage table. Oracle maintains pointers between the tables. We can create a nested table as column in an object table as follows:

```
CREATE TABLE t_name OF data type NESTED TABLE
        Nested_column STORES AS storage_table_column
```

The rows of the nested table are stored in the separate storage table specified as above. If the table definition contains more than one nested table type, a separate storage table must be defined for each nested table type. We could use a nested table to store orderline data in an order as an object table to represent a variable number of line items. We already defined a type **line_t** as an object. The following statement creates a nested table type called **lineitem_list** using the **line_t** object type as the only attribute:

```
CREATE TYPE lineitem_list  AS TABLE OF line_t
```

Each row of the **lineitem_list** nested table type contains a **line_t** object type; creating the type does not allocate storage space. We can use this nested table type directly in a relational table such as an order table:

```
CREATE TABLE wine_order
(       order_id           CHAR(6) PRIMARY KEY,
        customer           person_t,
        orderlines         lineitem_list)
        NESTED TABLE orderlines STORE AS lineitem_list_tab
```

The column name orderlines is plural indicating it is a collection type and the storage table must be declared as well. An alternative implementation would be to create an order type, **wine_order_t**, and from that an object table. We can now see how the composite object that represents the wine order was built up using the **lineitem_list** collection type and the **person_t** object we created previously:

Note the unique use of line_t, line_table, lineitem_list. One is the name of an object type, one is the name of an object table and one is the name of a collection type.

```
CREATE TYPE wine_order_t AS OBJECT
(       order_id           CHAR(6),
        customer           person_t,
        orderitems         lineitem_list,
        order_total        NUMBER(6,2),
               MEMBER FUNCTION
               Get_total RETURN NUMBER);
```

Since this object cannot store data, we must create an object table with the following statement, which creates an object table with a primary key and allocates a storage table to the nested column **lineitems**:

```
CREATE TABLE wine_order_table OF wine_order_t
  (CONSTRAINT prim_wine order (PRIMARY KEY (order_id))
NESTED TABLE orderitems STORE AS lineitem_list
```

EXERCISE 6.3

List the advantages of specifying the line item component in the order object as the following:

(a) using a VARRAY;

(b) using a nested table.

In Oracle the user can define an **incomplete type** that has no attributes or methods associated with it. This is useful when all the user requirements are not finally specified for an object type but it needs to be created because another fully specified object type may depend on the existence of the first type before it can be created as in a compositional aggregation. An incomplete type can be referenced by other types through its object name but before we can use it in a relational table or an object table it must be fully specified. To define an incomplete type we would state

```
CREATE TYPE person_t
```

User-defined types are useful for multimedia data. We can also use **person_t** to encapsulate some of the attributes of the employee table, as follows:

```
CREATE TABLE employee
(                employee_number           CHAR(4),
                 employee_detail           person_t,
                 salary                    NUMBER(6,2) )
```

We have now used the same **person_t** type in both the **employee** and the **wine_reserved** tables. This causes no problems but we should note that there would be only one object table associated with a type. If we were to refer to the object table in more than one relational table we need to be very careful.

In a similar manner we can create an object to store metadata and media data together. For example the **pronunciation** column of the **wine_list** table is used for holding audio clips of the French pronunciation of the wine name. The metadata could be the originator, the text itself, the speaker and the date of the recording. This information can be combined in an object:

```
CREATE TYPE pronunciation_t AS OBJECT
   ( originator   VARCHAR2(30),
     text         VARCHAR2(50),
     speaker      VARCHAR2(30),
     take_date        DATE,
     recording        BLOB)
```

We can replace the existing column in the **wine_list** table with the object type **pronunciation_t**. Another example of adding more complex information would be to include a map of the region defined as the following object:

```
CREATE TYPE map_t AS OBJECT
(          region        VARCHAR2(20),
           nw            NUMBER,
           ne            NUMBER,
           sw            NUMBER,
           se            NUMBER,
```

```
        drawing      BLOB,
        aerial       BFILE)
CREATE TYPE map_tab AS TABLE OF map_t
```

We can now replace the columns in the original **wine_list** table to include the more complex media types and metadata:

```
CREATE TABLE wine_list
(  wine_code   CHAR(6),
wine_name    VARCHAR2(30) NOT NULL,
 year         NUMBER(4),
 category     VARCHAR2(20),
 grape        VARCHAR2(20),
 price        NUMBER(5,2),
 bottles      sizes,
 character    VARCHAR2(50),
 note         CLOB DEFAULT EMPTY_CLOB(),
 pronounce    pronunciation_t,
 picture      BFILE,
 region_map   map_tab
 ) NESTED TABLE region_map STORE AS map_nested_tab;
```

In the course of specifying some of the Fine Wine Shop in an object-relational design we have created a number of complex types that need to be well documented. Details about object and object tables can be seen in Oracle's Schema Manager. The data dictionary contains a number of views to provide information about Object types:

- ALL_TYPES;
- ALL_TYPES_ATTRS;
- ALL_TYPE_METHODS;
- DBA_TYPES;
- USER_TYPES;
- USER_TYPE_ATTRS;
- USER_TYPE_METHODS.

For example, the following statement can be used to display details of the user-defined types created, the identifier of the type and attributes:

Note that **type_oid** is the object identifier Oracle uses to identify the Object type.

```
SELECT type_name, type_oid, typecode, attributes
FROM user_types
```

6.3.1 Manipulating User-defined Types

In this section we will illustrate how complex data can be represented and manipulated using combinations of the simple types and collection types we introduced. When you use an object definition within a table definition, these are user-defined types that can be used in the same way as *built-in* types in SQL statements. These new data types require methods. We already mentioned there is an implicitly system-defined constructor method that makes a new object according to its object type specification. The name of the constructor method is the same as the name of the object type.

As a simple example, first we create the type as an object as follows:

```
CREATE TYPE two AS OBJECT(
num1  NUMBER(2),
num2 NUMBER (2));
```
                                                                    type_two

Once a new type has been specified then it can be used in a relational table. This type already has attributes so we can use it immediately in a relational table definition. For example, to create a table that uses the type to specify one column of the table

```
CREATE TABLE three
(x1    NUMBER(1),
x2     two);
```
                                                                  type_three

We can use an insert statement to add data to the table but we need to specify two numbers for the type **two**. This example shows the nested nature of the insert:

```
INSERT INTO three VALUES (1, two(2,3));
```
                                                                insert_three

The **two** in the INSERT statement **insert_three** is a constructor method for type **two**. Another advantage of using object types in relational tables is that we can also query the results in SQL in the normal way:

```
SELECT x2 FROM three;
```

which will display the result as

```
    X2(NUM1, NUM2)
---------------------------
    TWO(2, 3)
```

When object tables are based on user-defined types that only include built-in data types then SELECT, UPDATE and INSERT statements use the same format as relational tables. Collection types have constructor methods as well that can be used to insert data into the collection. For example, we could refine the customer details using the **person_t** object with their contact details (which we defined as a VARRAY) as follows:

```
CREATE TABLE wine_customer
(       customer_id        CHAR(4),
        customer           person_t,
        contact_detail     contact_t)
```

Data could be inserted into the table using an INSERT statement that includes the constructor method, as follows:

```
INSERT INTO wine_customer(customer,contact)
VALUES ( person_t ('John', 'Smith', '17-Mar-1972'), contact_t() )
```

This will insert the person's details but leave the contact details empty. The data attributes of the object type must be in the same order for the constructor method as in the definition of the type. Note that an empty collection type does not imply it contains nulls. The next example shows the use of both constructor methods:

```
INSERT INTO wine_customer
VALUES ('1234,' person_t ('Shailey', 'Patel', '17-May-1975'),
contact_t('077891234', '441189234508','01567891234') )
```

Rows can be inserted into nested tables in a similar manner, using the INSERT ... INTO statement with the constructor method. For example, we could have a nested table type **artist_list**, i.e.

```
CREATE TYPE artist_list AS TABLE OF person_t
```

that can be used in a table called **song_list** where each song could have a number of artists associated with it:

```
CREATE TABLE song_list
(songid             CHAR(6),
 title              VARCHAR2(30),
 artists            artist_list)
NESTED TABLE artists STORE AS artist_list_tab
```

We can insert rows into a nested table by using the constructor method for its data type, the **artists** constructor method. Inserting rows into the **song_list** table requires the use of the constructor methods for both **artist_list** and **person_t** constructor methods.

```
INSERT INTO song_list VALUES
('100123', 'The times are changing',
      artist_list(
```

```
                        person_t ('John', 'Smith', '17-Mar-1972'),
                        person_t ('Mary', 'Jones', '23-Jun-1966'),
                        person_t ('Viki', 'Williams', '6-May-1982')
        ))
```

We can treat an object table as though it was a relational table and add data with an INSERT statement:

```
INSERT INTO line_table
VALUES        ( '040316', 8 )
```

The constructor method is formally a function that returns a new object as its value. For example, the next expression includes both constructor methods for the **wine_order**:

```
wine_order ( 100345, person_t ('John', 'Smith', ' 17-Mar-1972'),
                    orderitems ('43107b', 1) 5.75 )
```

This expression can be used in an SQL statement that would construct a row object

Order_id	100345
Customer	person_t ('John', 'Smith', ' 17-Mar-1972')
Orderitems	'040316b', 1
Order_total	5.75

The expression **person_t** ('John', 'Smith', ' 17-Mar-1972') is an invocation of the constructor function of the object type **person_t**.

In the same way that data can be inserted into object types using their constructor methods we can use UPDATE statements with constructor methods to amend the data by using a table alias, as in the next example where the alias for **wine_customer_table** is A:

```
UPDATE wine_customer
SET  customer = person_t ('Sunila', 'Patel', '17-Mar-1972')
WHERE customer_id ='1234'
```

Earlier in the chapter we created a **person_t** type which we used in a number of tables and other objects. When we want to query a column with this data type we need to use a correlation variable (or alias) as follows:

```
SELECT customer_id, W.customer.first_name,
W.customer.second_name
FROM  wine_customer W
WHERE W.customer.first_name LIKE 'P%'
```

first_name and **second_name** are attributes of the **person_t** type that defines the data type of the **customer** column. The performance of this query would be better if there was an index available. To create an index on a column that is part of an abstract data type we must specify the full path to the column as part of the CREATE INDEX statement, for example:

```
CREATE INDEX i_customer_name
 ON wine_customer(customer.first_name)
```

Earlier we used the REF function to reference row objects. We can also use a REF to examine or update the object it refers to and also we can use REF to obtain a copy of the object. We created a **wine_reserved_t** table that referenced the **person_t** object table. We can insert data as follows:

```
INSERT INTO wine_reserved
SELECT '43107B',
REF(P)
FROM person_table P
WHERE FIRST_NAME = 'JANICE'
```

In this insert first the person table is queried and the REF function returns the OID for the row object selected. The OID is then stored in the **wine_reserved_tab** table as a pointer to that row object in the **person** object table. The **wine_reserved_tab** table will not store the actual data and we can confirm this if we

```
SELECT * FROM wine_reserved
```

since only the OID data will be displayed.

We can query an object table in a SELECT statement to display the OID values assigned by using the REF function as in the next example when the **line_table** is given the alias A:

```
SELECT REF(A)
FROM line_table A
WHERE wine_code = '00456b'
```

The REF function takes as its input the alias given to the object table. It can only reference row objects, not column objects. Also, since it only returns the OID values it is not particularly useful. It needs to be combined with another function DEREF that takes the OID value provided by REF and returns the value of the row object:

```
SELECT DEREF (customer_id)
FROM wine_reserved
WHERE wine_code = '43107B'
```

The contents of a REF can be replaced with a reference to a different object or to replace it with a NULL.

Rows can also be deleted but problems may arise because, where this involves a row object that contains REFs from other object types or relational columns, the references will become invalid. The REFs from the associated object types or relational attributes are known as dangling REFs.

6.3.2 Implementation Issues

In most ODBMSs the OIDs become physical so that the logical identifiers are converted to specific pointers to memory addresses. No such construct exists in relational databases and the addition of this kind of navigational access violates the principles of normalization because OIDs make no reference to keys. Before we leave object-relational design we need to comment on the OIDs we mentioned in this section. These would correspond to the object identifier in UML. However, OIDs are really an implementation issue. Date (2000) lists a number of issues to be aware of including:

- OIDs are addresses and are hidden from the user.
- OIDs are not surrogate keys. Surrogate keys are values that are visible to the user which are system-defined keys such as the **rowid** in Oracle tables.
- OIDs do not avoid the need for "user" keys.
- What would be the OID value of a view or even a projection of a table?

In addition, in Date's review of object-oriented databases he considers the object model in terms of desirable versus undesirable properties which can be summarized as follows:

Object classes	Essential and equivalent to a type
Objects	Can be mutable or immutable and are "values"
Encapsulation	Just means scalar, e.g. SQL data type
Containment hierarchy	Misleading because they just contain OIDs not actual objects
Methods	Essential but he deprecates the use of constructor methods because these are pointers to constructed variables rather than to the values themselves
Views	Essential part of the database concept and not well supported by object systems
Ad hoc queries	Essential but not supported by pure object systems because such queries need to break encapsulation
Foreign keys	Essential but not supported by object systems except by procedural code
Catalog/metadata	Essential but not clear what it consists of in an object system

In many ways Date (2000) views object-oriented databases as a "huge step backwards" because the focus is on object manipulation which is equivalent to a record-at-a-time processing and not the set-at-a-time processing provided by relational databases. The other great loss is referential integrity which is provided by the relational model and implemented by virtually all commercially available RDBMSs. Object databases do not employee SQL style languages that operate a set at a time. Normally a 3GL language is employed for both the database and the non-database operations. The "host" language we mentioned in Chapter 1 and the database language are tightly coupled; in fact they are the same. It is argued that this avoids the "impedance mismatch" between the procedural language and the declarative semantics of the database language. This has given rise to practical problems but it would seem that the solution is not to reduce the capability of the database language to operate a set at a time.

The object-relational approach we adopted for the Fine Wine Shop has turned out to be quite complicated and it is not clear that it will be easier for the user to comprehend than the relational model. It also needs to be carefully documented when both objects and relational tables are in use.

Using Views and Object Views

Another important concept is that of the **object view**, which is a virtual object table. The rows are row objects. Object identifiers are generated from primary keys in the underlying table or view but are not stored persistently.

Views are an important part of relational design. A view is a table with defined columns and, at any time it is used, it *appears* to contain rows of data although in fact it contains none. Since no data is stored in a database for a view, all that exists is its definition which consists of a query that produces the rows of data that are its apparent content. A view, or rather just its definition since that is all that persists, can be created and dropped in a similar way to base tables. A view is created with a CREATE VIEW statement that includes a query specification. This defines the data that the view will display when it is used. The values in each column of the view are the values in the corresponding columns of the base table after processing by the query specification at the time the view is used. A view having been defined, it can be treated like any other table in the database. In particular, data can be retrieved from it in the same way as from any other table just as if it actually contained data. However there are a number of restrictions on updating views.

In a similar manner, object views are a means of viewing object tables. Object views are particularly useful for using object-relational concepts with existing relational tables without needing to recreate or redesign the database. Before we can create an object view the object types it will be based on must be defined.

All object views must have:

- a valid schema object name;
- the name of the object type on which the object view is based;
- an object identifier based on a unique identifier for the underlying data;
- a SELECT statement that assigns each row an object identifier.

Object views must have an object type to define the structure of the data to be retrieved. The next example creates an object identifier for each row of the view. The view itself will contain rows of objects and can be selected in the same way as a relational view. In Chapter 4 we created the department table with the structure

```
CREATE TABLE department
(department_number    CHAR(4) CONSTRAINT prim_dept PRIMARY KEY,
department_name       VARCHAR2(10 ))                        prim_dept
```

We can use the following statement to create an object view of the relational table **department** by creating an object first:

```
CREATE TYPE dept_t AS OBJECT
     (department_number      CHAR(4),
     department_name    VARCHAR2(10 ))
```

We can now create an object view based on the department table. An object view statement must specify the query that forms the view. To create the view we would add

```
CREATE OR REPLACE VIEW dept_OV(dept) AS
     SELECT dept_t(department_number, department_name)
     FROM department
```

This view will have one column **dept** defined by the **dept_t** type. The query statement includes the constructor method named **dept_t**. An alternative approach would be to create an object view and assign OID values to the rows of the department table:

```
CREATE OR REPLACE VIEW dept_view OF dept_t
WITH OBJECT OID(department_number) AS
     SELECT A.department_number, A.department_name
     FROM department A
```

The line containing WITH OBJECT OID(department_number) creates object identifiers for each row of the object view. This will allow rows within the department table to be referenced as though they were row objects within an object table. Object views can coexist with relational tables and object-relational components. The structure of an object view can be checked using

```
DESCRIBE  dept_view
```

This is important because it is possible to update the object view using INSTEAD OF triggers which can be created in a similar way to INSERT triggers on relational tables. However, there needs to be a one-to-one mapping between the attributes of the object view and the columns in the base tables. This will not be the case if the query the view is based on includes a join of more than one table, an aggregate function or GROUP BY clauses. With this constraint, object views can still be useful in multimedia tables when we wish to display only certain data because of restriction of size or hardware limitations. The key advantage is that when we impose an object-relational structure on an existing relational table we can also use methods on the user-defined types which can be applied to new tables and existing tables. The object views provide two different ways of entering data as well, adding to the flexibility of the data manipulation.

Using Oracle interMedia

Oracle *interMedia* is an alternative approach to using SQL:1999 data types for developing an MMDBMS. Oracle has developed ***interMedia*** as a way of building multimedia applications rather than providing an end-user application. It has been designed to support existing media standards but is extensible so that it supports a base set of popular multimedia data characteristics but can be extended to cope with new codecs, data sources and even specialized data-processing algorithms for audio and video data. In ***interMedia*** Oracle has created a set of multimedia user-defined types to make it easier for the database designer to create multimedia applications. The user-defined object types have associated methods which cover common multimedia requirements, for example it provides methods getContent() and process(). This also has another advantage that it allows databases to be developed in a generic style so that multimedia data can be exchanged between applications. Another advantage is that the data types can be accessed through a relational approach using PL/SQL and OCI or an object approach can be used based, for example, on C++ or Java. Since Oracle ***interMedia*** uses object types, an instance of these object types will consist of the media data itself, the methods associated with it and metadata about the instance.

The metadata might include information about the object's size, compression or format. Methods will be the special procedures needed to manage the object and will be the same for all instances of the object. The metadata and the methods are always stored in the database. The metadata includes the information about the source of the media data, source type, location, source name and whether the media data is stored locally (in the database) or externally. Examples of metadata used by the different types of media are included in Table 6.4. It also shows what kind of media data it applies to and the purpose of the metadata in separate attributes. *interMedia* manages the metadata for all the media types and may automatically extract it for audio, image and video. Some of the reasons for the metadata selected are connected with network performance, which is discussed in Chapter 9.

interMedia is based on an ORDMultiMedia abstract superclass that contains methods and attributes that are common to ORDAudio, ORDImage and ORDVideo. In addition, it contains ORDSource that holds the digital media data. The subclasses ORDAudio, ORDImage and ORDVideo contain specific attributes and methods for their kind of media. In addition to specific attributes another advantage is that the package includes a number of data manipulation methods for example for image media:

- image matching, format and compression conversion, scaling, cropping, copying.

Details of the *interMedia* attributes are listed in the file of that name on the CDROM

Table 6.4   Metadata and *interMedia*

Media data	Metadata	Purpose/comment/note
Audio, image, video	Update time stamp	Needed for real-time nature
Audio, video	Data description	Needed for semantic nature
Audio, image, video	MIME type	Needed for real-time nature; however, it is used for non-real time communication. MIME – multi-purpose internet mail extension – is used to wrap content retrieved from the web which has been transferred by SMTP or HTTP protocols (see Chapter 9). When MIME is used all the media is retrieved and then played using a single local clock
Audio, video	Comments	Semantic nature – text-based retrieval
Audio	Encoding type, number of channels, sampling rate, sample size, compression type, play time (duration)	Size – needed for issues related to performance for delivery across networked systems. This is particularly because poor performance will result in distortions that are not acceptable to the user
Image	Height and width, image content length, format, compression type	Size – needed for issues related to performance for delivery across networked systems
Video	Frame width and height, frame resolution, frame rate, play time (duration), number of frames, compression type, number of colours, bit rate	Size – needed for issues related to performance for delivery across networked systems where jitter becomes a problem

A database designer can also use *interMedia* to

- create new object types or composite object types based on the basic *interMedia* types combined with other LOBs;
- create new methods such as specialized plug-ins to support new external sources of media data such as new data formats, using a special ORDPLUGINS schema;
- process audio or video data in new ways.

interMedia includes object types for the different media, i.e. ORDAudio, ORDImage and ORDVideo, that all have a common data storage model. The media data can be stored as a BLOB or outside the database. In that case a pointer is stored in the database and the media itself stored in a BFILE or HTTP server-based URL or the source may be located on a special media server such as Oracle Video Server. Storing media data outside the database is a convenient way of managing media data that is already in existence. This data can be imported into a BLOB in the database when it is required for transaction processing.

To develop an application using Oracle *interMedia* the developer would firstly need to create an object-relational model and include a number of object types:

- ORDAudio for audio data;
- ORDImage for image data;
- ORDVideo for video data.

These three all store data in an object relational type known as ORDSource. By using these data types we can then use the methods provided to manipulate the types, including:

- manipulating data about the source and comment attributes;
- getting and managing data from web servers and other servers;
- performing file operations (open, close, trim, read and write) for audio and video only;
- extracting attributes from media data;
- processing commands for audio and video;
- manipulating image data.

We will now briefly look at the way *interMedia* can be used with the different types of media but in this chapter we will focus on image data as the main example and deal with the other media data in later chapters.

Audio

interMedia has facilities that can be used to integrate the storage, retrieval and management of digitized audio data in the database. Applications can then process or play the data depending on the hardware and the processing power available. As well as the audio metadata described in Table 6.4, the database may hold specific metadata such as a description of the audio clip, date recorded and artist depending on the actual application domain. This metadata can be stored by creating a user-defined type to store all this information together as we did with the pronunciation column in the **wine_list** table or by creating additional columns in the database table. Audio data processing involves passing an audio processing command and a set of parameters to a plug-in using the *processAudioCommand*() method.

For example, we could use **interMedia** data types to develop objects for the wine shop – by adding metadata to the pronunciation column:

```
CREATE TYPE pronunciation_t AS OBJECT
   ( originator   VARCHAR2(30),
      text         VARCHAR2(50),
      speaker      VARCHAR2(30),
      record_date      DATE,
      audioSource ORDSYS.ORDAUDIO)
```

We would still add the audio data using PL/SQL declaring ORDSYS types in procedures as follows:

```
CREATE OR REPLACE add_pronounce
      audioObj    ORDSYS.ORDAUDIO
```

Image

Oracle **interMedia** supports two-dimensional, static, digitized images. As well as the image metadata described in Figure 6.9 the database may hold specific image metadata such as persons featured, photographer, a description of the image. Image interchange formats are useful for allowing different applications to create, exchange and use images stored in different formats. Interchange formats are often stored themselves as disk files and are sometimes called image protocols.

For example, we can change the employee table to use **interMedia** types:

```
CREATE TABLE employee
(employee_number       CHAR(4),
employee_name          VARCHAR2(30),
salary                 NUMBER(6,2),
```

```
d_o_b                   DATE,
employee_picture        ORDSYS.ORDIMAGE)              new_emp_table
```

The employee table could be populated using the ORDSYS.ORDIMAGE constructor method with a BFILE image for file, Smith.gif, as follows:

```
INSERT INTO employee
VALUES
('7990', 'John Smith', 2400.78, '15-May-1979',
ORDSYS.ORDIMAGE(ORDSYS.ORDSOURCE(EMPTY_BLOB() , 'FILE',
'PHOTO_DIR', 'Smith.gif', SYSDATE,0),
NULL, NULL, NULL, NULL, NULL, NULL,NULL))
```

This uses the ORDSYS.ORDIMAGE and ORDSYS.ORDSOURCE constructor methods to insert data. Many of the attributes are specified as NULL if the values are not available or relevant. This is one of the problems of using "one-size-fits-all" data types. We can also process the *interMedia* data types by using the DBMS_LOB package. The next example is a procedure that adds image data by using the user-defined data type ORDSYS.ORDIMAGE:

```
DECLARE
        Image               ORDSYS.ORDIMAGE;
BEGIN
        INSERT INTO employee
        VALUES
                ('7990', 'John Smith', 2400.78, '15-May-1979',
                ORDSYS.ORDIMAGE(ORDSYS.ORDSOURCE(EMPTY_BLOB() ,
                'FILE', 'PHOTO_DIR', 'Smith.gif', SYSDATE,0), NULL,
                NULL,
                NULL, NULL, NULL, NULL,NULL));

        SELECT large_photo INTO Image
        FROM employee
        WHERE employee_name ='John Smith' FOR UPDATE;
        --set property updates for image data
        image.setProperties;
        UPDATE employee SET employee_picture = image
        WHERE employee_name ='John Smith';
END;
```

The method includes **image.setProperties** that can then be used to manipulate the image data retrieved by the SELECT … INTO statement. The image information that can be manipulated by ORDImage methods includes:

Table 6.5 Methods available for ORDImage

ORDImage method	Parameters	Purpose	Example
Process() With BLOB	IN VARCHAR2	Processes BLOB and writes image back on to itself – it can change <ul><li>compression format, e.g. JPEG to HUFFMAN3;</li><li>compression quality, e.g. low, medium, high;</li><li>file format, e.g. TIFF,JFIF,PICT,BMPF;</li><li>fixed scale to specific size of pixels</li></ul>Scale, e.g. specific scale factor 0.5, 2.0 etc. xScale – x axis default is 1 – to +ive float yScale – y axis default is 1 – to +ive float	Image.process(' CompressionFormat = JPEG, xScale = "2.0" ') Image.process ('fileFormat = GIFF') Image.process (maxScale = "32 32") ... Will produce a thumbnail image of 32 pixels square*
Process() With RAW (foreign image file formats)	IN VARCHAR2	Deals with: <ul><li>channel order;</li><li>input channels;</li><li>interleave;</li><li>pixel order;</li><li>scanline</li></ul>	
ProcessCopy()	IN VARCHAR2 INOUT ORDImage	Copies an image to an internal BLOB	Image.process Copy(Mycommand,image2) Mycommand := 'CompressionFormat = JPEG, xScale = "2.0" '
SetProperties() With BLOB		After an image has been copied or stored this reads image data to get current attributes, set them to new and stores them to attribute fields	
SetProperties() With RAW (foreign image file formats)		Deals with data offset, channel selection, interleave, pixel order	
CheckProperties()	RETURN BOOLEAN	Used to verify actual attributes match image	
GetHeight()	RETURN INTEGER	Does not read the image – checks attributes	
GetWidth()	RETURN INTEGER	Does not read the image – checks attributes	
GetContentLength()	RETURN INTEGER	Returns length	

(continued)

Table 6.5 *Continued*

ORDImage method	Parameters	Purpose	Example
SetUpdateTime()	Current time DATE	Sets time when image last updated	Default is SYSDATE
GetContent()	RETURN BLOB	Returns BLOB within ORDImage object	
Import()	ctx IN OUT RAW	Transfers image data from an external source	ctx is the source plug-in context information ⋯⋯⟩

* When the methods require floating numbers we must use double quotation marks ("") around the values otherwise the wrong parameters may be passed

- image height in pixels;
- image width in pixels;
- data size in bytes;
- file type;
- image type, e.g. monochrome, grayscale;
- compression type (JPEG, LZW, etc.);
- MIME type (based on file format).

The advantage of using ***interMedia*** is that procedures and functions are already developed and some of these are listed in Table 6.5.

We can use these methods to query the image data in an SQL statement, as follows:

```
SELECT employee_name. E.employee_picture.getWidth()
FROM employee E
WHERE employee_name = 'John Smith'
AND   E.employee_picture.getWidth() > 32
```

The following procedure will exploit features to copy and convert the format of an image. For example, the procedure will generate a thumbnail image (fixedScale=32 32) that is used to display sets of retrieved images for relevance feedback as described in Chapter 5.

```
DECLARE
        Image_1            ORDSYS.ORDIMAGE;
        Image _2           ORDSYS.ORDIMAGE;
BEGIN
        SELECT employee_name, employee_picture
        INTO    image_1, image_2
```

```
            FROM employee
            WHERE employee_name = 'John Smith' FOR UPDATE;
            --CONVERT THE IMAGE TO A THUMBNAIL AND STORE IN IMAGE_2
            IMAGE_1.PROCESSCOPY('fileFormat=TIFF fixedScale=32 32',
                                                      image_2);

            UPDATE employee SET employee_picture = image_1
            WHERE employee_name ='John Smith';
      END;
```

We can now change this procedure because we find we need a large photograph for the website and a small badge size image which is the large photograph, cropped and scaled. First we need to modify the **employee** table by
adding a badge column:

```
CREATE TABLE employee
(employee_number   CHAR(4),
employee_name      VARCHAR2(30),
salary             NUMBER(6,2),
d_o_b              DATE,
employee_picture   ORDSYS.ORDIMAGE,
badge              ORDSYS.ORDIMAGE)
```

The columns that were given types derived from ORDSYS.ORDIMAGE will
need their BLOBs initialized in the normal way so that we would use the following INSERT statement which sets the badge to empty:

```
INSERT INTO employee
VALUES
('7990', 'John Smith', 24000, '15-May-1979',
ORDSYS.ORDIMAGE(ORDSYS.ORDSOURCE(EMPTY_BLOB() , 'FILE',
                'PHOTO_DIR', 'Smith.gif', SYSDATE,0), NULL, NULL,
NULL, NULL, NULL, NULL,NULL),
ORDSYS.ORDIMAGE(ORDSYS.ORDSOURCE(EMPTY_BLOB(), NULL, NULL,
      NULL, SYSDATE,1), NULL, NULL, NULL, NULL, NULL, NULL,NULL))
```

The procedure carries out the insert and then gets the image details to
change the image:

```
DECLARE
      Image ORDSYS.ORDIMAGE
BEGIN
      INSERT INTO employee
      VALUES
      ('7990', 'John Smith', 24000, '15-May-1979',
      ORDSYS.ORDIMAGE
```

```
         ORDSYS.ORDIMAGE(ORDSYS.ORDSOURCE(EMPTY_BLOB() , 'FILE',
         'PHOTO_DIR', 'Smith.gif', SYSDATE,0), NULL, NULL,
         NULL, NULL, NULL, NULL,NULL)),
         (ORDSYS.ORDSOURCE(EMPTY_BLOB() , NULL, NULL, NULL,
         SYSDATE,1), NULL, NULL, NULL, NULL, NULL, NULL, NULL)
         NULL)
         SELECT employee_name, employee_picture
         INTO      image
         FROM employee
         WHERE employee_name = 'John Smith' FOR UPDATE;

         IMAGE.SETPROPERTIES;
         DBMS_OUTPUT.PUTLINE('image width = '|| image.getWidth()
         DBMS_OUTPUT.PUTLINE('image height = '|| image.getHeight()
         DBMS_OUTPUT.PUTLINE('image size = '||
                                          image.getContentLength()
         DBMS_OUTPUT.PUTLINE('image file type = '||
                                             image.getFileFormat()
         DBMS_OUTPUT.PUTLINE('image type = '||
                                          image.getContentFormat()
         DBMS_OUTPUT.PUTLINE('image compression = '||
                                      image.getCompressionFormat()
         DBMS_OUTPUT.PUTLINE('image mime type = '||
                                              image.getMimeType()
         UPDATE employee SET employee_picture = image
         WHERE employee_name ='John Smith';
      END;
```

Example output would be

Image width = 360
Image height = 490
Image size = 66 318
Image file type = JFIF
Image type = 24BITRGB
Image compression = JPEG
Image mime type = image/jpeg

Video

In order to process and play video data it is essential to know the media characteristics such as frame rate, frame size, frame resolution, etc. depending on the hardware characteristics available. Video data processing involves passing an audio processing command and a set of parameters to a plug-in using the *processVideoCommand*() method.

Oracle provides facilities for processing media data though ORDPLGINS. For example, video data processing involves passing a command and a set of parameters to a plug-in for processing using the VideoCommand() method.

Some complex multimedia information systems may integrate more than one of these basic types. Examples of multimedia databases can be currently found in the following application areas:

- video on demand (VoD);
- multimedia document management system;
- multimedia mail.

In terms of requirements for a VoD application, the system may need to store a video clip, an associated audio clip, two still images and text details. Video applications and the support available from *interMedia* are studied in Chapter 12.

6.3.3   Object Methods

If we create our own multimedia user-defined types instead of using those provided by *interMedia* we need to develop methods to process the types. In addition if we create object views of relational tables we can define methods to standardize the processing of existing data. As shown in Figure 6.9 an object consists of member methods as well as attributes. An object-type method may be written in PL/SQL and stored within the database or it can be written in JAVA or C++ and stored outside the database. In Oracle these methods are called members. In Chapter 4 we looked at how functions and procedures are developed in PL/SQL and now we will look at the way PL/SQL routines can be used as members of object types.

Using stored procedures as methods gives a number of advantages. Since stored procedures only require the calling parameters, the transmission of whole results sets or intermediate tables required for SQL statements is avoided and network traffic can be reduced. Stored procedures are executed in compiled format which greatly reduces code execution times. Stored procedures are also a way of controlling development and are an essential part of object-relational development.

Two different kinds of methods can be created:

- Function or procedure member methods are used to process information and can accept arguments. Methods that are functions always return a value.
- Comparison methods have a distinct purpose: to deal with the comparison of object types that are much more complex than the traditional data types.

Methods fall into three categories – member, order and static. Object-type methods are called members because they are important means of encapsulating the behavior of object types. A MAP MEMBER METHOD is defined by the keyword MAP in its function declaration. A MAP method returns the relative position of a given record in the ordering of all records within an object type. A type body can contain only one MAP method which must be a function. PL/SQL can use this ordering to evaluate Boolean expressions and to perform comparisons. When we specify an object we can create only one map method which must be a function. The result type must be a predefined SQL built-in scalar type. The map method can have no arguments except implicitly the object itself.

An ORDER MEMBER METHOD performs the comparison between two object types. One frequent requirement for database systems is to retrieve data matching a value. Whereas *built-in* data types have methods for valid comparison which are part of the SQL language, it is not possible to compare user-defined types unless the developer has specified methods to do this. An object specification can contain only one ORDER method, which must be a function that returns an integer. If the returned value is negative, zero or positive the implicit "self" argument of the function is respectively less than, equal to or greater than the explicitly specified record – that is the order method returns:

- negative value – the record is less than the specified record;
- zero – the record is equal to the specified record;
- positive value – the record is greater than the specified record.

Multiple rows within an object can be compared by including an ORDER BY clause. In this case the ORDER method is automatically executed to order the rows returned. If the developer has not specified any comparison methods Oracle tries to work around this problem by providing two methods of comparison for objects:

- Map method is a function that must return a value and that can exploit *built-in* data types.
- Order method uses internal logic to compare two objects of the same object type.

These are functions which usually accept an object type as the input argument to be compared with the object type of which it is a member. For example, we could define an object type for **address** with the attributes street, city, state and post code. This could be used to create objects that hold both the customer's address and the address to which, for example, wine is to be delivered. These addresses could be different, if the wine were a gift, and we would need a method that checked whether the addresses were equal. When a specific comparison method has not been defined, Oracle compares two objects of a type by comparing corresponding attributes, according to the following rules:

- If all the attributes are not NULL and are equal, Oracle reports that the objects are equal by returning the value zero.
- If there is at least one attribute for which the objects have unequal values that are not NULL, Oracle reports that the objects are unequal by returning the value +1 or −1 indicating a higher or a lower ordering between the object types.

In all other cases Oracle reports that the comparison is not available.

Note the we can only define either a MAP method or an ORDER method but not both when we define an object type. For example, we can define a MAP method for a customer type that returns the customer_id as a unique identifier of the instances of the object.

The next statement creates the type `customer-t`:

```
CREATE TYPE customer_t AS OBJECT
(customer_id      CHAR(4),
customer_details   person_t,
MAP MEMBER FUNCTION retn_value RETURN CHAR);
```

While the following statement creates the body of the `retn_value` method:

```
CREATE OR REPLACE TYPE BODY customer_t AS
MAP MEMBER FUNCTION retn_value RETURN CHAR IS
BEGIN
      RETURN customer_id ;
END;
END;
```

Alternatively, we can create an ORDER MEMBER function:

```
CREATE OR REPLACE TYPE BODY customer_t AS
ORDER MEMBER FUNCTION retn_value RETURN NUMBER

. . . . . . .
```

However, when we specify an ORDER method we want to identify an attribute of the object that could be used to do "greater than" or "less than" comparisons as well as identifying equivalence. In the case of the **wine_order** we could use the order total to decide whether one order was larger than another as follows:

```
CREATE OR REPLACE TYPE wine_order_t AS OBJECT
(     order_id           CHAR(6),
      customer    person_t,
```

```
            lineitems    lineitem_list,
            order_total NUMBER(6,2),
ORDER MEMBER FUNCTION
Wine_total (x IN wine_order_t)
RETURN INTEGER)

CREATE OR REPLACE TYPE BODY wine_order_t2 AS
ORDER MEMBER FUNCTION
Wine_total (x IN wine_order_t2)RETURN INTEGER IS
BEGIN
RETURN order_total - x.wine_total;
END;
END;
/
```

This ORDER function will accept another wine order as the argument of the function.

Members are defined by the CREATE TYPE BODY as follows:

```
MEMBER [function/procedure declaration];
MEMBER [function/procedure declaration];
MAP|ORDER MEMBER function declaration;
END
```

We can change the definition of an existing type to associate the type with a new method. The next example changes the definition of the **line** type to add a function **construct_line**

```
CREATE TYPE line AS OBJECT
(      wine_code       CHAR(6),
       quantity        NUMBER(2));
STATIC FUNCTION construct_line
       (quantity )
RETURN line)

CREATE OR REPLACE TYPE BODY line IS
STATIC FUNCTION construct_line
       (quantity )
RETURN line
       BEGIN
               RETURN line (SYS_GUID(), quantity)
       END;
END;
```

This construction method replaces the **wine_code** with a system identifier so that when it is used in an INSERT statement we can write

```
INSERT INTO line
VALUES (line.construct_line('2')
```

This is an example of a STATIC method which is a function or procedure that does not imply the use of the object itself as an argument. STATIC methods are used to develop customized constructor methods and methods that manipulate the attributes of the object. Earlier we introduced the method **get_total** for the **wine_order** type. This method can be used in SQL and PL/SQL statements that assign values to variables. For example, if **x** and **y** are **wine_order** objects then

```
w           =x.Get_total();
z           =y.Get_total();
```

The values of **w** and **z** will be different if **x** and **y** are different PL/SQL variables that have type **wine_order**. In each case the method will use the attributes of the object that it needs to return the value:

```
SELECT     wine_code.Get_total()
FROM       wine_order_table
```

Note that method invocations require the use of parentheses () even when the methods do not have explicit additional arguments.

Then variable **w** will hold the total value of order **x** and **z** will hold the total value of order **y**. We can say that the expression **x.Get_total()** is an invocation of the method **Get_total** of object order. In the invocation **Get_total** has an empty parameter list because its arguments are the attributes of the object of which it is a member. This is called a **selfish style** of invocation.

In general object methods are invoked by using the style type_name.method() or object_expression.method(). Using user-defined types gives a much wider choice to the designer but one question is what kind of type to select. Varying arrays are very limited for multimedia applications. They cannot include LOBs. In addition, when DBMS providers add functionality they tend to do so first to base tables. Varying arrays are difficult to manage when they include more than a few items as their performance decreases as they cannot be indexed and they are difficult to query.

Most of the examples in this chapter have been taken from Oracle. The way that DB2 handles objects and methods is slightly different. We can define a type

```
CREATE DISTINCT TYPE map AS BLOB (1M)
```

Then we can use the type in a table as follows:

```
CREATE TABLE places
(locid      INTEGER NOT NULL,
location    CHAR (50),
grid        map)
```

In addition we can write user-defined functions to operate on BLOBs such as to return the sampling rate of an audio object or the compression of an image. The next example uses a CREATE FUNCTION statement to specify a function that is applied to the map data type to identify the scale of the map but the code is written in C rather than PL/SQL:

```
CREATE FUNCTION map_scale (map)
RETURNS SMALLINT
EXTERNAL NAME 'scalemap'
LANGUAGE C
PARAMETER STYLE DB2SQL
NO SQL
DETERMINISTIC
NO EXTERNAL ACTION
```

The user-defined functions can then be used in SQL statements:

```
SELECT map_scale (grid)
FROM places
WHERE location= 'SAN JOSE, CALIFORNIA'
```

The full name of a DB2 function is *schema-name.function-name*, where *schema-name* is an identifier that provides a logical grouping for SQL objects. The schema name for DB2 extender UDFs is MMDBSYS. MMDBSYS schema name is also the qualifier for the DB2 extender UDTs.

The choices for dealing with multiple values are using a nested table or a separate relational table. Since nested tables are user-defined data types they have the advantage that specific methods can be associated with them so that this can make them preferable to relational tables when additional processing is needed in an application. However, relational tables are easily related to other tables. The table's columns can be indexed and queried easily. If the data in question is only related to one table then using a nested table type would be useful but if the design involves linking the table with many other tables it is preferable to use a relational table to give maximum flexibility.

6.4　Object-relational Approach

The object-relational approach offers the possibility of generic multimedia databases by combining the use of features such as type constructors, navigational access and user-defined functions to retrieve data as well as the features provided by relational databases such as set access, referential integrity and joins. In this way the database model can cope with unstructured multimedia data and in addition relational tables and complex relationships can be modeled. SQL3 offers the opportunity for *ad hoc* as opposed to application-specific querying of object-oriented multimedia databases. However, object-relational solution requires the ability to map the data model into a relational model. This is an additional development step and also may have performance significance, particularly if there is a mismatch between the way the data is stored and the way it is intended to be used.

The essential idea is that the database system should support both object and relational capabilities. Therefore there are several options:

- an equal integrated partnership;
- a data model based on the relational model;
- a data model based on the object model;
- two separate systems side by side.

Most database experts would reject the last option. The approach to the first option is not clear and it appears that in many cases what is happening is a prototyping approach where systems are been created as prototypes that evolve into the final systems.

It is an attractive proposition that we could develop a conceptual model based on UML classes and use cases that could then be implemented by mapping into a relational model that included an object implementation for some classes. This would be a pragmatic approach as we would retain all the database capabilities and could implement the design in Oracle or DB2. (We could implement a pure relational approach in MySQL.)

The option to implement using a object model would be difficult in a DBMS such as Oracle: we would need to define the objects, create object tables and then develop application code to support the operations. There would appear to be few advantages for this additional development cost.

Date (2000) claims that we need to do nothing to the relational model to exploit the most useful aspects of object-oriented design because the concept of domains has always been there. A column in a relational table is defined on a domain. These are usually the built-in SQL data types but it has always been part of the relational model that the domains could be more complex types. Let us review our list of classes in Table 6.6.

Table 6.6   Review of class model to relational model

Class	Implementation	Reason
Region	Relation with foreign key from country relation	In a compositional aggregation relationship with country *is a part* of country and may be joined to other tables as well so not suitable for a nested table Can be realized through referential integrity
Fine Wine	Base relation	This can contain complex data types
Individual and corporate customer	Relation that includes user-defined type person	Customer and employee are kinds of people, could be subtype of people superclass, so implement as user-defined types in a relation. Using the **person_t** type as an object table could turn out to be confusing
Catalog	Could be object table	Collection of wines
Vineyard	Relation	Is associated with producer so could be linked by referential integrity Does the producer have more than one vineyard? If it is one to one then we should combine producer and vineyard
Bottles	User-defined type in relation	Wines are available in different sized bottles so it could be a collection type
Producers	Relation	See vineyard
Events	User-defined type	Define as type
Wine tasting	Relation based on user-defined type	Is a kind of event
Dinners	Relation based on user-defined type	Is a kind of event
Lecture	Relation based on user-defined type	Is a kind of event
Case of wine	Could be object table	Collection of wine bottles
Grape varieties	Relation	Is a kind of grape
Country	Relation referred to by region	In a compositional aggregation relationship with region
Order		In a compositional aggregation relationship with Orderline. This can be achieved through object tables or relational tables
Orderline		In a compositional aggregation relationship with Order is a part of Order

One issue is how to represent an object relational model and how to show a complex set of domains. Naiburg and Maksimchuk (2001) discuss this and work through a comprehensive case study.

In Date (2000) and Date and Darwen (1998) the authors discuss object-relational design which is based on pre-UML classes. These authors discuss two options for object-relational design which can be summarized as:

- domain = object class;
- relation = object class.

In the above object-relational model we have generally used the domain = class approach. This involves defining a column in the table as a user-defined type. Note that SQL3 prefers the term type to domain.

Date deprecates a number of design practices that could be summarized as:

Note that Date has adopted the term relvar for relational variable instead of relation but it is not widely used as yet.

- declaring a user-defined type as a relational table which involves storing a set of pointers to another table in the rows of a table;
- using supertables and subtables because this might jeopardize the ability to use SELECT ... WHERE statements properly, particularly if methods are inherited from the superclass and the loss of closure – it is a vital property of the relational model that every operation on a relation produces a relation;
- using "relation-valued attributes" that is allowing attributes that are from some other relational table could undermine relational integrity.

Although Date includes a number of examples of poor object-relational design he does not include any examples of good object-relational design. This is a result no doubt of the immaturity of the technology.

The other issue is that if the relation consists of only one column which is defined as a user-defined type corresponding to an object class then we would appear to have the equation

relation = class = domain

Date (2000) does not discuss this but it would appear to be an implementation decision. As we become more experienced with the technology design decisions should become easier. Since MMDBMSs are inherently complex the best advice is always to pick the simplest design.

6.5 Notes

1. We created a number of tables and objects in this chapter. These require the Oracle user to have certain privileges. To be able to create a type the user needs to have the CREATE TYPE system privilege and EXECUTE ANY TYPE object privileges. These privileges can be granted explicitly or through a role.

2. It is possible to add a PRAGMA clause to an object method which is a compiler directive. The purpose of these is to deny member functions from certain database accesses, for example:
   - WNDS – specifies a constraint that writes no database state;
   - WNPS – specifies a constraint that writes no package state – does not modify packaged variables;
   - RNDS – specifies a constraint that reads no database state – does not query.

6.6 SUMMARY OF THIS CHAPTER

This chapter dealt with the different development approaches available for the multimedia databases. Initially we identified the need for expressive design notation that could represent complex data and their relationships and we looked at approaches using

- Semantic data modeling
- Object oriented design.

We reviewed the development of object-oriented methods in relation to databases and the advantages that adopting a standard approach based on UML may give the database designer. In particular we looked at the transformation of classes into relational tables.

Object relational design was then introduced in terms of practical object implementation in Oracle including the capabilities of *interMedia*. Finally the object relational approach was reviewed and drawbacks of the approach discussed.

SOLUTIONS TO EXERCISES

Exercise 6.1

(a) They all have the same attributes and same operations.

(b) A class is a definition of an object that represents the attributes and operations of an object. It is not a set of things.

(c) Generally in this text they mean the same thing. Objects can change the values of their attributes frequently.

(d) This is a difficult point. Many computer scientists would view a type as a set that has a particular membership that the type defines. Even SQL data type would be regarded as sets of valid integers or character strings. A class in UML is, however, not regarded as a set of objects but just a definition of what an object of a particular class would be. When we created an object in Oracle we called it a type so it is all quite confusing.

Exercise 6.2

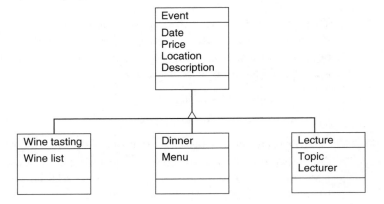

Recommended Reading

For general coverage of Oracle SQL and particularly object types:

Loney, K., Kock, G. (2000) *Oracle8i. The Complete Reference*, Oracle Press. Osbourne/McGraw Hill.

For many examples and a full reference on Oracle:

McCullough-Dieter, C., with Prem, J., Chandak, R., Chandak, P. (1998) *Oracle8 Bible*, IDG Books Worldwide.

Object-oriented Database Design

Britton, C., Doake, J. (2000) *Object-Oriented Systems Development*, McGraw-Hill International.

Heinckiens, P. M. (1998) *Building Scalable Database Applications. Object-Oriented Design, Architectures and Implementations*, Addison-Wesley.

Naiburg, E. J., Maksimchuk, R. A. (2001) *UML for Database Design*, Addison-Wesley.

Stevens, P., Pooley, R. (2000) *Using UML*, Addison-Wesley.

chapter *7*

Using Multimedia Metadata

Chapter aims

This chapter reviews the role of metadata and why it is important in the development of multimedia databases. This is a wide-ranging topic which encompasses such topics as XML, MPEG-7 and RDF. Through a study of this chapter the reader will develop knowledge of the main features of metadata in relation to multimedia data and within database development. At the end of the chapter the reader should be able to understand:

- the main features of metadata in relation to multimedia data;
- the classification of metadata;
- the generation and extraction of metadata;
- the role of the different standards relating to metadata;
- modeling metadata and how to developing an ontology.

7.1 Introduction

Metadata is literally "data about data". The development of huge database systems has created the need for effective ways to manage data. The web has also made the issues of the provenance (i.e. origin), quality and integration of data from different data sources key issues that it is claimed can be solved or at least alleviated by the effective use of metadata.

Its importance to multimedia databases was introduced in Chapter 2 and emphasized again in Chapter 5 when we considered the role of metadata in retrieving multimedia data. The term metadata is becoming somewhat ubiquitous so we will need to be careful when we define it, what we mean and its context of use. There is an important distinction between the use of metadata in multimedia databases and in "traditional" databases. Metadata has been an important part of databases in describing the database schema and constraints, seting up value sets and domain range limits for a long time. It has also been extensively used in distributed RDBMSs to describe the location and distribution of data. In the case of multimedia databases the metadata also concerns descriptions of the individual objects in the database, for example there could be metadata associated with every row of a table. This is sometimes termed associative metadata as it links to individual instances and has a different purpose which is usually to support an application.

In Chapter 5 it became apparent that metadata could be linked with media data so that it supported processing, especially for querying, retrieving, navigating and browsing the media. In particular we looked at the three ways multimedia data was retrieved:

- attribute-based retrieval;
- text-based retrieval;
- content-based retrieval.

Metadata is essential for all three of these different types of retrieval. Metadata allows the processing of queries that just could not be possible with the media itself.

Since individual objects will have their associative metadata, this will need to be maintained along with the original data in order to maintain consistency and integrity. Metadata can also be there to improve performance and give assistance to the end-user. Advanced multimedia applications can involve the composition of media of different types. Metadata can serve to match data structures and content when it is used to create representations involving heterogeneous media obtained from heterogeneous data sources, for example in biomedical applications. When metadata exists and is stored in the database we need to know how to update it and this involves a knowledge of the structure and semantics of the metadata. When the media data is updated the metadata must also be changed to remain consistent with the description of the media. For example, when images are changed the features extracted to create metadata may also have changed and therefore there must be a means to monitor and update the metadata and its related indexes. Associative metadata is also very important in indexing media data. There may also be occasions when changes in processing make it necessary to change the metadata even if there has been no change to the raw media. The structure and granularity of metadata (how much is enough and how much is too much) and its organization – such as in hierarchies – is an important design issue.

A large section of this chapter deals with metadata standards and introduces the currently most important. These standards are essential for any application where the domain is governed by a set of standards and interoperability is an issue. Interoperability is the capability to exchange machine-understandable information on the web between applications. It would obviously be foolish to develop a database that would not be able to access or exchange information easily with other applications in the same domain. If you are not concerned with this kind of application then this section can be skipped. As well as the information in this chapter, Appendix B gives a list of metadata standards and web sources of information on each one.

Metadata forms an essential part of any database, providing descriptive data about each stored object and is the key to managing data objects. In the case of multimedia objects it forms the main basis for their retrieval. For example for text, metadata would typically include catalog information such as the object's creator, form and date of creation. This could also be applied to applications based on collections of image or video media when it may also contain information about the object's content. The first type of metadata is significant for attribute-based retreival while the second is involved in content-based retrieval. Later on we will see how the development of standards in the metadata field could relate to content-based retrieval, but, at the present time, its impact is limited.

The purposes of metadata are numerous:

- *Administrative*. Managing and administrating the data collection process.

- *Descriptive*. Describing and identifying for retrieval purposes, creating indexes.

- *Preservation*. Managing data refreshing and migration. The multimedia objects may need to have a much longer lifespan than transaction data. Achieving this involves issues of whether the format will be readable over time.

- *Technical*. Formats, compression, scaling, encryption, authentication and security

- *Usage*. Users, their level and type of use, user tracking, multi-versioning. Digital media enables multiple and variant versions of the objects to be created (a high resolution version and a thumbnail). There must be metadata to link the multiple versions and to capture what is the same and what is different.

We need to understand how metadata can be classified, modeled and extracted in order to support multimedia database systems. Later in the chapter we discuss the role of ontologies in identifying and describing metadata attributes. The concept of domain ontologies has existed for sometime in knowledge-based systems (KBSs) and we will study one way of developing an ontology later in this chapter.

7.2   Classifying Metadata

The formal term schema, used in traditional relational databases, describes the intentional part of a relation such as database (name, size, security authorizations) and attributes (name, type, constraints). It relates to the individual instances of the relation through the intentional component. Some of the constraints relate to the attribute's type, some to relationships between the attributes. This kind of metadata is based on the formal logic of the relational model. In contrast, associative metadata relates to the extensional part of the relation. It describes the characteristic features of the data instances. Associative metadata does not have a formal logical relationship with the media objects although it may have been created by a systematic association such as the processes used for feature extraction.

It is also possible to recognize navigational metadata. We can see this kind of metadata in web systems such as AltaVista which can locate the URL of an information source through this kind of metadata. There is no formal logic relationship between navigational metadata and the data instances.

Classification of metadata can be:

- specific to the media involved;
- specific to the processing;
- content specific metadata.

In Table 7.1 we illustrate the types of metadata specific for different media. The examples contrast the different kinds of metadata needed for a photographic image, text document and a video. This variation causes a problem when we want to design a structured metadata database. Another problem we have to consider when we are developing a metadata structure is that a media object can be of interest to a wide range of specialists who were not in

Table 7.1   Metadata information for different kinds of media objects

Image object	Text object	Video
Image capture	Title	Time based
Image storage	Author	Play rate
Caption	Abstract	Camera motion
Genre	Table of contents	Camera lighting
Period	Full text indexes	
Subjects		
Photographer		
Intellectual property rights		
Texture		

the domain that originated the object. A nineteenth-century photograph can be of interest to historians, social scientists or family historians or even medical researchers and this will affect the way the data is retrieved. There will also be metadata concerning the age, history and quality of the media data. The origin of the media may dictate the format of the media. This information is termed **original** metadata. If the media format is changed in the course of further processing information about the new format would be **derived** metadata. The processing history of the media may be required for certain applications such as medical imaging.

Metadata can describe the functions designed for the specific processing of the different media. Metadata may be created specifically for search and retrieval functions which involve different processes for the different media. For example, a storyline may be available for a video object. Some metadata is required for interoperability requirements (see Chapter 8).

In Chapter 5 we learned to classify metadata as content dependent, content-descriptive and content independent. In addition to these classes we should recognize that content-descriptive metadata could be further subdivided into:

- domain-independent metadata which is independent of the application or subject topic;
- domain-dependent metadata, which is specific to the application area.

EXERCISE 7.1

In Chapter 4 we introduced the **wine_list** table which had the following columns for multimedia data:

pronunciation BLOB
picture BFILE.

Suggest five attributes that would be appropriate to provide metadata for attribute-based retrieval for both columns.

7.3   Generating and Extracting Metadata

The generation of metadata can be achieved in a number of ways, for example:

- analysis of raw media data;
- implicit metadata generation;

- semi-automatic generation;
- manual augmentation.

The creation and management of metadata can become a complex issue when we wish to provide metadata for text- and content-based retrieval. Unlike text documents, images make no attempt to tell us what they are about and often they are used for purposes not anticipated by their originators. In terms of manual augmentation, it is very difficult to express in words what a work of art is about when it is based on a wordless medium. Metadata based on manual addition of keywords to image objects is very time consuming. The Getty Information Institute, which has contributed a great deal to the development of metadata standards for their large art collections, reported an average time of seven minutes per image. Manual systems for video will be even longer. The use of manually created metadata has also not proved very reliable as a means of retrieving an object. The process of describing an image is highly subjective. Not only can an image mean different things to different people, it can mean different things to the same person at different times. A study of interindexer consistency found a wide range of disparities in the way that different individuals used to describe the same picture. There is also a mismatch between the user's terms and those of the indexer. This is particularly true when it is a domain which requires a special vocabulary. Another problem is that over time common vocabulary changes and evolves in a domain.

Although the problems of manual augmentation are still not solved there are a number of common-sense approaches, for example:

- stick to plain and simple terms accepted by the users;
- use a thesaurus with many lead-ins;
- provide support for "near to" matches rather than just exact match retrieval as described in Chapter 10;
- select attributes of metadata that will provide useful groupings of images;
- recognize that some metadata attributes will be useful when the user has located the object (e.g. intellectual property rights) and include these in the metadata specification.

Multimedia objects may acquire layers of metadata as they move through their lifecycle so when we design the structure of the metadata we need to consider how it would be updated. Where will the metadata be stored in the database? There are a range of ways in which metadata can be associated with the media object:

- contained within the same envelope as the media, for example through the header of an image file, as part of the object definition in Oracle *interMedia*;

- bundled with the media object, e.g. universal preservation format (UPF);
- attached to the information object through bi-directional pointers and hyperlinks;
- stored separately in a metadata registry – that is a special kind of data dictionary for metadata.

EXERCISE 7.2

(a) We have noted the problems of manually annotating media data particularly because the annotator can have a very different perception of the object than the end-users. One technique that can be applied to overcome this is associative group analysis (AGA). This is used for an in-depth analysis of perceptions and attitudes. The purpose of the analysis is to identify subjective images and meanings, elements of cognition and systems of mental representation. It is an unstructured open-ended approach. It attempts to collect **free associations** to strategically selected **stimulus themes**. Present the three images displayed in Figure 2.6, one at a time to a small group of database users. Ask each user to complete the following list. (Alternatively, substitute three similar images of your choice.)

> Look at each image in turn and write down the first five words or short phrases which come into your mind and you associate with it. Complete the task quickly without spending too long thinking about it. You can add more words to the bottom of the list if you wish.
>
> 1.
> 2.
> 3.
> 4.
> 5.

(b) From the results of (a) you should have a list of five terms (the terms that occurred most frequently) that could be used to annotate each image. Write the SQL statements required to modify the structure of the animal table to add a column with a suitable data type to hold the metadata.

7.4 The Role of Metadata Standards

Standards for metadata are important because they are a way of achieving a common representation and essential for the interoperability of systems and particularly those with gigantic information spaces such as the web. They are essential if metadata is to be exploited effectively in distributed systems (see Chapter 8). A number of metadata standards are currently being developed. Some of these have been motivated by the prevalence of the internet and the issue of how to search this huge information space effectively.

As a consequence of the recognition of the essential role of metadata a number of different organizations have put forward different standards. At the moment it is not clear which standard approach will be the most significant in practice. The standards include many similar ideas but differ in detail. Some have originated from attempts to address the problems of particular domains, for example, online libraries, and their application to non-text media has been somewhat fudged. Standards about metadata usually refer to structured metadata. Unstructured metadata in the forms of notes and annotations can, however, be part of structured metadata. There are some standards for metadata that relate to its structure. In addition, a small number of standards relate to the semantic aspects of metadata, for example AAT Art & Architecture Thesaurus and ULAN (see Appendix B).

7.4.1 Domain-independent Metadata Standards

We will consider a number of these standards in some detail because when we develop a metadata ontology it is obviously sensible to develop a structure that will be compatible with the information required to support the different standards. Recently, as metadata has become increasingly important, a number of international standards have been developed. Some of these standards relate to domain-independent metadata such as the following.

ISO/IEC 11179

One of the most important standards to consider is ISO/IEC 11179, especially Part 6, which covers the specification and standardisation of data elements. This set of standards are intended to provide:

- a conceptual framework;
- a logical explanation of the processes that would enable an organization to describe the semantics of the data contents of its databases in a consistent way across organizational units;
- the exchange of data and metadata between different organizations.

There are six parts to the FDIS ISO/IEC 11179-1 standard:

Part 1 – Framework for the Specification and Standardization of Data Elements;
Part 2 – Classification for Data Elements;

Part 3 – Basic Attributes of Data Elements;
Part 4 – Rules and Guidelines for the Formulation of Data Definitions;
Part 5 – Naming and Identification Principles for Data Elements;
Part 6 – Registration of Data Elements.

The ISO/IEC 11179 standard provides a logical capability for establishing unique identifiers for what it terms fully characterized data elements across different data systems and organizations. It also provides a standard structure of attributes that enable data elements to be compared in an unambiguous way. The information is held in what is called a "data registry" to differentiate its capabilities and scope from a data dictionary. A data registry, therefore, contains the metadata that is necessary to clearly describe, analyze and classify data elements in a way that is common across organizational boundaries and to be able to maintain an inventory of the metadata.

ISO/IEC 11179 standard specifies basic aspects of data element composition, including metadata. Part 1 introduces and discusses fundamental ideas of data elements essential to the understanding of ISO/IEC 11179 and the context for associating the individual parts of the standard. It also contains a glossary of terms, the fundamental model of data elements, a description of the other parts, an informative annex describing the relationship between data modeling principles and the standard and other useful information. Part 6, which relates to the registration of data elements, is particularly relevant to metadata. However, the standard was not intended to address any issues about metadata that relate to instances of data. Although it does not address the problem of semantic retrieval, it does provide an important framework that needs to be taken into account by all designers of MMDBMSs.

A data registry supports data sharing with cross-system and cross-organization descriptions of common units of data. The purpose of the data registry is to give users of shared data, for every elemental data unit, a common understanding of

- meaning;
- attributes;
- unique identification.

The data registry is only a subset of the complete metadata that can be included in a data repository. However, that metadata subset needs to be structured in a way that supports administration and retrieval of registered data. According to the standard a data registry is definitely more than just another data dictionary. A data dictionary is not adequate since, if for no other reason, it has no obvious structure. It is certainly true that in the past database experts such as Date (2000) have stressed the importance of the data dictionary – the system tables – the structure has depended on the approach taken by the individual DBMS providers.

The ISO/IEC 11179 (ISO 11179) standard for the description of data elements provides a set of ten attributes as set out in Table 7.2. Although ISO/IEC 11179 was not meant to deal with our principal concern, which is associated metadata, it provides a fundamental model of data elements that could be adopted for associated metadata as well. When we look at developing an ontology, we will use very similar concepts. The standard divides data elements into three constituent parts:

- object class – the thing the data describes, such as a person, airplane or chemical plant;
- property – a peculiarity that describes or distinguishes objects, such as sex, length or name;
- representation – the allowed values (value domain) and other information for a data element (for example, units of measure such as male or female, positive real numbers measured in meters, or character string).

This viewpoint of the standard shows data elements organized through classification. The object class and property are viewed as nodes in one or more classification structures. This view also corresponds to the way data modelers think about data. This standard, moreover, does not specify the representations or formats used for storing or communicating data and metadata within and between systems. In this view, a data element has a concept and a representation. The conceptual part contains the definition,

Table 7.2   ISO/IEC 1179 attributes

Attribute	Description
Name	The label assigned to the data element
Identifier	The unique identifier assigned to the data element
Version	The version of the data element
Registration Authority	The entity authorized to register the data element
Language	The language in which the data element is specified
Definition	A statement that clearly represents the concept and essential nature of the data element
Obligation	Indicates whether the data element is required to always or sometimes be present (contain a value)
Datatype	Indicates the type of data that can be represented in the value of the data element
Maximum Occurrence	Indicates any limit to the repeatability of the data element
Comment	A remark concerning the application of the data element

names and other identifiers. The power of this view is that data elements are organized by their definitions and their value domains, much the way programmers and analysts think about data.

EXERCISE 7.3

(a) What are the advantages and disadvantages of storing the metadata together with the media object?

(b) What are the advantages of storing the metadata in a metadata registry?

Other important standards to consider are:

● *Metadata Coalition Interchange Standard.* This is intended to address problems of exchange, sharing and management of metadata. This resulted in 1997 in the Metadata Interchange Specification (http://www.he.net/metadata).

● *Meta Content Format* (*MCF*). This addresses the abstraction, standardization and representation of structures for organizing information. The concept is based on relating media objects through the people and organizations related to them. MCF provides a general-purpose information framework for determining what data from one schema can be automatically and dynamically converted into another using its own structure description language. It provides syntax and semantics but not a standard schema. There is a standard vocabulary for describing people, organizations and meetings so that information from different sources can be integrated even when the data is derived from very different schema.

7.4.2 The Dublin Core Metadata Set (http://purl.org/metadata/dublin_core)

The Dublin Core Metadata Element Set was developed to provide simple resource description records in the context of online libraries in order to give improved access to the internet. The Dublin Core has been updated (the current standard is version 1.1) partly to broaden the scope of the original standard to other media and also to provide a link to the ISO/IEC 11179 standard. The object again is to promote interoperability which is a need that has partly been created by the spread of the web.

We have all experienced frustration in trying to search for documents on the web but retrieving many irrelevant documents which have to be sifted through. A number of initiatives are being directed at solving this problem through metadata. At present there are two types of resource descriptions in common use for electronic documents:

- Automatically generated indexes are used by locator services such as Lycos and WebCrawler. These automatically index every source available on the web and maintain up-to-date databases of these locations. However, these indexes often contain too little information to be really useful.

- Catalog records are created by professional providers such as MARC, a data interchange format for bibliographic data. These are costly to create and maintain and are not always adequate to describe complex web documents.

The Dublin core is intended to be a compromise between these two extremes by providing a simple structured record that can be mapped to more complex records or linked to more elaborate records. The Dublin core recognizes the existence of document-like objects (**DLO**s) that could be, for example, an electronic version of a newspaper article. This would not cover objects such as an annotated set of slides or complex geological data.

Although not an official standard, this set of metadata elements is now widely used for describing web documents. The standard was originally developed to cope with text documents. The only image-related aspects of the element set are the ability to define the existence of an image in a document ("DC.Type = image") and to describe an image's subject content by the use of keywords. This framework is limited and it is difficult to envisage that it could be extended to handle content-based retrieval. The definitions utilize a formal standard for the description of metadata elements. This formalization helps to improve consistency with other metadata communities and enhances the clarity, scope and internal consistency of the Dublin Core metadata element definitions.

There are four main advantages for adopting the Dublin Core:

- It encourages authors and publishers to provide metadata in a form that electronic search engines can utilize.

- It encourages the development of tools to support the standard.

- A Dublin Core record can be extended to cover more complex documents.

- Users from different domains can understand the Dublin Core without special training and can exchange information with each other.

Each Dublin Core element is now defined using a set of ten attributes from the ISO/IEC 11179 standard for the description of data elements. Six of the ten ISO/IEC 11179 attributes, described in Table 7.2, are common to all the Dublin Core elements. These are, with their values:

Version	1.1
Registration Authority	Dublin Core Metadata Initiative
Language	en
Obligation	Optional
Datatype	Character string
Maximum Occurrence	Unlimited

In addition a set of 15 metadata elements (known as the Dublin Core) has been proposed in Version 1.1 as described in Table 7.3. This has been suggested as the minimum number of metadata elements required to support retrieval of a DLO in a networked environment.

Table 7.3   Dublin Core elements

Core element	Semantics
Subject	Topic addressed by the work
Title	The name of the object
Creator	Entity responsible for the intellectual content
Publisher	The agency responsible for making the object available
Description	An account of the content of the resource
Contributor	An entity responsible for making contributions to the content of the resource
Date	A date associated with an event in the life cycle of the resource
Resource type	The nature or genre of the content of the resource
Format	The physical or digital manifestation of the resource; format of the file, e.g. Postscript
Identifier	Unique identifier
Relation	A reference to a related resource
Source	A reference to a resource from which the present resource is derived
Language	Language of intellectual content
Coverage	The extent or scope of the content of the resource. Coverage will typically include spatial location (a place name or geographic coordinates), temporal period (a period label, date, or date range) or jurisdiction (such as a named administrative entity)
Rights	Information about rights held in and over the resource

EXERCISE 7.4

(a) Write an SQL statement to create a table to hold the elements of the Dublin Core shown in Table 7.3 specifying suitable data types. Write an

SQL INSERT statement for the set values for this book for the elements – identifier, subject, title, creator, publisher, date.

(b) All the elements of the Core are optional – are there any disadvantages to this from the point of view of the database designer?

(c) All the elements of the Core are multivalued – are there any disadvantages to this from the point of view of the database designer? How would you now change the answer to part (a)?

There are two concepts within the Dublin Core proposals that cause some dilemmas for designers of distributed databases. The use of the two concepts described below is optional. This adds to the complexity because in a distributed environment some data may have been described using these refinements and some may not. The DBMS will need to acquire a mechanism for dealing with both situations. The concepts which were introduced to improve retrieval by increasing the specificity of the meta-data descriptions are:

- element refinement – the use of additional attributes to qualify the meaning of the orginal element;
- encoding scheme – the use of controlled vocabularies, formal notations and parsing rules.

Element Refinement

Each core element is optional and may be repeated. Each element also has a limited set of qualifiers, attributes that may be used to further refine (not extend) the meaning of the element. The Dublin Core Metadata Initiative (DCMI) has defined standard ways to "qualify" elements with various types of qualifiers. A set of recommended qualifiers conforming to DCMI "best practice" is available. These qualifiers make the meaning of an element narrower or more specific. A refined element shares the meaning of the unqualified element, but with a more restricted scope. The reason for this is that in a network system a client that did not understand a specific element's refinement term should be able to ignore the qualifier and treat the metadata value as if it were an unqualified (broader) element. This ability to ignore the unknown qualifiers and fall back on the broader meaning of the element in its unqualified form is known as the "dumb-down principle". A client should be able to ignore any refinement and use the description as if it were unqualified. While this may result in some loss of specific meaning, the remaining element value (minus the qualifier) must continue to be generally correct.

The use of qualifiers as an additional level of detail introduces the situation where a client can encounter collections of resources that are described using the Dublin Core with qualifiers that are unknown to the client application. This can happen either because the client does not support qualifiers and the collection does or because the collection supports specialized qualifiers developed by implementors for specific local or domain needs. This raises the issue of how the Dublin Core will be implemented. It would be better if there were a way of adding the element values automatically when the media object was added to the database collection.

Encoding Scheme

The purpose of the qualifiers is to aid the interpretation of an element value. These schemes are much more tightly specified and include using controlled vocabularies and formal notations or parsing rules. These features combined are termed an encoding scheme. When an encoding scheme is in operation, the value of an element will have been selected from a controlled vocabulary. This could range from a term from a classification system (or set of subject headings) to a string formatted in accordance with a formal notation (e.g. "2000-01-01" as the international standard expression for a date). If an encoding scheme were not understood by a client or agent, the value may still be useful to a human reader. The definitive description of an encoding scheme for qualifiers must be clearly identified and available for public use.

In order for the system to work the definitions of element refinement terms for qualifiers must be publicly available. Content data for some elements may be selected from a "controlled vocabulary", which is a limited set of consistently used and carefully defined terms. This can dramatically improve search results because computers are good at matching words character by character but weak at understanding the way people refer to one concept using different words, i.e. synonyms. Without basic terminology control, inconsistent or incorrect metadata can profoundly degrade the quality of search results. For example, without a controlled vocabulary, "candy" and "sweet" might be used to refer to the same concept. Controlled vocabularies may also reduce the likelihood of spelling errors when recording metadata.

The Dublin Core excludes extrinsic data, which it regards as data that describes the context in which the work is used – for example cost and access. It is extensible so that other data elements can be added for specialized domains.

Another way to look at Dublin Core is as a "small language for making a particular class of statements about resources" (Baker, 2000). In this language, there are two classes of terms (elements (nouns) and qualifiers (adjectives)) which can be arranged into a simple pattern of statements. The resources themselves are the implied subjects in this language. In the diverse world of the internet, it has been suggested that the Dublin Core is "metadata pidgin for digital tourists: easily grasped, but not necessarily up to the task of expressing complex relationships or concepts". Therefore we might have reservations about the suitability of the Dublin Core for non-text media. What would be the title of a satellite or medical image and who would be the creator? It is now possible to list a service as the creator so that Version 1.1 has adapted to the needs of non-text media to some extent.

Although the Dublin Core favors DLOs, it is intended to be applicable to other resources as well. Its suitability for use with particular non-document resources will depend to some extent on how closely their metadata resembles typical document metadata and also what purpose the metadata is intended to serve. It is worth looking at the solution of Exercise 7.5 because trying to apply the Dublin Core elements to a multimedia document with several components is not easy. From the above descriptions we can see that the Dublin Core proposals are tightly focused on attribute-based rather than text- or context-based retrieval. The very complexity of the proposals in practice highlights the limitations of an attribute-based approach.

EXERCISE 7.5

(a) We could regard the rows of the **grape** table described in Chapter 4 as representing DLOs. Redefine the columns of the table to include the Dublin Core elements and add default values where appropriate.

(b) Write a PL/SQL procedure to automatically insert the default data.

7.4.3   Resource Description Framework

Before we leave the topic of standards we must also consider the potentially greater relevance of another standard – the Resource Description Framework (RDF). The World-Wide Web Consortium is developing a standard, the RDF, for metadata. RDF allows multiple metadata schemes to be read by humans as well as parsed by machines. The RDF is a foundation for processing metadata; it provides interoperability between applications that exchange machine-understandable information on the web. RDF has a number of objectives as well as creating a metadata standard for:

- *resource discovery* to provide better search engine capabilities;
- *cataloging* for describing the content and content relationships available through *intelligent software agents*;
- *content rating*, in describing *collections of pages* that represent a single logical "document";
- describing *intellectual property rights* of web pages;

- expressing the *privacy preferences* of a user as well as the *privacy policies* of a website;

- *digital signatures* to create a "web of trust" for electronic commerce, collaboration and other applications.

The aim of the RDF is to provide a foundation for processing metadata in web documents, allowing interoperability between applications exchanging machine-readable information. It will specify a framework for detailed description of all kinds of objects stored on the web, allowing search engines to identify relevant content with much greater precision than is at present possible. The specification allows users to define attribute types and values relevant to their own needs, with the objective of providing sufficient extensibility to meet a whole range of specialist needs.

The preferred language for writing RDF schemas is the Extensible Markup Language (XML). This, like the better-known web page authoring language HTML, is in fact a derivative of the original generalized text markup language, SGML. XML is described in more detail in Chapter 10 but we will introduce its main concepts here. It provides a flexible language in which to define a whole range of document types (unlike HTML, which can define only a single type) and their associated metadata. XML breaks down a document into components also called elements. Elements can have attributes and can contain other elements. There is a root element that contains all the others. Elements contained in others are subelements, branches contain subelements and leaves do not. Root elements and document elements are interchangeable terms (see Figure 10.4).

The essential concept of XML can be summarized as

DATA + MARKUP = TEXT

XML allows text reuse through a feature called external entities. XML entities "keep track" of the location of the bytes that make up the document, i.e. the physical structure of the document. A data entity has a notation explaining whether it is JPEG, GIF etc. The way these features are managed in XML is through the document type definition (DTD). The DTD defines the element types in a class of documents by specifying entity types, attributes and notation. Although HTML has SGML DTD definitions, these are rarely seen in practice. In contrast XML and SGML require authors to think about the structure of a document and not how it is to be rendered. XML is also international in concept. Whereas the ASCII character set caters for the English-speaking nations, XML is intended to operate internationally since its character set is UNICODE. In addition, entities do not have to be stored in files.

RDF uses XML to express structure, thereby allowing metadata communities to define the actual semantics as illustrated in Figure 7.1, which provides an RDF description of an audio file using XML style. This decentralized approach recognizes that no one scheme is appropriate for all situations and further that schemes need a linking mechanism independent of a central authority to aid description, identification, understanding, usability and/or exchange.

RDF allows multiple objects to be described without specifying the detail required. The underlying glue, XML, simply requires that all namespaces be defined and, once defined, they can be used to the extent needed by the provider of the metadata. Attributes whose names start with "xmlns" are namespace declarations as used in Figure 7.1. RDF uses the proposed XML namespace mechanism to implement globally unique identifiers. The namespace name serves as the identifier for the corresponding RDF schema. An RDF processor would then use the schema universal resource identifier (URI) to access the schema content. Note in Figure 7.1 the expression

```
<rdf:Description
rdf:about="http://media.example.com/audio/guide.ra">
```

The **Description** is an important RDF element that names, in an **about** attribute, the resource as a URI, to which the statements following it apply. If the resource does not yet exist (i.e. does not yet have a resource identifier) then a **Description** element can supply the identifier for the resource using an ID attribute. A **Description** element without an **about** attribute represents a new resource. Such a resource might be some physical resource that does not have a recognizable URI. If another **Description** or property value needs to refer to the resource it will use the value of the ID of that resource in its own **about** attribute. The ID attribute signals the creation of a new resource and the **about** attribute refers to an existing resource; therefore either ID or **about** may be specified on a description but not both together in the same element. The values for each ID attribute must not appear in more than one ID attribute within a single document.

```
<rdf:RDF xmlns:rdf="http://www.w3.org/1999/02/22-rdf-syntax-ns#"
 xmlns:dc="http://purl.org/dc/elements/1.1/">

 <rdf:Description
rdf:about="http://media.example.com/audio/guide.ra">
 <dc:creator>Rose Bush</dc:creator>
 <dc:title>A Guide to Growing Roses</dc:title>
 <dc:description>Describes process for planting and nurturing
different kinds of rose bushes.</dc:description>
 <dc:date>2001-01-20</dc:date>
 </rdf:Description>
</rdf:RDF>
```

Figure 7.1   RDF definition fragment expressed in XML

Although RDF and XML are essentially text based, their extensibility implies that it should be possible to use them to encapsulate most types of data required for content-based retrieval. Non-XML entities would be graphs, movies, raw text, pdf, HTML, MPEG, JPEG, etc. How elegantly this can be accomplished remains to be seen. For example, the color histogram of an image might be specified by defining a ColorHistogram data type within XML. Each instance of this type would then be defined by indicating parameters such as the color space on which the histogram was based, and the number and extent of bins on each axis, followed by a tagged array of numbers representing the actual histogram.

Content-based retrieval search engines could access such definitions via appropriate APIs such as W3C's Document Object Model, translate them into their own internal format and compare them with corresponding data from other images.

The RDF data model representation can be used to evaluate equivalence in meaning. Two RDF expressions are equivalent if and only if their data model representations are the same. This definition of equivalence permits some syntactic variation in expression without altering the meaning. The RDF basic data model consists of three object types:

- resources;
- properties;
- statements.

Resources are all things described in RDF expressions such as:

- entire web page, e.g. HTML document;
- part of a web page – HTML or XML element;
- entire website – a collection of documents;
- object not directly accessible by the web – printed book.

Resources are always named by URIs plus optional anchor IDs. Anything can have a URI; the extensibility of URIs allows the introduction of identifiers for any entity imaginable.

Properties are specific aspects, characteristics, attributes, or relations used to describe a resource. Each property has a specific meaning, defines its permitted values, the types of resources it can describe, and its relationship with other properties.

Statements are resources with properties that have specific values. An RDF statement is specific resource together with a named property plus the value of that property for that resource. These three individual parts of a statement are called, respectively the *subject*, the *predicate* and the *object*. The object of a statement (i.e. the property value) can be another resource or it can be a literal, i.e. a resource (specified by a URI) or a simple string or other primitive datatype defined by XML. In RDF terms, a *literal* may have content that is XML mark-up but is not further evaluated by the RDF processor.

Qualified Property Values

Often the value of a property is something that has additional contextual information that is considered "part of" that value. In other words, there is a need to qualify property values. Examples of such qualification include naming a unit of measure, a particular restricted vocabulary or some other annotation. For some uses it is appropriate to use the property value without the qualifiers because the context is obvious. For example, in the statement "the price of that pencil is 75 US cents" it is often sufficient to say simply "the price of that pencil is 75".

Containers

Frequently it is necessary to refer to a collection of resources, for example to say that a work was created by more than one person, or to list the students in a course or the software modules in a package. RDF containers are used to hold such lists of resources or literals.

Container Model

RDF defines three types of container objects:

Bag	An unordered list of resources or literals. *Bag*s are used to declare that a property has multiple values and that there is no significance to the order in which the values are given. *Bag* might be used to give a list of part numbers where the order of processing the parts does not matter. Duplicate values are permitted. For example, we could have a bag with 2 apples, 1 orange and 2 pears in the order apple, orange, pear, apple, pear.
Sequence	An ordered list of resources or literals. *Sequence* is used to declare that a property has multiple values and that the order of the values is significant. *Sequence* might be used, for example, to preserve an alphabetical ordering of values. Duplicate values are permitted.
Alternative	A list of resources or literals that represent alternatives for the (single) value of a property. *Alternative* might be used to provide alternative language translations for the title of a work or to provide a list of internet mirror sites at which a resource might be found. An application using a property whose value is an *Alternative* collection is aware that it can choose any one of the items in the list as appropriate.

Note: The definitions of *Bag* and *Sequence* explicitly permit duplicate values. RDF does not define a core concept of *Set*, which would be a *Bag* with no duplicates, because the RDF core does not mandate an enforcement mechanism in the event of violations of such constraints. Future work on the RDF core may define such facilities.

To create a collection of resources, RDF uses an additional resource that represents the specific collection (an *instance* of a collection, in object modeling terminology). For example, we could define a collection called **fruit** as a bag. A particular bag would be fruit_1, another fruit_2.

Any collection resource must be declared to be an instance of one of the container object types defined above. The *type* property, defined below, is used to make this declaration. The membership relation between this container resource and the resources that belong in the collection is defined by a set of properties defined expressly for this purpose. These membership properties are named simply "_1", "_2", "_3", etc. Container resources may have other properties in addition to the membership properties and the *type* property.

A common use of containers is as the value of a property. When used in this way, the statement still has a single object regardless of the number of members in the container; the container resource itself is the object of the statement. The formal model of the RDF framework is:

1. There is a set called *Resources*.
2. There is a set called *Literals*.
3. There is a subset of *Resources* called *Properties*.
4. There is a set called *Statements*, each element of which is a triple of the form {pred, sub, obj}.

The statement always follows the pattern where **pred** is a property (member of *Properties*), **sub** is a resource (member of *Resources*) and **obj** is either a resource or a literal (member of *Literals*).

RDF can also be used with the Dublin Core proposals. The example below represents the simple description of a resources in RDF using vocabularies defined by the Dublin Core Initiative. Here is a description of a website home page using Dublin Core properties:

```
<rdf:RDF
  xmlns:rdf="http://www.w3.org/1999/02/22-rdf-syntax-ns#"
  xmlns:dc="http://purl.org/metadata/dublin_core#">
  <rdf:Description about="http://www.dlib.org">
    <dc:Title>D-Lib Program - Research in Digital
    Libraries</dc:Title>
    <dc:Description>The D-Lib program supports the community of
    people with research interests in digital libraries and
    electronic publishing.</dc:Description>
    <dc:Publisher>Corporation For National Research
    Initiatives</dc:Publisher>
    <dc:Date>1995-01-07</dc:Date>
```

```
      <dc:Subject>
        <rdf:Bag>
        <rdf:li>Research; statistical methods</rdf:li>
        <rdf:li>Education, research, related topics</rdf:li>
        <rdf:li>Library use Studies</rdf:li>
        </rdf:Bag>
        </dc:Subject>
      <dc:Type>World Wide Web Home Page</dc:Type>
      <dc:Format>text/html</dc:Format>
      <dc:Language>en</dc:Language>
    </rdf:Description>
  </rdf:RDF>
```

Note that the multivalued subject is described by a bag container.

Before we leave the subject of XML-based metadata, there is a potentially important XML document type for multimedia. The Synchronized Multimedia Integration Language (SMIL) is provided to describe multimedia presentations. It allows the sequencing of audio, video, text and graphic components to be described.

7.4.4 MPEG-7

Until this point we have focused on metadata standards that were really developed with text media in mind and on attribute-based retrieval that could be extended in some fashion to cover other media. Unlike most of the standards discussed above, one emerging standard – MPEG-7 – is set to make a major impact in content-based retrieval as well. MPEG-7 is the emerging standard for audio, video and image data. Its description definition language may in the future also be based on XML. In this respect, therefore, RDF and XML may well influence (and be influenced by) future developments in content-based retrieval.

Its importance stems form the fact that it is the only standard specifically aimed at representing multimedia content – the core of content-based retrieval technology. Previous standards from MPEG as outlined in Chapter 2 have concentrated on image compression (MPEG-1, MPEG-2) and ways of separately representing foreground objects and background (MPEG-4). These standards have had little impact on the database community, even those members dealing with image data. The new MPEG-7 standard is the first to address the issue of multimedia content at all seriously. It aims to set up a standard framework for describing all aspects of a multimedia object's content, including:

- low-level descriptions of each individual object in a scene, such as shape, size, color, position and movement;

- high-level abstract descriptions of the scene, the objects it contains and the event(s) taking place;
- audio information such as key, mood and tempo.

Thus an MPEG-7 description of a video clip might consist of a set of codes conveying information such as: "This scene contains a cellar containing shelves of wine with white walls and subdued lighting." It would also contain associative metadata such as the format of the video, when and by whom it was recorded and copyright information. In principle, then, the MPEG-7 specification will cover the entire range of features required for content-based image retrieval (CBIR) and content-based audio retrieval (CBAR).

The standard aims to define a Description Definition Language (DDL) in which to write Descriptor Schemas (DSs), specifying the set of features which describe a video's image and audio content. It is not intended to cover either the methods of feature extraction or the way in which search engines make use of the features for retrieval. Any level of feature may be defined in the standard – not all will be suitable for automatic extraction. While the most common use of MPEG-7 will probably be to describe the content of digitized video, no limits are set on the medium of the data being described. MPEG-7 codes can quite legitimately be used to describe the content of still images recorded on paper, using terms assigned by a human annotator.

The potential benefits of the new standard are considerable. It should make the process of searching for a desired image a great deal easier, since future MPEG-7-based search engines will simply need to process values of defined standard parameters, rather than computing search features from scratch. For the same reasons, the standard will enormously enhance interoperability, since all search engines will potentially be using compatible features. This is likely to have a major impact on image searching on the web, which will become a far more efficient process once a significant number of images enhanced with MPEG-7 metadata become available. Although the benefits of MPEG-7 are considerable there has been a worry that the field of image retrieval is not yet sufficiently mature for a set of preferred retrieval features to be defined. Consequently the MPEG development team is aiming to submit all proposals to impartial evaluation. There is another problem in that current methods for comparing the retrieval effectiveness of different retrieval techniques are still relatively undeveloped, and it cannot be guaranteed that the "best" representations will always be selected. Another worry is that the MPEG policy of rigorously distinguishing between image representations and the feature extraction methods used to generate them cannot always be implemented in practice. This is discussed in more detail in Chapter 12.

Whatever its merits and drawbacks, it seems certain that MPEG-7 will dominate the development of the next generation of image retrieval systems. It has the support of an impressive range of academic and industrial backers, including systems designers such as IBM and Virage and large-scale video users such as the BBC and INA, the French national film and TV archive.

It is important to remember that MPEG-7 will not of itself offer any solutions to the problems of feature extraction and matching discussed in Chapter 5. Issues such as how to identify the most appropriate similarity measures for image matching and how best to combine evidence from different sources into a single matching score will remain within the research domain well into the future. In particular, the semantic gap will remain as wide as ever. It is likely that if MPEG-7 compliant systems want to use semantic retrieval cues, these will still have to be added manually.

An important issue to note is that there are initiatives that aim to cut across the interoperability aims behind many metadata standards. Digital rights management (DRM) becomes a necessity to protect the value of content as digital multimedia spreads to many different outlets. In its current form, DRM could unfortunately work against the very goal of interoperability, as it locks up the "standardized content" using non-standardized protection mechanisms. This development is actually not even recent: many proprietary conditional access (CA) systems make standard MPEG-2 TV content inaccessible to people that happen to own the wrong set-top box – even when they can receive the signal and are willing to pay the associated content fees. In this context, MPEG-4 already provides a set of standard interfaces to proprietary intellectual property management and protection (IPMP) systems. These were a step towards a solution so that for a user to play content the user would only need to plug in the right DRM system (IPMP system). However, currently there is a problem with users downloading an IPMP system. Since 2000, MPEG started to work on more interoperable IPMP for MPEG-4 with the aim of finalizing it in 2002, while work on MPEG-21 which will include standards for Intellectual Property Management, a Rights Expression Language, and a Rights Data Dictionary is scheduled to be completed by July 2003. DRM is a very difficult issue. Content owners must be able to trust all the players that consume the content. This type of trust is very difficult to standardize; the necessary trust infrastructure is still not readily available.

7.5 Digital Rights Management

The management and protection of digital rights is currently of great concern to the providers of digital content. In the early stages of the internet there was no restriction on copying and distribution, which was actively encouraged for marketing purposes. Since it has become a serious commercial concern a variety of solutions have been suggested including:

- controlling and tracking access to and usage of digital information objects;
- securing the digital information object itself by using cryptography and watermarking technologies.

It is not always clear whether the main requirement is prevention or detection and tracking. With prevention "leakage" of the objects into the environment must not occur whereas with detection and tracking "leakage" can occur and may be regarded as inevitable but will be tracked to the redistributor. Digital watermarking is used to mark the object with identifiers such as the author's name, date and usage right. There are problems with embedding different fingerprint watermarks in each copy of original objects in the case of mass production.

There are two metadata languages that are relevant to digital rights:

- XrML – this is based on XML for describing rights, fees and conditions together with message integrity and entity authentication information (www.xrml.org) and is also based on Xerox's Digital Property Rights Language.
- Open Digital Rights Language (ODRL).

7.5.1 Usage Control Model (UCON)

UCON is a framework for all aspects of controlling and tracking access to and usage of digital objects. This includes policies, models, architecture and mechanisms employed as shown in Figure 7.2.

It deals with access control, trust management and DRM. It is intended to enable fine-grained access control whether in a centrally controlled environment or in the absence of central control, for example peer-to-peer networks (Chapter 8). The basic components of UCON models are:

1. Subject:
   - an entity that exercises rights on objects.

2. Object:
   - a digital information resource that a subject holds rights to;
   - it can be original or derivative.

3. Rights:
   - a subject's privilege to an object;
   - it can be legal or procurable;
   - it has a functional classification (read, play, print, copy rights, etc.).

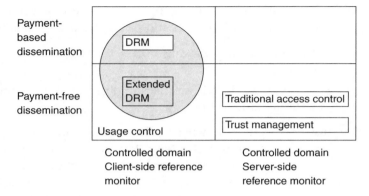

Figure 7.2   UCON security model

4. Authorization rules:
   - a set of requirements that need to be satisfied before allowing access to or use of digital objects.

5. Condition:
   - a set of decision factors that the system should verify before allowing usage of rights on a digital object, providing finer-grained authorization – these can be dynamic conditions or static conditions.

6. Obligation:
   - a mandatory list of requirements that a subject has to do **after** the exercise of rights on an object;
   - a consumer may have to accept metered payment.

The UCON model includes the following concepts:

1. The server provides the digital object and the client who receives/uses it.

2. *Control domain*. This is the area of coverage where the rights and usage on the digital objects are controlled. There are two kinds of reference monitors:
   - *Server-side reference monitor (SRM)*. This provides access control on behalf of the provider of the digital object, whether within the same organization or outside. The digital object can be stored centrally or locally. Any changes to a centrally controlled digital object are allowed. The user can copy their bank statement and annotate it – there is no control over client-side copies of digital objects. Access control and trust management are responsibilities of the server.
   - *Client-side reference monitor (CRM)*. There is no central control authority. The client needs to verify access on behalf of the provider. The control

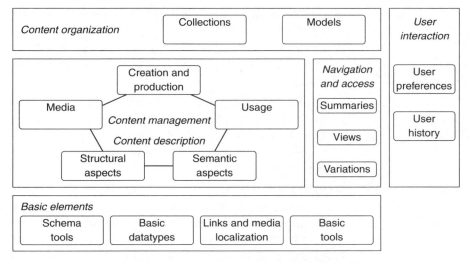

Figure 7.3   Overview of components for domain-independent metadata

mechanism is likely to be distributed. The digital object can be stored centrally or locally and changes to the digital object can be controlled.

DRM is focused on payment-based dissemination of digital objects. It can relate to client-side control without involving SRM. However, there is currently a lack of well-defined policies and models. Access control is a concept that primarily deals with access by users who are already known to the system. There is no control on strangers so this is an issue for peer-to-peer systems (Chapter 8).

Trust management deals with the authorization of previously unknown users for access purposes. It is focused on the control of the domain using SRM.

Before leaving the topic of domain independent metadata it is useful to reflect on the different components required for an effective system. Figure 7.3 provides an overview.

7.6   Domain-dependent Metadata

In addition to the general standard there are specific metadata standards being developed for some domains:

- Digital geospatial metadata (US Federal Geographic Data Committee, FGDC, http://www.fgdc.gov/metadata/metahome.html) provides a common set of terminology and definitions for the documentation of geospatial digital data. It defines a set of data elements and groups of data elements. It also defines the values the data elements can hold.

- Environmental data (UDK) was a proposal from the European Environmental catalog to enable collections of environmental data to be navigated.

- Product data exchange (PDES) was developed in the US and is related to STEP, the international standard for the exchange of product model data. This is an ANSI standard for the exchange of product model data approved by 20 countries. This is interesting because it uses the EXPRESS language.

- Rich Site Summary (RSS) is a lightweight XML vocabulary for describing metadata about websites, ideal for news syndication. RSS has evolved into a popular means of sharing content between sites (including the BBC, CNET, CNN, Disney, Forbes, ZDNet, and more). RSS is currently used for a number of applications, including news and other headline syndication, weblog syndication, and the propagation of software update lists. It is generally used for any situation when a machine-readable list of textual items and/or metadata about them needs to be distributed. A certain amount of havoc occurred when Netscape removed the RSS DTD that many sites were referencing in April 2001.

- Medical information (HL7) provides a specification for hospital records and medical information management. It was accredited by ANSI.

One of the key issues with the development of domain-dependent metadata from which different standards are evolving is whether, even though details such as element types would be different, the metadata would be based on the same basic data model and language. This would allow cross-domain interoperation.

Another interesting approach to metadata is from the ICOM/CIDOC (see Appendix B for details). This group has produced the *International Guidelines for Museum Object Information*, published in June 1995. This is a description of the information categories that can be used when developing records about the objects in museum collections. The *Guidelines* can be adopted by an individual museum, national documentation organization or system developer as the basis for a working museum documentation system. The group also developed a relational model for the organization of the metadata.

This raises the question of what kind of data model is suitable for the organization of metadata. The ICOM and early metadata standards focused on the relational model while more recently developed standards such as the RDF express concepts more akin to object-oriented approach. In Chapter 6 we looked at semantic modeling and object-oriented approaches to the design of MMDBMS. However, we recognized that there were only a few constructs available to capture relationships in the real world. We also noted the problems that are caused by multivalued attributes that feature in a number of metadata standards. These are difficult to accommodate in the traditional relational model and require the specification of collection types. The other issue with the standards is that they focus on providing a syntax for expressing metadata usually for the purpose of interoperability. This focus has nothing to tell us about the semantic nature of the metadata. In the next section we will focus on the development of domain ontologies as a means of answering this question.

7.7   Developing Ontologies

Ontology is not a new concept. The term has a long history of use in philosophy, in which it refers to the subject of existence and particularly a systematic account of existence. It is also often confused with epistemology, which is about knowledge and knowing. An ontology represents information entities such as person, artifact and event in an abstract way. We design ontologies so that we can share knowledge with and among people and possibly intelligent agents.

Ontology has both theoretical and practical aspects. It is important in content-based retrieval as we shall discover in later chapters. It is also used by intelligent mediators as we will outline in Chapter 8 (client–server architecture). In Figure 7.4 such a system is presented where wrappers are used as a means of allowing different media sources to be combined.

Ontology can provide a meaning for all conceptual modeling constructs within a domain. Therefore the development of an ontology can be useful for object-oriented modeling of the domain for database development as well as creating the ontology itself. We will look at one ontological framework in order to understand the process of constructing a domain ontology for the wine shop. There is a long tradition of ontology stretching from Aristotle to Russell. While there is a range of ontological frameworks available from different philosophical approaches we will use one that is exact and can be formally expressed because our purpose is to develop a domain ontology that would be of use to structure the semantics of the metadata of a domain.

The specific ontological constructs we will use are listed in Table 7.4, which gives the construct, its short definition and an example from the wine shop domain. The domain is based on someone's view of existing reality. Ontology distinguishes between concrete things which are called substantial individuals or entities and conceptual things. When we look at this frame-

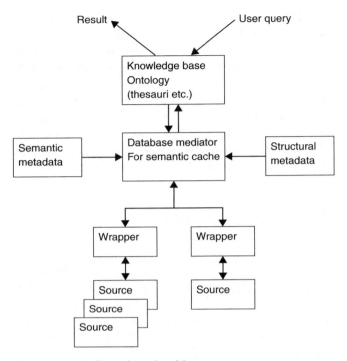

Figure 7.4   Mediator-based architecture

work we need to note that there is an overlap between the terms used in UML but also some important differences. For example, the framework distinguishes between the concepts of "property" and "attribute".

We will assume the domain can be described in terms of concrete things and the linkages between them. The idea of a concrete thing is based on it existing in physical reality in someone's mind. Therefore a bank account would qualify as a concrete thing just as much as a bottle of wine. Properties of concrete things are called properties and exist whether or not humans are aware of them. No two things can have the same set of specific properties so that a customer and an employee may be of the same kind but must have different properties. When humans conceive conceptual things in modeling, their properties are termed attributes. Humans are deemed to be aware of things only through their attributes. The notions of property and attribute are different. Attributes are characteristics assigned to models of things according to human perceptions. An attribute may or may not reflect a substantial property. Not every substantial property will be represented as an attribute. The scope of a property is the set of things that possess that property.

Table 7.4 Ontological definitions

Ontological construct	Definition	Example
Thing	Substantial individuals or concrete things	Wine bottle Winemaker
Property	All things have properties. Properties cannot have properties	Size
Mutual property	Depends on the existence of more than one thing	Being an employee depends on being a person in an organization belonging to the wine shop
Attribute	May not represent a substantial property May represent many properties that are not known explicitly Can be formalized by a predicate	Name Price (reflects quality, vintage and vineyard) Works_for(p,c,d) means person p works for company c at date d
Functional schema	Sequence of attribute functions defined on the domain	
State	The set of values of all the functions at a certain point	A combination of values such as size, price and vintage
Law	Govern the instances of natural kinds	A restriction on the values of an attribute. The location of a vineyard in a particular region is fixed
Interaction	When one thing causes another thing to change its value set. It may be indicated by a mutual property	A customer buys a bottle of wine which results in its stock decreasing
Class	A set of things	Chardonnay is a member of the grape class
Kind	The intersection of the scopes of a set of properties	All grapes belong to the same species
Composition of things	A thing can be a part of a composite thing. The composite has some properties not possessed by the individual parts	Champagne is a blend of wines from different grapes subjected to a special treatment

In Figure 7.5, concrete things (shown in bold) and some of their properties are shown as an example for the Wine Shop case study. Note we do not include any information just needed for processing and coding purposes.

In this ontology we include things with different natures – some are people, locations, organizations and biological things. If a set of things is a subclass of another set of things all the things in the first set must possess the properties of all the things in the second set, the subclass. Some members of the class will have an additional property that also makes them members of the subclass. For example, we could have a class of persons some

Wine bottle		Employee	
Properties	price	Properties	name
	bottle_size		address
	picture		salary
Wine		**Manager**	
Properties	character	Properties	name
	name		address
	pronunciation		responsibility
	category		
Cellar		**Vineyard**	
Properties	location	Properties	location
	temperature		history
Grape			address
Properties	name	**Proprietor**	
	category	Properties	name
	habit		address

Figure 7.5   Concrete things and their properties in the Wine Shop

of whom are employees who gain additional properties. Subclasses are formed by adding properties to a set of properties possessed by the class. Superclasses are formed by subtracting properties from a set of properties possessed by things in the subclass.

The concrete things – employee, manager, proprietor – have a number of common properties but each also has a special property that distinguishes them. Therefore we can recognize a superclass "people" with subclasses employee, manager, proprietor.

A kind may be different from a class. In formal terms for a particular set of properties, a kind is the intersection of all scopes of the set of properties. For example, there are different classes of grape but they all belong to the same species. A kind is defined by a set of properties and a natural kind is defined by a set of lawfully related properties. The instances of a natural kind are subject to laws that cannot change. For example, the region that a wine is associated with is fixed and determined by the location of the vineyard. Therefore type definitions that include integrity constraints can be viewed as natural kinds. UML class definitions that include methods can also be viewed as representing natural kinds. However, we should note that a class in UML is not a set or collection of actual objects; rather, it is a specification of an abstraction for generating an instance of the class. When a thing is named it will keep that name unless there are changes to its natural kind that calls for a change of name. When a thing gains or loses some properties it may change its class. When an employee buys wine from the wine shop he or she becomes a customer.

A functional schema is a finite sequence of attribute functions defined on the domain. The functional schema is defined over the set of properties that all the things in the set possess. Suppose we have a set of employees in the wine shop; we can define a function that represents the salary of the employees in a particular currency. At a particular time the function will have a value for an employee. There will be other functions to represent the employee's educational qualifications and another for their work experience. However, the functional schema may be based on a partial set of properties. The properties represented in the schema depend on the circumstances and purpose of the modeling activity.

The state concept is useful in reasoning about how things may change. The set of values of all the functions in the functional schema at a certain point represents the state of the domain. When two things interact one may cause the other to change which can be seen as a change to the value of its properties resulting in a change of state. When a customer decides to buy a bottle of wine its availability changes and therefore its state changes. There is an interaction between the customer and the wine inventory. The existence of a mutual property may indicate an interaction. When a person is employed by an organization the existence of the organization affects the state of the person. If the company ceases to exist the person will become unemployed. When a mutual property involves an interaction it is termed a binding property.

Any combination of values of the functions may represent a state. However, not all possible combinations might ever occur. When there is a restriction on the possible values this is termed a law. A law may restrict the combinations of an employee's job title and salary.

A composition is fundamental to the concept of an ontology. It deals with the concept that a thing is made of other things. A thing can have parts. It is then a complex thing. Each part is a *component_of* or *part_of* the composite thing. A composite thing can be composite if and only if at least two concrete things combine to form it. The reason we assemble things into composite things is that we are interested in some property of the composite. The composite has some property that is not possessed by any of its component parts, which we then term an emergent property. Every composite will have emergent properties such as its number of components, its structure and its overall history. As far as multimedia things are concerned it is very useful that ontology allows us to model emergent properties. The history of a composite depends on one or more of its components. It can also be useful to distinguish between connection relationships and *part_of* relationships. For example, a marriage represents a connection between a husband and a wife but both are *part_of* a family. The relationships can be:

- topological – representing a connection relationship;
- mereological – representing the *part_of* relationship.

Wines are connected to regions through topological relationships. Some wines are blends from several different vineyards or wines derived form different grape varieties – these have mereological relationships.

These categories both depend on mutual properties. A composite and its components are related via a binding mutual property. It is also possible that a mutual property that is shared by a set of components will order the components into some kind of sequence.

Identifying things in a domain is essential for eliciting the semantics of a domain. The purpose of setting out the rules is to provide a precise meaning and to reduce the semantic ambiguity. In order to develop an ontology using this framework we need to follow a set of rules. For this ontological framework the rules are:

Rule 1	Things are represented as instances. Events cannot be a thing. An event is a change of state of a thing. Properties cannot be things. Things can only be linked by mutual properties not by other things.
Rule 2	Both simple and composite things are represented by the same construct.
Rule 3	A class or a kind of thing is defined in terms of a given set of attributes and relationships. A specific thing can be an instance of several classes. Gaining or losing a property indicates that a thing has become or ceased to be an instance of a class.
Rule 4	An aggregate type must have properties in addition to its component types. A component thing must have emergent properties not possessed by any of its components. Things that are part of another thing may play different roles. When a thing has a specific role it will also become a member of a subclass.
Rule 5	All attributes and relationships of a class represent properties of things in that class. Class definitions in an ontology are based on substantial properties.
Rule 6	Intrinsic and mutual properties must have values for all possible instances. There are no optional relationships. There are no nulls.
Rule 7	Both binary relationships and higher-order relationships are represented by a mutual property/attribute.

Pragmatically, a common ontology defines the vocabulary in a level of detail that can be used in content-based queries. It also provides a set of assertions about the domain. Ontological commitments are agreements to use the shared vocabulary in a coherent and consistent manner. In short, a commitment to a common ontology is a guarantee of consistency, but not completeness, with respect to queries and assertions using the vocabulary defined in the ontology.

Returning again to the mediator architecture in Figure 7.4 we can see how the ontology can be incorporated into the design. The mediator may include the use of intelligent agents to handle the user's query. The agents need to share a common vocabulary but do not need to share the knowledge base; each knows things the others do not, and an agent that commits to an ontology is not required to answer all queries that can be formulated in the shared vocabulary.

EXERCISE 7.6

Generate an ontology based on Table 7.4 and Figure 7.5 for a family history application using the framework given above. The application should be able to include photographs and letters of members of a family over several generations. Videos may also be available for some of the younger members.

7.8 Summary of Chapter

In this chapter we considered the importance of metadata to multimedia databases. We learned how metadata standards should govern the data models and storage of multimedia data. We found how metadata could be generated and extracted from the media by the application of automatic or semi-automatic methods.

A large part of the chapter was taken up with outlining the numerous metadata standards and how they interrelate. Both domain-independent metadata standards, such as RDF, the Dublin Core and XML, and domain-dependent metadata standards were studied.

Finally we considered how domain ontologies related to metadata and how an ontology could be developed and specified for a domain.

SOLUTIONS TO EXERCISES

Exercise 7.1

Pronunciation
    Caption
    Speaker
    Format
    Duration
    English text

Picture
   Caption
   Subject
   Photographer
   Image capture
   Format

Exercise 7.2

The table needs to have an additional column with a collection data type to hold the metadata. This could be a VARRAY or a NESTED TABLE. Either could be used but the advantages of using a nested table in this case are that the order of the elements is not important, the elements can be queried and indexed.

```
CREATE TYPE picture_list AS TABLE OF VARCHAR2(25)

ALTER TABLE wine_list
ADD (meta_picture  picture_list)
```

We also need to specify a storage table.

Exercise 7.3

(a) In this case when the media object is located for update the metadata will be in the same envelope and can be updated at the same time. In this case the media object can also be retrieved by accessing the metadata first. However, there may be occasions when we want to change the metadata but not the original media object. On those occasions this may not be the optimum solution. Another issue is that if the media is stored as an external BLOB then we would be locating the metadata outside the protection of the database.

(b) This can be a better way of storing metadata particularly for external BLOBs. In addition, some retrieval processes could proceed through their early stages just based on the metadata so that the media data itself is only retrieved after a match or near match has been made to the user's query. As this is a data dictionary for metadata it may be better to store this as a central repository so that only the **dba** can change this data, which is vital for retrieval and integrity of the raw data.

Exercise 7.4

(a)
```
CREATE TABLE dublin_core
   (identifier      CHAR(10),
```

We could not create tables in Oracle with column names **resource** as this is a reserved word and we would need to change the attribute to something else for example **dc_resource**. This illustrates one of the problems of interoperability across the internet.

```
subject              VARCHAR2(80),
title                VARCHAR2(80),
creator              VARCHAR2(80),
publisher            VARCHAR2(60),
description          CLOB,
contributor          VARCHAR2(80),
subject_date         DATE,
resource             VARCHAR2(100),
format               VARCHAR2(30),
relation             VARCHAR2(100),
source               VARCHAR2(100),
language             CHAR(10),
coverage             VARCHAR2(100),
rights               VARCHAR2(100),
PRIMARY KEY(identifier))


INSERT INTO dublin_core
(identifier,subject,title,creator,publisher,subject_date)
VALUES
('1001001001','multimedia databases','Lynne
Dunckley'.'Multimedia Databases - An Object-relational
Approach','Addison-Wesley','1-Jan-2003')
```

(b) In the table above we have specified identifier as a primary key. If this were optional it would create obvious problems as it cannot be null.

(c) Allowing multivalued elements may mean that many columns would need collection data types. This would give problems for queries.

Exercise 7.5

A simple solution could be:
```
CREATE TABLE grape_dlo
(grape_name          VARCHAR2(30),
subject              VARCHAR2(80),
title                VARCHAR2(80),
creator              VARCHAR2(80),
publisher            VARCHAR2(60),
grape_description    CLOB DEFAULT EMPTY_CLOB(),,
grape_picture        BLOB DEFAULT EMPTY_BLOB(),
contributor          VARCHAR2(80),
subject_date         DATE,
resource             VARCHAR2(100),
```

```
format                 VARCHAR2(30),
relation               VARCHAR2(100),
source                 VARCHAR2(100),
language               CHAR(10),
coverage               VARCHAR2(100),
rights                 VARCHAR2(100),
PRIMARY KEY(grape_name))
```

However, the solution really needs to be more structured. The grape DLO consists of both textual description and an image. These may have different creators, dates, coverage and rights. Simply making these multivalued only adds to the confusion as we need to know which value in the creator column refers to the text and which to the image.

Exercise 7.6

In the family history ontology, events such as births, deaths and marriages are not concrete events. People in the family can take on roles such as father, mother, child. There are also links to uncles, aunts and cousins. However, these are secondary relationships. Following the rules gives a class of child with a set of substantial properties. When a child marries they acquire more properties so there must be a change of class.

Thing	Property	Mutual property
Child	Name	Mother's name
	Location of birth	Father's name
	Date of birth	
	Date of death	
	Occupation	
	Picture	
	Video	
	Gender	
Married_child	Date of marriage	Partner's name
	Location of marriage	
	Wedding picture	
	Date of divorce	

Functional Schema:

Married_to(a,b,c) means a married b at date c.

Mother_of(a,b,c) means a gave birth to b at date c.

Father_of(a,b) means a is father of b

Sibling_of(a,b) means a is the sibling of b, if and only if

Father_of(a) = Father_of(b) and Mother_of(a) = Mother_of(b).

All the other relationships can be deduced.

Recommended Reading

Applequist, D. K. (2002) *XML and SQL*, Addison-Wesley.

Baker, T. (2000) *A Grammar of Dublin Core*. GMD-German National Research Centre for Information Technology Scientific Library and Publication Services, Schloss Birlinghoven, Germany.

Boll, A., Klas, W., Sheth, A. (1998) In *Multimedia data management. Using metadata to integrate and apply digital media*, pp. 1–4.

Bunge, M. A. (1979) *Treatise on Basic Philosophy*, Vols 3 and 4, Reidel, Dordrecht, The Netherlands.

Chang, B., Scardina, M., Karun, K., Kiritzov, S., Macky, I., Ramakrishnan, N. (2000) *Oracle XML Handbook*, Singapore

Wand, Y., Storey, V. C., Weber, R. (1999) An ontological analysis of the relationship construct in conceptual modeling. *ACM Transactions on Database Systems*, **24** (4), 495–528.

Details of the RDF can be found at http://www.w3.org/TR/1999/REC-rdf-syntax-19990222

Multimedia Database Architecture and Performance

Chapter aims

This chapter reviews the role of database architecture in terms of the needs of multimedia databases. This topic is important because multimedia objects place a burden on database management systems in terms of managing storage and processing. The chapter will discuss what is meant by database architecture and why we should consider it. We will then look at the alternative architectures available in general terms and how they relate to the characteristics of multimedia data. We will need to review the extent to which architectures used for "normal" databases will be adequate to support the additional requirements of multimedia database management systems (MMDBMS). The effective management of MMDBMSs requires constant attention and involves choosing between a number of options and constraints. It will involve monitoring the performance of the database system and tuning this to fulfill its multimedia requirements.

Following this introduction we will look at specific implementations based on Oracle, DB2 and MySql to understand how choices in terms of architecture affect the performance of the database system. The contribution that different styles of architecture can contribute will then be discussed. The reader should then be able to understand in relation to multimedia data the roles of:

- multimedia architecture requirements;
- multimedia server requirements;
- distributed DBMSs;
- client–server systems;
- peer-to-peer systems;
- heterogeneous DBMSs;
- tuning and performance;
- storage parameters.

8.1 Introduction to Multimedia Architecture Requirements

There are a number of excellent texts devoted to database architecture and distributed systems. Some of these are suggested at the end of this chapter. The chapter cannot cover the whole scope of database architecture and the related performance issues. Therefore the approach has been selective, highlighting issues that are particularly important for the performance of multimedia databases.

The objective of database architecture is to obtain the best performance possible for the users of the data, paying particular attention to the specific requirements of the application. We can think of a database architecture as a structure that facilitates the database to complete a transaction. Before we consider the architecture we need to recap on what we expect from a database transaction. As a way of thinking about transactions there are four basic properties that all transactions should possess:

Atomicity	The all-or-nothing property. A transaction is an indivisible unit that is either performed in its entirety or it is not performed at all.
Consistency	A transaction must transform the database from one consistent state to another consistent state.
Independence	Transactions execute independently of one another. Transactions should not be aware of the effects of other incomplete transactions.
Durability	The effects of a successfully committed transaction should be permanently recorded in the database and must not be lost because of subsequent failure.

This is the so-called ACID test of transaction reliability. When we consider these properties they are fairly obvious requirements to keep our database reliable and consistent.

When we are using a single-user PC database where only one person is carrying out transactions at any one time the circumstances for the ACID test may appear irrelevant. However, once we are dealing with a commercial-size database with large numbers of users who may be accessing the same data at the same time these issues become important. A transaction can then only be achieved by locking the data rows involved to stop other users changing the data while our transaction is running. In a replicated database there may be more than one copy of the data that needs to be updated at the same time. The property of atomicity means that the whole transaction must be completed or it will have to be rolled back.

It is because of these issues that the architecture of multi-user databases can become complex and, with multimedia data, recognizing which architecture would be the best option is even less clear. A transaction involving multimedia data will in general be expected to take longer because of the size of the data involved. This means locks will have to be maintained for longer periods and we may also be concerned to avoid transmission of media data across networks during a transaction.

The first formal proposal for database architecture was by the DBTG (Data Base Task Group) who were appointed by the Conference on Data Systems and Languages (CODASYL, 1971) and who recognized the need for a two-layer approach to separate the user view from the system view. In 1975 this was superseded by the three-layer architecture proposed by ANSI-SPARC. Although this never became a standard it was very influential in recognizing the need for three levels of abstraction to provide data independence and a data dictionary as outlined in Figure 8.1. The external level provides the user's view of the database and consists of a number of external views of the database. The user's view is a partial view. The users will not be aware of the objects in the database that do not belong to their view. This is the way the data is seen by the individual user.

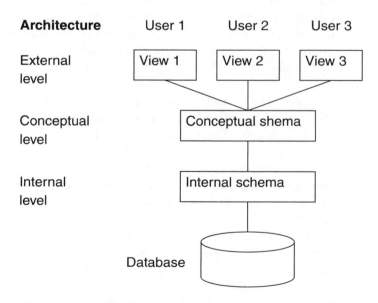

Figure 8.1 ANSI-SPARC three-level architecture

The conceptual level is the community view of the database – what data is stored and what relationships represented. This view will include constraints and semantic information about the data as well as security and integrity information. This is often known as the logical level and is the view seen by the database administrator.

The internal level is also known as the physical level. It is concerned with the way data is physically stored. Most users and even technical database staff and database developers are unaware of the details of the internal view of a relational database because there is no need for them to know about it.

In a relational database we would expect the conceptual level to be relational, consisting of tables and supporting data dictionaries. However, even in a relational database the internal level is not expected to be relational; rather, tables are stored as records, pointers, indexes etc. The relational model has nothing to say about the internal level and is ideally kept completely separate from it in the sense that the user will experience the relational model without any knowledge of the underlying physical storage. However, we would expect to see the internal view including a specification of indexes.

The organization of the physical storage will be specific to a particular DBMS. For example, later we will look at some of the issues relating to Oracle systems. For multimedia objects, performance will often depend on the rate at which information can be transferred from storage to memory for processing. The block or page is a unit of I/O – the amount of data transferred between secondary and main memory in one fetch. The block size can affect the performance of the database and we will consider it later in this chapter. In Oracle the maximum size of a block is 32K therefore even a modestly sized media object will require a number of fetch operations.

We would expect that users in multimedia systems would be restricted to interaction with the conceptual/logical level in the same way as those using a relational database because dealing directly with the internal schema would involve the risk of bypassing security and integrity constraints. However, although this strict separation is recommended in theory, dealing directly with the internal level may be the only way to obtain the required functionality and performance from multimedia systems.

In addition to operations traditionally required for databases, such as open, read, write, close and delete, in a multimedia database there will be a need for operations relating to the individual media such as play, fast forward and reverse for video while zoom and rotate are examples of operations for images. In addition, access methods are significantly different for different media, for example:

> one-dimensional objects – text and audio data are accessed in a contiguous manner (examples are ASCII strings and signal waves), which applies to text and speech;
>
> two-dimensional objects – image refers to spatial locations in two directions;
>
> three-dimensional objects – video, refers to two spatial directions and time.

The architecture of the database system will be strongly influenced by the underlying computer and network systems. For example, we shall look in turn at alternative solutions provided by:

- Centralized databases systems run on a single computer system that does not interact with other computer systems.

- In client–server systems, networking computers allows a division of work so that some tasks relating to database structure are executed on server systems and others relating to presentation to users on client systems

- Distributed database systems have been developed to handle geographically and administratively distributed data spread over multiple computer systems.

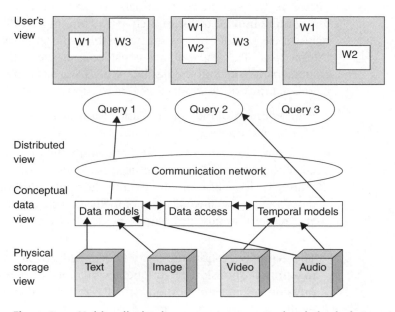

Figure 8.2   Multimedia databases – user, conceptual and physical storage views

In Figure 8.2 there is added complexity to the three-level architecture shown in Figure 8.1. The physical storage view presents the concept that multimedia databases are likely to require different storage devices with separate storage schemas that specify how the data is stored and accessed. Although the storage schema is still logically related to the conceptual data model the access, operations and file structure of the media have significant differences which have to be integrated spatially and temporally before the result can be presented to the user.

8.1.1 Multimedia Server Requirements

Multimedia databases are expensive to establish so that they are often large-scale applications, supporting thousands of users and stored media objects. The design of the media server must take into account:

- user access behavior;
- bandwidth;
- storage requirements.

Centralized databases supported the first multi-user databases, usually located in a single organization. A typical multi-user database system would need large storage capabilities and memory, may have multiple CPUs and a multi-user operating system. It serves a large number of users who are connected to the system via terminals. These terminals could be PCs or currently more limited facilities such as TVs and mobile devices. These systems may utilize parallel processing to enable a faster response to queries and transactions. This capability is considered at the end of this chapter. The characteristics of multimedia data which we have met a number of times before require any centralized system to support the following requirements:

- High volumes of information and real-time requirements – high volumes of information need large amounts of disk space.
- Real-time requirements imply bandwidth (bits per second, which is discussed in Chapter 9) and the need for policies for scheduling disk access requests. This will normally require the application of special multimedia database servers. Since the size of media objects influences storage capacity and retrieval bandwidth requirements, data compression is an important issue.
- The temporal requirements of video add considerably to the storage, making compression techniques even more important. However, compression systems must produce media – video and audio – of an acceptable quality.

In addition, the MMDBMS must support a very diverse user group, complex media formats including audio and video that require relatively large communication bandwidth and storage space. In addition, the creation and storage of multimedia objects is of little interest or value to the user in itself. The value is enhanced if the user can retrieve information quickly and on demand. We are used to existing alphanumeric databases supporting extensive interactivity. However, traditional methods of access are poorly equipped to handle the display needs of audio and video. One peculiar aspect of MMDBMSs compared with traditional databases is that the physical model may not be constant. In fact, it may need to be flexible and adaptive to predicted user demands. This is partly because the different media have different characteristics in terms of data rates and timing requirements.

There are currently three ways of realizing multimedia databases:

- using traditional data types where certain items refer to files of media data so that these act as pointers;
- based on object-oriented or object-relational database with multimedia data types but where the database is fragmented so that the media data is stored on different servers to the traditional data;
- using a fully integrated multimedia database – an ideal concept at present?

One of the important design decisions is what type and size of storage media to use. The bandwidth of the storage medium is a measure of how fast the stored data can be retrieved. Another important consideration is cost. Multimedia servers have a high capacity and they usually consist of a number of different types of storage media. A single server may include a tape library and RAM modules as well as magnetic and optical disk storage. These components have different storage and bandwidth capacities. The storage media with the best bandwidth (RAM modules) is also the most expensive. When we look at the problem of storing a database with a large number of video objects there will be a problem of how to store them as cheaply as possible. Some video objects are likely to be more popular with users than others. A cost-effective design has to take these issues into account to accommodate high demand without increasing the cost of the storage media. For example, for a video-on-demand system (see Figure 8.3), a solution would be to store very popular movies in expanded storage with the least popular stored on tape. This leads to the design of a storage hierarchy for multimedia servers. The customer demand profile must be known or at least guessed. This means there has to be an estimate of the probability of requests for the video. Highly demanded videos are then stored in the storage media with the highest bandwidth. A storage manager can act as an interface between the logical and physical layers. Above this level all accesses

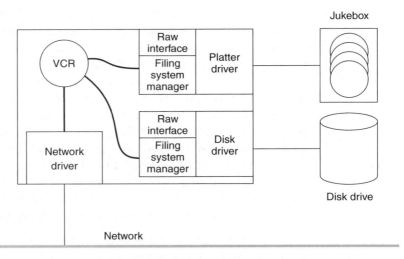

Figure 8.3   Storage devices for video-on-demand services

are to logical entities and below this level the access is to physical entities. The problems of video-on-demand applications are discussed in more detail in Chapter 12.

Continuous media such as audio and video because of their large transfer rate and storage requirements cause special storage and retrieval problems. Disk scheduling is used to achieve low service latency and high disk throughput. The bandwidth of a storage medium is a measure of how fast the stored data can be retrieved. Performance measures include total throughput, latency (time to first byte of response) and response time (time to last byte of response). For example, video-on-demand server architecture delivers video information on a schedule specified by the customer. A video stream is dedicated to each customer request. Video playback requires the periodic delivery of video frames; audio requires periodic delivery of audio samples. What is termed real-time delivery means the supplier – the disk storage system – must stream the data at a rate where the consuming display device does not suffer from "starvation". In addition, because of the large size of the media file it is also desirable to try to minimize the size of any buffer required. The ability to pause and then continue to play back continuous media will mean the system must support cueing as well. Any difference between the rate at which the media is delivered from a source to that which it is consumed must be covered by buffering. Cueing is not possible if the buffer space is limited. One way round this is to provide what is called "media on schedule" where the media is delivered on a frequent schedule. Video-on-schedule limits the customer's control over the video delivery time because the video streams are controlled by the server. The advantage is that if the timing of data retrieval is known in advance this can be used to minimize the buffer size. If the data stream can be put into the next available time slot then cueing will not be necessary if the user will accept a short delay before playback is resumed.

A video server needs to cope with both approaches and switch between them when demand requires. This means when the system is loaded the server will switch to video on schedule. If the scheduling interval is 1 minute all the requests made in that time interval will be stored up to receive the same stream so that the maximum wait for any customer is 1 minute. The picture quality of the video files depends on the video compression technology which was introduced in Chapter 2.

The characteristics of multimedia data which we have met a number of times before require any multimedia server system to support the following requirements:

- **Minimal response time**. A crucial factor for the success of multimedia services is the response time seen by the client. The server must be able to minimize response times to live up to the expectations of the user.

- **Fast processing capability and low data access rates**. To guarantee fast response times, client requests should be processed rapidly and data access rates should be minimized.

- **Reliability and availability**. Like any other kind of server, a multimedia server must be reliable. The larger the number of users and volume of data handled by the server, the more difficult it is to guarantee reliability. To provide fault tolerance, special hardware and software mechanisms must be employed. Since client requests may arrive at any time, the time the server is unavailable should be minimized. Data access refers here to fetching data from storage disks. Disks operate hundreds or even thousands of times slower than other parts of the computer system. Therefore minimizing the need for physical data access is a primary objective of database design.

- **Ability to sustain guaranteed number of streams**. Another important factor is the maximum number of data streams the server can simultaneously handle. This affects the total number of clients the server can serve.

- **Real-time delivery**. To be able to deliver multimedia data, the server should support real-time delivery. This poses profound requirements on the resource scheduling at the operating system level. The server should be able to guarantee real-time delivery for individual streams as well as for all the streams combined together. For this accurate real-time operating systems have to be developed.

- **High storage capacity**. To be able to store multimedia data and a large variety of information the server must have a large storage capacity. To sustain the delivery requirements of multimedia data, the server may be required to compress and encode video and image data prior to transport or storage. The performance of compression and signal processing should be optimized. This might require special hardware to be incorporated in the server.

- **Quality of service (QoS) requirements**. The QoS is a set of parameters describing the tolerable end-to-end delay, throughput and the level of reliability in multimedia communication and presentation. This is discussed in detail in Chapter 9 from the viewpoint of delivering multimedia data across network systems. QoS requirements of clients are an important factor that affects the usage of the server. The server should be able to provide and adapt itself to different QoS requirements, according to the characteristics of the client's terminal, the network connection and the requested data type.

- **Exploit user access patterns**. The server should also be able to trap and exploit dynamic user behavior, minimizing system load and network traffic. For example, by analyzing data access rates and times, popular data could be distributed closer to users in periods of low network load.

- **Ability to handle different types of traffic**. A multimedia server should be able to serve multiple real-time data streams simultaneously, as well as control data encountered when loading new data from other servers or storage repositories, billing and accounting data and communication between application processes.

- **Cost effectiveness**. A very important requirement governing the future of multimedia servers is cost effectiveness. The server must be affordable.

Distributed Multimedia Systems

In a distributed database system the database is stored on several computers that communicate with each other via a high speed network or telephone lines but do not share main memory or storage. A distributed multimedia system consists of three basic components – servers, networks and user terminals. The development of this architecture was driven by the need for an organization to integrate and control access to its data. The single database is split into fragments each of which is stored on one or more computers (nodes) under the control of a separate distributed database management system (DDBMS). The computers are linked by a network. Although the individual DBMS can handle local applications each DBMS will also participate in at least some global applications. However, the design adds significantly to the complexity of the system. In Table 8.1 we summarize the advantages and disadvantages of DDBMSs.

Table 8.1   Summary of advantages and disadvantages of DDBMSs

Advantages	Disadvantages
Structure can match organization	Complexity
Shareability and local autonomy	Cost
Improved availability – data can be located where needed	Security – can be accessed in range of locations
Improved reliability as more than one server involved	Integrity – difficult to maintain
Economics – cheaper individual components can be used.	Lack of experience
Modular growth – the system is not limited	Database design more complex

In a relational database that is distributed a table may be divided into a number of subrelations or fragments which can then be distributed to the various nodes. There are two main ways of fragmenting a table:

- horizontally – so that the fragments consist of all the columns but only some of the rows;
- vertically – so that the fragments consist of all the rows but only some of the columns.

This process is known as partitioning the data. As well as the types of fragmentation described above it is possible to follow a mixed strategy. The objective of the design of a DDBMS is to optimize the allocation of fragments so that they are situated where they are most needed and network traffic is minimized. Another approach to minimizing network traffic is to replicate a fragment so that duplicates are stored on several sites. Replication can improve reliability since there is another copy that can be accessed if one node fails. However, the duplicate copies of the data have to be maintained in a consistent state, so updating becomes more complex. In the case of multimedia data we need to know how often the data is updated in order to make these design decisions. If the media objects are never updated as in the case of video on demand then a distributed DBMS can be a great advantage as none of the problems associated with maintaining multiple copies of updated data consistent – the problems of record locking and deadlock – will matter. In multimedia databases where objects are liable to transaction updates more frequently there may have to be a decision to compromise between consistency and performance. In addition, replication of video objects can greatly improve performance. A user's request for a video can be directed to the server with the lightest load.

With conventional database systems the location tables in physical storage are relatively static but in the case of multimedia location is likely to be dynamic with LOBs moved to where they are likely to be requested even on a daily basis. Bad allocation of data to servers can lead to poor performance when a site becomes inundated with requests for data. Therefore design of the storage component of an MMDBMS cannot be ignored.

Factors that need to be considered include:

- using storage hierarchies that can support distributed and heterogeneous databases;
- user access to wide variety of information, including layered access and mechanisms to enable quick retrieval;
- staging, clustering and caching methods.

The example shown in Figure 8.4 has several repositories interconnected by networks. In addition to normal consideration of distribution and replication the storage hierarchy has to consider the real-time nature of the information transfers. The distributed implementation increases the availability of the information to the user by supporting several access points.

Each local subsystem can be tuned independently for user tastes within a geographical domain to give better overall performance. The system can be constructed in a regional–piecemeal fashion that supports scalability. The user may also have restricted interactivity that changes over time. This can involve scaling down the user sessions gracefully during periods of overload. Batching is the process of delaying user sessions a finite duration so that requests for a given media object can be accumulated and then satisfied *en masse*. The batching delay depends on the available bandwidth and user behavior such as reneging. In near video on demand the time is slotted and users receive movies only at the beginning of a slot. Users are allowed to perform interactive functions by switching channels. When the interaction is complete the system matches the user to a near-video-on-demand channel that is closest in time. Smooth merging is achieved by buffering. Division of time into slots allows the system to bound the merges, thereby simplifying

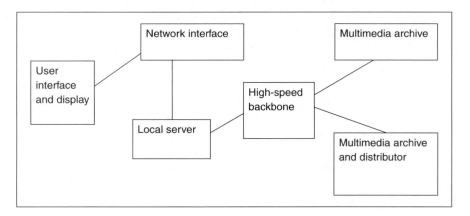

Figure 8.4   Hierarchical storage servers architecture for distributed multimedia

the operation. However, there is no guarantee that all users will get the channel they want. By understanding user behavior one can design a storage system and select an architecture that can perform as required.

The design process for multimedia systems becomes more complex since it is essential to take into account the access requirements before the distributed design is finalized.

8.1.2   Scalability in Distributed Multimedia Systems

There are a number of multimedia applications that provide interactive services for a wide range of users. To maintain the clients the system must work quickly and reliably all the time and withstand unexpected changes in the number of users and amount of data. When designing interactive multimedia systems, special attention should be paid to the scalability of the system. It might be the crucial factor for the success or failure of the service. In a distributed multimedia system scalability is extremely important. The term scalability refers to the ability of a system to continue to work even though some variables in the system change. This is important because it is well known that a solution that works well with a small problem may turn out to be impractical for the same problem when scaled up to larger size. This can happen when a system has to cope with large numbers of users or a sudden large increase in the number of transactions, or the size and number of media objects can suddenly increase. The objective of scalability is to minimize the impact of change on the system of variables.

The main factors causing scalability problems in a distributed multimedia systems are:

- **Increasing numbers of users**. Requests from users add to the network traffic in proportion to the number of requests, which is proportional to the number of users. The performance of some multimedia protocols deteriorates as the number of users increases. This issue is looked at in detail in Chapter 9.

- **Size of the data objects**. In particular, the size of audio and video files strains the network and I/O capacity, causing scalability problems.

- **Amount of accessible data**. The increasing amount of accessible data makes data search, access and management more difficult. This causes processing problems.

- **Non-uniform request distribution**. The interests of users may not be evenly distributed over the day and available servers. This puts strains on the servers and network at certain times of the day or at certain locations. Video-on-demand applications are particularly sensitive to this as different video objects tend to be requested at different times of day.

8.1.3 The Super Server Concept

Most of the existing scaling methods try to distribute the load among several servers. Problems arise with these schemes when the server selection is mainly based on system defaults or on the choice of the user. This kind of static selection can cause uneven load distribution and unnecessary network load. Instead, it would be better if an appropriate server were dynamically selected for the user.

Dynamic server selection can be implemented by the method of alternatively by mapping the requests to different servers in a local cluster. This might solve local load problems, but it cannot be used to effectively distribute the load in a widely distributed system. A scheme where the requests are directed to an appropriate server according to the location of the requested data, the current load of the servers, the location of the servers and the available network bandwidth might bring improvements to the above-mentioned schemes. This kind of approach could better adapt itself to the current state of the system. The super server concept is based on a group of servers distributed in the network. In a normal client–server system the client makes the decision which is the most appropriate server and contacts a specific server. In the super server concept the user would contact the multimedia server as a normal server, and it would then make this decision. If the requested media object is not found on the server, the server has high load or a closer server could be used, the request will be redirected to a more suitable server. The client will use this new server for future requests, as long as the server has the requested media object and its load is not too high.

This scheme will distribute users among all the available servers. If the locations of the users are taken into account, the users will in addition be directed to the closest available server having the media object in order to minimize transmission times and the number of "hops" across the network (see Chapter 9). As long as the load is low the users will be using the closest server. When the load increases some of the users will be transferred to another server. Thus all users are guaranteed service. This concept enables servers taking part in the service to provide different sets of media objects and different services. This is particularly good when servers might have different storage capacities or be specialized in some specific service.

The performance of the concept can be improved through caching. A cache is just a portion of memory that can be reserved for specific purposes. When a server does not have the media object and has a low load, the media object can be retrieved from another server and be cached. This will help distribute the load, especially if the caching scheme is constructed so that it will favor popular media objects. In the same manner, a server having problems with a high load can replicate a media object to another server and redirect clients to it.

These schemes suit only static and non-changing dynamic data. If a server providing changing dynamic data cannot sustain all requests, new distribution points could be activated. The new distribution point will distribute material from the same source. For example, if a database search engine cannot manage all requests, the service could be activated at another server. Both will, however, still use the same database for their searches. To decide where to redirect, the location of the requested media objects and information about server loads and locations must be available. The processing and gathering of this system information can be done in a distributed manner at all servers or in a centralized manner at some specified servers.

Distributed versus Centralized Super Server Architecture

There are two ways in which the processing and gathering of the location and system information could be done: in a distributed manner at all servers, or in a centralized manner at some specific servers. In the distributed super server architecture, presented in Figure 8.5, each server participating in the service gathers location and system information. To distribute the information, all servers must communicate with each other. For this a specific communication protocol is used.

In the centralized super server architecture presented in Figure 8.5, there are two kinds of servers participating in the service: normal servers, which serve the clients, and super servers, which gather location and system information. The number of super servers would depend on the size of the service. The ordinary servers monitor their own load and they know which clients to accept. If a request needs to be redirected, the information for making this decision is asked from the super server.

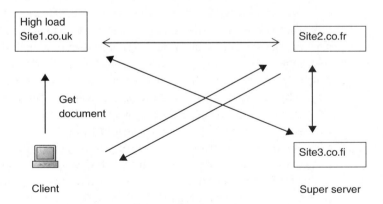

Figure 8.5   Super server architecture

One problem is that distributed architecture might cause a significant amount of network traffic, since all servers need to gather the location and system information. All servers are also taxed with the processing and gathering of requested information. The centralized server is likely to cause less network traffic, but, on the other hand, the super server can be a vulnerable point. If it fails, the whole system fails. To avoid this, there should be one or more back-up servers for the super server.

8.1.4 Client–Server Systems

It is possible to view client–server systems as a special case of distributed systems where certain sites are designated as clients and others as servers. All data resides at the server site but all applications execute on the clients and the system does not provide full location independence. While we will not cover client–server systems in any detail in this book there are two developments that are relevant to MMDBMSs. These are:

- the DataLinks specification part of the SQL3 standard (management of external data);
- the development of intelligent middleware.

Although the DataLinks concept has been implemented by a number of database providers we will illustrate the approach with one, DB2.

DataLinks DB2 Universal Database
The idea of DataLinks is to enable organizations to store large unstructured and semi-structured data objects in a file system located near a relational database. This approach it is claimed gives good speed of access and allows existing applications to incorporate multimedia with no changes to them. Some large objects, particularly video and audio objects, need to be streamed out to the client within a specified timescale. Database servers do not generally have these capabilities. Database functions such as the parser and optimizer (discussed later) slow data transmission to a level that is not acceptable for the real-time nature of some media. Location of large objects is critical to minimize network traffic. However, a key reason for wanting to incorporate large objects within the database is the need to manage access and security. DB2 solves this problem by using DataLinks to enable SQL to provide a transparent interface to the data stored in both the DBMS and the external files. It can be thought of as extending the reach of the database to the operating system files. It provides referential integrity that ensures that users cannot delete or rename any external file that is referenced in the database. It also provides access control to grant or deny a user the ability to read a referenced external file. DB2 also exerts transactional control over the external

data to preserve the logical consistency of the data as well as back-up and recovery.

In a DataLinks environment DB2 provides the metadata repository for external data. Attributes and subsets of the external data are stored in external files and maintained as DB2 tables within the database along with logical references to the external files (e.g. server_name.file_name). SQL can be used to query the database in the normal way using metadata attributes to locate the external files requested. In order to enable the linkage the table specification must include a DATALINK data type. In addition there must be "DB Links Manager Software" on the file server. This can run on a variety of platforms so that it facilitates heterogeneous database systems. A single DB2 database can access media files stored in multiple distributed file systems.

Before linking an external file to the database the application independently of the DataLinks Manager creates the file in the file system. A column defined with a DATALINK datatype is included in a CREATE TABLE statement. We can show how the employee table could be altered to enable this, as follows:

```
CREATE TABLE employee
(employee_number  CHAR(4),
employee_name     VARCHAR2(30),
salary            NUMBER(6,2),
start_date        DATE,
picture           DATALINK(200)
                  LINKTYPE URL
                  FILE LINK CONTROL
                      INTEGRITY ALL
                      READ PERMISSION DB
                      WRITE PERMISSION blocked
                      RECOBERY yes
                      ON UNLINK restore
)
```

This statement creates a table that includes a column picture with a DATALINK data type with read access control over the referenced files by the DBMS named DB2. This would be followed by an SQL INSERT statement that causes DB2 to initiate a LinkFile operation through the data links file manager (DLFM) shown in Figure 8.6 which inserts a URL value into the DATALINK column. This establishes the correct level of DBMS control over the file. An SQL DELETE statement will delete the row as well as the URL link. The DataLinks Filesystem Filter (DLFF) intercepts certain file system calls (file open, rename, file delete) issued by the database applications. The

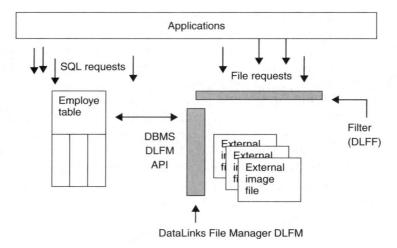

Figure 8.6 DataLinks architecture

DLFF will enforce referential integrity on any file referenced in the database. This avoids dangling pointers to files that no longer exist.

Intelligent Middleware

After client–server systems were developed, it was recognized that there was a need to exchange information across systems developed by different vendors, e.g. Oracle, Ingres and DB2, so the information could be integrated between them. In order to achieve this so-called "three-tier systems" were developed that included a gateway to manage the connections between the databases and deal with the semantic mismatch across the disparate systems. The gateway will need to make use of dynamic SQL or use a call-level inter-face such as SQL/CLI or ODBC. These systems are now called middleware or mediators, as illustrated in Figure 8.7.

There are two relevant standards that are applicable:

- ISO Remote Data Access (RDA) which defines formats and protocols for client–server systems;

- IBM's Distributed Relational Database Architecture (DRDA) which is a *de facto* standard based on IBM's protocols and formats.

In a large system there will be many servers, providing data from local and from external resources. There are a number of terms that are used in this area that we can distinguish:

- multi-database systems – allowing queries to address more than one independent source database;

- federated databases – integrated schemas to support joins over multiple, consistent databases;
- wrappers – server front-end software to provide SQL access to non-database files or legacy databases;
- knobots – software agents search for relevant data through multiple databases or the web.

However, mediators which would operate in the mediation layer shown in Figure 8.7 are expected to offer more facilities, such as:

- resolution of scope mismatches – scope mismatch occurs when the rows kept in a table from source **A** do not cover the same set of items collected in source **B**;
- abstraction to bring material to matching levels of granularity for integration;
- omission of replicated information that exists on more than one source but in differing forms;
- interpolation or extrapolation to match differences in temporal data.

Most of the activity in terms of mediators has been focused on business applications, particularly OLAP where there is a need to aggregate data from different systems, some of which are likely to be legacy systems. In terms of multimedia the main issues until now have been compression formats and applications that involve composing media. However, metadata standards

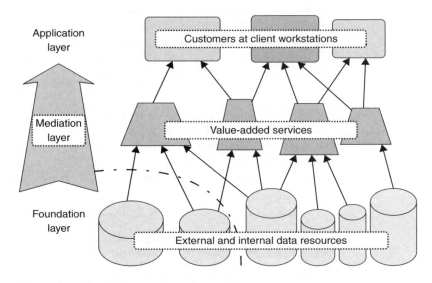

Figure 8.7   **Three-tier systems using mediators**

such as RDF and DCI (Chapter 7) allow qualifiers to modify the values of attributes. A mediation layer may be one way to reconcile the use of different qualifiers across networked systems. These issues are particularly important for medical imaging applications and are covered in more detail in Chapter 11.

To be effective mediators should also agree on the vocabulary and its structure, i.e. the ontology. For this purpose a Knowledge Query and Manipulation Language (KQML) has been developed with support from DARPA, which provides further desirable features, but some of them are now appearing in CORBA and its successors as well.

8.1.5 Peer-to-Peer Networks

This is a type of network in which each workstation has equivalent capabilities and responsibilities. The concept differs from client–server architectures, in which some computers are dedicated to serving the others. A peer-to-peer (P2P) application is different from the traditional client–server model because the applications involved act as both clients and servers. That is to say, while they are able to request information from other servers, they also have the ability to act as a server and respond to requests for information from other clients at the same time. This approach increases the amount of value that each node on the network can add because it not only takes information from a source but also has the ability to share that information with other sources.

P2P networks are generally simpler, but they usually do not offer the same performance under heavy loads. P2P is an architecture that is intended to link and exploit all available networked technology, including CPUs, storage, files, data, metadata and network availability. It enables users, applications and systems to centrally find and locally bind all network resources (i.e. transfer, translate or integrate them).

In the client–server model, the web server cannot arbitrarily contact the browser. The "conversation" is always initiated by the client. In a client–server system, the application finds other peers by registering with a central server that maintains a list of all applications currently willing to share and giving that list to any new applications as they connect to the network. Peers can be located by means such as network broadcasting or discovery algorithms.

A typical P2P application will display the following key features:

- *Discovering other peers*. The application must be able to find other applications that are willing to share information.
- *Querying peers for content*. Once these peers have been discovered, the application can ask them for the content that is desired by the application.

Content requests often come from users, but it is highly likely that the P2P application is running a query independently as a result of some other network request that came to it rather than a specific request made by a user at that machine.

- *Sharing content with other peers.* In the same way that the peer can ask others for content, it can also share content after it has been discovered.

There are a number of design options to consider when designing a P2P application. The decisions made about the architecture for a P2P application will have a significant impact on the type of features that the application is able to offer and, therefore, the users' experience. The range of applications in this area can be thought of as a continuum from what could be called pure P2P to pure client–server.

As shown in Figure 8.8, a pure P2P application has no identifiable central server in control of the system. A node dynamically discovers other peers on the network and interacts with each of them by sending requests and receiving content. The strength of this type of application is that it does not rely on any one server being available to accept a node's registration and location in order for other peers to be able to find it. At the same time, the lack of a central discovery server poses a problem because a relatively low number of clients can be discovered, thereby limiting the application's reach. In this scenario, a peer can either use information from a local configuration scheme to discover the clients (for example, a configuration entry that tells it who to talk with) or employ network broadcasting and discovery techniques such as IP multicast (see Chapter 9) to discover the other peers.

The core features of a P2P application would include:

- A P2P application should be able to locate other peers in the network.
- Once an application is able to locate other peers, it should be able to communicate with them using messages.
- Once the communication is established with other peers, the application should be able to receive and provide information, such as content.

One problem is that P2P creates an inherently unstable environment because of the nature of the connectivity and unpredictable network addressing. None of the control expected in traditional database systems

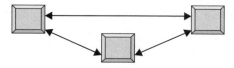

Figure 8.8   P2P network

is necessarily present. This chaotic state complicates authentication, authorization and access management.

Another P2P limitation is that the paradigm is based on the assumption that metadata will be pervasive, timely and accurate. Access to structured metadata within a central repository is required to enable P2P systems to find relevant content spread across a distributed network. P2P could eliminate the costs and management problems associated with more resource-intensive distributed approaches. Metadata, as we know, if well designed, could facilitate rapid attribute-based search and retrieval. However, at this point metadata is not commonly available and there are a number of competing standards. Therefore, for P2P applications to be effective in the present circumstances, data providers need to maintain their own discipline in systems, data and metadata design.

The first P2P systems developed (such as Napster, Gnutella and Freenet) were bottom-up technologies that led to the development of *ad hoc* communities that wanted to take advantage of rapidly decreasing communication costs to share information without centralized coordination or control. File sharing in P2P systems involves increased network bandwidth requirements that must be balanced against reduced time in information access, calculation and processing. By contrast, distributed computing offers a top-down approach that allows a computing problem to be spread across large numbers of processors.

It is possible that P2P technology will radically change business models and enterprise technology management approaches since it addresses an exponentially growing demand for more and faster information. When centrally coordinated, P2P computing may have dramatic implications for solving complex and costly IT problems, including data discovery, acquisition and life-cycle management. However, P2P computing may have a minor impact in multimedia retrieval because as we have seen in Chapter 5 this can be very computationally intensive.

The Peer-to-Peer Working Group, formed in October 2000, was put together to aid in the advancement of infrastructure standards for P2P computing. This group is a consortium of corporations dedicated to developing industry standards and non-proprietary norms for P2P computing technology as this is viewed as essential to promote the adoption of P2P technologies. The Working Group plans to provide specification definitions for such issues as:

- interoperability and performance of computing devices;
- security;
- management;
- privacy of data stored in web devices;

- common protocols for the way that information flows between, and is shared by, users of P2P devices.

  A number of problems have been predicted for P2P systems:

- *Network bandwidth.* If companies use P2P and web services based applications, it may severely slow down their network connections and hamper core business activities. By definition, P2P applications eliminate central servers and create a loose, dynamic network of peers. For any content retrieval operation, such as a search for a specific item in a catalog, all the peers in the network are searched, using a lot of network bandwidth. As the P2P network size increases and becomes more distributed, it may be affected by poor and slow connections.

- *Security.* The most important feature of the P2P-based application – decentralized, distributed architecture – is also its weakest link. P2P systems typically have very strong security if they are run as a closed system, as in enterprise application integration. However, with P2P open systems for business-to-business integration (B2Bi) the security risks are much higher.

- *Complex architectures leading to difficult maintenance.* The architecture of P2P-based applications with or without web services is extremely complex as it involves use of distributed resources in an optimal way, making decentralized and independent systems work as one. Security is also an issue. Maintenance of such applications is much more difficult since it is extremely tough to identify, replicate and fix network-related problems.

8.1.6   Heterogeneous Distributed DBMS

A distributed database may be classified as homogeneous or heterogeneous. In a homogeneous system all the sites use the same DBMS system and therefore the schemas and underlying data model will be consistent. In a heterogeneous system there may be different DBMS products and several different data models may be included. For example, there could be networked, relational, object-oriented and object-relational data models within the system. This may be the result of individual sites developing individual databases that were later integrated. It can also be the result of combining legacy systems with newer systems that may be object-oriented or object-relational databases. A number of MMDBMS applications tend to fall into this category.

The user interface or the terminal deals with the issues related to presentation and manipulation of multimedia objects and the interaction with the user. The network provides the communication mechanism between the user and the server. The server is responsible for managing multimedia

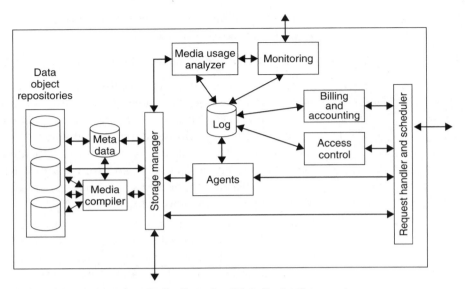

Figure 8.9   Heterogeneous distributed multimedia database system

databases and composing general multimedia objects for the users. The composition of an object is a complex process of integrating and synchronizing
multimedia data for transport, display and manipulation. The system
usually consists of multiple users, servers and networks as illustrated in
Figure 8.9. This shows an MMDBMS that includes data repositories linked to
both metadata and media compliers that would be responsible for interpreting the query and composing the result set. A storage manager is responsible
for dynamically managing the internal schemas. Other utilities deal with
access control and accounting functions.

8.2   Performance Issues in Specific Implementations

Earlier in the chapter we mentioned that normal database functions such as
parsing and optimizing queries could reduce the performance of multimedia
systems. We will start this topic by looking at the way Oracle's architecture
processes users' requests. For example, the following statement will be executed by SQL*PLUS (which can be regarded as a user process that will request
data from the server process):

```
SELECT    wine_name, price
FROM      wine_list
WHERE     region = 'Chile'
ORDER BY  price
```

The way Oracle fetches data from disk depends on whether it uses an index. In the case where there is no index Oracle processes the table one row at a time. This is called a full table scan. Processing with an index will significantly reduce the I/O processes. Oracle will then be able to locate a row in an index, read the **rowid** and retrieve the correct block from this address into memory.

Tuning involves managing the allocation of memory and the I/O stream. Performance of I/O has not improved at the same pace as improvements in CPU. Therefore one of the objectives of database tuning will be to minimize the amount of I/O processing. This is particularly the case with multimedia. We may be dealing with huge objects so any way we can avoid a full table scan will be a great benefit.

In an Oracle system a user process such as the SQL statement above will request information from the database. We describe the processing of an SQL statement by the DBMS in three steps – **parsing**, **planning** and **execution**. The first step in processing an SQL statement is parsing, which accepts a statement as just a string of characters and checks that it is valid SQL. This involves examining each term in the statement to ensure that it is an SQL keyword, such as SELECT or WHERE, the name of a table or column that already exists in the database or a literal string convertible to a data value; all terms must be correctly sequenced according to the rules of SQL grammar. Checking names is done by reference to the system tables (the data dictionary). These can be used to confirm that the names relate to valid tables and columns and that data types are compatible with their use in the statement. The result of this step is either a valid statement for input to the next step or termination of processing together with a message identifying any errors that have been found.

The next step is **planning**, which is concerned with producing a processing plan that specifies how a statement should be executed in terms of a sequence of basic table operations, such as restrict or project. In this statement

```
SELECT      wine_name, price
FROM        wine_list
WHERE       region = 'Chile'
ORDER BY    price
```

there is a restriction operation specified by *WHERE region = 'Chile'* and a projection operation so that the result set only consists of the columns **wine_name** and **price**. Processing will be faster if we can deal with smaller tables at every step. In this case the region column is required for the restriction so this has to be carried out before the projection which would result in the loss of the information in the region column.

While there may be just one way of executing a very simple query or update, a more complex query may be executed in several different ways depending on alternatives such as the sequence in which basic operations are executed and whether indexes are to be used. Thus different plans are possible, and a DBMS uses system tables to obtain details of how data is stored and accessed, and chooses one plan as the "best". This evaluation of plans is often referred to as **optimization**. It is a complex topic that we shall consider separately in the next section.

All SQL statements are processed in three phases

- parse – the most time-consuming and costly in processing terms since it involves optimizing the query, checking the syntax, determining execution plan and access path;
- execute – performs the reads, locks and writes required by the plan;
- fetch – rows are retrieved, formatted and displayed.

Performance, as we shall see later, can be improved by using queries already in the shared SQL pool. So we need to ensure that there is adequate space to accommodate an optimal number of ready-parsed statements.

During the process of executing a query Oracle uses the data dictionary to check who is allowed to log into the database and what tables and other objects the user can access. Oracle builds up an execution plan which is a kind of map that can be followed to get the data needed for the query. The plan is built up using statistics about the data that reside in the data dictionary. When Oracle builds the plan it looks for the shortest and lowest cost route.

In Oracle the SQL statement is passed to the server process through the system global area (SGA). This is a memory area that is shared by all the server and client processes. The SGA has four main components:

- data buffer cache;
- dictionary cache;
- transaction cache (also called the redo log buffer);
- program cache (also called the shared SQL pool).

The two largest areas are the SQL pool and the data buffer cache and they can directly affect database performance. In this case Oracle reserves SGA to do a specific kind of process. The server process takes requests from the user process and communicates with the database through a series of simple steps. The user statement must be transferred into the SGA before it is parsed (checked for validity) and then executed. The required data is read from the data file, retrieved into the data cache. The user process can then read the **wine_name** and **price** and pass this information back to the user.

When the next statement is executed the database is changed. The process will proceed as described above but the old value of the data to be changed will be stored in a rollback segment.

```
UPDATE employee
SET employee_detail=person_t ('John', 'Smith', '17-Mar-1955')
WHERE employee_number='1234',
```

All communications take place via memory but this has a finite size which becomes a serious issue for LOBs whether these are text-based CLOBs or BLOBs or BFILEs. Therefore memory needs to be used efficiently. Oracle maintains a shared SQL area known as the SQL pool. When an SQL statement is passed to Oracle it searches the pool to check whether there is an identical statement in the pool; if it finds a match it executes the statement already in the pool.

This process is illustrated in Figure 8.10 where we can see the following information flows:

User to memory	Requests for data from applications are assembled in memory where Oracle decides the most efficient way to retrieve the data
Memory to user	Results of queries are returned from memory to the user session
Disk to memory	As requests are received data required is transferred to memory
Memory to disk	Data changed or created is transferred to disk
In the case of Q1	The query can be satisfied in memory since the prepared SQL statement Q1 as well as the results reside in the SQL pool
In the case of Q2	There is no statement in memory so the query must be prepared but the query can be satisfied in memory since the results still reside in the SQL pool
In the case of Q3	The prepared SQL query is in memory but the results have been removed, new data must be read from disk and the results placed in memory
In the case of Q4	There is no statement in memory so the query must be prepared, the data read from disk, results put into memory, data returned to the user

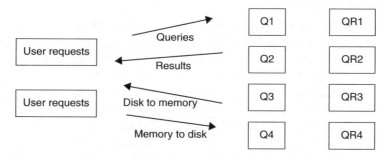

Figure 8.10 Flow of information from database to users

The last case is the most undesirable as it takes the longest. Access to data in memory is much quicker than access from disk. So it is desirable to get as much information as possible into memory. However, we know that multimedia data can include LOBs of gigantic size so this kind of process should involve LOB_locators not the data itself. When the statement is matched in the pool it is checked character by character. Therefore when we write code that we want to reuse in this way we will need to stick to strict conventions such as upper and lower case for key words and also watch spaces.

We can check what is in the shared pool by using a data dictionary view called v$sqlarea (owned by SYS), that has a column called sqltext, as follows:

```
SELECT sql_text
FROM v$sqlarea
WHERE lower(sql_text) LIKE ('%'||'&text'||'%')
```
show_pool

This will allow the user to specify any text at run time by using the *&text* substitution variable. For example, if we entered "wine_list" as the *&text* string this would be substituted in the query with the result that all queries in the shared pool that included **wine_list** any where would be displayed. The statement would then result in the following:

```
SQL_TEXT
------------------------------------------------------------
SELECT wine_name, price from scott.wine_list
WHERE region = 'Chile'
select * from scott.wine_list WHERE region = 'Chile'
```

We now understand that there are always a number of options a DBMS can select from when executing even a moderately complex query. When the query involves transmission of data across the network the performance issues can be even more significant. In the next section we look at the facilities available to manage the process of optimizing transactions.

8.2.1 Optimization

An action path is the method the database system, Oracle, determines to retrieve the data. The path depends on the locks in use and the session environment. The optimizer is a set of internal routines that decides on the most efficient path to the data. Early optimizers in Oracle used a rule-based approach to decide access paths. For example, if a query involves restriction and projection operations it may be more efficient to carry out the projection first so that the selection is carried out on a smaller set of data. This approach has generally been replaced by a cost-based approach that takes into account statistics such a retrieval times for different data. In a networked situation this is a better way for optimizing.

Cost-based optimization assumes that queries are executed on a multi-user system where the query is unlikely to be already available in the buffer cache. Thus, a plan being selected by the cost-based optimizer may not be the best plan for a single-user system with a large buffer cache. Furthermore, timing a query plan on a single-user system with a large cache may not be a good predictor of performance for the same query on a busy multiuser system. In Oracle the cost-based optimizer (CBO) carries out a process that weighs various factors that can affect the performance of executing an SQL statement and computes the cost for an execution plan. This includes the cost of I/O and CPU processes and the time to complete the execution. To work it needs information about the number of rows in each table involved, the distribution of keys, the number of data blocks occupied and allocated to the tables. This data has to be collected periodically and used to populate relevant tables in the data dictionary. The data can be collected or estimated. The problem is the collection process involves locking the tables. The keyword ANALYZE collects the statistics, for example

```
ANALYZE INDEX scott.wine_name_x COMPUTE STATISTICS;
```

Some tables will not have their statistics collected if they cannot have all their rows locked so it is important to use scripts that will report tables that fail to be analyzed so that the process can be repeated at another time.

Alternatively, the statistics can be estimated on a sample (e.g. 20%) of rows:

```
ANALYZE INDEX scott.wine_name_x ESTIMATE STATISTICS SAMPLE 20
PERCENT;
```

Analyzing a table uses more system resources than analyzing an index. It may be helpful to analyze the indexes for a table separately, or collect statistics during index creation with a higher sampling rate.

In addition, *Oracle8i* makes available DBMS_STATS, a package of routines to collect statistics of objects in the data dictionary.

The optimizing approach is set up when we start a session. The common alternatives are as follows:

all_rows	Involves whole tables of data and uses the CBO approach. This will take into account the size of the tables when it executes SQL statements
first_rows	Works as the previous option but is used for screen-based activity where users typically look at first few rows
choose	This is the default setting, if one table involved has statistics available the others will be estimated. If there are no statistics it will follow rule-based approach
rule	Follows a set of rules rather than any statistical data such as "is this table indexed?"

The following statement will alter the current session so that the "choose" approach will be adopted:

```
ALTER SESSION SET OPTIMIZER_GOAL =CHOOSE;
```

An alternative approach can be taken as the **system** user:

```
ANALYZE TABLE scott.wine_list ESTIMATE STATISTICS;
```

After running ANALYZE we can see the results by querying the system table called **user_tables** to view the statistics on the wine_list table:

```
SELECT num_rows, blocks, empty_blocks, avg_row_len, chain_cnt

FROM user_tables

WHERE table_name = 'scott.wine_list';

Sample output Statistics
------------------------------------------
      137 recursive calls
        0 db block gets
       48 consistent gets
       14 physical reads
       60 redo size
     1150 bytes sent via SQL*Net to client
      639 bytes received via SQL*Net from client
        3 SQL*Net roundtrips to/from client
        3 sorts (memory)
        0 sorts (disk)
        0 rows processed
```

Note that in order to carry out this process we need also to have the privilege granted:

```
GRANT ANALYZE ANY TO scott;
```

When we adopt an object-relational design it is important to note that user-defined structures, such as columns, standalone functions, types, packages, indexes and index types, are generally "opaque" to the optimizer. That is, the optimizer does not have statistics about these structures, nor can it compute accurate selectivities or costs for queries that use them. This is an area that needs attention because we need to know what impact adopting an object approach will have on the performance of the database.

For this reason, Oracle strongly encourages the developer to provide statistics collection, selectivity and cost functions for user-defined structures.

This is because the optimizer defaults can be inaccurate and lead to expensive execution plans. In addition users can be misled into concluding that using objects and other user-defined types will lead to poor performance.

Another utility that can help to provide insight is EXPLAIN PLAN. Its output shows how Oracle executes SQL statements. EXPLAIN PLAN results alone, however, cannot differentiate between well-tuned statements and those that perform poorly. For example, if EXPLAIN PLAN output shows that a statement uses an index, this does not mean the statement runs efficiently. Sometimes using indexes can be extremely inefficient. It is thus best to use EXPLAIN PLAN to determine an access plan and later prove it is the optimal plan through testing. Before we can use EXPLAIN PLAN we must be granted access to the **plan_table** which is created by running the script **utlxplan.sql**.

When evaluating a plan, we should always examine the statement's actual resource consumption. It is possible to check the plan Oracle is using to execute a statement in SQL*PLUS as follows:

```
EXPLAIN PLAN SET STATEMENT_id='Wine_1'
FOR
SELECT     wine_name, price
FROM  scott.wine_list
WHERE      region='Chile'
```

STATEMENT_id is the unique character string that identifies the code. The result of the request will be stored in the **plan_table** which belongs to the SYS user. This is a rather large table to check but it is possible to use the next statement saved as a script that uses the DECODE function to format the output of the **plan_table**:

```
SELECT DECODE(id,0,operation||' Cost = '||position,
       LPAD(' ',2*(LEVEL-1)||LEVEL||'.'||POSITION)||' '||
       OPERATION||' '||OPTIONS||' '||OBJECT_NAME||' '||OBJECT_TYPE)
                                                     QUERY_PLAN
FROM plan_table                         plan_table
```

This would produce a formatted single-column output called QUERY_PLAN as follows:

```
QUERY_PLAN
-------------------------
SELECT STATEMENT    Cost = 1
TABLE ACCESS FULL WINE_LIST
```

In the next example we use a statement that requires a JOIN from the employee and department tables. EXPLAIN PLAN will show how the data has been accessed and whether any indexes have been used.

```
EXPLAIN PLAN
FOR
SELECT employee_number,employee_name, start_date,
department_name
FROM employee, department
WHERE employee.department_number=department.department_number;
```

This time the output is more detailed.

```
QUERY_PLAN
--------------------------------------------------
SELECT STATEMENT     Cost = 2
NESTED LOOPS
TABLE ACCESS FULL EMPLOYEE
TABLE ACCESS BY INDEX ROWID DEPARTMENT
INDEX UNIQUE SCAN PRIM_DEPT UNIQUE
```

The output shows that a full table span which is a costly process was carried out on the **employee** table but an index based on the primary key of the **department** table was used to match the **department_number** in the **department** table to the value in the row retrieved by the full scan of the **employee** table.

Adding a multimedia component can significantly increase costs; for example, the following query from Chapter 10 involves processing a small amount of CLOB data:

```
EXPLAIN PLAN
FOR
SELECT DISTINCT category
FROM wine_list
WHERE DBMS_LOB.INSTR(note, 'Ideal as an aperitif')>0
```

This produces

```
SELECT STATEMENT     Cost = 3
SORT UNIQUE
TABLE ACCESS FULL WINE_LIST
```

This shows a much increased cost when CLOB processing is involved in a full table scan. Note that LOB data is not stored directly with the rest of the table data. Storing data out of line means the LOB data will not be scanned, only the lob_locator, and then the LOB data only read when it is required. It is also worth considering experimenting with indexing LOB columns and retesting.

A number of system tables are provided by Oracle to gather statistics that the database administrator can use for tuning the database. An alternative to EXPLAIN PLAN is to use SET AUTOTRACE ON.

SQL TRACE and **tkprof** are other utilities that provide performance information. They will tell us the time spent on parse, execute and fetch phases of statement execution. They will also tell us the percentage of logical reads and physical reads. Performance is improved if we can keep significant amounts of data dictionary information and data in memory.

This can be set in the session with

```
ALTER SESSION SET TIMED_STATISTICS =TRUE
```

At the start of an SQL script we can also add

```
ALTER SESSION SET SQL_TRACE= TRUE
```

While developing a program this is very useful but needs to be removed when the program is provided for users because this process generates a large trace file.

To summarize, by looking at the parse, execute and fetch lines in the output it is possible to see how the SQL statements are performing. User-defined types and functions need special routines to be developed to monitor their performance.

8.2.2   Tablespaces

The internal schema of a database (Figure 8.1) is generally stored in many files. In using the term "file", it should be noted that most relational DBMSs assign tables to some kind of storage area and use a separate specification to relate these storage areas to the usual operating system files. Terms such as **partition**, **tablespace**, **database space** or **dbspace** are used to refer to such storage areas. We shall continue to use "file" as a general term for a storage area for tables.

In Oracle a database is physically a collection of data files which are grouped together. It does this by using the concept of a tablespace. There must be a tablespace with a unique name in existence before a database can be created and objects stored in the tablespace. Table 8.2 lists an example of a typical tablespace arrangement.

Table 8.2   Example of a typical Oracle tablespace

Tablespace name	Purpose
System	Required tablespace for information about tablespaces, data files and contents
Temp	For temporary files
Tools	For storing the database objects needed to support tools
Users	For holding users' database objects
Data and index	Optional tablespaces for application data and index files
Rollback	For storage of data needed to undo an action on the database such as rollback segments so that the database can recover from aborted transactions

An important decision for the MMDBMS designer is the organization of the tablespace. Performance can also be improved by locating database files and indexes carefully. For example, tables can be stored on a separate disk to indexes. This is achieved by creating a tablespace for indexes. Separating tables from their indexes allows quicker access since read/write can then be simultaneous. All processes will involve accessing the system tables so ideally these should be on a different disk and users should not place their objects in the system tablespace. Temporary segments are objects the database creates to help them when performing GROUP BY clauses. These temporary objects should be in their own tablespaces. Rollback segments have a tendency to grow and shrink as transactions are being processed and therefore it is of benefit to have these in a separate tablespace.

A tablespace is related to a physical file that must exist within the system. It has to be created by a separate statement that relates it directly to a file, specified by the file's name which can include a path that enables the file to be located anywhere. The use of a tablespace name is just a way of simplifying references to a file. The following statement will create a tablespace called **users** providing the folders already exist in the operating system directory. Its size will be limited to 2M.

```
CREATE TABLESPACE users DATAFILE 'D:/oradata/users_01.dbf'
SIZE 2M EXTENT MANAGEMENT LOCAL AUTOALLOCATE;
```

This is another example:

```
CREATE TABLESPACE media DATAFILE 'D:/oradata/media_01.dbf'
SIZE 1M EXTENT MANAGEMENT LOCAL AUTOALLOCATE;
```

Note that, after the tablespace has been created this way, the files specified cannot be deleted through the operating system unless the tablespace is first dropped with the statement

```
DROP TABLESPACE users
```

However, this statement could fail because of problems with integrity constraints. The following statement should result in the removal of the tablespace **users:**

```
DROP TABLESPACE users INCLUDING CONTENTS CASCADE CONSTRAINTS
```

Since a DBMS usually allows a database to be stored in many files, we will need to specify where each table is stored. This specification is often included as part of the table definition in a simple syntax, such as

```
CREATE TABLE wine_list (wine_code ...)
   IN media
```

In this definition, the name **media** determines where data for the **wine_list** table is to be stored – the name **media** identifies a **tablespace**.

In Oracle any physical object is stored as a segment – an independent subunit. A segment may be made up of many extents within a single tablespace and can be spread across many data files. The AUTOALLOCATE parameter used in the example above will prevent users from specifying an extent size when creating objects in the tablespace. This statement will create a locally managed tablespace that uses bit maps to track extents and can manage space more efficiently. In Oracle a block can vary in size from 2K to 32K. The block size of the database is set when it is created. When a data block is too full to hold any more data Oracle places data in another block. It maintains a list in memory of free data blocks. With multimedia data large numbers of blocks (even when set at 32K) are likely to be involved. Note, however, that Lewis (2001) recommends small block sizes for LOBs. For example, in Chapter 4 we created the employee table but we could replace the definition to set the storage parameters when it was created as follows:

```
CREATE TABLE employee
(employee_number  CHAR(4),
employee_name     VARCHAR2(30),
salary            NUMBER(6,2),
start_date        DATE,
CONSTRAINT prim_emp PRIMARY KEY(employee_number)
      USING INDEX
      PCTFREE 2
      STORAGE (INITIAL 1M MAXEXTENTS UNLIMITED PCTINCREASE 0)
            TABLESPACE users)
```

Associated with each file there are many implementation parameters. For example, there is choice of block size, the amount of space to be allocated to data (the size of which is either fixed or increased automatically as data is added) and the number and size of input/output buffers (memory areas where file data is placed). As with other aspects of storage, for each such parameter an MMDBMS developer has to decide whether it should be fixed in the DBMS, or be the same for all databases or be different for each one. In the last case there is the further choice of how a parameter is decided for a given file – in particular, does a DBMS calculate it or should a database administrator be allowed to specify a parameter according to the requirements for their database? The main storage parameters available for Oracle are listed in Table 8.3.

In Oracle it is possible to set storage parameters at the time a table is created in this way. However, there are a number of constraints on these

Table 8.3 Oracle storage parameters

Storage parameter	Description
INITIAL	Size of the first extent to be created for a segment. The default is 5 which is too small for most tables. Calculating a reasonable size is important
MAXEXTENTS	The maximum number of extents allowed for a segment
PICTINCREASE	This can control table growth and fragmentation
PCTFREE	Reserves space in a data block for rows to grow in an update statement
PCTUSED	When new inserts are not allowed because the PCTFREE value is reached this value specifies when new inserts can occur – the amount of space that must be freed by deletes. Default value 40

settings which need to be balanced. PCTFREE and PCTUSED combined must not be greater than 100. The defaults are rarely correct. When PCTFREE is set to 10 the result reserves 10% of the space in a data block. New rows can be added into a block until the PCTFREE value is reached. For a database with a high transaction rate, PCTFREE should be increased but for a static database it should be decreased. The value of PCTUSED should not be set too close to that of PCTFREE because this will result in blocks being moved on and off the freelist of available blocks that the system keeps. On the other hand, if the value of PCTUSED is set too low block space will be wasted. One of the reasons that getting this right is important is that Oracle works on the basis that Oracle treats tables according to the maximum size ever reached even if most of the rows are deleted later.

In Chapter 4 we created the **wine_list** table with three LOB columns. We can specify the storage parameters and the tablespaces for the LOB data. The CREATE TABLE statement needs to be modified to include specifications for the out-of-line LOB data. (Putting the LOB data out of line prevents it being involved in full table scans.) This can be achieved by the addition of lines

```
LOB(note, pronunciation) STORE AS
(TABLESPACE media
STORAGE (INITIAL 100K NEXT 100K PCTINCREASE 0)
CHUNK 16K PCTVERSION 10 NOCHACHE LOGGING)
```

This LOB clause specifies the columns to be stored out of line, assigns the tablespace **media** and the storage parameters. The CHUNK parameter sets the amount of space to be allocated during each LOB value manipulation. The default CHUNK size is 1K and the maximum is 32K. The PCTVERSION parameter is the maximum percentage of overall LOB storage space used for creating new versions of the LOB. It means older versions of the LOB data will not be overwritten until 10% of the available LOB storage space is used. The NOCACHE parameter means the LOB values will not be stored in memory for faster access during queries. The LOGGING parameter specifies that all operations using the LOB data will be recorded in the database redo log files. The new statement would be

```
CREATE TABLE wine_list
(      wine_code    CHAR(6),
       wine_name    VARCHAR2(30) NOT NULL,
       region       VARCHAR2(20) NOT NULL,
       year         NUMBER(4),
       category     VARCHAR2(20),
       grape        VARCHAR2(20),
       price        NUMBER(5,2),
       bottle_size NUMBER(4),
       character    VARCHAR2(50),
       note         CLOB DEFAULT EMPTY_CLOB(),
       pronunciation    BLOB DEFAULT EMPTY_BLOB(),
       picture          BFILE,
CONSTRAINT prim_wine PRIMARY KEY (wine_code))
LOB(note, pronunciation ) STORE AS
(TABLESPACE media
STORAGE (INITIAL 100K NEXT 100K PCTINCREASE 0)
DISABLE STORAGE IN ROW
CHUNK 16K PCTVERSION 10 NOCHACHE LOGGING)
```

Indexing can improve performance. All large tables should have indexes. All primary and foreign keys will be indexed automatically but we can explicitly index other columns. The question is, which ones? It is better to index columns that are frequently featured in the WHERE clause by users. For example, most users will search for people using a surname and not a first name. We can index a column that has a LOB data type in this way and we may want to index metadata attributes. We can add an INDEX clause to the CREATE TABLE statement to make an index **note_lob_i** for the **note** column with

```
INDEX  note_lob_i
```

A LOB segment and its index could be stored in separate tablespaces in some older versions of Oracle. When LOB data is stored out of line the row holds a 20 byte descriptor that includes the ID generated by Oracle for the actual LOB content. To retrieve the data Oracle looks up the ID in the LOB index that points to the pages of the LOB segment that hold the current version of the LOB data. The LOB segment is broken up into pages of "chunk" size. A larger "chunk" size reduces the number of entries needed in the LOB index to describe the location of the LOB data, but the potential for wasted space increases because every write to a LOB is at least one chunk size. Even writing 1 byte of LOB data could result in a chunk of 32K. If the application involves lots of really large media objects then the chunk size should be set as large as possible.

In addition, we may want to generate a time-based index that has an element for each second of elapsed time for synchronization of audio and video data. The references associated with each element point to the index element whose time is closest to the number of elapsed seconds. This is discussed further in Chapter 9.

Columns with relatively few values that are repeated frequently are good candidates. Here is an example:

```
CREATE INDEX wine_name_x
ON wine_list
(wine_name ASC)
NOLOGGING
PCTFREE 80;
```

The primary key of the **wine_table** is the **wine_code** so an index may not exist for **wine_name** even though this is a way that many users will chose to search the table. When a number of columns are frequently queried together these are good candidates for composite indexes. However, unsuitable use of indexes can reduce the costs of physical I/O while increasing the costs of logical I/O (which involves CPU usage). In the example above we set a large value for PCTFREE in order to create space for new rows.

EXERCISE 8.1

Consider the **wine_list** table and identify:

(a) columns that could be indexed;

(b) likely storage parameters.

The **dba** can make changes to the database initialization files to tune the performance of the database by altering parameters. For example, the size of the shared pool can be increased. This is both the program and data dictionary cache. The larger the cache the more likely a previously parsed matching statement is likely to be found in memory. Therefore it is desirable to have this set as high as possible. However, in turn it increases the size of the SGA, which should not go beyond 50% of the available memory of the computer. To view the details of the SGA and the parameters we can connect to SERVICE MANAGER. In a Windows environment this would involve:

```
C:> SVRMGRL
CONNECT SYSTEM/MANAGER
SHOW PARAMETERS
SHOW SGA
EXIT
```

Some parameters from the output of the process are shown in Table 8.4

The **SORT_AREA_SIZE** parameter controls the allocation of memory to sorting. This is important for SQL statements that include ORDER BY and GROUP BY clauses. Activities such as CREATE INDEX also generate sort activity. When there is not enough memory available Oracle will complete the sort by processing on disk, which will be much slower. For multimedia data it is a good idea to try doubling the size of this parameter.

The **PROCESSES** parameter defines the number of processes that can simultaneously connect to an Oracle database. The default value is 50 but since this value has to include all the background processes it is a good idea to increase this value. The only reason to keep this value small is for business reasons or hardware capacity so it is worth experimenting with a higher value.

The **OPEN_CURSORS** parameter restricts the maximum number of cursors open at one time. When this value is exceeded applications will stop processing so it is a good idea to increase this to 2500.

The **TIMED_STATISTICS** parameter should be turned off unless it is a development database as it uses a lot of resources.

The tuning process is one of selecting from a number of trade-offs. It is possible to make one change at a time but more efficient is to apply a Taguchi method to improve the overall quality of the installation. The more memory Oracle has, the less will be available for other processes. Many of the changes suggested will affect the size of the SGA area.

We introduced CLOB data types in Chapter 4. In Chapter 10 when we consider text media we will need to add a CLOB to the employee table with

Table 8.4   Example of database parameters values

Parameter	Value
TOTAL SGA	18 087 348 bytes
FIXED SIZE	64 948 bytes
VARIABLE SIZE	17 539 072 bytes
DATABASE BUFFERS	409 600 bytes
REDO BUFFERS	73 728 bytes
SORT_AREA_SIZE	65 536 bytes
OPEN_CURSORS	50

the following SQL statement:

```
ALTER TABLE employee
      ADD (cv CLOB DEFAULT EMPTY_CLOB())
```

However, several storage parameters affect LOB performance. For example, the CLOB column could be placed in a separate tablespace **media** from the rest of the table data:

```
ALTER TABLE employee
 ADD (cv2 CLOB DEFAULT EMPTY_CLOB())
 LOB (cv2) STORE AS cv_segment
   (TABLESPACE media
 STORAGE (INITIAL 2K NEXT 2K PCTINCREASE 0)
 CHUNK 2K NOCACHE NOLOGGING ENABLE STORAGE IN ROW)
```

It is good practice to name the LOB segment. The significance of the other parameters is as follows:

TABLESPACE	This can reduce device contention and can allow SELECT for multiple LOB columns at the same time
CACHE | NOCACHE	NOCACHE will stop the LOB data passing through the database buffer cache. If you specify CACHE this will also effect the use of the redo log Buffer
LOGGING | NOLOGGING	For bulk loading of LOBs this should be set to NOLOGGING since this will make the load quicker. LOGGING needs to be used if changes to the LOB need to be recorded for recovery purposes
CHUNK	An integer specifies the number of bytes used for manipulation of the LOB. It should be set near to the expected size of a read or write to the LOB values. It must be less than the NEXT parameter
INITIAL..PCTINCREASE	See earlier discussion
ENABLE | DISABLE STORAGE IN ROW	ENABLE allows storage in line up to 4K. LOBs above this size will be moved out of line but may still have better performance since some control information will continue to be stored in line. DISABLE is a better choice if full-scan SELECTs are expected using the non-LOB data

8.2.3 Using Outlines

When it is necessary to migrate from one database to another, the execution paths of stored queries may change. This can have an impact on performance.

Oracle can automatically create outlines for all SQL statements, or we can create them for specific SQL statements. The main use of this is when we are upgrading the database such as changing parameters that affect the size of memory structures. Plan stability can be used to preserve execution plans for SQL statements prior to making any database changes. After the changes if some plans do not perform well then we can instruct the database to use the plans that were captured prior to the change. A stored outline stores a set of hints for a query. The outlines can be derived from either the rule-based or the cost-based optimizers. A set of hints is equivalent to the optimizer's results for the execution plan generation of a particular SQL statement. When Oracle creates an outline, plan stability examines the optimization results using the same data used to generate the execution plan. That is, Oracle uses the input to the execution plan to generate an outline, and not the execution plan itself.

We can use the following syntax to obtain outline information from the USER_OUTLINES view, where the outline category is **mycat**:

```
SELECT NAME, SQL_TEXT
FROM USER_OUTLINES
WHERE CATEGORY='mycat';
```

Oracle creates stored outlines automatically once we set the parameter

```
CREATE_STORED_OUTLINES to TRUE
```

When activated, Oracle creates outlines for all executed SQL statements. We can also create stored outlines for specific statements using the CREATE OUTLINE statement but we must already have the CREATE OUTLINE system privilege,

```
CREATE OUTLINE wine_out
FOR CATEGORY development
ON
SELECT     wine_name, price
FROM       wine_list
WHERE      region = 'Chile'
ORDER BY   price
```

Outlines are given a category name to simplify the management task. The CREATE OUTLINE statement allows for specification of a category. The **default** category is used if unspecified. To use stored outlines when Oracle compiles an SQL statement, we must set the system parameter USE_STORED_OUTLINES to either TRUE or to the category name. When we set USE_STORED_OUTLINES to FALSE, Oracle no longer uses the outlines.

However, when we set USE_STORED_OUTLINES to FALSE, followed by CREATE_STORED_OUTLINES to TRUE, Oracle would create outlines but not use them. If we specify a category name using the CREATE_STORED_OUT-LINES parameter, then Oracle assigns all subsequently created outlines to that category until we reset the category name.

Oracle stores outline data in the OL$table and hint data in the OL$HINTS table. Outlines are retained indefinitely unless they are specifically removed. Oracle retains execution plans in cache and only recreates them if they become invalid or if the cache is not large enough to hold all of them. The only effect outlines have on caching execution plans is that the outline's category name is used in addition to the SQL text to identify whether the plan is in cache. This ensures Oracle does not use an execution plan compiled under one category to execute an SQL statement that Oracle should compile under a different category.

Hints are specially formatted comments embedded into an SQL statement that tell the optimizer to modify its evaluation method for a specific statement. Hints apply only to the optimization of the statement block in which they appear. A statement block is any one of the following statements or parts of statements:

- a simple SELECT, UPDATE, or DELETE statement (not with INSERT);
- a parent statement or subquery of a complex statement;
- a part of a compound query.

For example, we can add a (very bad) hint to the query we used earlier with EXPLAIN PLAN to specify a hint that the query should use a full table scan with the "full" hint:

```
SELECT /*+ full(T)*/
employee_number,employee_name, start_date, department_name
FROM employee, department
WHERE employee.department_number=department.department_number;
```

When we activate the use of stored outlines, Oracle always uses the cost-based optimizer. This is because outlines rely on hints, and, to be effective, most hints require the cost-based optimizer. Information about outlines and related hint data that Oracle stores in the data dictionary can be seen from these views:

- USER_OUTLINES;
- USER_OUTLINE_HINTS.

For example, use this syntax to obtain outline information from the USER_OUTLINES view where the outline category is "media":

```
SELECT NAME,SQL_TEXT FROM USER_OUTLINES WHERE CATEGORY='media'
```

We can remove the previous OL$and OL$HINTS tables with the syntax:

```
CONNECT OUTLN/outln;
DROP TABLE OL$;
CONNECT OUTLN/outln;
DROP TABLE OL$HINTS;
```

We can also suspend outline generation during a session with the syntax:

```
ALTER SESSION SET CREATE_STORED_OUTLINES = FALSE;
```

EXERCISE 8.2

```
SELECT /*+ full(T)*/
employee_number, employee_name, start_date, department_name
FROM employee, department
WHERE employee.department_number = department.department_number;
```

Add a hint to the query above and run the resulting query through EXPLAIN PLAN to establish what difference it has made.

Another situation that could occur with a multimedia table is using a compound query consisting of two component queries combined by the UNION operator. This has two statement blocks, one for each component query. For this reason, hints in the first component query apply only to its optimization, not to the optimization of the second component query.

Before leaving the question of performance we need to consider the performance of stored procedures which are more likely to be used to manipulate LOBs than SELECT statements. Oracle has supplied DBMS_PROFILER to monitor user-defined procedures, functions and packages. This will report:

- the total number of times each line of code is executed;
- the total amount of time spent executing the line;
- minimum and maximum times spent executing a line.

I had problems with proftab.sql script but it is easy to read the table definitions and create them separately. The problem appears to be the extra blank line between the last column definition and the primary key declaration, which needs to be removed.

The package DBMS_PROFILER needs to be implemented by running two scripts (**proload.sql, proftab.sql**) that should be found in the RDBMS/ADMIN directory of the ORACLE_HOME directory. It also needs to access the file **prvtpbp.plb** which should be in the same directory. To implement the package, for example as **sys** user, execute the following statement in SQL*PLUS:

```
@C:\Ora8i\RDBMS\ADMIN\profload.sql
```

The @ symbol is a shortcut used to load and execute the SQL file. Running the next statement creates three tables (**plsql_profiler_runs**, **plsql_profiler_units**, **plsql_profiler_data**) to hold the timing information:

```
@C:\Ora8i\RDBMS\ADMIN\proftab.sql
```

Each profiler session can execute multiple named PLSQL routines. A profiler session could consist of the user starting the profiler, executing the application code and then stopping the profiler from the SQL*PLUS prompt. The script **profsum.sql** has been provided to demonstrate the operation of the profiler. It is wise to run this and study the output before looking at the results of executing a LOB procedure. The following statements demonstrate the facility. The **dual** table is a dummy table just used to complete the SQL statement.

```
SELECT DBMS_PROFILER.START_PROFILER('test_1')

FROM dual

EXECUTE  C:\Ora8i\plsql\DEMO\profsum.sql

EXECUTE  load_cv('1002','doc');

SELECT DBMS_PROFILER.STOP_PROFILER
FROM dual
```

The time fields are measured in nanoseconds. Interesting times are set out below that can be viewed by executing the next three statements.

Run_total_time	Total time of the profiler session
Total_time in units table	Sum of all total_time in data table
Total_time in data table	Total time for a particular line
Total_occur	Number of times line is executed
Min_time	Minimum execution times of a line
Max_time	Maximum execution times of a line

```
SELECT RUNID,RUN_DATE,RUN_TOTAL_TIME
FROM plsql_profiler_runs;

SELECT unit_type,total_time
 FROM plsql_profiler_units;

SELECT
UNIT_NUMBER,LINE#,TOTAL_OCCUR,MIN_TIME,MAX_TIME,TOTAL_TIME
 FROM plsql_profiler_data;
```

The last statement results in the following display:

UNIT_NO	LINE#	TOTAL_OCCUR	MIN_TIME	MAX_TIME	TOTAL_TIME
5	168	5	3087547	3162976	15657319
5	169	5	299200	319314	1546288
5	171	0	0	0	0
5	173	0	0	0	0
5	174	0	0	0	0
6	1	2	22519653	26444459	48964112
7	1	2	22785329	26255887	49041217
8	1	2	22960492	25825944	48786436
9	1	2	22199500	26395011	48594512
10	1	2	22664644	25716153	48380797
11	1	2	457600	22008414	22466015

8.2.4   Parallel Processing

Oracle8i introduced a parallel processing feature called PQO. Using this Oracle can parallelize many operations including sorts, joins, table scans, table populations and index creation. PQO should be used for:

- queries involving large numbers of rows (>1 000 0000);
- joins on more than one very large table;
- creating large indexes;
- bulk loads;
- copying large amounts of data between object types;
- data involving storage on many different disks or table partitions.

It is also a good idea when there is an under-utilized CPU (<40%) on the system. However, before deciding how much to parallelize we need to know the data and the users' behavior. Parallelization should be less if users predominantly query a small subset of tables frequently. Transaction systems will involve different kinds of retrieval to decision support systems so the nature of the application is also important in the choice.

Clearly with LOBs it would be a good idea if we could process these large objects in parallel. For example, *Oracle8i/9i* are capable of

- performing I/O operations in parallel;
- performing sort operations in parallel by taking advantage of multiple CPU machines.

Oracle can tune parallel execution automatically. It is also possible to process many queries in parallel so this can be an advantage for costly JOIN operations. The **dba** can set the level at which the optimizer will attempt to parallelize query processing when the table is created, for example

```
CREATE TABLE person
( name CHAR(20),
skills CLOB,
picture BLOB,
PARALLEL(DEGREE 8));
```

This defines how Oracle will try to separate the SQL by using multiple CPUs to complete the user's task.

```
ALTER TABLE person PARALLEL (DEGREE 16);
```

If multiple processes are available one is assigned as a dispatcher which then partitions the workload among the parallel processors up to the number specified in the table's degree of parallelization. Oracle will inspect the number of CPUs, the number of disks the data resides on and the degree of parallelization set on the tables.

8.3 Content Management

Before we leave the chapter on architecture and performance of multimedia databases, it is important to make a few comments about content management of multimedia. We have seen in the preceding sections that the creation of a multimedia database requires the integration of a number of technologies as well as design and implementation strategies that are more complex than those required for traditional database systems. The complexity derives from a number of key issues, such as:

- degree of semantics – ranges from information about artifacts (date, location) to content information (sentences, key frames, shapes, color histograms etc.) as well as domain concepts such as ontologies;
- decomposition of media into a database in terms of the production and storage of metadata should be as far as possible an automatic process.

In addition the costs of multimedia operations such as inserting, searching, creating must be planned and monitored as these will be much higher than those for traditional databases.

Managing the multimedia content of the database is another issue, for example:

1. *Multimedia collection.* This is the way a heterogeneous set of results can be presented as a single result, the way an unsorted collection of each media

type would be ranked:

- rank merging – how the technology judges and aligns uncertainty measures generated from independent sources;
- semantic rewrites.

2. *Semantic rewrites*. A multimedia query is essentially a set of constraints. A given query can be rewritten into equivalent forms. One reason for wanting to rewrite a query would be the cost so the rewrite maps the result set to a set of less expensive data items by looking at the cost of generating the different types of media. The other reason for rewriting might be availability. If the target data is not available or there were not sufficient resources to deliver the data, would the user accept a substitute set that was available? Cost rewriting introduces additional complexity over traditional database optimization owing to having to estimate/cope with costs of multimedia content.

To summarize, Figure 8.11 presents an overview of the many technological components that must work together to provide an effective MMDBMS. We have studied these components in the chapters.

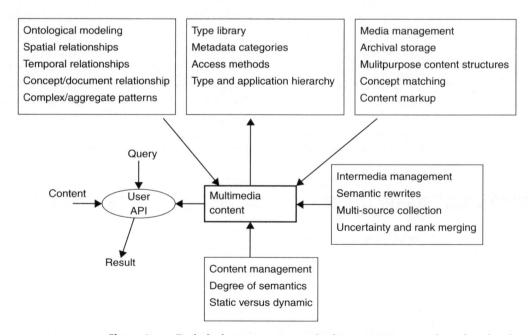

Figure 8.11   Technical components required to support content-based retrieval

8.4   Summary of Chapter

This chapter dealt with the different architectures available for the MMDBMS developer:

- multimedia super servers;
- distributed database systems;
- client–server systems;
- peer-to-peer systems;
- heterogeneous systems.

The choice of architecture will depend on the multimedia application, particularly the frequency with which the media data must be updated. We will return to this in later chapters when we consider particular applications involving text, image and video. We are likely to find that many applications will require a heterogeneous distributed approach.

We looked at the problems of tuning an Oracle multimedia database, the options available to the **dba** in terms of storage and processing parameters to optimize the performance of the database. We also looked at some of the utilities provided to investigate system performance. In reality there will always be a trade-off between the cost of processing a multimedia query and retrieving the data from disk. These factors need to be constantly monitored in multimedia systems and in addition we need to monitor user behavior and changes in their data requests.

Retrieving and delivering multimedia objects to the user can be very resource intensive. One way of improving performance is to exploit metadata retrieval, particularly where the query is not straightforward and could involve relevance feedback so that several sets of rows will be required as the user refines the query. The use of thumbnails is also important at the early stages of a multimedia query, so that only at the point when the user has located the data requested will the results actually be delivered.

SOLUTIONS TO EXERCISES

Exercise 8.1

(a)

```
(YEAR, REGION)
```

(b)

```
STORAGE (INITIAL 1M MAXEXTENTS UNLIMITED PCTINCREASE 0)
        TABLESPACE users
```

Exercise 8.2

The result is a much poorer performance.

```
QUERY_PLAN
---------------------------------
SELECT STATEMENT    Cost = 3
HASH JOIN
TABLE ACCESS FULL EMPLOYEE
TABLE ACCESS FULL DEPARTMENT
```

Recommended Reading

Oracle Systems

Ault, M. (2002) *Oracle Administration and Management: Revised Edition*, John Wiley & Sons, Inc.

Lewis, J. (2001) *Practical Oracle8i: Building Efficient Databases*, Addison-Wesley.

Scherer, D., Gaynor, W. Jr, Valentinsen, A., Cursetjee, X. (2000) *Oracle8i Tips & Techniques*, Osborne/McGraw-Hill.

General Distributed Issues

Burleson, D. K. (1994) *Managing Distributed Databases*, Wiley-QED.

CODASYL Database Task Group Report (1971) ACM, NY, April 1971.

Edwards, J., Orfali, R. (1999) *3-Tier Client/Server at Work*, Wiley.

Elmagarmid, A., Seth, A., Rusinkiewicz, M. (1998) *Management of Heterogneous and Autonomous Database Systems*, Morgan Kaufmann.

Furht, B. (1998) *Multimedia Technologies and Applications for the 21st Century*, Kluwer Academic Publishers.

Howard, P., Hailstone, R., Versant, J. (1996) *Distributed and Multi-Database Systems*, Artech House.

Linthicum, D. (2001) *B2B Application Integration*, Addison-Wesley.

Ozsu, M. T., Valderiez, (1999) *Principles of Distributed Database Systems*, 2nd edition, Prentice-Hall.

Serain, D. and Craig, I, (translator) (1999) *Middleware*, Springer Verlag – Practitioner Series, Springer, Berlin and Heidelberg.

Wijegunaratne, I., Fernandez, G. (1998) *Distributed Application Development*, Springer Verlag – Practitioner Series, Springer, Berlin and Heidelberg.

Multimedia and the Internet

Chapter aims

In Chapter 1 we found that the problems of multimedia database management systems (MMDBMS) stem from the nature of the different media and the way they interact. In dealing with multimedia on the internet it is essential to take into account the size of the media objects, their real-time nature and the requirement to synchronize different media. These factors will affect the storage, delivery and presentation of multimedia objects. When we discuss the transmission of multimedia data we will need to start by reviewing a number of terms that have specific definitions in communications systems. The reader should then be able to understand:

- transmission of multimedia data across the internet;
- main features of the Transmission Control Protocol/Internet Protocol (TCP/IP) and User Datagram Protocol (UPD) in relation to multimedia data;
- quality-of-service issues for the transmission of multimedia data;
- main features of other internet protocols used for the transmission of multimedia data;
- network architecture in relation to the delivery of multimedia;
- requirements of applications involving multicasting and interactivity.

9.1 Introduction

The internet's driving force is currently the world wide web, which we will refer to simply as the web. It features multimedia capabilities with video, audio, images, graphics and text. The expansion of the web followed the development of graphical viewers, called browsers, in 1993. The web has now become a vast network of data, news, shopping guides, periodicals and interest-group home pages. Many of these applications involve the presentation and delivery of multimedia data held in database systems. However, recently several new kinds of distributed applications, such as video teleconferencing, video on demand and virtual reality, have been developed which are sensitive to the quality of service they receive from the network with the result that these applications are hardly viable on the internet. Thus, before these applications can be widely used, the internet infrastructure must be modified to support real-time quality of service (QoS) and controlled end-to-end delays. This is likely to happen with the advent of the current internet protocol, IPv6.

In this chapter we will look at the reasons why using the internet for multimedia applications is not always satisfactory. The reasons are complex. Some problems arise from the quality and design of the network equipment, the capacity of the routers, switches and physical channels. Other problems arise from the software employed, particularly the protocols. The demands of multimedia have resulted in a change in the basic philosophy of the internet which is still unfolding. In order to understand what the problems of multimedia delivery are and the changes that have been introduced to the internet we will first look at the original system and the protocols TCP and UPD in some detail. We will understand why they were inadequate for multimedia and look at some of the recent developments. In addition, as we found in Chapter 8, the TCP/IP protocol is very important because it has been adopted by many organizations for linking clients to servers in local networks and intranets.

The basic concept behind communication via the internet is to have two remote sites or computers connected together via a network (local area network (LAN) or wide area network (WAN)) or a transmission line (wires,

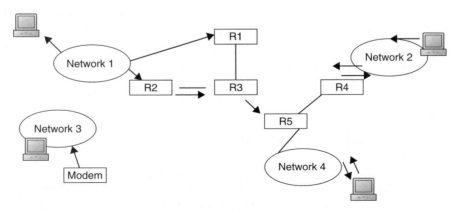

Figure 9.1   WAN of computers, routers and networks

telephone, coax cables, twisted pairs etc.). Figure 9.1 shows an example of a typical configuration – four networks, five routers, one modem and four computers. The four networks resembling the internet could be LANs, WANs, regional, national or international networks. The computers are connected to the networks via dedicated lines such as TV cables or T1 lines. The networks are connected via routers. A router is just a device which forwards packets of data between networks. The routers decide how to route and direct the data transmitted through the network lines. They find the shortest and the best way to deliver the data, utilizing sophisticated routing software and algorithms.

9.2 Delivery of Multimedia Data

In a multiuser database system, whether it is distributed or based on a client–server system, network capacity affects the performance of the database and can constrain design choices. The characteristics of the digital traffic across the network can affect quality and acceptability of the result. Therefore the configuration and integration of the distributed multimedia system need to be carefully designed. The technical requirements of the different media can have significant effects on the way the database is organized and developed. We can understand some of the problems of data transmission by looking at a simple example in the next exercise.

EXERCISE 9.1

In this practical exercise to demonstrate how data is transmitted we need two human volunteers but we will limit their normal very efficient means of communicating to demonstrate certain important requirements of computer networks.

The two human volunteers (friends or family) should be placed back to back at a little distance apart. One is supplied with a pencil and paper and the other should have the diagram shown in Figure 9.2. The human with the diagram (the sender) verbally describes the diagram (the data) to the other human who has the pencil and paper (the receiver) but the human receiver must not communicate in any way with the sender. Allow about 10 minutes for the activity, observe the interaction and then compare the information received with what was sent.

WHAT YOU WILL PROBABLY OBSERVE
- The sender splits the information up into packets, usually the separate

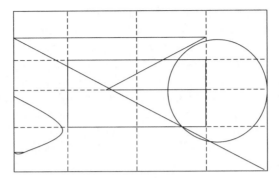

Figure 9.2 Data for transmission

lines, describing each one separately. The sender may pause between the transmission of the different packets.

- The sender has no idea whether the receiver has received and recorded the packet of information before he/she transmits the next packet.
- The receiver often seems confused and has trouble recording the packet before the sender attempts to deliver the next packet.
- Some of the packets of information get lost in the process.
- The resulting information is not likely to be an accurate copy of the information sent.

The way the information was sent in Exercise 9.1 was not successful. In the following sections we will look in turn at the way similar problems have been tackled in the case of computers exchanging information. In the case of humans the channel of communication was the human voice. In the case of computers a range of different channels can be used.

In the human receiver the data was stored in short-term memory (STM) before transmission to permanent storage on the paper. We know from Chapter 3 that STM is much more limited than long-term memory. We can regard STM in this case as a buffer that allows the storage of a limited amount of data. If the buffer capacity had been larger then less data would have been lost and transmission would have appeared smoother as the receiver would have been able to keep up with the delivery of data from the sender.

The internet involves a number of different channels of communication. We need to remember that the term channel is used in a number of different ways. In unaided human communication, channels can be referred to as audio (largely verbal and musical), visual (largely non-verbal and iconic) and tactile. In modern society channels are differentiated mainly by the technical devices used, for example writing, printing, telephone, photography, television (video and audio channels), satellite communication and, of course, computer networks. Each has its own limitations and properties.

In the context of this book, the term **channel** refers to a communication path between two computers or devices. It can refer to the physical medium (the wires) or to a set of characteristics that distinguishes one channel from another. For example, **TV channels** refer to particular frequencies at which radio waves are transmitted.

In the delivery of multimedia data we will be concerned with the channel capacity of different parts of the communication network. In the example in Figure 9.1, the network included routers, modems, computers and the transmission lines communicating between them. A channel is the part of a communication chain in which signals are transmitted from a sender to a receiver. In Figure 9.1 the channels could include coaxial cables, twisted pairs, optical cables, satellite links and so on. Unlike other processes in a communication chain (for example encoding, decoding, translation and transformation which we studied in Chapter 2), a channel involves a single physical medium that spans the difference in time and in space which separates senders from receivers. A channel is characterized by the physical properties of its medium and imposes a constraint on the capacity to transmit information because of its:

1. selective capability to store, retain and transmit certain kinds of signals;

2. sensitivity to non-systematic distortions and decay (*such as noise*).

There are quality-of-service issues and aspects of networks that are especially important to the delivery of multimedia data through real-time services, for example:

- bandwidth;
- jitter;
- capacity to switch or route nodes.

The **channel capacity** is very similar to the concept of information processing capacity; the number of messages per unit time handled by either a link or a node (system, element). The messages transmitted may be either similar or different. It is usually measured in bits per second. (It is often confused with bandwidth but as we shall see later this is a slightly different concept.)

Within any communication medium higher transmission speeds mean greater costs. Aggregate data rate refers to the amount of information being transmitted per unit time. Table 9.1 summarizes the performance of different media associated with the different channels.

All transmission media are liable to errors in data through signal distortions. For example white noise which results from the normal movements of

Table 9.1 Performance of different media

Media	Security	Errors	Common transmission speeds
Switched line	Fair	Fair	3000, 1200, 9600, 19 200, 38 400 bps
T1	Fair	Fair	1.5M, 6.3M, 46M, 281M
Twisted pair			
• 100Base TX	Fair	Fair	1M, 10M, 16M, 100M, 1G; 1 Gbps at distance limit of 220 meter
Coaxial cable	Fair	Good	1M, ... 400M
• 10Base2			10 Mbps at a distance limit of 185 meters
• 10Base T			10 Mbps at a distance limit of 100 meters
• 100Base T			100 Mbps at distance limit of 100 meters
Fiber optic cable	Good	Good	Over 2 Gbps
Microwave	Poor	Fair	To 45M
Spread spectrum radio	Poor	Fair	2M
Infrared	Poor	Fair	1M, 4M
Satellite	Poor	Fair	To 50M

electrons in the media is more significant in radio frequency links than in cable. Impulse noise is noticeable as a spike in a signal and is usually the result of switching equipment. A bit error is much more likely to occur at higher transmission speeds. Unfortunately high speeds are required for multimedia data.

9.3 Media Streams

An important objective of multimedia systems design is to transfer data in a predictable manner and often at a constant speed. However, we have already found that networks consist of different components with very different channel capacities linked together. Streaming is a technique for transferring data so that it can be processed as a steady and continuous stream. Streaming technologies are becoming increasingly important with the growth of the internet because most users do not have fast enough access to download large multimedia files quickly. For example, although streams of real-time video traffic have a constant average rate, the traffic consists of patterns of regular bursts. By using streaming, the client browser or plug-in can start displaying the data before the entire file has been transmitted out just like the human receiver in Exercise 9.1.

For streaming to work, the client side receiving the data must be able to collect the data and send it as a steady stream to the application that is processing the data and converting it into sound or pictures. This means that, if the streaming client receives the data more quickly than required, it needs to save the excess data in a buffer. If the data does not arrive quickly enough, however, the presentation of the data will not be smooth. These transient delays caused by queues at routers even in real-time streams lead to jitter. The characteristics of the digital traffic across the network for steaming digital media objects and their impact on the network are crucial. A critical feature of video is synchronization. Packet loss can cause loss of lip synchronization or may even stop the client playing but this is still much higher loss than the level of loss at which humans find the video pleasing to watch.

This can be understood by looking at a specific example. Organizations often have switched Ethernet intranets. Suppose a media server is connected at 155 Mbits/s to a high performance ATM network; the bursts of data are much faster than many of the smaller downstream links can cope with in an Ethernet network of PCs – note the different transmission speeds quoted in Table 9.1. For successful delivery of packets of data, whenever there is a step down in the bit rate of the network link, the network device doing the step down must have sufficient buffer capacity to hold the entire packet. For example video traffic from a server may travel at 155 Mbits/s through an ATM switch. When the Ethernet switch passes the traffic to the client at a much lower rate of 10 Mbits/s, a data packet with the usual size of 16 Kb would take 13 milliseconds to deliver. This means the Ethernet switch must have sufficient buffer capacity to store the entire video data packet when it arrives to ensure no data is lost. When this buffering capacity is insufficient it can result in almost 100% packet loss. The system would need to be reconfigured so that it only streams traffic out at the right rate and there is no mismatch in speeds of the traffic entering and leaving. This means buffering capacity must be shifted to the areas of the system that can cope. In any node in the network where a bit rate drop is required and the device in question is not able to provide the buffering required there needs to be an upstream device which does have the capacity and can be configured to drop the rate there. Although this is a solution it is an undesirable workaround because it places a limitation on the bandwidth available for use by other applications between the inadequate node and the more capable upstream node.

Jitter is defined as the variation in the time taken by a network to deliver a packet of data from a source to a destination. For real-time video streaming where packets enter the network at regular intervals, jitter is the variation in inter-arrival time of the packets as they exist in the network. Transmission is smoother when jitter is maintained at a low level. The tolerance of the application to network jitter is a function of the buffering capacity of the decoder. This is because packets of data that are stored in advance allow the decoder to continue normal operation when packets are delayed. The client has to have adequate buffering to ensure smooth play-out, for example 500 Kb of buffering capacity is sufficient for streaming over switched Ethernet networks.

These limitations of networks make streaming video (as, for example, in video-on-demand applications) from one central site inadequate and uneconomic. One solution is to stream the video to local servers from the central repository in non-real time so that the local servers can then deliver real time to clients across LANs. Access and authorization would then be handled by the central site. This means a distributed server architecture such as that described in Chapter 8 is required. Several competing streaming technologies are emerging. For audio data on the internet, the *de facto* standard is Progressive Network's *RealAudio*.

When we are discussing the delivery of multimedia data to the user we often use the term session. This is a collection of communication exchanges which together make up a single overall identifiable task. There is no need for the different media making up a session to be carried in the same packet. Multiple streams of different or the same media data can be carried from source to target over a single channel by using the multiplexing function. For example, four video streams can be carried across a 10 Mbits/s Ethernet trunk. It simplifies receivers if the different media streams are carried by separate flows. This has the advantage that the different media can be given different quality of service standards. For example, with certain applications some users could just have audio while others could have video as well. Real-time applications need to buffer real-time data at the receiver for sufficient time to remove jitter and to recover the original timing relationships between the media data. In order to know how long to buffer, each packet must carry a timestamp which gives the time at the sender when the data was captured relative to the other data packets.

EXERCISE 9.2

Give a one-sentence summary of the following terms:

(a) channel capacity;

(b) router;

(c) streaming;

(d) jitter.

Explain why each of the above terms may be of interest to the multimedia database developers of a video-on-demand application.

9.4 Network Protocols

When we completed Exercise 9.1 we discovered that there were a number of problems that needed to be solved before information could be successfully transmitted. There must be a set of rules that are agreed between the sender and receiver. For computer networks these rules are captured in a set of software known as protocols. When we consider the delivery of multimedia data we also need to take into account the protocol that is operating. A protocol is just an agreed-upon format for transmitting data between two devices. The protocol determines:

- type of error checking to be used;
- data compression method, if any;
- how the sending device will indicate that it has finished sending a message;
- how the receiving device will indicate that it has received a message.

The internet uses a communication protocol called TCP/IP (**Transmission Control Protocol/Internet Protocol**). TCP is the standard protocol used by the internet and many other networks. TCP/IP refers to a suite of protocols not just the TCP and IP protocols. The IP's main job is to find the best route through the internet from the source to the destination. It obviously needs the address of the sending and receiving destinations. IP uses IP addresses to identify the host machine and the network. TCP is used to guarantee end-to-end delivery of segments of data, to put out-of-order segments in order and to check for transmission errors. TCP/IP originated as the network portion of Unix. It solves many of the problems we recognized in Exercise 9.1. It has mechanisms to control the flow of data, keep the data packets in the right order and give the transmission some reliability.

TCP rules are as follows:

- TCP breaks the data to be transmitted into TCP packets, each with a maximum size of 1500 bytes.
- TCP numbers these packets sequentially.
- TCP puts each packet into a standard TCP envelope (called encapsulation).
- TCP encloses the TCP envelope inside an IP envelope. An IP envelope has the IP address of both the sender and the recipient.
- TCP transmits the IP envelope across the network.
- When the IP envelope arrives at the receiver, the data is extracted from the envelopes, and the receiver puts the data packets into the correct order.

All networks share common functions even though many different computer networks have been introduced by manufacturers. In order to manage this diversity the ISO recommended a reference model known as the Open Systems Interconnection reference model (OSI model). This described a seven-layered set of functions for transmitting data from one user to another. In terms of the internet three layers of the model are more significant and are presented in Figure 9.3. The top layer is the applications layer and the functions of this layer are application dependent. The individual applications determine the data being exchanged. The transport layer is responsible for generating the end-user's address and for the integrity of the receipt of the message blocks. The bottom represents the data link/network layer which must establish and control the physical path of communication to the next node. These functions are accomplished by different protocols that control the different layers of the OSI model.

In the different layers of the model the packets of data are referred to by different names because they are slightly different. In the next paragraphs we will set out the different terms. "Packet" is a generic term used to describe a unit of data at any layer of the OSI model but it is most correctly used to describe application layer data units (APDU). In contrast, "segment" is the term that is used to describe the data that is transmitted and received at the **transport** level of the OSI model where TCP resides. A technique is used by layered protocols in which a layer adds header information to the protocol data unit (PDU) from the layer above. As an example, in internet terminology, a packet would contain a header from the physical layer, followed by a header from the network layer (IP), followed by a header from the transport layer (TCP), followed by the application protocol data. A "frame" is another important term associated with the data link layer (DDL) – a "packet" which contains the header and trailer information required by the physical medium. That is, network layer packets are encapsulated to become frames.

A frame is a block of bits that is recognized by the DLL as a single unit. This means that the DLL is able to compose and decompose frames in order

OSI model	TCP/IP suite of protocols					
Application	HTTP	SNMP	FTP	SMTP	Telnet	NNTP
Presentation		161	20			
	80	162	21	69	23	119
Transport		TCP			UDP	
Data link	IP					
Physical						

Figure 9.3   Simplified OSI model and TCP/IP

to send and receive data using the underlying physical layer. This process is carried out in a bit-oriented fashion. It provided the capability to communicate using frames with the network layer. For example, a message is constructed from the application layer and is put into the DLL in one or more frames, and the DLL then transmits it by sending the bit-oriented (i.e. a stream of 0s and 1s) message using the physical layer. The DLL at the receiver will convert the bits to one or more information blocks and offer them to the upper layers. This is called framing/deframing and can have important consequences for synchronization of multimedia data streams. In order to compose frames from the bit-stream received from the physical layer, the DDL could put some synchronization "things" in the bit-stream.

In Figure 9.3 the IP is shown as the only protocol in the data link/network layer whereas there are two different protocols, TCP and UDP, which provide different kinds of service in the transport layer. TCP is a transport layer protocol known as a connection-oriented service. It is responsible for reliable end-to-end delivery of segments of information. TCP also redirects the data to the appropriate port (upper level service) that is required. The different network programs and services that use TCP and UDP protocols, use different so-called **well-known port numbers** as decreed by the protocol. A port is an abstraction to allow transport protocols like UDP and TCP the capability of handling communications between multiple hosts. It allows a communication to be uniquely identified. Ports are identified by a positive integer. TCP and UDP use these port numbers to indicate where the segments should be sent. For example, web servers use **port 80** to indicate that the **http** protocol is used. (A **socket** is just another name for a well-known port. This is why web users sometimes experience confusing error messages about sockets and socket layers.) The redirection of data to the upper level service is accomplished by using source and destination port numbers. Multiple connections to the same service are allowed. For example, you may have many users (clients) connected to a single web server (http is normally port 80). Each client will have a unique port number assigned (typically above 8000) but the web server itself will only use port 80.

The reliable end-to-end delivery of data by the connection-oriented service is accomplished because:

- When segments are received at the destination, the receipt of each segment is acknowledged to the source. If there are missing segments the source can re-send them.
- Data is broken up into segments that are numbered (sequenced) when transmitted. The destination TCP layer keeps track of the received segments and places them in the proper order (re-sequences).

- Retransmission of lost data can be requested if a segment is lost in transmission (missing sequence number). The destination will timeout and request that all segments starting at the lost segment be retransmitted.
- Error checking is used. Segments are checked for data integrity when received using a 32-bit CRC check.

Although TCP's rules are good for checking the accuracy of data in a way that is good for database transactions these are counterproductive for multimedia traffic because the error checking process is very slow for large multimedia objects. It is also very difficult to use for many-to-many communications. Some multimedia objects would still be useable even if some packets are lost, because of the way human perception works (see Chapter 3).

9.5 User Datagram Protocol

User datagram protocol (UDP) is an alternative to TCP. This is intended to provide interactive and real-time data support through data such as local time and name look-up services but it is not really powerful enough, in terms of functionality, for satisfactory multimedia data transport. UDP is a simple protocol as shown in Figure 9.4, which illustrates what is contained within a UDP packet.

In contrast to TCP, the UDP provides a connectionless host-to-host service that operates at the same transport layer of the OSI model. This results in a low overhead, fast transfer service that relies on the upper layer protocols to provide error checking and delivery of data. A datagram is a self-contained, independent entity of data carrying sufficient information to be routed from the source to the destination computer without reliance on earlier exchanges between this source and destination computer and the transporting network. If each transport layer (UDP) packet carries 16 Kb of information, at 2 Mbits/s bandwidth the loss of one UDP packet out of every thousand will typically result in the loss of a visible artefact on part of an image, seeing on average one noticeable glitch each part of a second or an

0	8	15	19	24	31
UDP source port (16 bits)			UDP destination port (16 bits)		
UDP message length (16 bits)			UDP checksum (16 bits)		
Data					

Figure 9.4   UDP packet

Table 9.2   Components of UDP packets

Source port

The source port is a 16-bit number that indicates the upper level service that the source is transmitting. UDP allows port numbers to be in the range from 0 to 65 535. The source port is optional and, if not used, a field of zeros is inserted. Clients will have a unique port number assigned to them by the server. Typically the number will be above 8000.

Destination port

The destination port is a 16-bit number that indicates the upper level service that the source wishes to communicate with at the destination.

Length

The length field is 16 bits long and indicates the length of the UDP datagram and has a maximum value of 65 535 bytes and a minimum value of 8 bytes. UDP packets can vary in length and can exceed the 14.6K limit imposed by TCP.

Checksum

The checksum field is 16 bits long and calculates a checksum based on the UDP header, data field and what is called the UDP pseudo-header. The UDP pseudo-header consists of the source IP address, destination IP address, zero, IP protocol field and UDP length.

Data

The data field contains the IP header and data.

audible click or squeak. Therefore UDP is used by applications that only need a connectionless, best effort transport service. Most real-time CORBA systems are currently implemented on UDP/IP connectionless protocols.

Since UDP is more likely to be used for the transfer of multimedia data than TCP we will look at its components in more detail in Table 9.2 as an example of a multimedia packet. The major uses of this protocol are DNS and multimedia file transfer through TFTP (see Table 9.3). UDP has a small header and for all intensive purposes adds port addressing to the IP header. The IP header routes datagrams to the correct host on the network and UDP routes the datagram to the correct application.

In the **application layer** shown in Figure 9.3, there are many hundreds of programs and services which are governed by their own protocols. Some of the most important are listed in Table 9.3.

In order to use UDP, the application must supply the IP address and port number of the destination application. TCP/IP does not allow fragmentation of IP packets, only re-assembly, whereas some implementations of UDP modules allow for fragmentation. The maximum allowable UDP packet size is 1460 bytes. Therefore, although the TCP/IP will not allow outgoing UDP packets to be greater than 1460 bytes, it can handle larger incoming UDP packets.

Table 9.3 Well-known port numbers of the application layer

Protocol (port)	Application
HTTP (80)	HyperText Transport Protocol which is used for transferring web pages
SNMP (161/162)	Simple Network Management Protocol which is used for managing network devices
FTP (20/21)	File Transfer Protocol which is used for transferring files across the network
TFTP (69)	Trivial File Transfer Protocol which is a low overhead fast transfer FTP protocol
SMTP (25)	Simple Mail Transfer Protocol which is used for transferring email across the internet
Telnet (23)	An application for remotely logging into a server across the network
NNTP (119)	Network News Transfer Protocol which is used for transferring news

However, UPD does not always provide enough functionality for multi-media data transport. Some additional features are required, such as:

- basic framing service defining unit of transfer, common with the unit of synchronization;
- multiplexing so that it is possible to identify separate media in separate streams but also to stack media together in the same IP packet;
- timely delivery, traded against reliability.

We have seen that an error detection and timeout/retransmission-based error recovery scheme is not appropriate for multimedia data. It needs a media-specific forward error recovery system which can be provided by more recently developed protocols discussed in the next section.

9.6 Quality-of-service Issues – Internet Service Models

Originally the internet quality of service (QoS) was based on **best effort** delivery of datagram traffic from senders to receivers. This does not guarantee when or whether a datagram will be delivered. It also does not assume a first-in-first-out (FIFO) queuing system, although some routers adopt this. Best effort service implies only delays caused by serialization (at each hop) and propagation. However, datagrams can be dropped when the queue size allowed at the router is exceeded so when a link is congested packets will start to be lost. Real-time internet traffic is defined as consisting of datagrams that are sensitive to such delays. Multimedia is not usually real-time critical and can afford to lose some data if this does not mean losing much information since human users can tolerate small delays in delivery. However, best effort service can seriously degrade the service of multimedia data, particularly because the size of the data is likely to congest links. Recently several new kinds of distributed applications, such as video tele-conferencing, video on demand and virtual reality, have been developed which are sensitive to the quality of service they receive from the network. In particular, their treatment in the traditional manner by trying to ensure correct and fair delivery by trading this off against delay is not acceptable. Thus, before these applications can be widely used, the internet infrastructure must be modified to support real-time QoS and controlled end-to-end delays.

Therefore better-than-best service is required for some data flows. A flow is identified as a tuple (source, destination, source port, destination port, protocol) where any of these could be a wildcard. What is needed for multimedia is long-lived data flow and then to set priorities so that some flows can be degraded to **best effort** service. One solution is to classify real-time traffic separately from non-real-time giving real-time traffic priority treatment so that it suffers the minimum delay. The resource reservation protocol RSVP is now being developed for this purpose.

Criteria for the selection of a prototype for multimedia would include:

- simplicity;
- reliability;
- speed;
- synchronization;
- availability of hardware/software components.

We have seen that in a network situation packets are lost in transit, reordered or delayed so that some simply do not make it. The degradation of the received and perceived signal will increase when compression has been applied to the data and since compression removes redundancy it removes the signal's tolerance to loss. Lossy compression reduces the signal to its bare essentials as we saw in Chapter 2. The designer has to choose a compression scheme and ratio to minimize the impact of loss for the average delivered rate. One way is to use smart protection by re-adding redundancy to the packets in a way that is designed to protect against packet loss. Multimedia packets are large so the loss of one is usually significant.

RSVP is used by applications to request specific QoS from the network. If a network has sufficient capacity when a request arrives from a real-time traffic source then a reservation for that capacity can be put in place. If there is insufficient capacity the admission to the network is refused but will still be forwarded at the default level of service. When a reservation sets aside resources for a flow other traffic is denied access. Some negative feedback is required to prevent pointless denial of service to other users. This may result in additional charging. RSVP is not a routing protocol, but rather an internet control protocol. Its task is to establish and maintain resource reservations over a distribution tree, independent of how the reservation was created. It is important that the reservation is set by the receiver, not the sender. Each receiver is responsible for choosing its own level of reserved resources, initiating the reservation and keeping it active as long as it wants to. This achieves a distributed solution for the resource reservation problem and enables heterogeneous receivers to make reservations specifically tailored to their own needs. A source-initiated reservation cannot deal with heterogeneous receiver requirements. For example, certain receivers may be using better hardware, or others may have low bandwidth paths to them. As the source does not automatically know about receiver specifications, it can only instruct a uniform level of reservation throughout the network. Source reservation, in contrast, would lead to unfairness and would often cause wastage.

The presence of different network layers which are an essential feature of the OSI model actually causes problems of multimedia data transmission. This is because as we have seen each layer adds extra header data as it encapsulates the package so further increasing the size and number of packets required. Collapsing protocol layers to increase performance and reduce copying and buffering is straightforward in principle, but getting the implementation right requires overcoming specific performance obstacles in existing systems:

- cache performance;
- dealing with unusual protocol semantics (ordering/fragmenting, etc.);
- dealing with the CPU-to-memory gap;
- different "views" of data at the different levels in the protocol (the level below's headers are part of the next level's data);
- preserving modularity.

EXERCISE 9.3

Write a one-sentence explanation to distinguish the use of the following terms:

(a) packet;

(b) segment;

(c) frame.

9.7   Packets and Datagrams – Sequence and Loss

Multimedia applications fall into two groups in relation to delivery requirements. In the first group of applications the multimedia is present to enhance and promote another product and is not inherently of value itself. In this case the accuracy and security of the media data is not critical. Alternatively, the multimedia component can be the main product being delivered to the user through the network in applications such as video on demand and media on demand. In this case accuracy and quality of the media are critical but so is security. Therefore we need to note that IP Security (IPSec) is a set of protocols being developed by the IEFT to support secure exchange of packets at the IP layer. IP Sec is expected to be deployed widely to implement virtual private networks (VPNs). IP Sec supports two encryption modes: transport and tunnel. Transport mode encrypts only the data portion (payload) of each packet, but leaves the header untouched. The more secure tunnel mode encrypts both the header and the payload. On the receiving side, an IP-Sec-compliant device decrypts each packet. For IP Sec to work, the sending and receiving devices must share a public key. This is

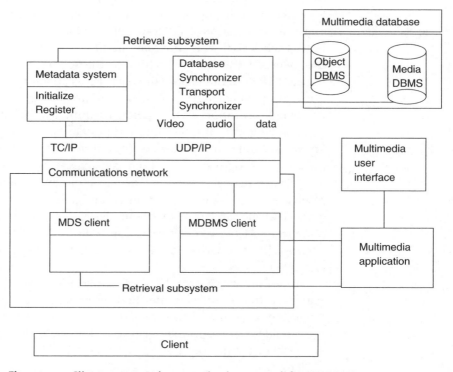

Figure 9.5   Client–server and communication network for MMDBMS

accomplished through a protocol known as internet Security Association and Key Management Protocol/Oakley (ISAKMP/Oakley), which allows the receiver to obtain a public key and authenticate the sender using digital certificates.

In this chapter we have discovered the importance of metadata and the way it is essential to virtually all media retrieval. This means there has to be a way of storing and organizing the metadata associated with the media database. One solution is shown in Figure 9.5 – this shows a multimedia database composed of two separate databases. The metadata is located in the registry as described in Chapter 7. In this example the metadata is held in an object-oriented database because the structure of an ontology lends itself to object-oriented design. The media data is held in a different database which could have a different data model. The retrieval subsystem delivers the query data and the related metadata. The media data is delivered via a protocol such as UDP while the metadata can be adequately delivered by TCP/IP.

Another important protocol, RTP, is the preferred carrier/framing protocol for multimedia traffic. It is normally carried on the top of UDP. It carries source identifiers and provides a standard format packet header, which gives media-specific timestamp data, payload format information and sequence numbering. It includes a media timestamp for the sample carried which is formatted specifically for each media type. This is used for media play-out and synchronization. RTP does not provide any enhanced reliability over UDP. Each RTP flow is supplemented by RTCP packet types that provide a link between the real-time clock of the sender and the RTP media timestamp. RTP does not ensure the packet's reachability to the destination and is not aware of congestion along an intermediate path.

Synchronization is an important requirement for multimedia. One way of achieving this is a common timestamping arrangement. The sender knows the times the packets were sent and the receiver needs to play the media in the right order without gaps, gasps or jitters. Synchronization is also needed between different media. Audio and video flows will therefore receive different amounts of jitter and possibly QoS. Audio and video grabbed at the same time by the sender may not arrive at the receiver at the same time. At the receiver each flow will need a play-out buffer to remove network jitter otherwise packet loss can be so high that the video is too annoying to watch.

Interflow synchronization can be performed by adapting these play-out buffers so that samples/frames that originated at the same time are played out at the same time. This means the times that the different flows from the same sender were captured needs to be known at the receivers.

Other new approaches to the problem include:

- Application layer framing (ALF) is a solution to these problems based on the idea that an application can best select the "element of synchronization" and that this is suitable as the protocol data unit or packet size to be used.

- Integrated layer processing (ILP) can also be applied based on the idea that "much of the protocol processing carried out over the PDU/packet can be rolled together".

ALF can be combined with ILP so that it can be applied to multimedia units of data sent as RTP/UDP/IP encapsulations.

Another issue is how to select the best combination of network protocol and compression method. Network transport itself uses up bandwidth, for example 2 Mbits/encoded video transported onto a network with associated packed headers can use approximately 2.3 Mbits/s. Compression systems must produce video of an acceptable quality for multimedia. Experimental user trials of video on demand reported impairments in aliasing of lines, blotches on backgrounds and loss of definition of facial features. Jerky frame rates result in very noticeable defects. MPEG1 and MPEG2 can produce high quality video in different circumstances, so which should be used? Network capacity affects the performance of both and acts as a constraint of their selection. For example, MPEG2 requires more than 3 Mbits/s capacity whereas in some cases MPEG1 compressed video can work with 1.5–2.5 Mbits/s. MPEG2 only gives a better quality of delivery for rates greater than 4 Mbits/s. MPEG1 uses progressing compression schemes, which lose vertical and temporal resolution, while MPEG2 uses interlaced compression schemes and will give better quality eventually. In addition the nature of the network topology also affects performance so that bus networks are tending to be replaced by star networks.

9.8   Network Architecture

The performance of a multimedia database system can also be affected by the network architecture of the physical/DLL layers. Asynchronous transfer mode (ATM) provides high speed switching of data packets across networks. In ATM the data sent by the user is broken down into 48-byte data packets. Control data (5 bytes) is added to create a 53-byte transmission frame (sometimes called a cell). These frames are transmitted separately, possibly by different routes. Packet switching is a term used to describe the transmission of a message by splitting it into packets of fixed length and then routing these to the recipient over different paths so that they may arrive out of order. The actual route is determined during transmission of the packet. ATM solutions are reliable and technically desirable and can be linked to cheaper solutions such as switched Ethernet. Networks that are wholly switched Ethernet are acceptable but care must be taken to ensure all pairs of devices being connected are correctly matched. A network that is adequate for non-real-time data applications may not be suitably configured for real-time services because despite less than optimal configuration some packets still get through successfully so that the result is poor quality data. Transport protocols like TCP make sure that data traffic is still delivered reliably even with lower than predicted performance whereas UDP, which is usually used for real-time services, does not perform any retransmission of lost packets. The reason for this is that a retransmitted packet would arrive too late to be of use and would only be discarded by the application anyway, which wastes valuable bandwidth.

Packet loss on Ethernet trunks is more pronounced than on ATM trunks. When traffic builds up jitter is much greater, which increases the buffer requirements for the client. The higher level of jitter can be explained by different ways that information is interleaved between streams on the two networks. With ATM the interleaving is done at the cell level (53 bytes) so that with 155 Mbits/s trunks the jitter introduced is of the order of 1–10 microseconds. With switched Ethernet where IP fragments are carried in a single frame (of the order of 1000 bytes) the jitter introduced can be of the order of hundreds of microseconds.

Shared media networks like traditional Ethernet tend not to be suitable for streaming video because of the potential contention for the use of the bus between the multiple clients attached to the network. Cable modem delivery can be unreliable because of inconsistent bandwidth availability. One solution is only to use cable modems for the last leg of the delivery to the client. The cable is a shared medium so it could be expected to be unreliable with heavy loading and video delivery would suffer.

The details of the network configuration can also affect multimedia performance. Routers and switches operate at different layers in the network protocol. Switches operate on the data link layer and routers on the network layer, which therefore requires more interpretation of the contents of the packet. Switches make more use of hardware so it could be expected that routers are usually less able to cope with the demands of real-time traffic. Routers will tend to cause problems in any other than lightly loaded networks.

As we noted earlier the internet works by degrading everyone's performance smoothly as load increases rather than blocking access. For a variety of reasons samples may arrive at different times from when they were sent. A play-out buffer can accommodate a fixed variation in arrival. The throughput and delay on the internet can vary drastically as other traffic comes and goes. When the network is overloaded packets get lost leaving gaps in the information flow at a receiver.

There are two possible solutions to these problems:

- Audio and video (and interactive applications) receivers could use an adaptive play-out scheme where the size of the buffer is continually recalculated by the system.
- Senders fall back to lesser quality of service (best effort) as the network becomes highly loaded and increase the quality and subsequent load only as the network is perceived to have spare capacity.

This real-time flow for media data can work because RTP places a timestamp on each packet sent. All receivers use the timestamp to monitor the inter-arrival time distribution. By monitoring the inter-arrival times and adding this to a play-out buffer that is used for sending data between the receiving application and the output device (video window, audio, whiteboard, ...) the receiver can be assured that it will not be starved of data.

9.9   Requirements of Applications Involving Multicasting and Interactivity

In applications such as video on demand the media object must be delivered to multiple users at the same time. Multicasting is the ability of a network to deliver information to multiple recipients. IP unicast packets are transmitted between a source and one destination. IP multicast packets are transmitted with one source and a group address, providing delivery to a set of receivers. IP multicast is important in P2P networks. This can result in many-to-many datagram distribution. For multimedia this is so common a requirement that unicast is regarded as a special case. Multicast packet delivery is a similar concept to TV and radio broadcasting but superior. Group addressing is an extension of the internet addressing scheme and can provide dynamically assigned addresses with a single identifier. When a host joins an IP multicast group:

- The host re-programs the network interface to receive packets from additional group addresses used for multicast.
- The host informs all nearby routers that there is at least one recipient for packets to the multicast address.

Multicast address assignment is usually dynamic. Anyone can send a packet at any time to any group. The receiving applications have to deal with multiple receptions. This raises two problem areas – addressing and network capacity. It is possible to flood a receiver with traffic just by knowing its address. With multicast a receiver can pull down more traffic than they can handle by joining multiple groups. Routers use a delivery tree to get packets from the source to the receiver. The tree is usually optimal in terms of the number of links. Packets are not usually transmitted multiple times on the same link anywhere but copied at appropriate points. internet multicast distributes both the group control and the data distribution tasks into the network.

Some multimedia applications are described as being collaboration aware – they are specifically written to be used with multiple simultaneous users. This adds a layer of complexity to what we have discussed so far because the users can manipulate and update the media data, for example to create a shared text editor that could be used in a "meeting" with a number of people geographically distributed. Although the number of people making changes to data at any one time will be small we need to avoid placing constraints on the number of people able to participate in such a meeting. The text editor must be resilient to packet loss, link failure and failure of participating systems. Therefore a distributed replicated data model is appropriate. Resilience to packet loss can be achieved through redundancy, through retransmission or through network reservation. When applications use multicasting there can be some unexpected consequences. For example, conventional network schemes rely on recipients notifying senders of missing packets through negative acknowledgment packets (NACKs). This would cause problems if the loss of a packet were recognized by a host of recipients who then all sent NACKs with disastrous effects on traffic at a node.

Experiments with multi-user whiteboard systems suggest that users will tolerate temporary inconsistencies between one view of a document at one site and the view of it at another as long as eventual consistency is achieved and so long as the time they have to wait is predictable. Total consistency would at the moment cause unacceptable delays. One approach to design of collaboration software is to recognize that consistency of views for all users is simply unachievable within finite resources. For example, to simplify the system we could define a set of operations that each user could carry out on the whiteboard, each of which is idempotent (can be repeated without danger).

As a general rule we want constraints on interactivity kept to a minimum, for example multiple users should be able to edit a shared document simultaneously. Any lock should be imposed on as small a part of the data as possible, although imposing locks does increase resilience.

When all changes to the document are multicast and all changes are timestamped there can be a simple mechanism for clock synchronization among members of a group:

- If a site has not sent any data and receives data from another site it sets its clock (application clock) to the timestamp in the received message.

- If a site has not received any data and needs to send data it sets its application clock to its own local clock time.

- If a site then receives a message with a timestamp greater than its current application clock time it increases its application clock time to match that of the received message.

These rules ensure that all sites' application clocks are synchronized sufficiently accurately. This assumes that all local clocks run at the same rate. When a source joins and immediately sends a message all the existing sources in the network adjust to its clock which will be close to its local time. If this is not true the worst that can happen is all the clocks adjust to the fastest clock. This will not synchronize the system clocks to real time but the most important thing is that the time cannot decrease.

Another recently proposed protocol is RWANDA (Parr and Curran, 2000) which is intended to support large-scale isochronous multimedia applications. Objects are transmitted by senders using IP multicast or unicast. Receivers subscribe to channels to receive the objects such as audio/video postings. The aim of the protocol is to support a wide range of multimedia applications with increased performance by decreasing protocol complexity.

Another issue is the degree to which controlled access is an issue. There are two different approaches:

- The term *lightweight sessions* is used to describe multicast-based multimedia conferences without explicit session membership and control mechanisms. These allow many-to-many data streams supported by RTP, RTCP using IP multicast. RTP payload types indicate what the media type encodings are in use in a real-time internet session.

- Tightly coupled conferences may also be multicast based on RTP and RTCP with explicit conference membership and explicit control mechanisms. The rendezvous mechanism provides information on multicast addresses, ports, media formats and session times. A session directory allocates multicast addresses and the control mechanism to be used to join the conference. RTCP conveys information such as participant details and statistics of packet arrivals and losses. It is typically sent on a UDP port one number higher than the UDP port used for the associated RTP packets.

9.10   Summary of Chapter

The chapter focused on the problems that arise when we transmit media data across networks, particularly the internet. These problems arise from the size of the media and its real-time nature. Communications across the network are regulated by the protocols in use. In this respect the virtues of TCP/IP for transactional data make it unsuitable for media data. The way in which TCP checks for package loss and reorders packets cause unacceptable delays in the transmission of real-time media data. In addition the way the internet traditionally operates in terms of QoS is difficult for the transmission of media data where long-lived data flows are required. For these reasons we studied a number of alternative protocols.

SOLUTIONS TO EXERCISES

Exercise 9.2

(a) Channel capacity is the number of messages per unit time handled by either a link or a node (system, element). Video-on-demand applications require high channel capacity not usually obtainable on the internet at present.

(b) A router is a device which forwards packets of data between networks by deciding the shortest and the best way to deliver the data. Networks other than the internet use routers and for video on demand these need to be effective and have large buffering capacities.

(c) Streaming is a technique for transferring data so that it can be processed as a steady and continuous stream. Video on demand will require long-lived data streams.

(d) Jitter is defined as the variation in the time taken by a network to deliver a packet of data from a source to a destination. If packets arrive late there will be a loss of synchronization which will be very noticeable to users of video on demand.

Exercise 9.3

(a) Packet is the generic term for data unit for any level of the OSI model.

(b) Segment is the term used for the data unit transmitted by the transport layer.

(c) Frame is the term used for data units transmitted by the DDL – data layer that can incorporate flags for synchronization.

Recommended Reading

Crowcroft, J., Handley, M., Wakeman, I. (1999) *Internetworking Multimedia*, Morgan Kaufmann, San Francisco, CA.

Fluckiger, F. (1995) *Understanding Networked Multimedia*, Prentice Hall, London.

Dealing with Text Databases

Chapter aims

This chapter looks in detail at the way text data is manipulated, queried and processed in multimedia databases. The general principles of processing and querying media data were introduced in Chapter 5. What we are looking at in this chapter are techniques that can be applied to text media, particularly those that currently support context-based retrieval (CBR) or could support it in the future. A number of techniques for processing text have been derived from research in AI and KBS and focus on the analysis of single text objects. We need to focus on techniques that can operate on a set-at-time basis so that mostly we will be using techniques based on indexing technologies and statistical methods. As well as considering the techniques available we will look at the way actual database implementations such as Oracle have incorporated these techniques and approaches. The reader should then be able to understand:

- manipulation of text data types;
- techniques for CBR of text media including text retrieval (TR), schema-directed extraction (SDE) and query-directed extraction (QDE);
- statistical methods of textual analysis;
- implementations based on Oracle and XML.

10.1 Introduction

Firstly we will consider what we mean by text media and what it is that distinguishes it from other media data, what is the nature of text that causes problems and what are the solutions available to us. In English text objects consist of words, units of natural languages that we can easily recognize because within the body of the text they can be delineated by spaces. Words consist of character strings that are specified in a dictionary for a given language. These features of text should enable us to process text relatively easily by using queries expressed in text-based languages such as SQL. This advantage is unlikely to be paralleled by image and video data, although audio objects may consist of spoken words. However, there are some problems with words. Some occur so frequently that they are meaningless from an information viewpoint – for example "and, but, the, from, to". These are called stop words and we will usually deal with them by removing or ignoring them. The main difficulty with words is that they change their appearance, spelling and meaning depending on context and location. There are the problems of:

- synonymy when a word has the same meaning as another word;
- polysemy when a word has more than one meaning in different context, for example "lead" in general English or "memory" in the specialist context of computing and the brain.

Although there will be many words and phrases that could be used to describe the same concept users are unlikely to be willing to input exhaustive lists of synonyms in order to express a query. In addition, different users may employ different terms to describe the same concept.

The distinction between words and phrases is blurred in some languages such as German and Dutch. In some Asian languages there are no specific word separators. In both cases the text needs to be processed by breaking it up into "words" or word groups that can be indexed. Here we will stick to English for the examples but it is worth noting that it has been proposed to split text into n-grams where an n-gram is a string of fixed length, n character bytes (Damashek,1995). This approach has the advantage of tolerating mis-spellings as well as being more sensitive to changes in words by the addition of prefixes and suffixes.

(This polymorphism is paralleled by objects within images and videos that change depending on spatial and temporal location. One of the advantages of dealing with text data first and then moving on to study image and video in later chapters is that the results of the manipulations on text data can be relatively easily observed and understood. The process of feature extraction using text can show what and how much data has been lost or summarized by the feature extraction processes much more transparently than in the case of visual data.)

End-users want to access text objects based on concepts existing in the domain of interest and semantic patterns that may exist both within a single text object and across sets of media. The objective is for the user to be able to achieve meaningful information through access to diverse information sources that may by distributed across networks. Evaluating retrieval for text media databases traditionally focused on the ability to compare the performance of alternative system designs, for example through what are called "workbench tests". This involves using standard collections of text that can be up to 2 Gb in size with over one million uncompressed documents. Test collections are listed by the TREC conferences.

However, the behavior of the user has a significant effect on the overall retrieval success because the tasks of media retrieval are no longer single transactions but sessions of many retrieval cycles with the user actively involved in refining the query a significant problem for effective evaluation is the difficulty of being able to judge the quality of any retrieval by simply inspecting the result set. Recently evaluations have included user-based and work-based studies (Pejtersen, 1996). These have found that users tend to find interesting information at many stages in the retrieval session. This information is used to modify their query formulations and may also change their goals and relevance judgements. In this context, goals refers to the first stage of Norman's seven stages of action, set out in Figure 3.2. If we want to study, measure, and optimize the useful work done with a text database, we must measure the retrieval done by an interactive user over a set of retrieval cycles. The effectiveness will depend partly upon the DBMS, but also partly upon what the user does. In other words we no longer have behavior that fits the simple linear pattern of Norman's seven stages of action. The last three stages deal with feedback from the system after the user's action – perceive, interpret and evaluate the resultant state of the system. This evaluation when the user judges the relevance of the result set to their original objective, causes a redefinition of the user's goal. Features of the user interface may prompt the user to formulate "better" or "poorer" queries or to even give up the attempt before the best result set has been retrieved. Consequently the quality of a single transaction may be relatively unimportant in determining whether the session converges on a high quality result set but using the result set in further queries may be essential. Some interesting research in this area has been carried out by Borland and Ingwerson (1997) and Rasmussen *et al.* (1994).

Usability metrics for multimedia retrieval need development – ideas put forward as quality issues for retrieval from multimedia database management systems (MMDBMSs) include:

- data accessibility;
- interpretability;
- usefulness;
- believability.

In this chapter we will begin by a study of the principles of techniques specialized for text:

- text retrieval (TR);
- schema-directed extraction (SDE);
- query-directed extraction (QDE).

In content-based retrieval of text objects, the query is focused on the extraction from collections of semi-structured text. Most of the content-based approaches to text can be classified as follows.

Text retrieval is the simplest form of processing that would return a set of documents from a query. Documents are returned in the result set if they are considered relevant to the query. In practical terms we will study specific methods to achieve:

- exact matches to words or phrases;
- inexact searching;
- proximity searches;
- intelligent searches such as discovering themes, sorting by relevance and weighting terms;
- getting the gist of a document;
- classifying and clustering text objects.

Query-directed extraction uses queries that are based on the domain ontology by mapping the elements of the ontology to structural text elements. It is useful for semi-structured text documents such as those found in business or scientific domains where documents are laid out to conform to a pattern.

Schema-directed extraction is a process that manipulates large collections of related text objects, for example e-mails. SDE systems proceed document by document, extracting information to fill slots in a predefined schema, ignoring most content of the document. It focuses on content that matches set criteria. The objective is to fill a schema rather than answering a query. This method can pull out representations of objects, properties and relations that exist in the domain ontology. In the case of analyzing all the e-mails accepted by an ISP a schema such as that shown in Table 10.1 could be used. In Chapter 7 we discussed the development of a domain ontology. From this an extraction schema could be developed for certain kinds of frequently posed queries. The schema could include a specification:

```
e-mail {sender, receiver, date, subject, persons, places}
```

A large collection of documents can then be processed by automatically searching and extracting the information to fill a relational table. The table

Table 10.1 Schema extracted relational table

Schema	Instance	Instance
Sender	Shirley Jones	Chris O'Toole
Receiver	Matt Smith	Matt Smith
Date	30–Jan–2002	30–Mar–2002
Subject	Award Board	Arrested in London
Persons	Ray Miller, John Chang	Alan Smith
Places	Room A406	Buckingham Palace

corresponding to the e-mail schema that could be held as metadata or output directly to the user. Users can refine the schema incrementally as their interests change. This is the basis used for software for searching collections of employee e-mails and file systems. SDE works well if there already exists a good knowledge of the domain and the user requirements. Statistical methods such as those we study later can be used if these are not clear in order to discover the concepts of interest buried in a collection of documents.

However, at the moment SDE still does not deal with the body of the text but merely slots easily recognized names into slots in the schema. We therefore need to consider methods that can pick out important words or phrases from the contents. SDE can be combined with some of the techniques described later that reduce individual documents to a tuple of the schema. The resulting filled schema forms the metadata that can be queried. Metadata standards described in Chapter 7 also need to be taken into account as these specified a number of different, sometimes related, schema that can form part of the predefined schema. These schemas may also be filled automatically by the techniques developed to support SDE.

In processing text objects we will need to abandon the concept of simple predicates that return a result set consisting of members each of which completely satisfies the predicate. Rather we will have a result set that is relevant to the query. A very difficult issue is determining the relevance of a document in a result set to a query. Ideally the process would not miss any relevant documents and not return any irrelevant ones. The quality of the retrieval process can be measured in terms of two metrics, namely **recall** and **precision**. Recall is a measure of how well the retrieval engine performs in finding relevant documents. The recall of a system is defined as how much of the information that ideally could have been retrieved or extracted by the system was in fact retrieved or extracted by the system.

Precision is a measure of how well the engine performs in not returning irrelevant documents. If every document is relevant the precision is 100%. The precision of a system is defined as how much of the information that ideally could have been retrieved or extracted by the system belongs to the information that should have been retrieved or extracted by the system. The retrieval engine must balance recall against precision. High precision means few unwanted documents are retrieved, while low recall means many relevant documents are missed. We can all think of examples of web search engines that result in very high recall but very low precision. In order to judge the overall performance of text retrieval systems recall–precision graphs are generated by calculating a value pair for each relevant document in the result set, obtained from each test retrieval. A retrieval engine may perform well for low recall (when it is finding a small percentage of the relevant documents) but perform worse than other retrieval engines when required to find 50% of the relevant documents so that there is often a trade-off between precision and recall. The order in which the documents are presented to the user is also relevant. Often we want to know the relevance of the first ten documents retrieved and this information cannot be extracted from recall–precision graphs.

Stop lists can be used to improve precision. Commonly occurring words are removed but it is also possible for the users to provide a list of stop words which can be excluded for indexing. Stop themes are a similar idea that can exclude whole subject areas.

Performance results in terms of recall and precision are available for systems using TR and SDE: also, to a limited extent, for QDE systems which have been developed more recently. (Much of the development of this technology has been sponsored by DARPA. Text Retrieval Conferences, TRECs, and the Message Understanding Conferences, MUCs, are useful sources of information on the evaluation of extraction and retrieval systems.)

In *Oracle Text* there are several storage options for the data. Note Oracle's treatment of text is different in some details between *Oracle8i* and *Oracle9i*. It can be stored in the database in both systems. It can be stored in the file system. It can be stored on the web. It is possible to create a text index on any text that can be referenced by a URL that exists on the internet or any specified intranet. Text objects can be stored within a database table which has a column defined as a CLOB data type. It is also possible to store the text using a user-defined data type.

We will start by recapping how we can insert and update CLOB data. Recall the employee table we introduced in Chapter 4. We can add a column to hold the employee's CV with a BLOB data type using the following statement:

```
ALTER TABLE employee
    ADD (cv BLOB DEFAULT EMPTY_BLOB())
```

Alternatively, and preferably, we could add a column with a CLOB data type which will allow us to use some character functions:

```
ALTER TABLE employee
    ADD (cv CLOB DEFAULT EMPTY_CLOB())
```

add_cv

We recall that LOB data types must be initialized before use so that any existing rows will need to be updated, for example,

```
UPDATE employee
SET cv=EMPTY_CLOB()
WHERE employee_number='1001';
```

initial_cv

Although it is possible to load text information into a CLOB (but not a BLOB) using an INSERT or an UPDATE statement it is better to use the DBMS_LOB package because these SQL update statements are restricted in terms of the text format that they can accept. For example, we can add plain text as follows:

```
UPDATE employee
SET cv='An excellent employee with a good range of professional
qualifications'
WHERE employee_number='1001';
```

update_cv

The following procedure in contrast loads a Word document from an external file into the **cv** column that has been specified as a BLOB. The Word document is loaded from a BFILE. The procedure accepts the **employee_number**. The BFILENAME function returns the BFILE locator that will be used as a pointer to the Word document in the file system. The document must exist in a directory for documents which has been created as a directory object and the user needs to be granted access to the directory, as follows:

```
CREATE DIRECTORY "TEXT_DOCUMENTS" AS 'C:\TEXT_DOCUMENTS';
GRANT READ ON DIRECTORY TEXT_DOCUMENTS TO SCOTT;
```

(Note that Oracle is case sensitive to directory names.) Here is the PL/SQL to create the procedure, called **load_cv**, which accepts the employee's number and the file extension of the text document. The BFILENAME function loads the data into a temporary variable **v_document** after checking that it exists in the directory. The SELECT .... FOR UPDATE locks the row specified for update and retrieves the lob_locator which must already exist. Routines from the DBMS_LOB package are used to open and load the file.

```
CREATE OR REPLACE PROCEDURE load_cv
(my_employee_number t_employee.employee_number%TYPE,
  my_file_extension VARCHAR2 DEFAULT '.doc')
AS
        v_document          BFILE;
        v_cv                employee.cv%TYPE;
BEGIN
  v_document :=BFILENAME('TEXT_DOCUMENTS',
'my_employee_number'|| '.'||'my_file_extension');
 IF DBMS_LOB.FILEEXISTS(v_document)=1 THEN
   SELECT cv
   INTO v_cv
   FROM employee
   WHERE employee_number=my_employee_number
   FOR UPDATE;
   DBMS_LOB.OPEN(v_document, DBMS_LOB.LOB_READONLY);
DBMS_LOB.LOADFROMFILE(v_cv,
v_document,DBMS_LOB.GETLENGTH(v_document));
   DBMS_LOB.CLOSE(v_document);
 END IF;
EXCEPTION
      WHEN OTHERS THEN
      IF DBMS_LOB.ISOPEN(v_document)=1 THEN
      DBMS_LOB.CLOSE(v_document);
 END IF;
END
/
```

It is important to close the BFILE in the exception clause of the procedure. We may recall that in Chapter 4 the following records are in the employee table:

```
EMPL  EMPLOYEE_NAME
----  -------------
1001  John Smith
1002  Mary Jones
```

Therefore we can add the CV of Mary Jones as a Word document with the following statement:

```
EXECUTE load_cv('1002');
```

EXERCISE 10.1

Write a PL/SQL procedure based on the example above to check how much data is held in the original document for the CV of an employee with a given employee number and compare this with the amount of text in the CLOB; then send a message to the messages table about the number of characters in the CV and added to the CLOB.

10.2   Querying Character Data Using SQL

Thus by adapting SQL functions and procedures we can insert and update CLOB data but to what extent can we use SQL built-in functions to manipulate text data? First we will review the SQL functions available to query character data types before checking on the equivalent functions for CLOBs, listed in Table 10.2.

In this section we will briefly review the way SQL is used to query character data in relational databases and then see how similar queries could be used with text data.

10.2.1   Exact Matching

SQL was designed for exact matching using Boolean queries. The WHERE clauses that we have used earlier in Chapter 5, such as **where_France**, used search conditions involving only single conditions. These conditions are referred to as predicates in relational theory because they must have a truth value that is either true or false. It is possible to use multiple predicates combined as the next query shows. The **logical operators**, comprising **AND**, **OR** and **NOT**, can be used to combine predicates into composite search conditions for more complex restrictions:

```
SELECT      wine_name, price
FROM        wine_list
WHERE       region='France' AND category='Chablis'
```
Boolean

Although this is a very simple way of retrieving information using conventional data types we will not be able to use the method with LOBs. However, it is important because we would be able to use this kind of query on the

Table 10.2   SQL built-in functions for text processing

SQL built-in functions	Objective
SOUNDEX('string')	Matches to the sound of a string
IN(...)	Matches to any member of a list of strings
LIKE	Matches to a string pattern
INSTR('string',column)	Locates a substring within a string
SUBSTR	Extracts a substring of a specified length from a string

metadata that is held in scalar data types, for example in SDE derived tables. Therefore we shall now describe some SQL query operators and *built-in* functions that are particularly useful for text data.

```
SELECT      wine_name, price
FROM        wine_list
WHERE       region IN ('France', 'Chile', 'USA')              in_query
```

We would use this statement to answer the query "List the name and price of wines in the **wine_list** table having a region of France, Chile, and USA". In this example, the predicate involving IN is satisfied when a value in the column being compared is equal to any one of the values given in the list.

10.2.2 Inexact Matching

Exact matching is no use when the user does not know the exact term to search for in the database, does not know the spelling or wants to search about an idea rather than a particular word. The uncertain spelling problem can be solved by using the SOUNDEX function. When processing text, this allows for searching for the sound of a word rather than its appearance. SOUNDEX uses an algorithm to return text that sounds like the sample provided by the users. It is particularly useful for names. The next example shows how it works:

```
SELECT wine_name, SOUNDEX(wine_name)
FROM wine_list
WHERE SOUNDEX (wine_name)=SOUNDEX ('Errazuriz')
```

```
                                                            sounding
WINE_NAME                              SOUN
-------------------------------        ----
Errazuriz                              E626
```

The SOUNDEX code for a string is derived by taking the first (English) alphabetical character in the string and appending it to between one and three numbers right padded with zeros to a total length of four characters (see Table 10.3). Any non-alphabetic characters at the beginning of the string are

Table 10.3 SOUNDEX codes

Character	SOUNDEX value
B,F,P,V	1
C,G,J,K,Q,S,X,Z	2
D,T	3
L	4
M,N	5
R	6

ignored. Each of the numbers represents a syllable. A syllable for this purpose is defined as a consecutive string of equivalent characters, not separated by any other characters. However, the vowel sounds represented by the letters "A,E,H,I,O,U,W,Y" are not assigned a value.

Examples of SOUNDEX codes are:

- ACCESS – SOUNDEX code = A220;
- AKKEZZ – SOUNDEX code = A220.

This is particularly useful when documents include errors that frequently arise from OCR.

10.2.3 The LIKE Operator

This SQL predicate can be used in both exact and inexact search conditions. LIKE is used to match a column with a known string or part of a string. There is one characteristic of this predicate to note – that it can only involve a column name and not an expression.

```
SELECT wine_name
FROM wine_list
WHERE wine_name LIKE 'Erraz%'
```

The predicate in the query needs a little explaining. The LIKE keyword is used in a situation where we wish to compare character string values in a column with a pattern in the form of a constant character string. The matching of the strings need not be complete. To allow it to be incomplete, the underscore character, _, stands for any single character, while the percentage sign, %, stands for any sequence of zero or more characters. For example, the next query will allow the user to search for any wines with the phrase "Pale ... medium bodied ... " in any category of wine:

```
SELECT DISTINCT category
FROM wine_list
WHERE character LIKE 'P_b%medium_bodied%s'
```

medium

With this interpretation, the pattern 'P_%medium_bodied%s' can be matched as follows. The string must start with "P", the underscore following "m" means that any character including a space can follow but the next letter must be "b". The "%" sign followed by "s" means that any sequence of zero or more characters can then follow as long as the string ends in an "s".

The LIKE operator is useful for achieving stemming. Stemming is the way we can use the essential part of a word, its root, but remove the endings that may change depending on the word's position in a sentence. For example, "computer", "computing", "computed", "computation", "compute" are all based on the stem "comput." Therefore it is better to search for the stem "comput" than the particular words. In addition some stems are common to different languages and can be used to overcome variations in spelling, for example, between "UK/USA" English and French.

10.2.4   Proximity Searches

We can also use LIKE to search for topics within character data, for example

```
SELECT wine_name
FROM wine_list
WHERE character LIKE '%Medium Bodied%'
```

medium2

This query can be expressed formally as

Give the name of each wine that has a character that is described by a string that contains the substring "Medium Bodied" with any number of characters before or after.

The SQL standard defines the equivalent function POSITION instead of INSTR.

However, although this will return a set of wine names, including "Chablis Billaud-Simon" there is no indication of the actual location of the substring "Medium Bodied" within the **character** text. To find the location of a substring, Oracle SQLPLUS provides the capability with a function named INSTR, which has two string arguments (separated by a comma) and finds the position of the second string in the first:

```
SELECT wine_name, INSTR(wine_name, 'au') AS position
FROM wine_list
```

position

The result of this query shows that, for each wine's name that does not contain the substring "au", the INSTR function gives the value 0, while for "Chablis Billaud-Simon" the function would give the value 13, because the start of the string "au" occurs at the thirteenth position in this string.

EXERCISE 10.2

(a) Give the SQL query to locate the stem of "body, bodied" in the character column of wine_list.

(b) Give a query that uses the INSTR function in a WHERE clause to select only those wines whose character contains the text string "medium bodied" to obtain the same result as the query **medium** using LIKE.

(c) Give the SQL query to locate the stem of "programming" in the CV column of employee.

While the solution to Exercise 10.2(b) shows how in this example, the INSTR function can be used to give the same result as using the LIKE operator, they have different capabilities. In particular, note that the substring being searched for using INSTR cannot contain any pattern symbols in the way LIKE uses % and _. Moreover, neither the LIKE operator nor the INSTR function can be used with CLOB DATA so the next query would not be valid:

```
SELECT DISTINCT category
FROM wine_list
WHERE note LIKE '%Ideal as an aperitif%'
```

Instead we will need to use the DBMS_LOB package as follows:

```
SELECT DISTINCT category
FROM wine_list
WHERE DBMS_LOB.INSTR(note, 'Ideal as an aperitif')>0
```

The requirement of giving just part of some text is satisfied in Oracle by using a function SUBSTR that has three arguments separated by commas, meaning the substring is FROM the named column, starting at the second argument, FOR the length of the third argument. ()

Note: this is a variation from the SQL standard which provides the equivalent capability through the function SUBSTRING.

```
SELECT wine_name, SUBSTR(wine_name,1,3)
FROM wine_list
                                                    substring
WINE_NAME                            SUB
------------------------------       ---
Ch.Haut-Rian                         Ch.
Errazuriz                            Err
```

The SUBSTR function gives the part of the first string argument that starts at the position in the string specified by the second argument. It has a length specified by the third argument (the second and third arguments must be integers, but do not have to be constants as in the example). The last argument can be omitted, with the effect that the result is the substring starting at the position given by the second argument and including the rest of the first string argument. We can combine SUBSTR and INSTR to cut out just a section from a large text as follows:

```
SELECT wine_name,
SUBSTR(character, INSTR(character, 'Medium Bodied'),300) AS
cut_out
FROM wine_list                                        cut_out
```

This query will locate the wines where the **character** column contains the phrase "Medium Bodied" and displays the name of the wine followed by a section of text that follows the phrase to a specified length of 300 characters. This will give a list of medium-bodied wines and some information about them, as follows:

```
WINE_NAME CUT_OUT
--------------------  ---------------------------------------
Ch.Haut-Rian          Medium Bodied, Dry, Ready, but will keep
```

The problem with this simple query is that it starts at an arbitrary point in the text when "Medium" occurs and stops after a fixed length even if this is the middle of a sentence or even a word. So the result table will not be very satisfactory but does form a basis for the user to interrogate the database. (We have also ignored the issue of case – "medium" versus "Medium". There are two functions UPPER and LOWER to ensure differences in case can be eliminated.)

These functions cannot be used with CLOB data types and instead we have to use the DBMS_LOB package. We can construct another query statement for the **note** column which will result in a character string from the CLOB of length 5:

```
SELECT DBMS_LOB.SUBSTR(note,10,5) cut_out
FROM wine_list
                                              cut_out_LOB
```

EXERCISE 10.3

Give the query in natural language corresponding to the following statement:

```
SELECT wine_name,
DBMS_LOB.SUBSTR(note, 80,DBMS_LOB.INSTR(note, 'citrus fruits
and gooseberries')) cut_out
FROM wine_list
WHERE DBMS_LOB.INSTR(note, 'citrus fruits and gooseberries')>0
                                              cut_out_clob
```

Before leaving these simple queries we should mention the problem of missing values and how to deal with them.

10.2.5 Missing Values

Using null is an accepted way of indicating that there is no value for a given column in a particular row of a table. It is a practice that causes problems in database implementation and good database design should always try to minimize the use of nulls. In a relational database consisting of tables with a fixed structure missing values cannot always be avoided, particularly in multimedia databases because these missing values can arise from a user perspective in two different ways:

- There is a value but it is not known at the time, for example no pronunciation clip yet available.
- There is no value because the column is not applicable for that row, for example in the **wine_list** table the pronunciation column will only hold data in the case of French wines.

SQL does not provide any means of distinguishing these two situations. When using null in SQL, the results can often be inconsistent and misleading, as we shall show. The internal storage of a null, the SQL keyword NULL and the symbols used to display nulls are all distinct and are different in different DBMS implementations. You may recall that in Chapter 2 we introduced the idea of a LOB locator. The locator is also important in Oracle since before data can be added to the LOB the locator must be non-NULL. This is done by initializing the locator with the function EMPTY_BLOB as we showed above when we added the **cv** column. In the same way the BFILE column must be made non-NULL by using the BFILENAME() function.

For example, the query

```
SELECT wine_name,DBMS_LOB.GETLENGTH(note)
  FROM  wine_list;
```

will result in

```
WINE_NAME                         DBMS_LOB.GETLENGTH(NOTE)
------------------------------    ------------------------
Ch.Haut-Rian                                           183
Errazuriz                                                0
```

When the table wine_list was created in Chapter 4 the **note** column was defined using the default value function EMPTY_BLOB, therefore when rows have been inserted with no values for **note** such as for "Errazuriz" wine, the length of the note is zero (if it was null the length would also be null).

10.2.6 The IS NULL Operator

Even though we may have set up the LOB columns to be non-NULL we may still find we have nulls in other columns. Since nulls can cause misunderstanding and errors SQL provides a method for testing whether a particular value is null. A special operator called IS NULL is used to check this, as in the following example:

```
SELECT wine_name
FROM wine_list
WHERE note IS NULL                                           is_null
```

This will result in no rows being returned because the column was set with a default value but the picture column was not given a default value so that

```
SELECT wine_name
FROM wine_list
WHERE picture IS NULL
```

This results in a final table which answers the request "List the wines from the wine list in which there are no pictures (**picture** is null)". This is another example of the use of these operators

```
SELECT wine_name
FROM wine_list
WHERE pronunciation IS NOT NULL                             isnt_null
```

In considering the effect of null on queries, we can distinguish two situations. The first is where the query is explicitly concerned with searching for null in a table, in which case you have to use a predicate involving IS NULL. It is not possible to use a simple comparison predicate of the form <column> = NULL, as SQL will not allow the use of the keyword NULL as if it were a value that could be compared with other values.

The second situation we need to consider is much more general. Any query may be affected by nulls in the tables being searched or nulls arising during processing. We will need to consider both how a query involving nulls is processed and what impact this may have on the results of the query. The use of nulls can have unplanned consequences so that the user is led to believe whole sections of data are missing. In Appendix C there is a list of the effects of nulls in different situations that users find particularly confusing.

Text retrieval is usually based on Boolean operators (AND, OR, NOT) although some extra facilities can improve recall, for example the thesaurus operators that extend the match to synonymous words, proximity operators such as PARAGRAPH, SENTENCE, PHRASE and NEAR/n. When these techniques are used instead of the result set representing an exact match, we have a set that is to some extent relevant to the query. Retrieved documents are therefore assigned a relevance score – the degree to which they match the query.

At the start of the chapter we noted that text retrieval relies on statistical methods and index technology. In the next sections we will study both these issues.

10.3   Statistical Methods for Text Analysis

In terms of database requirements there are two distinct type of processing:

- dealing with a single document as a collection of words;
- dealing with a collection of documents.

We will start by looking at the processing of a single document and then at dealing with sets of documents.

10.3.1   Single Document Processing

The next stage is to consider how the use of LOBs by themselves or as components within objects could be combined so that text data could be manipulated within the conceptual framework of SQL that the user is already familiar with.

For a single document the user may want to:

(a) find a single term (word or phrase) and its location;

(b) count the number of times the term occurs as a measure of the relevance of the document;

(c) reduce the document to its essential terms and rank them in order;

(d) locate a term and make a selection from the document on that basis.

A number of quite effective statistical methods have been used for text queries. These exploit computational power by taking a large text document and reducing it to a set of terms. These terms may be single words or related groups of words that can be recognized in the text. A weighting is given to each term corresponding to the number of times it occurs in the text relative to the size of the document. In this way a collection of documents can be compared. However, even though linking and stop words are ignored there is a danger that this list of terms can get quite large. The process can be further refined and the number of terms reduced by combining synonymous terms and by using a thesaurus to combine equivalent terms. The result is a set of terms and their weights which is called a **term vector** that can be stored as metadata. The whole process can be carried out automatically on a collection of documents. One way of recognizing these terms is to:

- Split the text into manageable chunks.
- Remove the stop words. These are very frequently occurring words that have no specific meaning, for example *"the", "and", "but"*. We can also remove most of the common adjectives such as *"large"* and *"small"*.
- Try to recognize words that always go together as these may be phrases or composite terms.
- Count the number of times the remaining words occur in the chunk.
- Consider combining words based on a thesaurus.

Figure 10.1 gives an example of using this technique to compare two sequences of text. The result of this exercise is the discovery of a number of terms that could be used directly in queries or stored in indexes. This process could be carried out when a document is added to the database and the

---

SAMPLE SEQUENCE 1
More and more application areas such as medicine, maintain large collections of digital images. Efficient mechanisms to efficiently browse and navigate are needed instead of searching and viewing directory trees of image files.

REMOVE STOP WORDS
application areas medicine collections digital images. mechanisms browse navigate searching viewing directory trees image files.

TERMS
application (1); area (1); medical (1); collection (2); digital (1); image (2); mechanism (1); browse (1); navigate (1)

SAMPLE SEQUENCE 2
Advances in techniques for obtaining images of the body's interior have greatly improved medical diagnosis. New imaging methods include various X-ray systems, computerized tomography and magnetic resonance. The introduction of computerized tomography was a major advance in visualizing almost all parts of the body particularly useful in diagnosing tumors and space-occupying lesions. These new techniques lead to accumulation of masses of digital medical images stored in medical image archives.

REMOVE STOP WORDS
techniques obtaining images body's interior medical diagnosis. imaging methods include X-ray systems, computerized tomography magnetic resonance. computerized tomography body diagnosing tumors space-occupying lesions. techniques digital medical images medical image archives.

TERMS
techniques (1); images (4); body (2); interior (1); medical (3); diagnosis (2); method (1); X-ray (1); computerized tomography (2); visualising (1); tumor (1); space-occupying lesion (1); digital (1); archive (1)

TERMS IN BOTH
medical (1, 3); image (2, 4); digital (1, 1)

Figure 10.1 Comparing two text sequences for chunking

terms stored at that point in an index or as metadata. When the user specifies one of these terms in a query the whole document or a sample section of the document can be retrieved. In addition, terms can be weighted either by the user or by the term extraction process. A simple weighting can be based on the frequency of occurrence of the term in the document. By using a thesaurus with the text in Figure 10.1 we may conclude that "technique" and "method" should be combined and that in this domain "tumor" and "lesion" could be combined.

The concepts **term expansion** and **term normalization** are often referred to in text processing. Term expansion is when one term is expanded into a set of terms. For example, whereas in stemming we recognize a root that can be used to represent a lot of words, in other cases words in natural languages are inflected, for example "buy" and "bought". In these cases the query terms need to be expanded to include all the inflected terms. It may then be possible to use stemming on these as well. Related terms that belong to the domain can also be dealt with by term expansion. Documents about the "Bay Area" may also be related to the term "Silicon Valley". This is accomplished by using a thesaurus that includes knowledge about these relations.

In Oracle the user can extend the internal knowledge base using one or more thesauri following the format of the ISO-2788 standard (which covers synonyms, broader terms, narrower terms, related terms and translation terms). Term normalization describes the process that takes place when several related terms are collapsed into a single preferred term. This will also cover abbreviations and acronyms which are replaced by their full forms. In this way controlled vocabularies that are being established by a number of metadata standards can be incorporated (see Chapter 7).

Recall and precision are measures of how well the retrieval engine performs in finding relevant documents. Term expansion and term normalization increase recall values. Term expansion and term normalization decrease precision.

The technique we illustrated in Figure 10.1 has been variously called chunking, zoning, scanning and segmenting. The objective is to discover structures in the document larger than a sentence. This means segmenting documents into passages corresponding to sentences, paragraphs, headings and section borders. Semi-structured documents can be more easily chunked because headings can be recognized and given extra weighting on the basis that they refer to a whole section of text. This is based on recognizing formatting cues, punctuation and SGML tags. It is helpful to treat passages as if they were separate documents. The assumption is that a smaller part of a large document is more likely to be focused on a single topic. However, chunking has not been studied or applied systematically.

This method of generating metadata is based on using text tiling algorithms that assume terms describing a subtopic will occur together in the same local area of the text. A switch to another subtopic would be recognized by the co-occurrence of a different set of terms. A typical algorithm would proceed as follows:

(a) divide text into 20-word adjacent token sequences (ignoring common and connection words);
(b) compare adjacent blocks of token sequences for overall lexical similarities based on frequency count – if the frequency is localized to a block or set of blocks it can be identified as a topic;
(c) compute similarity values for adjacent blocks.

Figure 10.2   Subtopic boundary location

Subtopic boundary location is another method that can be used to create summaries of documents as shown in Figure 10.2.

Parsing refers to the analysis of the natural language sentences or similar structural units in terms of the syntactic structure as specified in a grammar. A parser usually works with a grammar, a lexicon and a part-of-speech (POS) tagger. In the case of the parser, it must be robust enough to cope with the presence of ungrammatical constructs, incomplete sentences and spelling errors. It must have speed, i.e. it must work in real time in the presence of structural ambiguity. Partial parsers are fast as they are capable of picking out common phrases even in sentences full of errors. Some of the fastest although computationally least powerful are finite-state parsers.

An interesting example is FASTUS (cascaded finite state automata), a system developed by Hobbs *et al.* (1996) that uses SDE by decomposing the process into several stages:

- initial stage – processing at word level, recognition of multi-word and proper nouns;

- second stage – identify phrases, segment sentences into phrases;

- third stage – scan for patterns of events of interest to the application, encoding information about events and entities;

- final stage – identify equivalent structures in an attempt to solve co-references.

Recognition of phrases is based on syntactic information, for example obtained by searching a noun group consisting of head noun, its determinants and other left modifiers. Contexts are used in identifying proper nouns as names of specific types, for example "*Vaclav Harel, President of Czech Republic*" which results in Vaclav Harel being recognized as a person.

FASTUS uses criteria for determining equivalence of two structures based on

- internal structure of noun groups;

- nearness along some metric;
- semantic compatibility of two structures.

All of this is done without employing natural language processing (NLP) and is effective when the domain is simple and the task well defined.

10.3.2 Processing a Collection of Documents

The techniques described in the previous section analyze separate documents. A collection of documents could be processed individually and then summarized for SDE. The next technique works on collections of documents.

Statistical Vector Space Methods in text access

Several statistical approaches based on vector space methods can be used very successfully in retrieval systems to provide a means of assessing the relevance of a document to a query.

Routines parse the target documents for unique terms so that each document is associated with a term vector as shown in Table 10.4. In a term vector each of a set of possibly occurring terms is associated with a weight which depends on how many times it occurs in the document. Stop words are ignored and an adjustment is made for document size to ensure large documents are not always preferred.

Documents are then ranked by ascending order of relevance. Since text retrieval can produce large result sets users want the documents to be sorted by their relevance to the query rather than just returned as a set. This requires the ability to rank the documents by a process called relevance ranking. With relevance ranking we can use a cut-off point to measure recall and precision. For example, it is a great advantage to include methods using the first twenty returned. Relevance ranking can be improved by being able to rank the relative importance of different terms in a document with respect to a query term. This requires a combination of statistical information and knowledge about the domain and the relationship between the terms.

Table 10.4 Term by document matrix

	Document 1	Document 2	Document 3	Document 4
Term 1	1	2	0	0
Term 2	0	2	3	1
Term 3	0	1	0	2
Term ...		0	1	0
Term ...				
Term t	1	0	3	1

The weakness of the method is that vectors themselves, as seen in Table 10.4 are quite large. Synonymous terms are not taken into account so terms such as "car" and "automobile" are classed as orthogonal. Topic vectors overcome these limitations by grouping terms by concept. Latent semantic indexing (LSI), which we introduced in Chapter 5, is one method of achieving this. LSI is a method that derives these clusters automatically by associating each term with a profile based on the occurrence in the same document of other terms with that term. Alternatively, a thesaurus can be used to group terms with other terms in thematic classes. It is based on providing a thematic profile of the document as a vector of terms or concept weights. This can be followed by a process to measure how close the documents are to each other in a way that can be visualized.

The resulting vectors are then compared for similarity or dissimilarity. A list of similarity/dissimilarity algorithms is given in Table 10.5. These algorithms can be used to generate an $n \times n$ matrix that describes the similarity or dissimilarity of each possible pair of documents.

The query can be analyzed in the same way to yield a vector of weights and a distance metric; typically a sum of squares is applied between the query on the one hand and each document on the other. The overall measurement of the document similarity lends itself particularly well to query by example. A sample text is provided with the request "give me documents that are like this document". The sample text is mapped to a vector profile in the same way as a query and similar documents returned. Most systems are based on this method or pattern matching.

LSI has not yet been incorporated in many commercial systems. A theme-proving technology is used by Oracle to try to prove the relevance of a query term to a query by searching for secondary evidence from related terms in the document. The related terms are evaluated by using a set of

Table 10.5 Similarity/dissimilarity measures

Algorithm	
Dice	$\text{Similarity} = \dfrac{2 \sum_{k=1}^{t} \text{term}_{ik}\,\text{term}_{jk}}{\sum_{k=1}^{t} \text{term}_{ik} + \sum_{k=1}^{t} \text{term}_{jk}}$
Cosine	$\text{Similarity} = \dfrac{\sum_{k=1}^{t} \text{term}_{ik}\,\text{term}_{jk}}{\sqrt{(\sum_{k=1}^{t}\text{term}_{ik}^2 + \sum_{k=1}^{t}\text{term}_{jk}^2)}}$
Overlap	$\text{Similarity} = \dfrac{\sum_{k=1}^{t} \text{term}_{ik}\,\text{term}_{jk}}{\min(\sum_{k=1}^{t} \text{term}_{ik},\ \sum_{k=1}^{t} \text{term}_{jk})}$
Asymmetric	$\text{Similarity} = \dfrac{\sum_{k=1}^{t} \min(\text{term}_{jk}\,\text{term}_{jk})}{\sum_{k=1}^{t} \text{term}_{jk}}$
Minkowski	$\text{Similarity} = \sqrt[r]{\sum_{k=1}^{t}(\text{term}_{ik} - \text{term}_{jk})^r}$

rules that are intended to give the best combination of precision versus recall. This will give better results than merely using a large thesaurus.

10.4 Querying Multimedia Text

We have seen how it is possible to query text by using SQL in the conventional manner. However, large text instances are difficult to display in a result set in a coherent fashion. An alternative paradigm is "query by example". The user can then present a text document or a fragment of text and present the query as "find documents like this one".

In order for this to work well we would need

- a set of sample data items with examples of the semantics of interest to users;
- knowledge of the general domain semantics;
- constraints describing patterns in and across the sample data items and domain semantics – this is the most complex aspect.

A number of different approaches have also been suggested for the way the user should be able to express a text query although currently few of these are available in commercial DBMSs. These include:

- *Cyclic incremental querying*. A set of text examples is labeled and then a similarity search match is performed against the examples. The output of one request is recycled into input of a follow-up request.
- *Result traversal* so that the result set may best be conveyed as a set of hyperlinked multimedia results.
- *Annotation interaction metaphors*. A user is provided with a way to annotate the results of a previous query and submit the annotated data as a new similarity search request.
- *Visualizing spatial relationships*. Multimedia queries and results are often highly spatial. The result set is viewed as a set of concepts or patterns, organized in multidimensional space.
- *Visualizing temporal relationships*. As above but with the focus on time rather than space.

An alternative means of achieving these objectives to using a text-based query language such as SQL is to use spatial data management systems that represent documents spatially in either two or three dimensions. The idea is that the configuration of the documents represents the underlying semantic relationships between the documents. The objective is to allow users to search more intuitively as similar documents are represented clustered together in space. The semantic content of each document must be assessed by the statistical methods described above and similarity measures obtained. Two examples of these systems are:

- JAIR (MIT AI Labs);
- PathFinder Network (Brunel University, UK).

Studies of these systems with users found evidence that the statistical algorithms provide a good representation of general human opinion of document similarity but there were wide human differences and the spatial representation was not always helpful.

A similar concept is to construct a two-dimensional thematic map of a set of documents but again evaluation of user performance in terms of search times and quality of retrieval has been mixed.

10.5   Content-dependent Metadata

We introduced the concept of content-dependent metadata in Chapter 7. In the next subsections we will look at content-dependent metadata in relation to text media, what it is, how it is generated and its role in content-based retrieval.

10.5.1   Metadata for Text

One of the simplest ways of generating metadata for text media is through SGML. An SGML editor automatically generates metadata according to the document type definition when the document is edited. Similarly, XML will result in the generation of automatic data about web documents that can be used by search engines. An example of the SGML definition of a journal paper is shown in Figure 10.3.

XML, which was introduced in this text in Chapter 7, provides a toolkit for text processing based on three ways of defining the structure of all XML documents:

- XML schema (XSD) – the way the information is organized;
- DTD – document type definition;
- XDR – Extended Data Reservation Standard for describing and encoding data.

The DTD concept existed in SGML but in XML the DTD becomes machine-readable. It is possible to link DTD elements to object classes through the use of an API. XML editors are a useful way of creating XML because, although

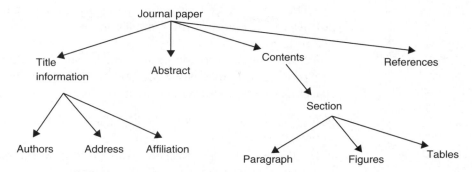

Figure 10.3   SGML for a journal paper

XML can be created by a text editor, XML editors enforce compliance to the specified DTD. A valid XML document conforms to the XML syntax rules and a parser can validate an XML documents against the DTD. An application can also validate an XML document from an external source, authored by one system and delivered and displayed by another. Individual XML instances can be validated against the DTD before further processing. An instance of XML is a self-contained well-formed "bit" of XML such as a tag nesting structure. A text file can be a combination of many XML instances. We can regard a DTD as a class with the XML document as an instance of the class; Table 10.6 illustrates the connection between the DTD and an XML instance. The reasons DTDs are used are as follows:

- The document is part of a larger set and we need to ensure that every member of the set follows the same rules.
- The document must contain a specific set of data.
- The document needs to match other industry-specific documents.
- It is possible to error check the document.

For example, take a sentence from earlier in this chapter:

The retrieval process can be measured by **recall** and **precision**.

Table 10.6   XML instance and corresponding DTD

XML instance	DTD
`<E-MAIL ID='1'>`	`<! ELEMENT E-MAIL (FROM,TO,SUBJECT, BODY)>`
`<FROM ID='2' sender's name</FROM>`	`<! ELEMENT FROM (#CDATA)*>`
`<TO ID='3' recipient's name</TO>`	`<! ELEMENT TO (#CDATA)*>`
`<SUBJECT A message</SUBJECT>`	`<! ELEMENT SUBJECT (#CDATA)*>`
`<BODY> some text here </BODY>`	`<! ELEMENT BODY (#CDATA)*>`
`</E-MAIL>`	

This sentence can be presented as a persistent parse tree that distinguishes the elements of the sentence in an hierarchical layout as shown in Figure 10.4.

XML schemas provide more control over XML documents than DTDs can provide. Schemas work with both XML documents and XML namespaces. XML schema was developed to overcome some limitations of DTDs:

- All DTD elements are global and not context sensitive. All elements must have different names.

- DTDs cannot be used to specify the kinds of information such as dates or e-mail addressed that go inside an element.

There are a number of options for linking XML and SQL databases together:

- *Persistent parse trees* (see Figure 10.4). In this approach the entire XML document is decomposed element by element into individual nodes and each node stored as a separate row in a table. Each node of the parse tree is put into its own row with relations built to the other nodes to reflect the structure and order of the XML. The XML is disintegrated into its constituent parts. This approach can allow queries such as listing by format, for example words in bold. However, this approach can be difficult to index and lacks relational integrity.

- *XML decomposition.* In this approach a schema is created for every element and every attribute forms a separate table. This allows for relational integrity but it is difficult to maintain consistency between changes in the XML and the SQL.

- *Partial decomposition.* In this approach the entire XML document is stored as an instance in the database. The XML document is maintained as the primary data source as a CLOB but some selected data from the XML is placed in relational tables.

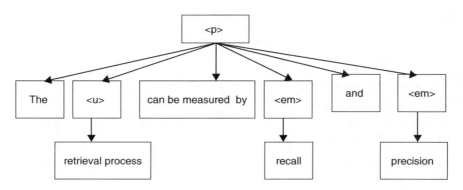

Figure 10.4 Hierarchical layout of XML example

We can illustrate how these concepts would work in practice by developing a text application for distributing headlines on the web. As mentioned in Chapter 7 Rich Site Summary (RSS) is a lightweight XML format designed for sharing headlines and other web content so we will use this as the metadata format. Developing the basic application involves the following steps (Figure 10.5):

(a) Create an XML document (xml.rss) using the RSS DTD standard, which can be validated against an external source, which defines the following classes:

Channel	{title, link, description, language}
Item	{title, link, description, weighting}

Item will hold the metadata for the document located at the URL stored in **link**.

(b) Create a PHP document (xml.php) that parses the XML document and the class definitions and sets up an array of items. It displays the metadata for the list of documents.

(c) Create an HTML document that dynamically displays the data about the documents using DHTML and a scripting language that allows the user to browse, make selections and display the results.

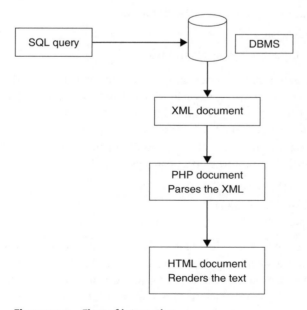

Figure 10.5   Flow of interaction

In Oracle there are explicit links to XML documents provided by functions such as HASPATH and INPATH that are used with CONTEXT indexes. INPATH is used when we want to search a text query within a path. HASPATH is used when we want to test for path existence. It takes a path as its only argument and returns 100 for a document if the path exists, 0 otherwise. For example,

```
SELECT       wine_name
FROM         wine_list
WHERE CONTAINS (note, 'HASPATH(/Media/Documents)')>0
```

will return all the wine_names where within **note** there is a top-level tag that is a media element which has a document element as a direct child.

10.5.2 Oracle Text Implementation

Oracle8i used *interMedia* to manipulate and retrieve text media. *Oracle9i* uses *Oracle Text* so that *Oracle Text* has replaced *interMedia Text* in *Oracle9i*. Both allow text data objects to be more fully integrated with the database so that text and structured queries can be combined in a straightforward manner. Both systems use indexing technologies to support text searching. In the next sections we will describe some of the facilities they both offer, making clear when certain operations are only available in *Oracle Text*.

In order to use these capabilities we must:

- load text media into the database;
- index the text;
- express queries about the text.

Text data can be loaded into the database as CLOBs, described at the beginning of the chapter. In order to use the services provided by *Oracle interMedia Text* the user must be granted the role CTXAPP. This will give the account the ability to make the necessary text calls to perform text indexing and processing. A column with a CLOB data type cannot be indexed in the normal way but can be indexed as follows in SQL:

```
CREATE INDEX index_note ON
wine_list(note)
INDEXTYPE IS ctxsys.context
```

This creates an index of type ctxsys.context that consists of a number of indexes and tables. Only one column may be indexed this way but nested table columns that include CLOBs cannot be indexed. Included in *interMedia Text* is a set of views, tables and stored code that are owned by CTXSYS. Many of the CTXSYS objects are prefixed with either CTX_ or DR.

There are a number of options that can be considered when indexing in this way:

- DATASTORE – specifies how the index is stored by using the PATH attribute;
- FILTER – specifies text filtering so that formatted binary documents such as Word documents can be turned into HTML, XML or plain text;
- SECTION – specifies how HTML and XML tags operate within a search;
- LEXER – specifies how the text is split into words.

Once the column has been indexed in this way it can be queried using the CONTAINS operator in an SQL PREDICATE as follows:

```
SELECT wine_code
FROM wine_list
WHERE CONTAINS (note, 'aperitif') >0
```

The CONTAINS function, which can only appear in the WHERE clause, checks the text index for the **note** column. If the term "aperitif" is found in the index a score greater than 0 is returned. The value of the score reflects how well the row value matches the criteria specified in the CONTAINS function. Oracle processes the SQL part of the query in a standard way and the text query separately and then the two result tables are merged to produce a single set of results. The symbol > is a threshold operator so the user can set the value that follows it to between 0 and 10. The value returned is displayed by the SCORE function; for example, in this inexact search the threshold is set as 1:

```
SELECT SCORE(1)
FROM employee
WHERE CONTAINS(cv, 'CGI scripts', 1) > 0
```

The SCORE function can be used in a SELECT clause or a GROUP BY clause.

```
SELECT SCORE(10), wine_code
FROM wine_list
WHERE CONTAINS(text, 'medium'), 10) > 0
```

Oracle interMedia Text includes a number of operators that will support term expansion that increase recall and a few that will narrow the search to increase precision; these are listed in Table 10.7.

The ACCUM (accumulator) function adds together the scores for individual searches for different criteria linked by AND or OR so that the query

```
SELECT wine_code
FROM wine_list
WHERE CONTAINS (note, 'aperitif' AND 'medium')>0
```

Table 10.7   Text manipulation operators provided by *Oracle Text*

Operator	Description
Term expansion operators	
ABOUT	Increases the number of relevant documents returned
ACCUMulate	Search for any that contain one search term
BT (broader term)	Expand query using thesaurus
EQUI	Expand query by including equivalent term:
	term1 term2 equiv
FUZZY	Expand with similarly spelled terms
RT (related term)	Include all related terms from thesaurus
SOUNDEX()	Expand to include words with similar sounds
STEM()	Search for words with same root
Term reduction operators	
NT (narrow term)	Use thesaurus to narrow terms
NEAR	Return score based on proximity
NOT	Contains one query term and not another
PT (preferred term)	Replace a term with one from thesaurus
THRESHOLD(----:)	Eliminates documents that score below a threshold number
WEIGHT(*)	Multiplies the score by a given factor
General operators	
HASPATH	Find documents on specified XML path
INPATH	Search for XML documents
SQE	Calls a stored query

becomes

```
SELECT wine_code
FROM wine_list
WHERE CONTAINS (note, 'aperitif ACCUM medium') >5
```

The threshold operator performs an analysis that uses the threshold value to compare the score calculated by Oracle with the specified threshold value "5". The weight operator enables the user to indicate the importance of different terms in the search. The following query will double the target search score for "aperitif" compared with the threshold score while "medium" remains the same.

```
SELECT wine_code
FROM wine_list
WHERE CONTAINS (note, 'aperitif*2 AND medium*1') >5
```

The ABOUT operator will find documents that match a concept or a theme. The concepts are created when the text index is created; for example, to search a fruit theme

```
SELECT wine_name
FROM wine_list
WHERE CONTAINS (note, 'ABOUT(fruit)') >0
```

The list included in the ABOUT clause consists of the terms the user thinks are relevant to their search. The documents returned will be matched using these criteria – the documents can include any of the listed terms but a document will appear higher in the result set if more terms are found in it. The ABOUT operator does not use stemming.

The SCORE function can be used in a SELECT, GROUP BY or ORDER BY clause, unlike CONTAINS which can only be included in the WHERE clause.

We can also create our own thesaurus for an application as a file shown in Figure 10.6. The items mean that discount is a synonym for sale and the foreign words included can also be used. After the thesaurus file is created then it can be loaded with the CTXLOAD program which is included in the CTXSYS.CTX_THES package.

We can check the list of thesauri available with the statement

```
SELECT *
FROM ctx_thesauri
```

Constructing effective queries for complex text data can be challenging for users. *Oracle interMedia* helps the user by providing the EXPLAIN procedure. This shows how the query has been parsed and how terms were expanded and normalized. It can also extract a summary of the document that includes some of the most salient paragraphs or sentences of the document and can also provide a theme summary.

To summarize, *Oracle Text* can

- search a document by theme such as "wines of the New World" whether or not the documents contain the word "wine";
- get themes from a document – extracting sentences or paragraphs that fit the major themes;
- get the gist of a document;
- extend the knowledge base with terms from a particular domain;
- extend the knowledge base with new associations between terms;
- classify a stream of documents according to a set of queries;
- cluster a set of documents according to their themes.

```
sale
    italian: saldo
    spanish: oferto
    french: solde
    syn discount
    italian: sconto
    spanish: descuento
    french: escompte
```

Figure 10.6   Thesaurus file

10.6 Indexing Technologies for Text

To use the text operators we must first create a text index on the column in which the text is stored. The text index formed will itself be a collection of tables and indexes that stores information about the text stored in that column, for example, for *Oracle8i*

```
CREATE INDEX wine_note
ON wine_list(note)
INDEXTYPE IS CTXSYS.CONTEXT
```

The column specified in the CREATE INDEX statement can have the following data types: CHAR, VARCHAR2, BLOB, CLOB or BFILE. Nested table types cannot be indexed.

The simplest type of text query is the exact match which we met at the beginning of the chapter for SQL character data types. In text retrieval the concept of the exact match is used when the user knows exactly what they want and having specified the term the whole collection of documents is searched one by one and those documents with at least one match are returned. This will be a very slow process if the documents or the collections are large. Therefore it would be much more efficient if the terms we have identified by the methods described above could be used instead to form the basis for an index. Oracle builds an inverted index in this way so that simple queries can be executed by using the CONTAINS predicate described above. The inverted index is a list of words from the documents with each word having a list of documents in which it appears. It is called inverted because it is the inverse of the normal way of looking at text – seeing a document as a list of words.

An index term might also be associated with its expected frequency of occurrence generated over many documents. A criterion can be applied such as more common terms being less important/relevant than less common words. Stop words are those that are so common they have no relevance and so are ignored.

Phrases are also indexed in a "theme" index together with information about the relative position of these words. When the user is interested in any of "Winston Churchill", Winston Spencer Churchill", "Winston S. Churchill", then *Oracle8i* can use the NEAR predicate. For example, the next query illustrates the use of NEAR to locate where there is "vintage" mentioned close to "Sauvignon Blanc" in the NOTE column:

```
SELECT score(1), wine_name
FROM wine_list
WHERE CONTAINS (note, 'vintage NEAR Sauvignon')>1
ORDER BY score(1) DESC
```

Score(1) will display the distance between near occurrences in each note CLOB.

The CTXRULE index type can be used to build document classification or routing applications. In a routing application documents are checked as they are added to a collection and matched with a user's persistent expression of interest.

In addition it can help the user refine their search by

- showing how the query was expanded;
- show other words that are alphabetically close to the search terms with their hit count;
- show words or phrases that are semantically close to their search terms.

The indexing process of text data will be relatively slow and so in Oracle it is carried out in batch mode. In order to ensure that the data table is synchronized with the index the following statement should be executed:

```
EXEC ctx_ddl.sync_index()
```

Alternatively, you can synchronize a partition **part_one** with size 2 Mb:

```
EXEC ctx_ddl.sync_index('text_idx','2M', 'part_one')
```

The synchronization may be carried out periodically, for example every 5 minutes, or immediately.

The text index is stored with the database and can span many columns. There are three index types for text as summarized in Table 10.8:

- context index type (CONTEXT) that provides a rich set of text search capabilities;
- catalog index type (CTXCAT) which is designed for small amounts of text typically found in e-business catalogs – this catalog searching provides performance suitable for web applications and the index it always synchronized with the tables;
- classification index type (CTXRULE) that is created on a table of queries for classification purposes.

With the CTXRULE index the process is quite different from CONTEXT. In query-directed expansion (QDE) we index a set of queries rather than the documents and find queries with the documents.

Table 10.8   Text index types

Index type	Application type	Query operator
CONTEXT	Content-based retrieval of text data types	CONTAINS
CTXCAT	Small text fragments	CATSEARCH
CTXRULE	Classification	MATCHES

The process is set up by creating a query table:

```
CREATE TABLE queries
(          username           VARCHAR2(10),
           query_string       VARCHAR2(80)  )
```

Rows are added that include some text representing the topics of interest for the different users, for example

```
INSERT INTO queries
VALUES ('JSMITH', 'text indexing')
```

We can then create the index:

```
CREATE INDEX queryx ON queries(query_string)
INDEX TYPE IS CTXSYS.CTXRULE
```

As new documents arrive in the database the query is run:

```
SELECT username
FROM queries
WHERE MATCHES (query_string, :note_text)>0
```

The incoming documents are used to query the queries. The index on the queries allows us to find just the queries that match the new document. However, we need to provide the classification hierarchy and the rules that govern the classification before processing documents. One approach would be to use the theme extraction features to carry out a classification.

Note that CTXRULE matches a single document against a set of queries. It is not a clustering method. The queries must be explicit, consisting of specific words and phrases. "Give some funny stories" is too vague.

10.7 Summary of Chapter

In this chapter we looked at text media, how it is stored, manipulated and retrieved. We have been concerned with its potentially large size but have noted that because it usually consists of character strings in the form of words we can split it up, look for themes and summarize it relatively easily. Techniques for retrieval focused on indexing technology and statistical methods.

At the end of this chapter the reader will have learned about:

- SQL manipulation of character and CLOB data types;
- text retrieval (TR);
- schema-directed extraction (SDE);
- query-directed extraction (QDE);

- statistical methods of textual analysis such as chunking, subtopic boundary location and vector space method;
- implementations based on Oracle;
- implementations based on XML.

SOLUTIONS TO EXERCISES

Exercise 10.1

```
CREATE OR REPLACE PROCEDURE check_cv2
( my_employee_number employee.employee_number%TYPE)
AS
    v_document    BFILE;
    v_cv    employee.cv%TYPE;
    lob_loc   CLOB; - TO HOLD LOB LOCATOR
    v_amount NUMBER;
    cv_amount INTEGER;
BEGIN
  v_document :=BFILENAME('TEXT_DOCUMENTS',
'my_employee_number'|| '.'||'my_file_extension');
  IF DBMS_LOB.FILEEXISTS(v_document)=1 THEN
    v_amount : =DBMS_LOB.GETLENGTH(v_document);
    SELECT cv
    INTO lob_loc
    FROM employee
    WHERE employee_number=my_employee_number;
    DBMS_LOB.OPEN(v_document, .LOB_READONLY);
    cv_amount : =DBMS_LOB.GETLENGTH(Lob_loc);
    DBMS_LOB.CLOSE(v_document);
  INSERT INTO MESSAGES (numcol1, numcol2,charcol1)
  VALUES (v_amount,cv_amount,'compare BLOB data');
  COMMIT;
  DBMS_LOB.CLOSE(v_document);
   END IF;
  EXCEPTION
  WHEN OTHERS THEN
   IF DBMS_LOB.ISOPEN(v_document)=1 THEN
  DBMS_LOB.CLOSE(v_document);
  END IF;
 END;
 /
EXECUTE check_cv2('1002');
```

Exercise 10.2

(a)

```
SELECT wine_name
FROM wine_list
WHERE character LIKE ('%bod%')
or
SELECT wine_name
FROM wine_list
WHERE character LIKE ('%body%') OR character LIKE ('%bodied%')
```

(b)

```
SELECT      wine_name
FROM        wine_list
WHERE       INSTR(character, 'medium bodied') >0
```

(c)

```
SELECT      employee_number
FROM        employee
WHERE       DBMS_LOB.INSTR (cv, 'program') >0
```

Exercise 10.3

Give the name of any wines with notes containing the phrase "citrus fruits and gooseberries" and display the corresponding section of note for up to 80 characters, located from the start of that phrase.

Recommended Reading

Borland, P., Ingwerson, P. (1997) The development of a method for the evaluation of interactive information retrieval systems. *Journal of Documentation*, **53**(3), 225–250.

Chen, C. (1999) *Information Visualisation and Virtual Environments*, Springer, London.

Goldfarb, C., Prescod, P. (2001) *The XML Handbook*, Fourth edition, Prentice-Hall PTR.

Perry, B., Chang, S.-K., Dinsmore, J., Doermann, D., Rosenfield, A., Stevens, S. (1999) *Content-Based Access to Multimedia Information*, Kluwer.

Rasmussen, J., Pejterson, A. M., Goodstein, L. P. (1994) *Cognitive Systems Engineering*, Wiley, New York.

Van Rijsbergen, C. (ed.) (1998) *Information Retrieval: Uncertainty and Logics*, Kluwer.

Dealing with Image Databases

Chapter aims

This chapter reviews the way multimedia databases deal with the retrieval and manipulation of image data. It follows from topics introduced in a number of earlier chapters. In Chapter 2 we looked at the characteristics of multimedia data in general, while in Chapter 4 we studied the way SQL3 enables multimedia data to be manipulated and we looked particularly at Oracle's object-relational capabilities in Chapter 6. Chapter 5 looked at the problems of multimedia retrieval and potential solutions that were common to all types of media data. However, there remained many problems we have not discussed about image databases. There are special issues of size and real-time nature but the main problem is the complex semantic nature of images. Furthermore we need to consider the distinct requirements of two-dimensional and three-dimensional images. At the end of the chapter the user will understand:

- technologies used for image processing;
- role of feature extraction;
- retrieval based on image features;
- role of object recognition;
- image analysis and segmentation;
- image classification;
- image query process;
- examples of image database applications.

11.1 Introduction

In addition to the above aims, later in the chapter we will introduce a new case study that requires the manipulation of image and video objects. A database professional may expect that, given any kind of data, semantics and operational requirements, a suitable database system could be designed and built. However, databases are most successful when the data already has an imposed structure. When we looked at text data we were often looking at semi-structured data where headings, sections and paragraphs could be easily recognized. The structure within an image is much less explicit so we need to apply techniques that will identify a structure that will facilitate the image's storage in a database. In a relational database the semantic content exists because the database developer takes trouble to ensure that every attribute in the relational model has a well-defined interpretation and that dependences between attributes faithfully reflect real-world problems. However, in visual data systems the semantic value is innate in the object and its association with other visual objects. In this respect it is very different from the text media databases we looked at in the previous chapter. Characterizing the content of visual objects is much more complex and uncertain. The similarity between two visual objects arises because they have similar appearance. This similar appearance may be the consequence of several factors such as color, texture and orientation. When we provide object A as a query we expect to be able to be provided with a matching object B whether it is a text or visual object. One way of achieving this is by giving every object a label and then matching the labels. These labels can be text based or content based. Content-based labels will not consist of words but numerical values of various attributes or features that can best be used to identify the appearance of an object in a given context. In Figure 1.4 we distinguished between linguistic and visual search modes. In this chapter we will be concerned with a combination of visual query and visual search modes.

In Chapter 5 we introduced three strategies for multimedia database retrieval, namely attribute-based, text-based and content-based retrieval (CBR), summarized in Figure 5.4. All these methods involve the storage of additional information about the image (associative metadata) as well as the image itself. This raises issues about the way this additional information should be integrated and stored within the database system and what the query process should comprise.

It is possible to take the simplest approach and annotate the image object with text metadata based on a human being's perception of the image but there are still no standards for developing image descriptions. Photographic images are not self-identifying since the information usually available for text objects such as title, author, abstract, list of contents, etc. is often not available. Image retrieval systems usually represent images by a collection of low-level features such as color, texture, edge positions and spatial relationships in the image. These features are used to compute the similarity between a picture selected by a user and the images in a database.

Query processing using a visual mode is based on matching a vector of the sample image's features with those of other images in the database. The methods used depend on the type of image. Satellite images, architectural images and facial images are treated in different specialized ways. Many methods rely on the recognition of the boundary of an object by seeking a set of points within the image that all have the same intensity.

11.2   Technologies for Image Processing

One of the significant problems we must address is a fundamental difference with the approach that can be taken with text. Text retrieval can be achieved by associating each document with a variable number of descriptors that represent the content of the document. Searching is achieved by matching documents with a set of descriptors, the term vectors, and the rules of symbolic logic can be applied. Boolean searches are possible and probabilistic searches still rely on a variable number of descriptors. Images are characterized by **feature vectors** which are described below. Each image will have a value for every feature in the database. CBR treatment of images is not usually based on Boolean logic. Numerical rather than Boolean operators are used to calculate the similarly of the images to the query. Boolean operations can be performed on images particularly when images are converted to binary images as in morphology.

Although we will be concerned mainly with the semantic nature of image data because our primary interest is database processing we will be selecting and applying techniques from other disciplines that are capable of dealing with large data sets – techniques that are efficient and multipurpose. A number of candidate techniques have been developed in the fields of image processing and computer vision. However, one problem is that work in both image processing and computer vision has tended to focus on seeking solutions to a restricted set of questions for very constrained data sources, for example counting the number of objects such as cars or people within a scene. This kind of problem can be approached by a combination of object detection and object recognition whereas our objective is a multimedia database management system (MMDBMS) capable of dealing with generic queries.

It is important here to distinguish between computer vision and image processing. Computer vision is a promising discipline because it is a way of collecting and oganizing visual information. Computer vision can be looked at as a branch of artificial intelligence combined with image processing. It is concerned with computer processing of images from the real world. Computer vision typically requires a combination of low-level image processing to enhance the image quality (for example remove noise, increase contrast) and higher-level pattern recognition and image understanding in order to identify features present in the image.

Image processing is the computer manipulation of images. There are many algorithms used in image processing. In contrast to computer graphics, which is usually more concerned with the generation of artificial images, and visualization, image processing attempts to manipulate real-world data such as photographs for humans to understand them better. There are three stages in a computer vision process as shown in Figure 11.1.

The image analysis stage will include the extraction of symbolic data such as the object's edges, regions, boundaries, colors and texture. Usually this process is performed by software but there are some dedicated hardware systems that could perform this task. Image understanding is more difficult to define but is concerned with the interpretation of the data to reach a decision. The decision can be a factual judgement which can be based on quantified data or it can be a value judgement based on morphology, heuristics or pseudo-quantified factors. For example, in the registration of medical images where images from different sources (magnetic resonance imaging or computerized tomography) are being combined the process may involve applying a "best fit" function with external reference points set by experts.

These technologies are capable of extracting large amounts of data from images in terms of feature extraction but there has been less progress in organizing this additional information into what we would describe in associative metadata that could be stored within the database. Research needs to be directed at transforming computer vision technology into algorithms that would be effective and perform acceptably with large databases. The human visual system, which we studied in Chapter 3, can recognize complex scenes rapidly. It appears that human classifications are based on fuzzy similarity computations that are often context driven. In addition, human beings are able to accumulate knowledge and combine features and from this make complex judgements. This is a computational dream (or nightmare) for artificial visual systems.

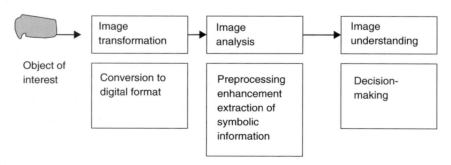

Figure 11.1 Computer vision process

11.3 The Role of Feature Extraction

We introduced the concept of feature extraction in Chapter 5. A **feature** is an attribute derived from transforming the original visual object by using an image analysis algorithm. The visual query mode involves matching the input image to pre-extracted features of real or idealized objects. The pre-extracted features are held in the database. The purpose of the feature extraction is to extract a set of numerical features that removes redundancy from the image and reduces its dimension. A well-selected feature set will have useful information that defines the information that discriminated the image from its collection. We can judge the set of features with the following criteria:

- small intra-class variance – this would mean that slightly different shapes which have similar characteristics should have numerically close values;
- large inter-class separation – feature measurements from the different classes should be quite different numerically;
- regardless of the object's scale, orientation and translation the extracted features must be invariant.

A feature characterizes a specific property of the image such as its color. Usually a feature is represented by a set of numbers often called a **feature vector**, although few vector operations are ever performed on them. Operations that are performed include:

- *Projection*. This is important in MMDBMS as it creates a smaller vector by choosing a user-specified subset. For example, it is possible to describe the shape of an object with about ten floating-point numbers but the user can specify the match by using the first five numbers which will match the overall shape but not the details.
- *Apply a function*. This operation takes the values of the feature and applies a function to all of them. For example, a filter function can be applied to a color content to focus on the red values.
- *Distance measures*. Given two objects, compute the distance between them in terms of the constituent features.

Although color histograms like those shown in Figure 2.6 are not vectors, the difference between two color histograms of different objects can be measured by a statistical process that results in the Mahalanobis distance which we met in Chapter 5. Another important feature called texture can be represented by three values for:

(a) randomness (how regular the pattern is);

(b) periodicity (repetitiveness in the pattern);

(c) directionality (are there stripes in one direction?).

The features of an object can also be represented as groups of points in the **feature space**. Whether the feature were represented by a vector or a histogram the feature would inhabit a space defined by its variables – this is called the feature space. When texture is used as a feature the space is at least three dimensional and some researchers have used hyper-dimensional space. As we add more images to the database the feature space becomes more densely populated. The feature space is a useful concept because we can use it to query the data. We can locate the images that are represented by a specific point in the space, or a specific area. Also, the feature space can give an overall impression of what the database contains, which is useful for users browsing the space. We can also perform operations on the feature space such as union, difference and set membership. Counting and ordering are important operations performed on the resulting subsets.

Other operations have been developed including:

- *Find boundary*. In this operation the user provides a number of examples of images of the same object and queries "show the part of the feature space that covers all these instances". Additional queries can then be framed such as what other objects belong to this region.

- *Selection by spatial constraint*. This is very useful in GIS where there are only two or three dimensions to consider. Then the user can specify a range or a rectangle.

- *Select by distance*. The user presents a query by picking a feature point in the space and a range around this point.

- *k-Nearest neighbor*. This is the most popular type of query in query-by-example systems (see Chapter 5). The operation finds the k nearest points in the feature space, often ranking them in the order of distance. Although this is the most popular type of query it is not very useful when the feature space is sparse because the nearest neighbor may be very different from the query example.

- *Partition space*. This is useful as it divides the space into regions. These are often described as clusters. There are several different ways of partitioning the data.

- *Aggregation*. Aggregate operations can be carried out on the groups to provide information about count, mean, standard deviation and the cluster diameter.

Since images are already large objects, adding feature vectors increases the size of each instance in the database. One way of reducing the amount of

Table 11.1 Feature extraction techniques

Feature	Main technique/measure/filter
Color	Color histogram
Texture	Luminosity, image intensity
Shape	Aspect ratio, moments, boundaries
Position	Spatial coordinates
Appearance	Curvature and orientation

data that needs to be compared is to combine features together into complex feature groups. This can also make the complex feature more expressive. Detecting bare-skinned human figures in images can be achieved by combining skin-color filters and luminescence features. We can also create domain specific features from a set of primitive features.

The objective is to use very simple computations on low-level features of an image, such as color or the edges of objects, to recognize the actual content. These features are used to compute the similarity between a picture selected by a user and the images in a database. Table 11.1 lists some of the features extracted. The most commonly used features for content-based image retrieval (CBIR) are shape, color and texture.

EXERCISE 11.1

This exercise and several of the later exercises in this chapter require you to take on the role of the user and experience a number of the image information retrieval demonstrations that are available through the web at university and research sites. This exercise uses the BLOBWORLD site that uses image segmentation for information retrieval (discussed later) at http://elib.cs.berkeley.edu/photos/blobworld/.

The objective of the exercise is to appreciate the way the user presents the queries. You should try first to locate the target image without using the keywords and then repeat the exercise using the key words and the images:

(a) Using "animals", try to locate a cat image, preferably a Siamese cat.

(b) Try to locate an image of a church with a spire.

Feature extraction methods can be classified into two main groups – global and local. Global features are based on characteristics of regions such as area, perimeter, Fourier descriptors and moments (described later). They can be obtained either for a region by considering all the points within a region or simply for those points that form the boundary of a region. Global features have a disadvantage in that small distortions in a section of an object's boundary can change the global features. Boundary and edge detection technologies are based partly on our own ability to recognize objects from their silhouettes and line drawings and to recognize objects even when only partial boundary information is available.

Local methods are region based and use local features such as critical points, holes and corners. These measures perform well at discrimination even when there is a lot of noise, distortion or partial occlusion. This is because these factors only alter local features leaving other features unaffected. However, recognition based on local features is computationally more intensive and time consuming. Extra computational time is required to calculate the features and extra space is needed to store them. We can use different filters to give measurements for different features of the image. The features extracted are then used as components of a feature vector. This is a concept which is used to reduce the information in an image to a manageable level in the feature space. Two images are considered similar if their feature vectors lie close enough in the feature space. A number of different similarity measures have been developed (see Jain *et al.*, 1999) When *n* different filters are applied to an image the result is known as an *n*-dimensional feature map. Image query processing is based on matching a vector of the sample image's features with those of other images in the database. If the system also knows the meaning of a scene a retrieval system may compute in advance the semantic category to which the image belongs in the database.

EXERCISE 11.2

Write a single sentence to explain the following terms and their function in CBIR:

(a) feature vector;

(b) feature space;

(c) feature map;

(d) invariant feature.

Feature extraction corresponds to intermediate level processing. The purpose is to reduce the bulk of the data by extracting certain characteristic properties that makes each data object unique. The most common weakness of most of the methods we have considered is their inability to cope with noisy images that can generate serious errors. An alternative is to use what is known as the **Hough transform**. This essentially involves the integration of the image's intensity along a set of lines. Fluctuations arising from noise tend to get cancelled out so that it can be better to carry out a shape detection using the transformed image. However, the computation of the Hough transform is costly with complex objects. An alternative that is less expensive is to use the **Radon transform** which, although it was developed in 1917 in Germany by Radon, was not exploited until the Russian mathematician Gel'fand and his associates explained that it could be used in image processing in 1966. (In fact the Hough transform is a special case of the Radon transform and they both use the same underlying equation.) Another advantage is that the Radon transform is used for image reconstruction. The Radon transform can be used to represent an image instead of the pixel values and has a smaller data size that is also more representative of the shape of the object (Adjei, 1996). The concept itself is very simple and is shown in Figure 11.2.

An object with an intensity distribution that can be expressed as a function $f(x, y)$ is bounded by the domain D. The line L is perpendicular to the line that makes the angle ϑ with the x axis. The distance from the line L to the origin is measured as p and ds is the infinitesimal element of integration performed along the line L. Although our example is in two dimensions the Radon transform can be generalized to any number of dimensions. In addition, shifting, rotation and scaling are possible. It is very simple and easy to implement and a summary of the algorithm is as follows:

(a) edge detect the image;

(b) rotate the image through ϑ (degrees);

(c) project the rotated image onto a projection plane;

(d) repeat for any angles ϑ selected.

The image can also be reconstructed from its Radon transform.

An image description generated by these methods could be used for searching and matching an image within a database. However, comparing numerical arrays of images with others can be computationally intensive so there has been some effort to find ways to speed this up. One approach is to look for key distinctive regions in an image initially and using this to find

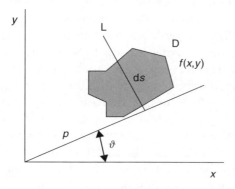

Figure 11.2   Graphical representation of a Radon transform

a set of images which are used then to refine the process. By using these different methods a set of features can be extracted for every image object in the database. The following sections give examples of retrieval using the main primitive image features set out in Table 11.1.

11.4   Retrieval Methods

These sections look at retrieval:

- based on color, using color histograms and color invariants;
- based on texture, using variation in intensity and topography of surfaces;
- based on shape, using aspect ratios, circularity and moments for global features or using boundary segments for local features;
- based on position, using spatial indexing;
- based on image transformations, using transformations;
- based on appearance, using a combination of color, texture and intensity surfaces.

11.4.1   Retrieval Based on Color

The color of an image conveys a lot of information, and therefore most image database systems support color content queries as an important cue for image matching and retrieval. Color can be expressed in terms of hue, saturation and intensity (HSI). Hue corresponds to the color content of a pixel, represented by an angular scale from 0° to 360° (red is at 0°, green at 120° and blue at 240°). Saturation corresponds to the "depth" of the color. A saturation value makes the color gray. Intensity corresponds to the brightness of the incident illumination and is seen as a gray-level image. In black and white pictures, only intensity is represented.

Color can often take the form of the distribution of colors based in an image. Several methods for retrieving images on the basis of color similarity have been described in the literature, but most are variations on the same basic idea. Each image added to the collection is analyzed to compute a **color histogram** such as the one we studied in Chapter 2. This showed the proportion of pixels of each color within the image. The color histogram for each image is then stored in the database. The user can query the database by either specifying the desired proportion of each color (75% olive green and 25% red, for example) or submitting an example image from which a color histogram is calculated. The matching process then retrieves a set of images whose color histograms most closely match those of the query. The matching technique most commonly used is called histogram intersection. Swain and Ballard (1991) developed a system called color indexing based on the similarity of color histograms. Their technique is used in many systems including QBIC which we used in Exercise 1.2. The color histogram is independent of many imaging conditions such as orientation of a scene, relative position of particular scene elements. However, a problem results because image colors depend on the lighting conditions. Small variations in lighting can lead to indexing failure. Three solutions to this have been suggested:

- Control lighting to remove dependence. It has been found that the ratio of adjacent colors independent of illumination is very useful.
- Use color constancy algorithms as a preprocessing step before indexing.
- Color invariant features, which are discussed later, are extracted from images and used for indexing.

Color distribution moments have also been used (moments are discussed later). Color image normalization is useful because it removes bias due to illumination but suffers from the problem that it does not recover the true colors of surfaces. Normalized colors are functions of the true color and the context of the scenes. Unfortunately, this means that the same object in different scenes would have different normalized colors so it cannot be used directly for color indexing. However, color normalization is important for analyzing local image regions where it can solve the problem of context of scenes. Local color normalizations are referred to as color invariants.

Swain and Ballard's indexing method divides an image into a set of bins along each of the R and G color dimensions. The chromaticity of each bin is compared with a test image. This can deliver a recognition rate of about 30–40%. Variants of this technique are now used in a high proportion of current CBIR systems. There are a number of methods of improving on Swain and Ballard's original technique including the use of cumulative color histograms (Stricker and Orengo, 1995), combining histogram intersection with some element of spatial matching (Stricker and Dimai, 1996) and the use of region-based color querying (Carson *et al.*, 1997). According to Eakins and Graham (1999), the results from some of these systems can look quite impressive.

11.4.2 Retrieval Based on Texture

The study of the texture of an image can be very useful. The ability to match on texture similarity can often distinguish between areas of images with similar color (such as sky and sea, or leaves and grass). The method uses pixel intensity values that result from the reflection of light from illuminated surfaces or the transmission of light through translucent media. This variation is the result of the nature of the illumination and the topography of the surface. The two-dimensional (2D) arrangement of the intensities defines the visual texture of the image.

A variety of techniques have been used for measuring texture similarity based on statistical analysis. Essentially, these calculate and compare the relative brightness of selected *pairs* of pixels from the query image with the other images, each in turn. From these it is possible to calculate measures of image texture such as the degree of *directionality* and *regularity*, or *periodicity* (Tamura *et al.*, 1978; Liu and Picard, 1996).

Alternative methods of texture analysis for information retrieval include the use of Gabor filters, and fractals (Manjunath and Ma, 1996). Gabor filters, which we will mention again later, are one of the most powerful techniques for image analysis.

Texture queries can be formulated in a similar manner to color queries, by selecting examples of desired textures from a palette or by supplying an example query image. The system then retrieves images with texture measures most similar in value to the query. For example, in processing images of faces it is possible to infer the shape of the surface topography from the variations in the intensity. This is called "shape from shading" or "shape from texture". In addition it is now possible to use a texture thesaurus, which retrieves textured regions in images on the basis of similarity to automatically derived codewords representing important classes of texture within the collection.

11.4.3   Retrieval Based on Shape

The ability to retrieve by shape involves giving the shape of an object a quantitative description which can be used to match other images. Unlike texture, shape is a fairly well-defined concept – and there is considerable evidence that in the brain natural objects are primarily recognized by their shape. The process involves computing a number of features characteristic of an object's shape that are independent of its size or orientation. These features are then computed for every object identified within each stored image. Queries are then answered by computing the same set of features for the query image, and retrieving those stored images whose features most closely match those of the query.

Two main types of shape feature are commonly used:

- *global* features such as aspect ratio, circularity and moment invariants;
- *local* features such as sets of consecutive boundary segments.

The 2D boundaries of three-dimensional (3D) objects enable object recognition. Shape representation is very difficult. A shape is defined by x and y coordinates of its boundary points. The similarity transformation could include translation, uniform scaling and orientation changes. If the camera changes its viewpoint with respect to the object the boundary of the object is deformed, for example a circle will be converted to an ellipse. Two medical images of the same object may differ from one another by rotation about an axis as well as differences in scale. The deformation can approximate to an **affine** transformation when, in addition to these transformations, shapes are also subject to non-uniform scaling and shearing.

In Figure 11.3 we can see an image of the Zinfandel grape from the wine shop application. In the case of the Zinfandel grape image the circular nature of the shapes is relatively easy to detect. In Figure 11.4 there are a number of examples that give problems for retrieval based on shape that human processors would not find difficult. Because of these problems quite a wide selection of different approaches have been tried.

Queries presented to shape retrieval systems are formulated either by identifying an example image to act as the query or by asking the user to draw a 2D sketch as in QBIC. There are several different challenges involved in developing these systems:

- How would the user formulate a 3D query? It could involve selecting an example 3D image or the user presenting a sketch, probably a 2D view-point.

- How is the 3D result set to be presented and its relevance evaluated?

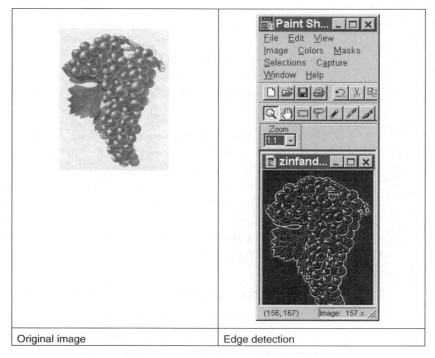

| Original image | Edge detection |

Figure 11.3 Zinfandel grape image and edge-detected image

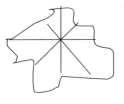

Successful
shape
representation
using radius
vectors.

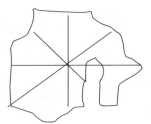

This shape has a convex
boundary. The horizontal line is
multivalued – so where does the
shape end?

The problem caused by
spikes may not occur
when the other methods
such as autoregressive or
statistical methods are
used.

A spike can cause a
boundary point to be
lost resulting in a wrong
target profile when the
centroid method is
used (see figure 11.5).

Figure 11.4   Problems retrieving shapes

● Can 3D images be effectively retrieved based on one or more 2D viewpoints
of an object?

There is no general solution to this problem, but some progress has been
made based on images of objects from different viewpoints, especially in
facial recognition systems. One approach has been to build up a set of plausible 3D models from the available 2D image and match them with other
models in the database. However, this method involves defining 3D shape
similarity measures. Another is to generate a series of alternative 2D views of
each database object, each of which is matched with the query image
(Dickinson *et al.*, 1998).

11.4.4   Retrieval Based on Position – Spatial Location

Using spatial location is one of the oldest image retrieval methods and is an
essential aspect of geographical information systems and biological systems.
However, to exploit this method the image collections must contain objects

in defined spatial relationships with each other. It is possible to impose a spatial structure on an image of a natural system by using the Voronoi tessellation (Blackburn and Dunckley, 1995). One of the advantages of this approach is that many of the established methods work in 2D and 3D. Spatial indexing is seldom useful on its own, although it can be effective in combination with other cues such as color and shape.

11.4.5   Retrieval Based on Image Characteristics – Transformations

Several other types of image features have been proposed as a basis for CBIR. Most of these rely on complex transformations of pixel intensities which have no obvious counterpart in any human description of an image. These techniques aim to extract features which reflect some aspect of image similarity which a human subject can perceive, even if he or she finds it difficult to describe. The most well-researched technique of this kind uses the *wavelet transform* to model an image at several different resolutions may prove very effective.

11.4.6   Retrieval Based on Appearance

Visual appearance is an important part of judging image similarity. However, it is difficult to define exactly what we mean by an object's appearance. It will depend on the object's 3D shape and also the viewpoint of the image but it will be independent of color and texture. Ravela and Manmatha (1998) have proposed that an image's intensity surface has features that could be used to compute appearance similarity. In their method, in order to compute global appearance similarity, features are extracted from pixel neighborhoods and their distributions over the image are compared. Histograms are used to represent distributions of features and correlation is used to compare histograms.

Two versions of this method have been developed, one for whole-image matching and one for matching selected parts of an image. Global appearance similarity is computed using differential features of the image. A differential feature is a feature computed from spatial derivatives of an image. They can give measures of curvature and orientation. Such features are obtained by transforming simple derivatives so that they are invariant or tolerant to factors affecting the object's appearance, such as rotations, scale and illumination changes.

The part-image technique involves local curvatures and orientation. Global image similarity is deduced by comparing distributions of these features.

Table 11.2 Features used in retrieval – summary of their uses and problems

Feature	Measures	Theory	Main use	Problems
Color	Histogram	Swain and Ballard	Color indexing	Lighting variations
Texture	Pixel intensity ● illumination ● topography Degrees of ● directionality ● regularity ● periodicity	Gabor filters Fractals	Indexing Texture thesaurus	
Shape	Global features ● aspect ratio ● circularity ● moments Local features – boundary segments	 Active contours	Shape indexing Object recognition	Spikes and holes in objects cause errors in indexing
Appearance	Global features ● curvature ● orientation Local features – local curvatures and orientation	Transforms	Image classification	
Position	Spatial relationships	Tessellations (Voronoi)	Object recognition	

We have introduced a number of features that can be of use in image retrieval. Table 11.2 summarizes the features, how they are measured, the theory relating to the measurement, their uses and associated problems.

EXERCISE 11.3

Demonstrations of image retrieval by appearance

The first site uses black–white images. Access the site illustrated below at http://cowarie.cs.umass.edu/~demo/Demo.html. Carry out the following queries and assess the effectiveness of the system to locate

(a) an image of a "mini" automobile;

(b) an image of a baby;

(c) an image that is similar to the face of a male colleague.

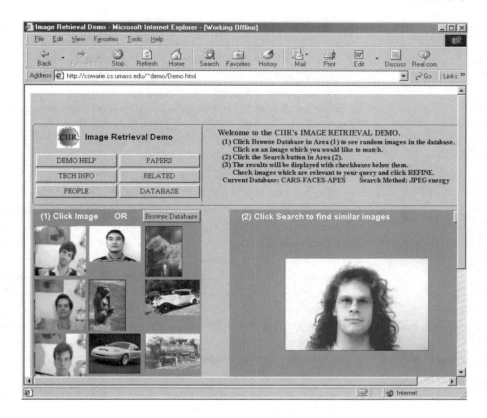

The retrieval here is done using retrieval by example, i.e. an example picture is presented as a query. There are two kinds of retrieval:

- whole-image matching – where the entire image is used as a query;
- part-image matching – where part of the image is used as a query.

This system if you try the demo is more precise for face recognition but not so good for whole human figures or for cars or trains, which it can confuse. In general the concepts of precision and recall introduced for evaluating text retrieval are not usually applied to image systems. Using retrieval by appearance means using the intensity structure of the image. Appearance may be represented in different ways. Two representations are demonstrated here, one uses curvature and phase information and the other what the developers term **jpeg energy**.

Technical information about the site

There is a collection of approximately 1600 images: cars, locomotives (steam and diesel), apes, people, faces and sundry.

The system operates in a similar manner to the text-based systems we met in Chapter 10. The system computes differential invariants at three scales and five pixels apart. Invariant vectors and coordinates are sorted and inverted file lists are generated and indexed. Query invariant vectors are compared with the database using simplex search per invariant per scale and then composed. A spatial consistency check is performed on retrieved points and the final score is computed. Sorted results are displayed in order.

We have covered what can seem a confusing list of techniques that use a number of image features. Because image retrieval is so challenging it is tempting to use as many features as computationally feasible. Generating the features can be difficult and time consuming so ideally these feature extraction methods need to be applied when the image is acquired and indexed into the database. In order to help to select the most useful features for an application Table 11.3 sets out the main advantages and disadvantages of each feature. To summarize the advantage of all these techniques, they can describe an image at varying levels of detail. In addition these methods can be applied to the whole image and so avoid the need to segment the image into regions of interest. As we will see later, image segmentation is a troublesome problem.

In the following sections we will look at why the features described above are useful and how some of the different types of features are extracted from an image.

Table 11.3   Advantages and disadvantages of feature methods of retrieval

Feature	Advantage	Disadvantage
Color	Can be applied to all colored images, 2D and 3D	
Texture	Distinguishes between image regions with similar color, e.g. sea and sky	Large feature vectors each containing 4000 elements have been used
Shape	Important in image segmentation Can classify images as stick like, plate like or blob like	Representation is difficult Viewpoints change an object's shape Spikes and holes 3D is very difficult
Appearance	Important way of judging similarity Can generate invariant measures Describe an image at varying levels of detail	
Position	Can be applied to 2D and 3D images	Images must contain objects in defined spatial relationships Spatial indexing not useful unless combined with color and texture

11.5   Image Analysis and Object Recognition

There are two main approaches to analyzing an image. The reason we want to analyze the image is to produce the equivalent of the kind of syntactic analysis we can use with text to breakdown the image into its "words" and identify the relationship between these "words" to achieve the identification of structure within an image for database manipulation and storage.

When we describe an image in terms of color, texture, region, shape and 2D spatial relations we are dealing with syntax. In order to achieve CBIR this needs to be combined with semantic information about the context; in image terms this is the scene. There are two basic approaches:

- analyzing the image as a whole;
- segmenting an image into regions or objects.

The first approach involves measuring properties of the whole image and using these measures to classify the image. The image itself is just a numerical array of pixel values. The pixels are scalar values for "black and white" images and vectors for colored images.

Examples of measures that can be applied as a basis of representation that depend on pixel values include:

- histograms or color scattergrams;
- textual properties;
- moments;
- coefficients.

We have already discussed the first two measures. Moments are dealt with next.

Moments provide a useful method of generating a shape descriptor. There are a series of moments that can be calculated from a function that represents the pixel intensity. The simple moments (zero order and first order) cannot be used to match objects because they vary according to scale position and rotation but more mathematically complex moments have been discovered that exhibit invariance for translation and rotation. However, objects with irregular features such as those shown in Figure 11.4 require the calculation of high-order moments but this computation is difficult if the object is partially occluded. The process shown in Figure 11.5 is usually adequate for computing a set of moments that is adequate to distinguish between input images. Moments have been successful in a range of application domains including handwriting and 3D polyhedral objects. However, moments have several limitations because they cannot be used effectively in gray-level images and do not work well when the image suffers from noise. They work best for solid objects.

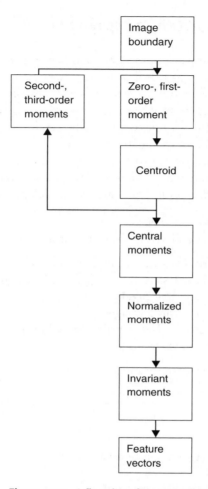

Figure 11.5 A flowchart for computing invariant moments

Segmenting an image into regions or objects results in groups of related pixels which are labeled separately. The segmented image is then an array of pixel labels. This is sometimes called a symbolic image. The segmentation can represent:

- geometry of the parts;
- topology;
- size;
- shape.

The term image segmentation is sometimes confused with the term image classification. It can be carried out manually by an expert or automatically by applying techniques. Manual segmentation can be time consuming, error prone and subjectively biased. The human expert may produce the most accurate result, for example a radiologist tracing the boundary of an organ in a radiographic image. A third way is to combine the two methods to produce an assisted or semi-automatic segmentation. The best semi-automatic methods are interactive and intuitive with effective mechanisms to allow the human and the computer to work collaboratively together.

One issue here is how to segment an image. When the segmented parts have a simple shape, this can be represented by unit vectors that specify the boundaries of the part. Another approach would consider the part as a union of more primitive pieces. These primitives can be represented by methods such as medial axis. McAuliffe *et al.* (1996) used this method to give an approximation of the boundary of an object (BASOC). This can be used to provide an initial guess to a method that uses "Active Contours" – also called "Snakes" because of the serpentine nature of the object after extraction. After an initial guess is provided for a boundary starting point snake algorithms search the region about the starting point and adjust the boundary until an optimal boundary is found.

Many shapes can be effectively described by their skeletonized version consisting of connected lines that run along axes of the object limbs. The axes are known as medial axes and enable the object to be represented as a simple geometrical shape that is defined by the shape of the original object. The theory was developed by Blum (1967). To produce the skeleton the image of the object is eroded repetitively and thinned in such a way that the connectivity is preserved and there is no shortening of the thinned limbs. The medial axis transform reduces the complexity of objects into a set of unique characteristics. However, it could be argued that the boundary of an object is a more natural representation than the skeleton.

Most of the approaches assume that the image can be segmented based on a simple model. The segmented image is represented be an attribute graph. The nodes of the graph are associated with property values that act as labels to the nodes. The arcs between the nodes represent relations between the parts. Finally the whole image can be described by propositions about the parts, their properties and relations. These 2D representations can be a very concise way of describing an image but they ignore the 3D aspects of a scene.

11.6 Image Classification

Whereas image segmentation is mainly of interest to the MMDBMS developer because it raises issues of storing segmentation data for later use, image classification is vital to image retrieval.

Image classification is usually performed after features are extracted and the image is segmented. There are different ways of classifying images. In a naive way images can be classed as:

- natural images such as photographs, medical images;
- artificial images such as computer graphics, drawings and paintings.

However, this is not always helpful as an image of a face could be a photograph or a drawing. The classification methods used depend on the type of image. Satellite images, architectural images and facial images are treated in different specialized ways. Many methods rely on the recognition of the boundary of an object by seeking a set of points within the image that all have the same intensity. As we noted when we reviewed the different features available it is important that the recognition processes used are not affected by image transformations such as scaling, illumination and precise object location.

In all present-day image databases the main process involved is to identify various features (color, texture, shape, etc.) of all the images in the database and to use these features to classify the images into groups. This has led to the development of a framework for image retrieval which we have seen two examples of in the practical exercises. It can be summarized as:

(a) Index images by their content while avoiding the segmentation and recognition issues. Several attributes such as color, texture, shape and appearance can be associated with image content.

(b) Apply operators to extract features that measure statistical properties of the selected attribute.

(c) Compile features into representations of images. An image is replaced by its feature representation, e.g. color histogram.

(d) Retrieve in a query-by-example fashion. A user selects an image as a query and its representation is compared with those in the collection to obtain a ranked list of images.

In the demonstration exercises this process was being followed.

11.6.1   Classification Methods

A number of methods are based on classifying images in the following ways.

Scenes can be represented by a collection of features such as texture, color or spatial frequencies. These can be computed on local areas of the image that has been **tessellated** (systematically divided into areas corresponding to a patterns); for example, in Figure 11.6 the edges of the cells are emphasized. This process can manage to classify images as indoor versus outdoor.

Growth after 40 time intervals

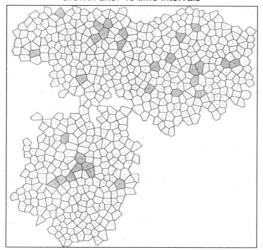

Figure 11.6 Tessellated image of cell growth

Lower-level features can be represented as a power spectrum template. The power spectrum of an image is the square of the magnitude of the Fourier transform. It gives global information about the basic elements that form in the image, such as the main orientation, dominant spatial scales. It answers such questions as which frequency band encodes most of the energy, whether there are poles or narrow lines. This uses the spectral content of an image to discriminate between images with different semantic contents and it can give information such as the main orientation, dominant spatial scales. It is possible to create broad semantic categories – cities versus mountains, city center versus streets, panoramic beaches or valleys, kitchens or bedrooms, etc. For example, a typical beach scene has strong horizontal organization so it will tend to have dominance of energy along the vertical axis at low spatial frequencies.

This allows a classification based on:

- horizontal shape – horizontal dominant line from low to high spatial frequencies – city scene with tall buildings;
- cross shape – vertical and horizontal – indoor scene living room of small objects;
- vertical shape – beaches and fields and panoramic scenes;
- oblique shape – mountain ranges, canyons, valleys;
- circular shape – all orientations equally represented – highly textured scenes such as forests.

In the future hierarchical classification seems the most promising. This would provide:

- a first-level discrimination between artificial and natural environments – horizontal and cross shapes represent artificial environments while the other three classes represent natural environments;
- second-level discrimination looks at natural scenes in terms of open (beaches/fields) or closed (forests mountains).

11.6.2   The Query Process

The problems of image retrieval can be summarized as:

(a) uncertainty about the query, how the user can express what they want – it is difficult to describe visual cues;

(b) uncertainty about how well the result set satisfies the query request, for example the image background affects the search;

(c) uncertainty about how to rank the result set – human beings are weak at weighting image features quantitatively.

In image databases, traditional SQL query styles cannot be used as it is difficult to describe an image in text. There is no concept of an exact match as there is in text searching. There are two alternative approaches:

- firstly, to use a query image;
- secondly, to use user-defined features.

As we have seen in the practical exercises in some cases the query will itself be in the form of a data object which could be an image. So we ask how we judge how similar the result set is to the query example. Human perceptions play an important part in defining the similarity in the image domain. In order to help the relevance check it may be required to provide the user with a reduced scale or sampled representation or even an abstraction based on selected features. We will also have found that the systems used demonstrate how difficult image retrieval is. The human visual system can recognize complex scenes rapidly so we have been slow to appreciate how difficult this is.

When using a query image the user can provide an image or compose a target image by selecting and clicking color palettes and texture patterns as in QBIC.

Studies of users searching through large collections of images show they have an imprecisely formed query. Users go through a number of explore–navigate–select–refine cycles before identifying objects of interest.

One recent approach to assist this behavior is to allow users to explore a distribution of images in virtual space where the axes are features the users have selected. Users usually opt to sample images from any part of the virtual space.

Another approach to using virtual space is to allow users to select a sample image. In the query process the distribution of image objects is then recomputed in terms of the distance from the sample image. This is the approach we have met in the practical exercises and we have experienced its limitations. A better approach is to allow users to select a set of images that are somewhat close to what is required, rather than just a single image, and ask the system itself to determine the similarity of the selected images and make a search based on this.

In most of these cases when users tested systems they reported the need for semantic information to assist searches. This involves finding the relevant semantic description of the concept and then matching this to the relevant low-level features. The objective is to use very simple computations on low-level features of an image, such as color or the edges of objects, to recognize the actual content. If the system also knows the meaning of a scene a retrieval system may compute in advance the semantic category to which the image belongs in the database. It is important that the recognition processes used are not affected by image transformations such as scaling, illumination and precise object location.

A more recent approach is to mimic the human processor to develop algorithms that reflect human cognition. A human does not see the whole image at once. Because of the Gestalt laws described in Chapter 3 most subsets of an image are indistinguishable from their backgrounds while some are very "salient". Humans are very sensitive to various things about an image such as color, texture and parts of an image that appear to "pop out". Humans have little conscious control over how they perceive an image.

Expectations can raise or lower thresholds by only a small amount. Humans appear to use those parts of an image that can be seen "at first glance" to form an initial hypothesis about the content of an image but the further verification of these hypotheses and analyses of the image is carried out under cognitive control. This hypothesis–verification loop could be used as a model for future content-based methods.

There are a number of strategies that can be followed in image retrieval.

One-stage Retrieval

The image set is retrieved in a single step using content-based methods. The images would then usually be represented by thumbnails but the result of one stage is usually low precision.

Two-stage Retrieval

In this method the first stage retrieves a set of images based on partial information. In the second stage the system accumulates knowledge from the results of the first stage retrieval and analyzes the result set in order to understand what the query is about. Statistical techniques that we met in Chapter 5 such as principal components analysis (PCA), latent semantic indexing and cluster analysis (CA) can be used. Both PCA and CA are difficult to use with large data sets because they both involve a large number of computations and comparisons. Therefore they are usually performed with a small number of images which have been previously selected.

One method would be to provide the user with a set of images which the user must sort into two groups, those similar to the image they want and those discarded. Both sets are then compared by PCA and CA. PCA will identify the most important features that the members of the sets have in common. CA will find groups of images that are very similar. By reapplying the strongly identified characteristics to the whole database a small result set can be retrieved.

Multi-stage Retrieval

One reason for needing multi-stage retrieval is that even more than in traditional databases the user may not have clearly formulated the query so it is essential that the user be able to refine and re-pose the search criteria. How can the system judge (weigh) the relevance of an object to the query? In some cases the query will itself be a data object – so, how similar is it to the results? Human perceptions play an important role in defining similarity in the image domain. In order to help the relevance check it may be required to provide the user with a reduced scale or sampled representation or even an abstraction based on selected features.

This approach considers the recognition problem as one of supervised learning. The learning module's input is an image. The learning module may be a simple binary classifier that gives an output of "yes" or "no". The learning module is trained by providing a set of input–output pairs (previously labeled images). Both positive and negative examples must be provided. This simple system would be able to distinguish a dog from a cat but to get it to distinguish a face it would have to be provided with images of a face. We would have to provide a number of images from different viewpoints. We have been making progress here. Early researchers in this area noted that their systems were unable to distinguish between an image of the researcher and an image of their coffee mug.

When objects have a simple shape – and this is particularly true for artificial objects – then there are standard computer graphics algorithms (called 2D affine transformations) that can transform an image by scaling, rotation and shearing. These kinds of images will only need one viewpoint. However, if the transformation is affected by the object's 3D shape then more than one viewpoint is needed. Illumination effects can be important too.

When an object is being studied we are looking for the properties of the object that are invariant under various transformations.

In the simple approach illustrated in Figure 11.7 (b) each unit stores one of the example views and measures the similarity of the input image with the stored example. The process of measurement is called a filter. The weighted outputs of all the units are then added. If the sum is above a threshold then the output is 1, otherwise it is 0. During learning both the values of the weights and the threshold are adjusted to optimize the correct classification. Scale and position invariance information is achieved in computer vision systems by serial scanning in which the whole image is searched for an object of interest sequentially at different positions and scales.

One recent approach is to use "overcomplete dictionaries". The idea is that if you had to describe an object with words from a very small dictionary of allowed words an object would need a long sentence to describe it completely. However, if we develop very large dictionary then objects can be completely described in a very few words or even a single word. (In signal processing this is the way overcomplete wavelet filters work.) Computer

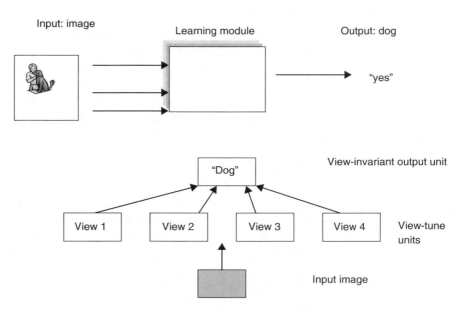

Figure 11.7 (a) The general learning module and (b) the specific classifier trained to respond in a view invariant manner to a particular object

vision algorithms now work quite effectively for facial recognition if just provided with three detectors, one trained for frontal faces, one trained for left profiles and one trained for right profiles.

As we have seen in the many different approaches above, content-driven recognition procedures usually assume a semantic classification can emerge from very simple computations based on low-level features. Knowing the meaning of a scene, an image retrieval system may compute in advance the **semantic category** to which the image belongs in the database. Scene categories should be invariant to transformations such as scaling, illumination and precise object location. A number of methods are based on classifying images into exclusive classes. Methods used include:

- encoding the global configuration of a scene by using spatial and photometric relationships within and across regions in the images – this method is good for static scenes such as snowy mountains with blue sky regions but not for scenes of rooms in which objects such as furniture can change position;
- representing scenes by a collection of features such as texture, color, spatial frequencies locally computed on tessellated images – this can manage simple classification of images as indoor versus outdoor.

11.6.3   Object recognition

Image retrieval systems at present find objects by using sets of easily measured image properties. The parts of the image can be classified as stick like, strip like, plate like and blob like. In a stick one dimension is much larger than the other two, while in a blob all three dimensions are comparable. This simple difference can be used for object detection. These characteristic regions can be rapidly detected in images by algorithms that use specialized hardware. These results can be used to form hypotheses about the content of an image. It has been suggested that the human processor goes through a similar process to rapidly identify objects "at a glance".

In an alternative approach we can identify objects by their functions rather than their appearance. A chair can be difficult to identify by shape because there are so many variations of design but functionally it consists of a horizontal surface, a means of support and a distance from the ground. A hand tool will have a handle for grasping. So affordance (see Chapter 3) can be used to recognize objects.

To summarize, this is a difficult problem with no "magic bullet". The future challenges include:

- automated and accurate segmentation of structures and features of interest;

- classification of image content;

- image enhancement means making certain features in the image more recognizable or prominent;

- quantitative measurement of image properties and features including a discussion of the meaning of image measurement.

11.7 Image Database Software

When we completed the practical exercises we used some of the software that has been developed for image retrieval. Table 11.4 lists well-known software systems available to support content-based retrieval and also indicates the features used by the system.

IBM QBIC (query by image content) uses features for color, texture and shape and is probably the best known. It offers retrieval by any combination of color, texture or shape as well as by text keyword. Queries based on color content of images work well. Texture features usually work better if an area is highlighted based on this. Shape queries are difficult because of the problem of describing a shape. QBIC has a color layout feature which combines elements of both color and shape in a query. There are two ways of

Table 11.4 Summary of software and the features supported

System	Color	Texture	Shape	Spatial resolution	Text	Reference	Organisation
			Image feature				
visualSEEK	×					Smith and Chang (1997)	Columbia University, USA
QBIC	×	×	×		×	Flicker (1995)	IBM
Photobook	×	×				Pentland (1996)	MIT Media Labs
Piction			×	×	×	Srihari (1995)	Buffalo
Chabot	×				×	Stonebraker (1995)	UCLA (Berkeley)
Virage	×	×	×			Jain (1997)	UCLA (San Diego)
NETRA	×	×	×	×		Ma and Manjunath (1997)	UCSB
Unnamed	×			×		Chang (1996)	University of Pittsburgh
MAVIS	×	×				Lewis and Hall (1996)	University of Southampton, UK

generating a query in QBIC:

- Start with an image and request to find other images which are similar in terms of color layout – "*query by similar image*".
- Draw a rough picture of the required image, i.e. to define the distribution of colors within it – "*draw color layout*".

The searching can be combined with other cues such as keywords. It is integrated with DB2. The system extracts and stores color, shape and texture features for each image added to the database. Efficiency is improved by the use of R*tree indexes. The system matches appropriate features from query and stored images, calculates a similarity score between the query and each stored image examined and displays the most similar images as thumb nails. Queries based on color content of images work well. Texture features usually work better if an area is highlighted. Shape queries are difficult because of the problem of describing a shape. Therefore, QBIC has a color layout search method which combines elements of both color and shape in a query.

In QBIC some features are collected automatically when the database is populated. This is based on object recognition using color histograms (see Chapter 2), texture contrast and directionality. Other features are also included to assist classification but the information is collected semi-automatically.

A **QBIC catalog** is a set of files that hold data about the visual features of images in the database.We would create a QBIC catalog for each column of images in a user table that we want to make available for searching by content. DB extenders allow the database designer to set up objects (user defined data types) with appropriate methods. The *Image Extender* within DB2 maintains information about the width, height and number of colors in an image, as well as information about attributes common to image, audio and video objects, such as the identification of the person who imported the object into the database or who last updated the object. When we create a QBIC catalog we would identify the features for which we want the Image Extender to analyze, store, and later query data. We can also add or drop features from a QBIC catalog after the catalog is created.

DB2 administrative support tables can also contain the contents of stored objects in BLOB format. Alternatively, an object can be kept in a file and referenced by the administrative support tables. For example, an image can be stored as a BLOB in an administrative support table or kept in a file that is referenced by the table. When you store an image, audio or video object in a user table, the object is not actually stored in the table. Instead, an extender creates a character string called a **handle** to represent the object and stores the handle in the table. The extender stores the object in an administrative support table or stores a file identifier in an administrative support table if you keep the content of the object in a file. It also stores the object's attributes and handle in administrative support tables.

Average color	The sum of the color values for all the pixels in the image divided by the number of pixels. For example, if 50% are red and 50% are blue the average value will correspond to purple.
Histogram color	This measures the distribution of color across a spectrum of 64 colors. It identifies the percentage of pixels in an image for each color.
Positional color	This measures the average color value for pixels in a specified area of the image.
Texture	This estimates the coarseness, contrast and directionality of the image. The coarseness is measured using the size of repeating items (pebbles versus boulders). Contrast measures light versus dark. Directionality looks for dominant lines as opposed to uniform, e.g. sand.

Virage is available as a set of independent modules that can be built into application development. This makes it easy to extend the system by building new types of query interfaces. It is also available as an add-on to Oracle and Informix. It is used by AltaVista in their AV Photo Finder.

Photobook aims to characterize images for retrieval by computing shape, color and texture. Unlike the other systems described above it aims to calculate information, preserving features relevant to a particular type of search, from which all essential aspects of the original image could in theory be reconstructed. This gives greater flexibility at the expense of speed. Although not commercially available it has been incorporated into several face recognition systems.

The **Chabot** system provides a combination of text-based and color-based access to a collection of digitized photographs. Since it was first developed it has been renamed Cypress and incorporated into Berkeley Digital Library (UCB).

NETRA is a system developed by *UC Santa Barbara* which allows images to be segmented into regions. NETRA in Sanskrit means "eye". Images are segmented into homologous systems. These regions can be treated as spatial objects with location, shape, size and neighborhood properties. Users can compose queries such as "retrieve images containing objects with color A, the texture of object B and the shape of object C that lie in the upper third of the image".

Informix Visual Information Retrieval DataBlade Module allows images to be retrieved via visual cues. Keywords can be used to aid the search. The system can retrieve images by similarity measures but does not take into account any semantic information except keywords.

MAVIS (University of Southampton, UK) allows the user to retrieve source anchors via media specific cues such as texture or color.

VisualSEEK is an experimental system. It offers searching by region, color, shape and spatial location as well as keyword. Users can build up image queries by specifying areas defined by shape, color at absolute or relative positions in an image.

Synapse is an implementation of retrieval by appearance using whole-image matching which we described earlier in the chapter (Ravela and Manmatha, 1998).

11.8   Developing Image Media Databases

This chapter has focused on the challenges of image retrieval but it is important to summarize what is involved with implementing an image database:

- *Image acquisition.* Images must be acquired by processes outlined in Chapter 2. In addition, if object recognition is required then some of the objects need to by captured in different viewpoints.

- *Image processing.* The images will need to be preprocessed to improve the quality of the image and to reduce noise arising from the acquisition process. In addition the images may be subject to edge detection, the computation of translation, scale and rotational invariance as part of the feature extraction.

- *Image storage.* This needs to be designed in terms of the requirements of the system.

- *Image classification.* One or more processes of classification will be applied to the whole database collection or subsets of it. This may include the development of a number of indexes.

- *The query process.* This will be designed by considering the application area and the user needs.

IMAGE AND VIDEO CASE STUDY

In order to apply the knowledge and skills introduced in this and the next chapter a new case study will be introduced. We can then develop a

small object-relational database to simulate the requirements of the
system.

The Sewage Information System

The objective of the sewage plant is to remove organic material from sewage
so that the effluent can be discharged into natural bodies of water without
disrupting the ecosystem. If untreated sewage were discharged into a natural
water system it would remove oxygen from the water, kill aquatic plants and
animals and create a health risk. In urban areas treatment is usually by the
activated sludge process. Solid wastes are first separated from the liquid so
that both may be treated. Bacteria are used to oxidize the organic carbon to
carbon dioxide (CO_2) and which must then be separated from the liquid
effluent prior to discharge. The bacterial population is kept high by returning some of these separated bacteria, the activated sludge, back to the start
of the liquid treatment phase. These elevated population levels demand that
the sewage be actively aerated during the process. The stages in the process
are shown in Figure 11.8.

In turn the bacterial colonies are consumed by protozoa. These are
small, single-cell organisms which feed on the bacteria by grazing. Protozoa
preferentially consume suspended bacteria encouraging bacterial growth in

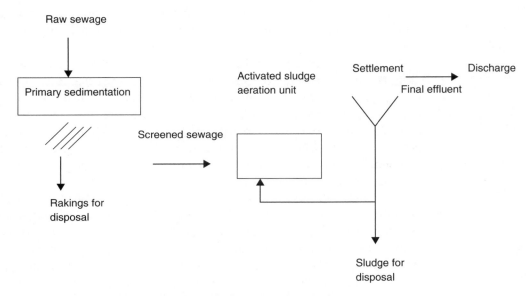

Figure 11.8   Diagrammatic representation of sewage treatment

clumps which sediment more efficiently and give a highly clarified final effluent.

The primary sedimentation process removes solid household artefacts such as bicycle frames from the sewage before it is treated.

Protozoa exist widely in nature, in aquatic habitats including the moist films surrounding soil particles. The main types are ciliates, flagellates and amoebae. In natural environments there may be millions per liter of water. Most protozoa feed on bacteria, algae, other protozoa and small animals.

To optimize treatment rates, the bacteria and protozoa need adequate oxygen. The flow of sewage is measured to control and monitor the treatment. The type of tanks used will be carefully designed to control mixing and enhance aeration.

Sewage works need to monitor the process of the breakdown of organic matter in sewage. Biochemical oxygen demand (BOD) is a measure of the amount of biologically available carbon present in the water. Treatment plants have a statutory duty to monitor regularly the quality of the effluent but the standard BOD test takes five days to complete. In the meantime problems can arise in the periods between sampling and analysis. For example, pollution by industrial solvents such as phenols or chlorocarbons can cause problems by poisoning the system and altering the species balance, so treatment plants could lose control of the process, making it difficult to keep within the statutory operating bounds. In addition, checks are also required in some countries that population levels of human pathogens, are below the statutory minimum in the final effluent. The protozoa present in activated sludge systems do not include any recognized human pathogens and there is no statutory requirement to monitor their populations.

A biological sewage monitoring system has been developed by microbiologists that can give rapid results. Research has shown that different bacteria and protozoa are dominant at different stages of the treatment and that monitoring the protozoa can give a good indication of the state of the treatment process. Also, the dominant species of protozoa change in response to pollution levels. Therefore monitoring the protozoan populations is an excellent and low cost method of monitoring, and consequently controlling, the treatment processes.

The monitoring system involves technicians sampling the effluent at sampling stations in the sewage plant at regular intervals. Samples of sludge are simply examined under a microscope. The microscopic examination can be as useful a tool as chemical analysis and other physical techniques. Much can be learned about the state of the sewage tanks based on the type of protozoa present. For example, in a healthy sample ciliates are expected to predominate as a result of aeration processes, with moderate populations of crawlers and creepers. Only small numbers of other protozoa such as flagellates and amoebae would be expected to be found. However, a mixture of protozoa is important in order to provide a stable environment. For example, if a pollution incident occurred that affected the population of one species another species that could tolerate the adverse conditions would thrive.

The skills to recognize protozoa are in short supply and the protozoa group suffers from a reputation of being hard to identify. In order to facilitate the identification, information and knowledge from taxonomic experts have been captured and incorporated in an information system so that technicians at the sampling points can use a database system to record the details of each sample and identify the species present. The sampling record includes details about the name and location of the sewage works, the specific plant involved, sample date, technician identifier and a description of the sample. A remark may also be added.

Studies of the identification process have shown that there is a degree of subjectivity involved in the identification of the protozoa, and, although trained identifiers are consistent in themselves, there may be some variation between different identifiers. Therefore tracking the technician identifiers is an important requirement. The identification of the protozoa is assisted by a database that includes images of protozoa species, their characteristics and video clips of the different species' behavior, particularly grazing and movement. Each protozoan species has a corresponding line diagram image such as the example shown in Figure 11.9. This component of the system is essentially a training aid and a reference work, since with a little practice technicians soon learn to identify the common species at a

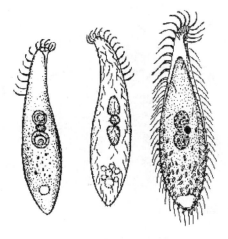

Figure 11.9   Line drawings of the protozoa – Acineria uncinata

glance.

It is important that the resolution of the images and video clips should be as high as possible. The considerable variation in the features present in different kinds of protozoa (see Figure 11.10) can be used to identify samples of the genera. Some protozoa are described as ciliates because of the tiny hair-like projections, called cilia found on their bodies. Other protozoa have "whip-like" projections called flagella that extend from their bodies. The flagella are used for movement and for capture of food. Yet another group, stalked ciliates are organisms that feed on suspended bacterial cells. They can be easily identified because the main body of the organism is attached to a stalk that is usually attached to a floc of bacteria.

Characteristics that can be used in identification include habit, shape and size, the appearance of the nucleus and whether the species has features such as spines, tentacles, cilia and vacuoles. Also important is the appearance of the protozoa body such as whether neck, nose and mouth regions can be recognized. Some characteristics are relatively easy to distinguish while others can be quite difficult and require a high level of skill and experience. Table 11.5 gives a selection of these attributes that can be included in a database for identification purposes.

Protozoa are defined as not being plants, animals, fungi or algae. They are mostly free-living and single celled. There are approximately 65 000 varieties so that identification is challenging. This compares with only 4500 bacteria. Their size varies from 1 to 300 μm, that is from the size of bacteria to the size of a fairly large human cell. However, some exist that are large

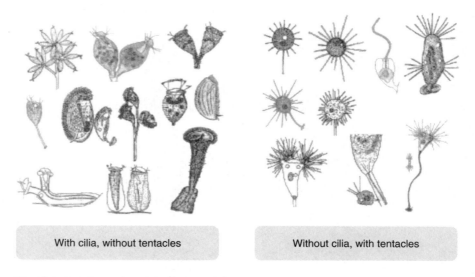

| With cilia, without tentacles | Without cilia, with tentacles |

Figure 11.10   Examples of the Protozoa genera

Table 11.5 Examples of attributes of protozoa used in identification

Attribute	Single/multi-valued	Main categories – Range of values
Anterior truncation	Multi-valued	Transverse; oblique: not truncated
Anterior direction	Multi-valued	Oblique; forward
Anterior beak	Single valued	Present or absent
Somatic cilia	Single valued	Present or absent
Somatic cilia rows	Multi-valued	Longitudinal; transverse; oblique; spiral; not applicable
Contractile vacuole	Single valued	Number in range 1, 2, or more
Habit	Multi-valued	Via tentacles, spine, stalk, body, lorica or not attached
Lorica type	Single valued	Mucilaginous; membranous; not applicable
Body stalk	Single valued	Branched; unbranched; not applicable

enough to see with the naked eye (3–4 mm). This is a very ancient category of life from which fungi, plants and animals arose. Animals can be regarded as modified protozoa.

EXERCISE 11.4

1. Outline the implementation strategy that should be followed in order to set up an image database for this application area.

2. Identify a list of features that would be likely to be most promising for future retrieval purposes.

3. Identify a candidate list of classes using the method set out in Chapter 6 and generate a set of classes in UML notation.

4. Specify a set of relations and object definitions to deliver the core information for the protozoa application.

11.9 Summary of Chapter

The chapter focused on the problems that arise in developing image databases to manipulate and particularly to retrieve image data. The chapter outlined the many different features that could be used to extract association metadata from image objects. There is no magic bullet yet. Most commercial systems use color, texture and shape features but there are a number of interesting possibilities using transforms and moments.

The image metadata will need to be stored in the database as well as the image instances. We also looked at image classification processes and considered the options for query strategies.

SOLUTIONS TO EXERCISES

Exercise 11.1

Most people find this quite frustrating even when using the keywords. However, after a while you may find you have learned to think about the shapes the way the system does and your retrieval success improves. This BLOBWORLD presentation is created by clustering pixels in a joint color–texture–position feature space. The segmentation algorithm is fully automatic and has been run on a collection of 10 000 natural images. An important aspect of the system is that the user is allowed to view the internal representation of the submitted image showing the segments and the query results. Similar systems do not offer the user this view into the workings of the system; consequently, query results from these systems can be inexplicable, despite the availability of means to adjust the similarity metrics.

Exercise 11.2

(a) A feature vector represents a specific property of the image such as its color by a set of numbers which can be acquired for a sample image and matched to others in the database.

(b) A feature space is the space a feature would inhabit defined by its variables that can be used in queries by performing operations such as union, difference and set membership.

(c) A feature map in n-dimensional space is the result of applying n different filters (feature extraction methods) on an image.

(d) A feature is invariant if its value set remains unchanged regardless of the object's scale, orientation and translation.

Exercise 11.3

This is a frustrating experience but it appears to be better at locating reasonable result sets for the face query than the other two options. The system provides a similarity rating for each image in the result set and this may help the user learn to work around the system and understand the kind of images the system regards as "similar".

Exercise 11.4

```
CREATE TYPE anteria_truncated AS VARRAY(3) OF VARCHAR2(15);

CREATE TYPE anteria_direction AS VARRAY(2) OF VARCHAR2(10);

CREATE TYPE somatic_cilia    AS VARRAY(5) OF VARCHAR2(15);

CREATE TYPE habit  AS VARRAY(6) OF VARCHAR2(12);

/* now create the protozoa table using user-defined types

CREATE TABLE protozoa
( protozoa_name VARCHAR2(40) PRIMARY KEY,
family_name    VARCHAR2(40) NOT NULL,
biological_name VARCHAR2(40),
anteria_trunc anteria_truncated,
anteria_d anteria_direction,
anteria_b CHAR(1),
cilia    CHAR(1),
vacoule NUMBER(2),
somatic_cil somatic_cilia,
protozoa_habit habit,
lorica    VARCHAR2(15),
bodystalk VARCHAR2(15),
remark  CLOB DEFAULT EMPTY_CLOB( ),
picture BLOB DEFAULT EMPTY_BLOB( ),
video BFILE )
/
/* create a table to hold the results of the tests for the
samples
CREATE TABLE sample
(
sample_no        CHAR(8) PRIMARY KEY,
protozoa_name    VARCHAR2(25) REFERENCES protozoa,
works_name       VARCHAR2(25) NOT NULL,
location         VARCHAR2(25),
plant            VARCHAR2(50),
technician_number CHAR(4) REFERENCES technician,
description      CLOB DEFAULT EMPTY_CLOB( )
 )
/
```

Recommended Reading

Chang, S. K. (ed.) (1996) *Intelligent Image Databases*, World Scientific.

Dobie, M., Tansley, R., Joyce, D., Weal, M., Lewis, P., Hall, W. (1999) "MAVIS 2: A New Approach to Content and Concept Based Navigation" in *Proceedings of the IEE Colloquium on Multimedia Databases and MPEG-7*. Institution of Electrical Engineers, **99**(056), January, pp. 9/1–9/5.

Eakins, J. P., Graham, M. E. (1999) Content-based image retrieval. Report to JISC Technology Applications Programme.

Flickner, M., Sawhney, H., Niblack, W., Ashley, J., Huan, Q., Dom, B., Gorkhani, M., Hafner, J., Lee, D., Steele, D., Yanker, P. (1995) "Query by image and video content: the QBIC system", *IEEE Computer*, **28**(9), 23–32.

Gong, Y. (1997) *Intelligent Image Databases*, Kluwer.

Gupta, A., Santini, S., Jain, R. (1997) In search of information media. *Communications of the ACM*, **40**(12), 35–42.

Lewis, P., Davis, H., Griffiths, S., Hall, W., Wilkins, R. (1996) "Media-based Navigation with Generic Links" in *Proceedings of the Seventh ACM Conference on Hypertext*, New York, 215–223.

Ma, W. Y., Manjunath, B. S. (1997) "Netra: a toolbox for navigating large image databases", *Proc. IEEE International Conference on Image Processing (ICIP97)*, **1**, 568–571.

Ogle, V. E., Stonebraker, M. (1995) "Chabot: retrieval from a relational database of images", *IEEE Computer*, **28**(9), 40–48.

Pentland, A., *et al.* (1996) "Photobook: tools for content-based manipulation of image databases", *International Journal of Computer Vision*, **18**(3), 233–254.

Robb, R. A. (2000) *Biomedical Imaging, Visualization and Analysis*, Wiley-Liss.

Smith, J., Chang, S. (1997) *Intelligent Multimedia Information Retrieval*, MIT Press, Cambridge, MA.

Srihari, R. K. (1995) "Automatic indexing and content-based retrieval of captioned images", *IEEE Computer*, **28**(9), 49–56.

Stricker, M., Orengo, M. (1995) "Similarity of color images" in *Storage and Retrieval for Image and Video Databases III* (Niblack, W. R. and Jain, R. C., eds) Proc. SPIE 2420, pp. 381–392.

Venters, C. C., Cooper, M. (2000) *Content-Based Image Retrieval*. Technical report JTAP-054, JSIC Technology Application Program.

Computer vision demos:
http://www-2.cs.cmu.edu/~cil/v-demos.html

Information retrieval demo:
http://www.ctr.columbia.edu/~sfchang/demos.html

Image retrieval using regions:
http://elib.cs.berkeley.edu/photos/blobworld/

Dealing with Video Databases

Chapter aims

This chapter looks at the challenges involved in developing multimedia databases for video and audio objects. In this case as well as the challenges of size and semantic content that we have had to address in the earlier chapters on text and image media we need to consider the challenge of managing the real-time nature of video and audio objects. Temporal and spatial attributes will be important. At the end of the chapter and the reader should then be able to understand:

- role of video feature extraction;
- video analysis and segmentation;
- metadata for audio and video objects;
- video classification;
- indexing video media;
- video query process;
- video database applications.

12.1 Introduction

The aim of a video database system is to provide capabilities for storing, retrieving and presenting video information in ways that are comparable with the performance of traditional databases. When video databases were first developed retrieval was based on sequential and time-consuming searches through a whole video. The large size of video objects provides a formidable challenge to database systems. Even when compressed a one-hour video using MPEG compression can require gigabytes of storage. In order to achieve the performance capabilities of traditional DBMSs we need to deploy technologies derived from not only databases but disciplines such as image processing, pattern recognition, data security, networking and human–computer interaction. Videos also differ from the other media we have studied in another respect – they are far more complex. Few videos consist purely of video data. A typical video will have a soundtrack containing music, speech and other sounds, text appearing in the video sequence and possibly *closed-caption text* used to provide subtitles for the hard of hearing.

The field of video data management has advanced rapidly in the last decade. For example, the automatic identification and separation of whole scenes from a video is now possible. Another advance is the ability to automatically extract short video clips representing the key features of much longer sequences, providing users with far more information than still frames could provide. Perhaps even more useful is the query-by-motion example provided by the experimental VideoQ system. This allows users to specify the way an object moves across the screen during a video clip, as well as its color or shape.

Video sequences are an increasingly important form of media data and pose special challenges to database designers and implementers because of their storage and retrieval requirements. Video images are complex and contain a wide range of primitive image types (see Chapter 11) as well as motion vectors. Video objects can take hours to review, while the comparable process for still images takes seconds at most. Therefore the process of video retrieval will contain aspects akin to the abstracting and indexing of long text documents as well as aspects encountered in image retrieval.

12.1.1 Role of Video Feature Extraction

Video can be processed to extract audiovisual features such as:

- image-based features;
- motion-based features;
- object detection and tracking;
- speech recognition;
- speaker identification;
- word spotting;
- audio classification.

12.2 Video Analysis and Segmentation

Even though there are these difficulties video sequences are an increasingly important form of visual data. Several groups of researchers have investigated

Clip			Attributes		
	Clip 1		Index		
			Category		
			Title		
			Date		
			Source		
			Duration		
Scene/story			Theme		
	Story 1	Story *m*	Duration		
			Frame start		
Segment			Frame end		
			Number of shots		
			Event		
			Keywords		
Shot			Theme		
Captured	Shot 1	Shot 2	Duration		
between a			Frame start		
record and		Shot *k*	Frame end		
stop camera			Camera		
operation			Audio level		
Frame			Frame Number		

Figure 12.1 Hierarchy of digital video

ways in which CBR techniques can be adapted for video retrieval. All the approaches start by segmenting the video into small objects. These can be classified as a hierarchy of clips, segments or scenes, shots and frames. A frame corresponds to a single image and the video is a sequence of frames. As shown in Figure 12.1 we refer to a digital video document as a clip that can last from a few seconds to a few hours. It is not efficient to use individual frames as a unit for database management. Segments in contrast serve as retrievable units while in terms of film production a shot is the fundamental unit. A scene consists of a series of shots focused on one event or location. The possible attributes of the video classes are also shown in Figure 12.1

A scene is a sequential collection of shots unified by a common event or locale. A clip can have one or more scenes. We call the process of automatically detecting the transition from one shot to another shot detection. Much research has focused on segmenting video by detecting the boundary between camera shots. A shot may be defined as a sequence of frames captured by a single camera in a single continuous action in time and space, for example two people having a conversation. It may consist of a number of close-up views of their faces interleaved to make the scene. Shots define the low-level syntactic building blocks of a video sequence.

EXERCISE 12.1

Use the information derived in Figure 12.1 to create a class diagram of the video hierarchy in terms of superclass and subclasses. Do not show any operations. Note that it is doubtful whether Frame constitutes an object as it has so few attributes.

There are two types of shot transitions – abrupt and gradual. Shot detection techniques can be classified as two approaches:

- detection on uncompressed or decompressed video;
- direct detection on compressed video.

Since uncompressed video is huge the first approach is computationally expensive. The second approach uses the information in the compressed video to locate shot transitions.

This is much more efficient than dealing with uncompressed video and involves spatially reduced images. As we found in Chapter 2 this could involve motion JPEG and MPEG; however, there are also direct current (DC) images where the image size is reduced 64 times and this is effective for video processing. At this low resolution global image features are still well preserved. Extraction from DC images does not require full decompression and is computationally very efficient. Spatially reduced DC images are useful for what is termed microscopic video browsing. This is when users want fast convenient access to individual shots and frames and at the same time want to conserve bandwidth.

A number of different boundaries can exist between shots. A cut is an abrupt transition between shots that occurs between two adjacent frames. A fade is the gradual changing in brightness either starting or ending with a black frame. A dissolve is similar to a fade except it occurs between two shots, so the frames of the first shot become dimmer and the images of the second shot become brighter until the second replaces the first. Other changes can be wipes or morphing which are computer generated.

In MPEG-encoded video the motion compensation vectors are used as parts of the temporal redundancy encoding and can be easily normalized and used to estimate camera motion. It is worth distinguishing between the different MPEG standards that are significant for video.

MPEG-1 is the standard on which video CD and MP3 are based. It has space-efficient encoding for spatial and temporal domains. MPEG-2 is the standard on which digital television set top boxes and DVD are based. It has space-efficient encoding for spatial and temporal domains and video quality, predictive coding of interleaved video, scalable modes for graceful degradation.

MPEG-4 has the above plus distributed processing and object recognition, abilities to support mobile channels and interactivity. This part will also be a standard of the International Telecommunication Union (ITU-T). It will define how to represent content and also provides interfaces to digital rights management systems. In MPEG-4 audiovisual scenes are composed of several media objects, organized in a hierarchical fashion. At the leaves of the hierarchy, there are primitive media objects, such as:

- still images (e.g. as a fixed background);
- video objects (e.g. a talking person – without the background);
- audio objects (e.g. the voice associated with that person).

A media object in its coded form consists of descriptive elements that allow handling of the object in an audiovisual scene as well as of associated streaming data, if needed. It is important to note that, in its coded form, each media object can be represented independent of its surroundings or background. The coded representation of media objects is as efficient as possible while taking into account functionalities such as error robustness, easy extraction and editing of an object. MPEG-4 opens the way for video manipulation in a way not considered before. For example, one visual object could consist of a person talking; this can be combined with the corresponding voice to form a new compound media object, containing both the aural and the visual components of that talking person. This kind of complex composition opens the way for authors to create complex video objects and individual users to manipulate them.

MPEG-7 is the standard for description and search of audio and visual content to provide support for search and CBR will complement MPEG-4, not replace it. MPEG-21 is the standard to provide an interoperable multimedia framework.

The MPEG-7 standard consists of the following parts:

- MPEG-7 Systems – the format for encoding MPEG-7 descriptions and the terminal architecture;
- MPEG-7 Description Definition Language for defining the description tools;
- MPEG-7 Visual – the description tools dealing with (only) visual descriptions;
- MPEG-7 Audio – the Description Tools dealing with (only) audio descriptions;
- MPEG-7 Multimedia Description Schemes – the Description tools dealing with generic features and multimedia descriptions;
- MPEG-7 Reference Software – a software implementation of relevant parts of MPEG-7;

- MPEG-7 Conformance – guidelines and procedures for testing conformance of MPEG-7 implementations;
- MPEG-7 Extraction and use of descriptions – informative material about the extraction and use of some of the description tools.

Interoperability, which is covered by the new standard MPEG-21, will mean that consumers will be able to use the content and not be faced with incompatible formats, codecs, metadata and so forth. MPEG-21 introduces some new viewpoints to the area of standards. It views the world as consisting of users that interact with digital items. A digital item can be anything from an elemental piece of content (a single picture, a sound track) to a complete collection of audiovisual works. A user can be anyone who deals with a digital item, from producers to vendors to end-users. The intention at present is that all users will be "equal" in MPEG-21, in the sense that they all have their rights and interests in digital items, and they all need to be able to express those. A driving force behind MPEG-21 is the notion that the digital revolution gives every consumer the chance to play new roles in the multimedia supply chain.

A scene is the logical grouping of shots into a semantic unit. A single scene focuses on a certain object or objects of interest but the shots can be from different angles. The segmentation of a video into scenes is a lot more useful than segmentation into shots because end-users visualize a video as a sequence of scenes not shots. Scene boundary detection requires a high-level semantic understanding of the video sequence and such understanding must take cues from such things as the audio track and the encoded data stream itself. Shot boundary detection plays a vital role in any video segmentation as it provides the basic syntactic elements. However, the use of these different shot transitions creates problems for the software.

Methods for shot boundary detection include:

- histogram comparison (see Chapter 11);
- motion vectors;
- edge detection (see Chapter 11);
- macroblock counting;
- combinations of them all.

There is a great deal of temporal redundancy in a video object so what is needed is motion detection. By identifying patterns across a group of frames we can identify the motion of the camera:

- for pans – primary motion will be constrained to horizontal direction;
- for tilts – primary motion will be constrained to vertical direction;
- for zooms – there is a focus of expansion and contraction.

Most of the methods to detect shot boundaries consist of analyzing consecutive frames to decide whether they belong to the same shot. A "running histogram" method can be used to detect gradual as well as abrupt changes. Other methods use information encoded in the compression format to detect shot boundaries, for example the ratio of intracoded (I) and predicted (P) macroblocks in MPEG frames which we looked at in Chapter 2. In general histogram-based approaches have been found to be more successful. One problem is that noise on the video or fast camera change within a shot can cause errors by causing a perceptual change that can be mistaken for a shot boundary. Zooming and panning cause particular difficulties, as do split screen interviews.

One of the problems is that during MPEG compression the order in which the individual video frames are placed in the coded stream is not the original order as illustrated in Figure 12.2. The reconstructed frames are not necessarily in the correct order for display. This leads to delays in encoder–decoder loop while the decoder corrects this – so this could cause a 0.5 second delay which is a long time for interactive purposes. The out-of-order processing can also introduce latency that is unacceptable for video telephony and video conferencing. This also means that if we want to detect shot boundaries in compressed video the methods used need to compensate for this.

Also, at least two layers of video are supported by the MPEG standard – the lower layer and the enhancement layer – spatial scalable extension. MPEG-2 provides scalable extension tools that are designed to support applications beyond that which can be supported by single layer video. Some decoders are more complex and have more capabilities than others. Scaleable video coding enables decoders to decode and display appropriate reproductions of coded video from the same encoded bitstream. In the case of basic scalability, two layers of video referred to as the lower layer and the enhancement layer are allowed. The basic scalability tools offered are: SNR

At the encoder input										
12	3	4	5	6	78	9	10	11	12	13
IB	B	P	B	B	PB	B	I	B	B	P
At the encoder output										
14	2	3	7	5	610	8	9	13	11	12
IP	B	B	P	B	BI	B	B	P	B·	B
At the decoder output										
12	3	4	5	6	78	9	10	11	12	13

Figure 12.2   **Example of frame sequence changes**

scalability, spatial scalability, temporal scalability and data partitioning. From a single video source two spatial-resolution video layers are generated so that the lower layer is coded by itself to provide the basic resolution and the enhancement layer provides spatially interpolated data and carries full spatial resolution of the input video source:

- The SNR scalable extension involves two video layers of the same spatial resolution but different video quality.
- Temporal scalable extension involves generating two video layers so that the lower one is encoded by itself to provide the basic temporal rate and the enhancement layer is coded with temporal prediction with respect to the lower layer. These layers when decoded and temporally multiplexed yield full temporal resolution of the video source.
- The data partitioning extension partitions the video into two parts: one part carries the more critical parts – headers, motion vectors, DC coefficients, the other carries less critical parts.
- Profiles and levels define subsets of the syntax and semantics and the decoder's abilities to decode certain streams.
- Five profiles and four levels are defined in MPEG-2. The resource-intensive bit of the process is the encoder – once encoding is done transmission and decoding are more straightforward.
- MPEG-3 has been dropped because it was intended for HDTV but MPEG-2 at higher rates is good enough for this.
- MPEG-4 is for low bandwidth or low storage capacity environments. It is derived from model-based image coding schemes – knowing what is in the picture and used for up to 64 Kbits/s.

There are a number of approaches to video compression. Intel's digital video interactive (DVI) compression scheme is based on region encoding. Each picture is divided into regions which in turn are split into subregions until the regions can be mapped onto basic shapes to fit the required bandwidth and quality. When transmitted the data includes a description of the region tree and of the shapes at the leaves. This is an asymmetric coding which requires a large amount of processing for encoding and less for decoding. Work is going on into wavelet, vector and fractal compression methods that could deliver high quality video in the future.

12.2.1   Video Segmentation and Object Recognition

Object recognition for faces and people in video is a fundamental aspect of the content description of many classes of scenes. Tracking an object over several frames provides an effective way of recognizing an object. When spatio-temporal segmentation is combined with camera motion estimation this can be used to identify objects, for example to count the number of people or cars in a surveillance application. The structure of a video is difficult to analyze. The structure of a scene deals with the interaction between objects within a scene in both space and time. While the division of scenes into shots has been well investigated, the semantic structure of a scene is much more difficult to deal with. One possibility is to create graphs with shots represented by nodes and transitions as arcs.

It is also possible to determine scene boundaries by using a set of heuristics:

- Sequential shots with a similar color content usually share a common background. The color content of the frames changes much more drastically at the end of a scene. Also, a change of camera angle has no effect on the background colors.
- The audio content is usually quite different in different scenes. The coincidence of an audio cut and a video cut suggests a change of scene.
- Consecutive shots are grouped into a scene if the shots can be identified as representing a dialog.

Video segmentation can also be used to create an object-oriented time-dependent video record. A video record is defined as a sequence that starts with a frame in which a target object appears and ends with the frame containing its disappearance. Each video record has:

- a unique identifier;
- annotation as a label (added manually);
- motion vectors of the objects described by a combination of primitive motions (e.g. rotate right, north).

The motion vectors can be identified as (x,y,t) tuples stored as metadata. The video records can then be used and indexed.

In Figure 12.3 we see a set of sequential frames from the protozoa database application introduced in Chapter 11.

Once a video has been segmented into its basic components it is possible to identify semantically rich events. This helps to identify sequences of frames that are important to abstract. However, for multimedia database systems the features frequently required which are additional to traditional object-oriented approaches are:

- set-oriented access;
- class hierarchy independent of the database schema;
- media-specific features.

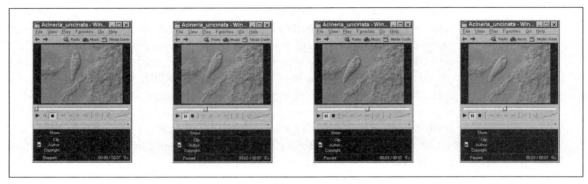

Figure 12.3   Sequence of frames in the protozoa video

An alternative model is provided by VDOM, the video object description model which is created from an entity relationship model. Each video object has a set of attributes (text for keywords, image identifiers).

An algebraic video data model has also been developed that defines a video stream by recursively applying a set of algebraic operations to the raw media data. The model focuses on a presentation which is a combination of video segments. The video operations are:

- create;
- concatenation, union and intersection (based on temporal and spatial conditions);
- output description.

12.3   Storage of Video Objects

When we think of applications such as entertainment, education and training with videos in the form of fragile tape and DVD it is understandable that storing these valuable objects in a database makes sense. However, the large data size of video presents serious problems for data management.

As we discovered in Chapter 8, one of the important design decisions is what type and size of storage media to use. The bandwidth of the storage media has to be weighed against its cost. A single server may include a tape library and RAM modules as well as magnetic and optical disk storage. When we look at the problem of storing a database with a large number of video objects there will be a problem of how to store them as cheaply as possible. Tape systems can be used to store terabytes of video data. Disk arrays can be used to store video data retrieved from tape to deliver to users. A disk array can consist of 1000 disks so that, with a transfer bandwidth of 4 Mbits/s, a

1000 disk system would be large enough to hold three hundred 90-minute MPEG-2 films and support 6500 concurrent users. RAM is used for buffering to ensure smooth playback. Some video objects are likely to be more popular with users than others. A cost-effective design has to take these issues into account to accommodate high demand without increasing the cost of the storage media. A solution would be to store very popular movies in expanded storage with the least popular stored on tape. The customer demand profile must be known or at least guessed. This means there has to be an estimate of the probability of requests for each video. Highly demanded videos are then stored in the storage media with the highest bandwidth. For video on demand the different video objects change during the day. This means that videos have to be swapped from tape to disk daily. A storage manager can act as an interface between the logical and physical database layers.

Even when video objects have been compressed the bandwidth required to deliver the object can still be high – 4–20 Mbits/s is not unusual. Video objects must also be delivered to the user and displayed at a constant rate. Jitter-free playback requires that the video frames should be at the user's machine before playback time. This places critical requirements not only as we have seen already on the network component of the architecture but also on the storage facilities, such as:

- large capacity with hierarchical structure;
- high performance I/O bandwidth for concurrent video streams.

One of the main problems is due to variations in access latencies from the storage component to the network system. This variation arises from both the physical constraints, devices, file systems as well as the operating system components. To manage this variation it is important to coordinate the system components through various scheduling schemes, particularly through resource reservation and using sufficient buffers to absorb latency variation arising from accessing different system components.

For example, a high density CD may hold about 650 Mb, so that in a UNIX system with partitions of maximum size 2 Gb we would find that a video file that was stored on three CD sides would fill a partition. Video and audio files tend to require hundreds of gigobytes while a single DVD can hold 17 Gb. Many operating systems were developed to cope with multiple small files while video applications would involve a very few gigantic files. For these systems when an actual video database is required as opposed to a single video magnetic disk drives are usually combined with jukeboxes of CDs and DVDs for video storage systems. Magnetic disks are characterized by high bandwidth and fast access while CDs have low bandwidth and slow access. In a storage system that combines both there will be a delay as the

CDs are changed. The jukebox storage manager needs to manage the data transfer properly so that the system calculates the total disk change delay and delays the initial playout so that the user will not notice the transitions.

12.4 Disk Scheduling

An important aspect of MMDBMS design is the actual placement of media data on the storage device. Video data needs to be stored in a continuous fashion and retrieved sequentially. Traditional file system data layout strategies do not take the characteristics of video data into account. A popular solution is to use data striping schemes to store video files. A separate processing and routing component then retrieves the video streams for the network. Multimedia data is striped across a set of disks that form the striping unit, not across a network. The server consists of a number of secondary storage devices with a similar performance. Multimedia data is striped in order to support multiple concurrent streams. The number of storage nodes across which an object can be striped has an effect on the number of simultaneous streams that can be supported. The retrieval of large video objects involves the objects being retrieved in rounds but at each round the data that is retrieved must be enough to support continuous presentation of the objects until the next round. The data is fetched by a sequence of service rounds when a stream goes in a round-robin fashion to retrieve B bytes where B is the buffer capacity of the user's workstation. The load is balanced so that the same amount of data is retrieved during service, equally among all disks. The client workstations may be equipped to prefetch data before playback and to support operations such as fast forward.

The strategies of disk striping and parallel placement are frequently implemented with delay-sensitive media such as audio and video. This can provide an uninterrupted service of multiple concurrent streams by giving aggregate bandwidth. The effectiveness of the data striping scheme depends on:

- the number of disks involved;
- the size of the striping unit;
- the consumption rate of each media stream;
- the performance of the disks on key operations such as seek, rotational delay and disk transfer rate.

Data replication can be applied as shown in Figure 12.4. Each disk stores a number of titles and a client who wants to view a title will be assigned to a particular disk for the viewing. Data streams retrieve from one disk only. For popular titles which may have more concurrent viewers than one disk can

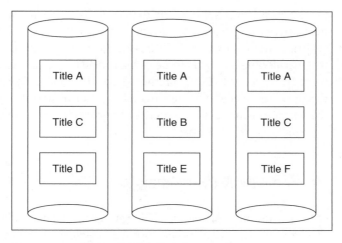

Figure 12.4 Disk striping schedule

satisfy, the title must be replicated onto as many as necessary. In the example shown title A is expected to be very popular and so is replicated on every disk; title C is less popular and is only replicated on two disks. The other titles are not replicated. Another advantage of replication is that a replicated system could economically support cueing and instant restart of paused streams and handle incremental growth by just adding another disk. The disadvantage of the system arises if a title predicted to have low popularity is suddenly accessed by many streams. The bandwidth capacity of the storage device must be sufficient to cope with this sudden increase in demand. Therefore popularity must be closely tracked and predicted. Unfortunately the popularity of a movie changes as the viewer's interest and profile changes in time. Some videos are highly demanded in the morning and others are demanded in the evening. In order to achieve a reasonable service it may be necessary to migrate titles between disks at different points in the day. Thus the cost of distribution will increase but increasing the number of customers will increase revenue. A typical video server can accommodate thousands of video files. In order to have a cost-effective service the video files must be allocated to the right place at the right time. Modeling the variation in customer demand is important in developing the file allocation policies. One way of classifying this is to consider the duration of the video as a measure of the storage required and the demand which is a measure of the number of simultaneous streams requested of the same file. The architecture of a general video server would include memory units, processors as well as a disk system and probably a tape system. So there is a storage hierarchy because the tape library is economic but has low bandwidth while "expanded storage" is expensive but has high bandwidth.

At first glance video on demand may appear one of the simplest of multimedia applications – involving no complex queries or data manipulation. It turns out to be quite complicated. The design and distribution of the media objects needs to be continuously monitored. The user preferences need to be recorded and predicted continuously. The amount of traffic on the network needs to be monitored to determine the service level that can be delivered to the users. The media objects themselves need to be relocated on an almost continuous basis.

12.5 Dealing with Moving Images

One of the main problems with modeling multimedia database systems is the need to deal with the temporal characteristics of much of the data. This means capturing relationships that involve:

- time;
- duration;
- synchronization.

It is much more efficient because of the huge size of video to deal with compressed video. However, in many cases compressed video has to be decompressed before processing. Compressed video processing can be achieved through fast extraction of spatially reduced image sequences from MPEG and Motion-JPEG.

12.5.1 Synchronization

There are several kinds of synchronization that are important for audio–video media as follows:

- *Lip synchronization.* The movement of the lips as seen on the video and the delivery of the audio persuade the viewer that the person is really speaking at that time.
- *Time synchronization.* The specification of time (which could be relative or absolute) is consistent in each stream of each linked media, regardless of the volume of data in the streams.
- *Inter-packet synchronization.* The packets transmitted across a network arrive at the media tools of the receiver for playout in the same order and with the same inter-packet gap as when they were transmitted by the sender. Where more than one stream is being played some kind of inter-stream multiplexing is required to maintain this synchronization.

These factors are particularly important for video conferences when the audio–video samples are being created and immediately transmitted. In order to deal with this effectively we need to deal with the real-time character of audio and video data. This involves synchronization such as:

- Intra-stream synchronization deals with the time structure within a media stream. The MPEG coding scheme specifies the way multiple streams are encapsulated but also how timing information is carried in the stream. In addition, the internet protocol that we considered in Chapter 9, RTP, includes a media-specific timestamp which provides for data being transmitted.

- Inter-stream synchronization deals with streams from different sites. This is usually achieved through a globally synchronized clock. Using NTP, the network time protocol that can operate between computers and continually exchanges messages to monitor clock offsets and network delays, may solve this problem.

- Inter-media synchronization, usually known as lip synchronization, is required. Although it is possible to use NTP to achieve this goal, it is better to encapsulate the media that needs to be synchronized in the same transmission stream. However, this relies on the recipient having the computational power to unravel the streams. Some hardware video codecs use the H221 set of protocols that were devised for ISDN equipment. H221 uses a bit-level framing protocol that is very hard to decode rapidly so that it may lead to jitter if the receiver cannot cope adequately. An alternative approach is to allow the audio decoder and the video decoder to exchange messages inside the receiver to synchronize play-out points. An interesting phenomenon is that a number of play stations can synchronize their own programs perfectly in real time but lose lip synchronization when playing DVD movies. This can be recovered by stopping the DVD momentarily and restarting to allow the clocks to be resynchronized.

In earlier chapters we covered metadata in some detail. In audiovisual media we need to be able to deal effectively with speech and video so that in the following sections we consider them separately.

12.6   Metadata for Speech

Speech media is much more difficult to deal with than image and text data and generally has to use automatic methods for generating content-dependent metadata. Human dialog makes use of mechanisms to facilitate smooth conversation, for example turn taking without frequent interruptions of one speaker by another. Speech recognition techniques are used for the identification of both the speakers and the spoken words. Factors which influence the complexity of the identification problems encountered include:

- isolated words (easier to recognize);
- single speaker (one is easier);
- vocabulary size (smaller is easier);
- grammar (tightly constrained is easier).

Deliberately creating a speech database is rare because at present it is impossible to locate speech information in large audio objects and CBR is not supported in the way we have seen for text or even for image data.

Recently structured metadata summaries have been extracted that include:

- names, places and organizations mentioned in spoken media objects as well as location, date, etc.;
- passages extracted automatically with topic labels.

The principle adopted is to try to impose a document data model on the spoken data object. The content can then be searched in the same way as text media and relevance feedback used. Users can use query by example by providing a coherent "story" and this frees the user from constructing a Boolean search.

The technologies used to achieve this have to be integrated and include:

- large vocabulary speech recognition;
- speaker segmentation;
- speaker clustering;
- speaker identification;
- name spotting;
- topic classification;
- story segmentation.

All these technologies are based on statistical methods and use training data from the domain that has been labeled by marking names, complete stories and topics.

The architecture for such a system is shown in Figure 12.5. The speech media sample is segmented and compressed before storage in the database on the audio server which is capable of streaming large media objects. Before storage, as the data is collected it is also processed by speech recognition

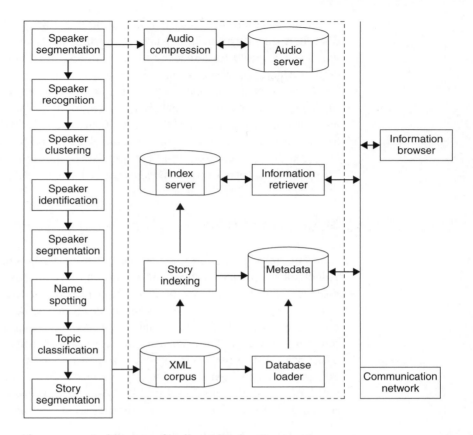

Figure 12.5   Architecture of audio retrieval system

systems, classified by clustering, processed for speaker recognition and segmented into speech stories that are equivalent to the video scenes. The result
of this is text-based metadata that can be treated in much the same way as
described in Chapter 10. The index created is organized around the stories.
Notice that this architecture uses different kinds of servers for the different
media. The data may also be organized using different data models. These
systems are currently in development so it is not clear what is the most
appropriate model.

Other requirements for an effective database system of this type would be:

- sufficiently robust to cope with the variability of spoken language;
- independent of the language used;
- capable of coping with large data sets.

Speech clustering is used to identify all segments from the same speaker and
assign them a unique label. It allows skimming audio by speaker identification.

Story segmentation turns a continuous stream of spoken words into document-like units and assigns a set of topic labels. Sets of four-word intervals are examined to detect for topic changes. Story boundaries are uncovered between regions of topic stability.

These systems involve some technologies that we have not mentioned previously. For example, speech recognition may use continuous-density Hidden Markov models (HMMs) HMMs are a particularly effective way of looking for patterns in one-dimensional data by looking for small changes. One of their celebrated applications is to mapping the genetic code. Probabilistic information retrieval can also use HMMs.

12.7   Metadata for Video

Video has to be processed for extracting the required metadata. This involves video shots, object motions and camera movements. Generating video metadata can be carried out by manual logging or through automatic or semi-automatic methods. This is often based on using a tool called a video parser that can detect any change in the information contained in a sequence of frames. The algorithm needs to capture the information content of a frame. If the metrics exceed a threshold for consecutive frames a shot boundary can be identified. The use of special effects such as dissolve, wipe and fade makes this process difficult because the shot boundary will then be spread over a series of frames. The metrics used include:

- comparison of pixel/blocks in a frame;
- comparison of histograms based on color levels.

Frame characteristics that could be used for metadata would include color histograms, brightness, color, texture and the objects themselves. Individual frames need to be defined using an array data type. In addition the video objects need deliberately mapping to the application domain. This can be done by using domain-specific models such as:

- domain–object relations (DO);
- domain–event relations (DE);
- image objects and relations (IE);
- image representation and relations (IR).

The video parser may have to work on compressed or uncompressed video data. We have noted above the problems that MPEG compression can create. However, it is possible to look for patterns of change. Both camera operations and object motion induce specific patterns. Panning and tilting (horizontal and vertical rotations) of camera angle cause strong motion vectors corresponding to the direction of the camera movement. However, object motion needs to be distinguished from camera motion. This is achieved by dividing the motion field of each frame into a number of blocks and then applying the analysis to each block. If the motion of the blocks agree this is considered to be camera motion, if not then it is concluded it is object motion.

Some video metadata can be captured automatically when a video is created by using a data camera. This will record a time code; camera position and voice annotation of the who–what–where type can be added.

When the video object is a film of an educational product important information appears in the opening sequence in the form of text. This is important to abstract for use in an index.

EXERCISE 12.2

Explain how the different classes of metadata described in Chapter 7 would be used in processing the query for a movie database described by

Show the details of movies where a character said "I am not interested in a semantic argument, I just need the protein".

In the examples in this and earlier chapters we have seen that metadata is essential for query processing of multimedia databases. Wherever possible metadata is generated automatically by setting various criteria. The process of generating the metadata for the various media involves different techniques which exploit the characteristics of the media but are also limited by them. However, all the methods which have been outlined involve similar objectives and strategies. Typically the processes involve

- distinguishing between objects of interest (topics, actors, speakers) and background information of less or no interest (parts-of-speech, image background);
- filtering out the background that adds little real information;
- partitioning the remaining data into subsets of data that are related (classification);
- storing key features that distinguish the subsets.

12.7.1 Indexing Video Media

This is very difficult to carry out automatically. There is no point in indexing the complete video object. What is needed are ways of indexing video clips, segments or scenes. It is difficult to identify attributes for attribute-based retrieval by automatic methods because keywords that could be used for indexing are very difficult to identify for spatial and temporal character-istics of a scene. Annotation is often used for text-based retrieval but this text is too large to index. Video metadata captured automatically by using a data camera has some potential for indexing.

A simple way of indexing once video segmentation has been achieved is to associate each video segment with a representative frame from the segment. These frames are then processed as images using the techniques described in Chapter 11, to create an index. This process involves dividing up the video into individual shots. Normally, the change from one shot to the next involves a sudden change in screen image content and camera angle. As described earlier such changes can be detected automatically through analysis of color histograms, texture and motion vectors from sequences of individual frames. From each shot, a **keyframe** is then selected by analysis of color and texture representing each. A keyframe is an annotated still image. The complete set of keyframes for the video thus forms a storyboard for the video, which can then be manually annotated or stored in a multimedia database for browsing or content-based retrieval. Several commercial vendors, including Excalibur and Virage, now have products automating at least part of the video data management process.

Another approach is to automatically extract short video clips repre-senting the key features of much longer sequences, providing users with far more information than still keyframes can achieve. This enables the users to carry out a process sometimes described as **video skimming**.

As mentioned before video can consist of a number of other media types. The Informedia project at Carnegie-Mellon University (Wactlar *et al.*, 1996) has demonstrated video retrieval when information from video, speech and closed-caption text is combined. The ability to use speech infor-mation to resolve ambiguities in video interpretation (and vice versa) has led to some quite impressive results.

12.8   Manipulating Video Data

In Chapter 11 we introduced the Sewage System case study which featured the protozoa objects. We can store data about the protozoa in the following table:

```
CREATE TABLE protozoa
( protozoa_name VARCHAR2(40) PRIMARY KEY,
family_name  VARCHAR2(40) NOT NULL,
biological_name VARCHAR2(40),
```

```
anteria_trunc anteria_truncated,
anteria_d  anteria_direction,
anteria_b  CHAR(1),
cilia   CHAR(1),
vacoule NUMBER(2),
somatic_cil somatic_cilia,
protozoa_habit habit,
lorica VARCHAR2(15),
bodystalk VARCHAR2(15),
remark CLOB DEFAULT EMPTY_CLOB( ),
picture BLOB DEFAULT EMPTY_BLOB( ),
video BFILE )
```

We add data to the protozoa table using INSERT statements, for example

```
INSERT INTO protozoa
(protozoa_name, family_name, remark, video)
values
('acineria_uncinata', ' acineria',
'Free swimmers are usually found when no large flocs have been
formed. They generally swim faster than flagellates and are
generally more efficient feeders.',
BFILENAME('PHOTO_DIR','acineria_uncinata.mov'))
```

In this case we have used the BFILENAME function to insert the small video file called **acineria_uncinata.mov** which must be already located in the specified directory. However, we could have added the video object by using a PL/SQL procedure, called **prot_blob** as follows:

```
CREATE OR REPLACE PROCEDURE prot_blob_write IS
    Lob_loc     BLOB; - TO HOLD LOB LOCATOR
    proto   VARCHAR2(32767) := '';
    image = acineria_uncinata.jpg
    OFFSET      INTEGER;
BEGIN
    /* Select the LOB: */
        SELECT picture INTO Lob_loc FROM protozoa
            WHERE protozoa_name = 'acineria_uncinata'
        FOR update;
    /*offset and amount parameters always refer to bytes in
BLOBS */

        OFFSET := DBMS_LOB.GETLENGTH(Lob_loc)+2;
        AMOUNT := LENGTH(reftext);
    /* Read data: */
        dbms_lob.write(Lob_loc,amount,offset,reftext);
```

```
          /*    */
          INSERT INTO MESSAGES VALUES (amount,'BLOB added','',offset);
          COMMIT;
       EXCEPTION
          when no_data_found
          then dbms_output.put_line('COPY operation has some
       problems');
       END;
       /
```

12.9 Video Query Process

In Chapter 6 we introduced the OVID database as an example of an object-oriented multimedia database system. In this schema a video object consists of a set of frames and their contents can be described in a dynamic and incremental way. An OVID object can be composed of a multiple of intervals. In OVID a video object would have a definition consisting of:

- an object identifier (OID);
- a set of intervals.

An alternative model is provided by VDOM, the video object description model which is created from an entity relationship model. Each video object has a set of attributes (text for keywords, image identifiers).

An algebraic video data model has also been developed that defines a video stream by recursively applying a set of algebraic operations on the raw media data. The model focuses on a presentation which is a combination of video segments. The video operations are:

- create;
- concatenate, union and intersection (based on temporal and spatial conditions);
- output.

Retrieval from video databases requires the active participation of the user and is potentially more demanding than any of the other media queries we have dealt with. Some video researchers have referred to it as involving "rich interaction" with users because they are required to visualize information by processing the video data.

The video query style is highly interactive because it involves query refinement and includes the following stages:

- finding the desired materials – this selection will depend on the efficiency of search and indexing techniques, the way the data is organized and stored in the database, the volume of data;

- the user's process of information gathering, browsing, understanding and extracting information from a set of candidate clips;
- video composing for special queries;
- delivery of query results – the video DBMS is more likely to be a heterogeneous distributed DBMS and delivery will be an issue.

An essential requirement is to minimize the cost of the retrieval process. The query presentation is likely to involve a combination of the use of keywords as well as visual and audio-based queries. The organization of both the video data and its metadata will facilitate search and indexing performance. The initial stage of the query is likely to use keywords that search the video annotation as in an SQL query. However, this type of query expression is likely to return a very large number of video clips – too many for a user to review manually. Tools need to be available to help the user navigate through a large result set. High-level abstractions of the content of the clips are needed so the user can select segments of interest and from these compose a result video document.

Video visualization and browsing are interesting issues. Both involve extracting and presenting high-level abstractions to users so that they can quickly browse the content of individual clips, navigate from document to document, select segments of interest and compose video documents from various sources without downloading full clips.

Access control is needed to protect the video database from unauthorized access and this is more of an issue than for other multimedia databases. It also has significance if the video objects were stored outside the database as operating system files such as BFILEs in Oracle. Access rights raise the issue at what level of granularity permissions will be granted. It may be necessary to set the access authorization at the data instance level. This technology can involve data encryption and digital watermarking technologies. Figure 12.6 illustrates how these components fit together in the video retrieval system.

A significant problem is presentation to the user because the process inevitably involves the user having to investigate each result in a one-at-time method rather than a set of results at one time. Video abstraction was devised to address this. Some systems distinguish between:

- syntactic browsing (frames and shots) and use DC thumbnails generated directly from the MPEG compressed image;
- semantic browsing (scenes and stories) – a more difficult issue so methods include scene transition graphs based on keyframes.

In Chapter 5 we stated that there were three levels of complexity associated with "what" information can be retrieved from multimedia queries:

- **Level 1** is retrieval of primitive features. In the case of images this involved color, shape, texture, spatial location. Video queries will involve

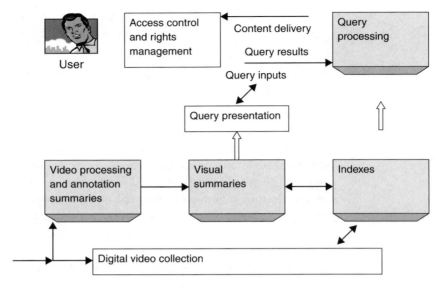

Figure 12.6 Video retrieval system

object movement as well. The query is posed in terms of features such as *"find clips of objects moving from top-right to bottom-left of screen"*.

- **Level 2** is retrieval of logical features related to the identity of the object within the media and for video include named types of action – query example would be *"find a clip of an aeroplane taking off"*.

- **Level 3** is for retrieval of abstract attributes associated with understanding the visual objects that differ little for image or video data: *"find a video clip of geographical disasters"*.

It is apparent from these examples that several factors distinguish multimedia database systems from traditional databases, particularly the size of media objects (large) and the real-time nature of the information content. For media such as video and audio the term real-time is used in a particular sense that there is a sequence of information that must be preserved. Multimedia data introduce different kinds of relationships between data. For example the relationships between the data items may be both spatial and temporal.

Temporal relationships describe:

- when an object should be presented;

- how long an object is presented;

- how one object presentation relates to others (audio with video).

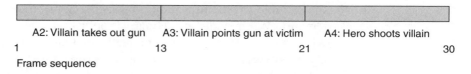

| A2: Villain takes out gun | A3: Villain points gun at victim | A4: Hero shoots villain |

1   13   21   30

Frame sequence

Figure 12.7   Example of identifying a video clip by content

The description of the video object's content is subjective in nature and usually held as metadata. The selection of what content will be needed to be stored also depends on the application area.

For example, when using a video-on-demand application the user may request a video clip from a film which shows fight scenes. There will need to be a way of identifying video clips based on the content. A typical request could be for a "clip with the hero fighting a villain". This is represented diagrammatically in terms of the relevant sequence of frames in Figure 12.7.

The full description of the video clip may also include the characters, background, etc. The designer will need to create a conceptual model based on a set of abstractions of the multimedia data. The conceptual view of the multimedia data will need to include:

- metadata (deals with the content, structure and semantics);
- indexing mechanism (needs to provide fast access to features);
- temporal model (describes time and duration);
- spatial model (representation and layout);
- data model.

As with other types of databases the conceptual data model must capture the essential nature of the data elements and their relationships. In order to use multimedia binary objects as meaningful data, it is necessary to identify their content.

12.10 Video Applications

Video applications tend to fall into two groups:

- information-intensive applications such as news management, in which the content is often in the audio rather than the video;
- data-intensive applications such as inspection systems and surveillance, earth observation, in which domain knowledge is involved in detecting unusual behavior in a static scene and the information is not structured by the user.

An example of an information-intensive application would be video on demand. While video-on-demand applications have limited interaction requirements other video applications require indexing, editing and advanced visualization. In video editing there needs to be the ability to add and remove objects from a scene. A video-on-demand application would have the following requirements:

- objective – to produce high quality synchronized video in order to generate playback at 30 frames per second;
- design – high speed disks with RAID technologies in order to get high volumes of data from storage to the user;
- focused on transmission, storage and delivery;
- additional requirements – admission control to multiple users.

There are two types of approach to video on demand:

- Video-on-demand server architecture delivers video information on a customer-specified schedule. A video stream is dedicated to each customer request.
- Video on schedule limits the customer's control over the video delivery time because the video streams requested by users are delayed for a short period of time.

A video server needs to cope with both approaches and switch between them when demand requires. This means that when the system is loaded the server will switch to video on schedule. If the scheduling interval is 1 minute all the requests made in that time interval will be stored up to receive the same stream so that the maximum wait for any customer is 1 minute. The picture quality of the video files depends on the video compression technology.

The design of the storage component of an MMDBMS cannot be ignored. Factors that need to be considered include:

- using storage hierarchies that can support distributed and heterogeneous databases;
- user access to a wide variety of information, including layered access so that those users with lower quality receivers experience graceful degradation;
- mechanisms to enable quick retrieval;
- staging, clustering and caching methods.

An example of data-intensive applications would be medical specialties such as biplanar angiography used in cardiology where the video would be of an acceptable quality. Video transmission by satellite usually involves such a high level of compression that it is not adequate for many biomedical applications. Advances in "firewire" networks developed for video production could deliver uncompressed video in the future. In addition, the 640 × 480 display provided by standard TV signals is not adequate for the spatial and intensity resolution required for many biomedical images. Even though TV and PC systems provide low cost equipment the quality of the signal network is at present too low for the effective transmission and sharing of biomedical images, which means that telemedicine is only possible in a very limited form.

12.11   Summary of Chapter

In this chapter we considered the challenges facing developers of video and audio databases. We learned how large amounts of audio and video data could be stored and retrieved. We also looked at the problems of browsing and posing queries for this kind of media.

In order to query audiovideo media there must be segmentation and abstraction. It involves expertise from many disciplines. In addition, it may involve many of the technologies that we studied in relation to image and text. Text plays an important role in the content-based retrieval of both video and audio objects.

SOLUTIONS TO EXERCISES

Exercise 12.1

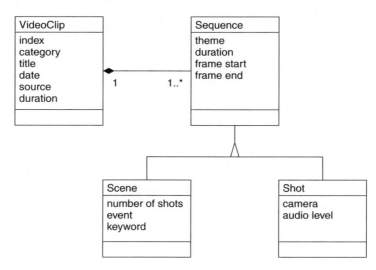

Exercise 12.2

1. Use video preprocessor to select film clips about ordering food, eating.
2. Identify film details from metadata text database.
3. Use text preprocessor to search scripts for topics.
4. Use meta correlation of text and video metadata.
5. Use video metadata to locate video clip.

Recommended Reading

Elmagarmid, A., Jang, H., Helal, A., Joshi, A., Ahmed, M. (1997) *Video Database Systems-Issues, Products and Applications*, Kluwer Academic Publishers.

Kubala, F., Colbath, S., Liu, D., Srivastava, A., Makhoul, J. (2000) Integrated technologies for indexing spoken language. *Communications of the ACM*, **43** (2), 49–56.

appendix **A**

Normalization and Relational Databases

Many of the textbooks on databases listed in the references provide comprehensive accounts of the process of normalization (e.g. Date, 2000; Connolly *et al.*, 1998). These notes are provided merely as a reminder of the theory.

Relational databases must be designed around integrity constraints which result from the nature of the data stored in the database. In addition, each relation in the database must be linked to a key (unique attribute). The data must be normalized, i.e. it must be in first normal form. Breaking down the data into normal forms must also be lossless.

A relation is a table in a database, which consists of a number of columns that represent attributes. Each attribute corresponds to a single column in the relational table. The rows across the table correspond to tuples in the relation. Data can be extracted from the relation by the operations of projection and selection (restriction). Projection selects particular columns (attributes), i.e. it cuts the table vertically. Restriction selects certain tuples only according to a particular condition (predicate), i.e. it extracts data horizontally. The result of these operations will always be another relation. This phenomenon is known as relational closure.

Keys

Candidate Keys

Relational databases use the fundamental concept of candidate keys. A candidate key for a relation is a subset of attributes which always has:

(a) the uniqueness property – no two distinct tuples in the current value of the relation can have the same value;

(b) the irreducibility property – no proper subset of the key has the uniqueness property.

A relation can have a number of candidate keys. A candidate key which involves a single attribute is called a simple key. One which involves more than one attribute is called a composite key.

The irreducibility property allows the integrity constraint to be enforced and foreign keys to operate.

Primary Key

A primary key is the candidate key chosen for a particular relation. The remainder of candidate keys are called alternate keys. Every base relation in the database must have a primary key.

Foreign Keys

A foreign key in a base relation R2 is a subset of the attributes of the relation R2 if there is a relation R1 with a candidate key such that each value of the foreign key in R2 is identical to the value of the candidate key in R1.

Foreign keys can be simple or composite. Foreign keys are sets of values. A foreign key need not be part of the primary key of either relation.

A foreign key represents a reference to a tuple containing the matching candidate key value. A database must not contain any unmatched foreign key values. The foreign key constraints should prevent this happening.

The problem of ensuring that the database does not contain any invalid foreign key values is therefore known as the **referential integrity** problem. The constraint that values of a given foreign key must match values of the corresponding candidate key is known as a referential constraint. The matches represent the relationship between rows in different tables.

Normalization

There are several different normal forms. Normalization is a technique to arrive at a relational model that will not result in anomalous update problems when implemented.

First normal form (1NF)

When a relation is in 1NF it has a primary key and every tuple contains exactly one value for each attribute.

In effect there are no repeating groups and a primary key exists.

Second normal form (2NF)

A relation is in 2NF if and only if all non-key attributes are dependent on all the primary key elements.

Third normal form (3NF)

A relation is in 3NF if and only if it is in 2NF and every non-key attribute is non-transitively dependent on the primary key. This means there can be no dependency between non-key elements.

However, even relations in TNF can have anomalies. Anomalies are unexpected update problems which can cause the integrity of the database to breakdown.

Boyce Codd normal form (BCNF)

This modification was intended to cope with anomalies, which result from functional dependencies (i.e. errors in 2NF). The normal form is intended to deal with the situations where:

- a relation: has two or more candidate keys;
- the candidate keys are composite;
- the candidate keys have at least one attribute in common (overlapping keys).

BCNF is defined as follows: a relation is in BCNF if and only if the only determinants are candidate keys. This should normally prevent anomalous updates so that database designers should aim to achieve a database where all the relations are in BCNF. However, there are a three further three normal forms that could be applied.

Fourth normal form (4NF)

A relation is in 4NF if it is in BCNF and has no multivalued dependencies.

Fifth normal form

5NF covers relations, which if they were split by projection into two would result in information loss, but would be alright if split into three other relations.

Domain key normal form (Fagin, 1981) (DK/NF)

A relation with no anomalies and a relation with no anomalous update problems is in DK/NF.

This is a different approach to normalization based only on domain constraints and keys. A relation is in DK/NF if every constraint on the relation is a logical consequence of the definition of the keys and domains.

A constraint is a rule which can be checked as true or false, e.g. functional and relational dependencies. A relation is in DK/NF if the enforcing key and the domain restrictions cause all the constraints to be met. Unfortunately there is no formal way of producing DK/NF. Designing DK/NF relations is more of an art than a science.

Note

You may have noted that the messages table which we created in Chapter 6 and used in other later chapters was not in fact normalized. It did not have a primary key declared. There is not logical reason for the messages table to exist – it is not part of the database. It is only there to assist in the development of the PL/SQL procedures by receiving data that can be used to check the operation of the procedures which can be quite difficult with multi-media data.

appendix B
Metadata Standards

AAT, TGN, ULAN:

www.gii.getty.edu/vocabulary/index.html

Dublin Core:

http://purl.oclc.org/metadata/dublin_core/

ICOM/CIDOC:
The Group has produced the *International Guidelines for Museum Object Information*

http://www.cidoc.icom.org/guide/

published in June 1995. This is a description of the information categories that can be used when developing records about the objects in museum collections. The *Guidelines* can be adopted by an individual museum, national documentation organization, or system developer, as the basis for a working museum documentation system.

The terminology work includes reviews of terminology resources. The Group has published a *Terminology Control Bibliography* (1990) and a *Directory of Thesauri for Object Names* (1994).

The data model work includes developing a theoretical data model, preparing publications and training workshops concerning the model and advising other projects about the application of the model. The files making up

http://www.cidoc.icom.org/model/relational.model/

itself are available online and in print (updated 1995).

The Group has also issued a *Data modelling bibliography*

http://www.cidoc.icom.org/model/datamodel.bibliog

published in 1994 and compiled by Jacqueline Zak and Linda Kincheloe (Getty Conservation Institute), with the help of Pat Barnett, Janet Goman and George Hickman.

The *Multimedia Group* is concerned with improving communication within the museum community about multimedia technologies and applications, formulating guidelines on the use of multimedia and representing the interests of museums with regard to multimedia. It has published a first public version of *Introduction to Multimedia in Museums:*

http://www.rkd.nl/pblctns/mmwg/home.htm

MARC (Machine Readable Cataloging) data interchange format for bibliographic data:

http://lcweb.loc.gov/marc/
http://www.loc.gov/marc/

[DCT1] type vocabulary:

http://dublincore.org/documents/dcmi-type-vocabulary/

[ISO11179] ISO 11179 – Specification and Standardization of Data Elements, Parts 1–6:

ftp://sdct-sunsrv1.ncsl.nist.gov/x3l8/11179/

[ISO639] ISO 639 – codes for the representation of names of languages:

http://www.oasis-open.org/cover/iso639a.html

[ISO3166] ISO 3166 – codes for the representation of names of countries:

http://www.oasis-open.org/cover/country3166.html

[MIME] Internet media types:

http://www.isi.edu/in-notes/iana/assignments/media-types/media-types

[RFC1766] Tags for the identification of languages, internet RFC 1766:

http://www.ietf.org/rfc/rfc1766.txt

[RFC2396] Uniform resource identifiers (URI), generic syntax, internet RFC 2396:

http://www.ietf.org/rfc/rfc2396.txt

[RFC2413] Dublin Core Metadata for Resource Discovery, internet RFC 2413:

http://www.ietf.org/rfc/rfc2413.txt

ULAN is the Union List of Artist's Names. It is recommended for use in the Creator elements of other standards:

http://www.gii.getty.edu/vocabularly/index.html

The Visual Resources Association (VRA) Core 2.0 is a set of 28 elements designed to describe works of art, architecture and other cultural works. It provides a template specially designed for visual resources collections.

http://www.Oberlin.edu/~art/vra/dsc.html

Uniform resource identifiers (URIs, also known as URLs) are short strings that identify resources in the web: documents, images, downloadable files, services, electronic mailboxes and other resources. They make resources available under a variety of naming schemes and access methods such as HTTP, FTP and internet mail addressable in the same simple way. They reduce the tedium of "log in to this server, then issue this magic command..." down to a single click. It is an extensible technology: there are a number of existing addressing *schemes*, and more may be incorporated over time. See also *A Beginner's Guide to URLs*, available at

http://archive.ncsa.uiuc.edu/demoweb/url-primer.html

- *URI.* Uniform resource identifier. The generic set of all names/addresses that are short strings that refer to resources.
- *URL.* Uniform resource locator. An informal term (no longer used in technical specifications) associated with popular URI schemes: http, ftp, mailto, etc.
- *URN.* Uniform resource name.

SQL Notes

The effects of NULLs are as follows:

1. If one of the columns involved in a value expression is null, the expression (such as price * quantity) evaluates to null. This means there will be no result set from the database and this can be misleading because some data may exist.

2. If an aggregate function is applied to a column, any row containing a null is ignored; thus COUNT only gives you the number of non-null values. This has led to many reported errors from databases.

3. If a comparison uses the comparison operators, <, = , etc. or LIKE, and involves nulls, the outcome is null. Only rows that evaluate to TRUE are included in the result, so null results are omitted. If a null occurs in a comparison that uses BETWEEN, the corresponding row will also be omitted.

4. Nulls in the processing of DISTINCT in a SELECT clause are considered identical.

5. Nulls in a grouping column of a GROUP BY clause are considered equal and are placed in a single separate group.

The way nulls are treated in a query depends on the implementation. All nulls are also considered equal to one another. For example, nulls in a query that contains an ORDER BY clause can be considered either greater than or less than all non-null values, depending on the implementation. This can lead to serious problems in heterogeneous databases where, for example, users may be using SQL to retrieve data from both Oracle and Sybase.

One way of solving some of the main problems with nulls is to use SQL functions to substitute another value. For example, the following row would cause an error with aggregate functions:

```
EMPL EMPLOYEE_NAME        SALARY START_DAT DEPA
---------------------      ----------------------
1001 John Smith                  12-MAY-01 1234
```

The result of the next query will be misleading because, while the AVG and SUM functions will ignore any rows with nulls for the salary, COUNT will include all the rows:

```
SELECT COUNT(employee_number),
SUM(salary)/ COUNT(employee_number), AVG(salary)
FROM employee
```

We can use the NVL function in *Oracle8i* to resolve this by assigning a default value such as 500.00 to any missing salaries:

```
SELECT COUNT(employee_number),
SUM (NVL(salary,500.00))/ COUNT(employee_number), AVG(salary)
FROM employee
```

The NVL function will accept any scalar data type as the second argument.

appendix D
Acronyms

ABR	Attribute-based retrieval.
ALF	Application-layer framing.
API	Application program interface.
ATM	Asynchronous transfer mode.
CBAR	Content-based audio retrieval.
CBIR	Content-based image retrieval.
CBR	Content-based retrieval.
CLI	Call language interface.
CORBA	Common object request broker.
CRM	Client-side reference monitor.
DBA	Database administrator.
DBTG	Data base task group.
DC	Direct current.
DCI	Dublin Core Initiative.
DDBMS	Distributed database management system.
DDL	Description definition language
DLL	Data link layer.
DLO	Document-like-object.
DNS	Domain name system.
DOM	Document object model.
DRDA	IBM's Distributed Relational Database Architecture.
DRM	Digital rights management.
DTD	Document type definition.
FDDI	Fiber-distributed data interface.
FTP (20/21)	File transfer protocol.
GDSS	Group decision support systems.
GIF	Graphics interchange format.
HTML	Hypertext mark-up language.
HTTP	Hypertext transport protocol.
ILP	Integrated layer processing.
ISAKMP/Oakley	Internet Security Association and Key Management Protocol/Oakley.
ISO/IEC 11179	Metadata standard.
JPEG	Joint Photographic Experts Group.
KLT	In computer vision and pattern recognition research PCA is also know as Karhunen–Loeve transform.

KQML	Knowledge Query and Manipulation Language.
LAN	Local area network.
LSI	Latent semantic indexing.
MCF	Meta content format.
MMDBMS	Multimedia database management system.
MPEG	Moving Pictures Experts Group.
NNTP	Network news transfer protocol.
NTP	Network time protocol.
ODRL	Open Digital Rights Language.
OLAP	Online analytical processing.
OSI	Open Systems Interconnection.
P2P	Peer-to-peer.
PCA	Principal components analysis.
PDES	Product data exchange.
PDU	Protocol data unit.
QBE	Query by example.
QDE	Query-directed extraction.
QoS	Quality of service.
RAM	Random access memory.
RDA	Remote data access.
RDF	Resource description framework.
RSS	Rich site summary.
RSVP	Resource reservation protocol.
RTCP	Real-time control protocol.
RTP	Real-time protocol.
SDE	Schema-directed extraction.
SGA	System Global Area (in Oracle).
SGML	Standard generalized mark-up language.
SMIL	Synchronized multimedia integration language.
SMTP	Simple mail transfer protocol.
SNMP	Simple network management protocol.
SRM	Server-side reference monitor.
TBR	Text-based retrieval.
TCP/IP	Transmission control protocol/internet protocol.
TFTP	Trivial file transfer protocol.
TIFF	Tagged image format file.
UCON	Usage control model.
UDP	User datagram protocol.
W3C	World Wide Web Consortium.
WAN	Wide area network.
XML	Extensible mark-up language.
XrML	Extensible rights mark-up language.
XSD	XML schema definition language.

Affordance	Design concept so that objects have an appearance and behavior that suggests to the user how they are intended to be used.
Attribute	A component of an entity or object type that represents a single property of that type.
Bandwidth	Bandwidth is the difference between the minimum and maximum frequencies in the analog signal.
Base table	A table containing stored data values.
Binary large object	A large unstructured data object that could contain text, image, audio or video data.
BLOB	⇨ binary large object.
Boolean search	A search involving a combination of search terms using the Boolean operators AND, OR and NOT.
Built-in data type	Data type used in relational tables such as VARCHAR, INTEGER.
Channel capacity	The number of messages per unit time handled by either a link or a node (system, element).
Class	A method of grouping sets of objects together that have similar attributes and behavior.
Clip	A sequence is made up of contiguous video frames.
Cluster	In Oracle a schema object that contains a group of tables which share one or more common columns (cluster key) that are stored in the same data block.
Codec	Coder/decoders – devices that encode, decode, compress and decompress all together.
Column	A component of a relational table that contains data of the same type.
Compression	The process of abbreviating any repeated information in a data object such as an image and eliminating information that is not required for the application, e.g. difficult for the human eye to see.
Computer vision	A branch of artificial intelligence combined with image processing. Concerned with computer processing of images from the real world.

Conceptual data model A formal representation of the properties of the data that a database should contain which is independent of the implementation of that data's representation and defines the domain of discourse for the database users.

Constraint A rule applied to a table or a column within a table that restricts the nature of the data that can be held in any row of the table.

Constructor method A system-generated method for each object type that creates an instance of the object.

Database A collection of data sharable between applications.

Datagram A general term for a packet of data.

Data model It is an abstract, logical definition of objects and operations that allow us to model the structure and behavior of the data.

Data type A set of values and the permitted operations on those values.

DBMS A system designed to administer and control one or more databases and to manage the storage and retrieval of data in the databases. Usually offering security, integrity, concurrency and recovery management.

Derived data Data which is generated (derived) from the processing of other data.

Derived table A table with values which are generated from a base table (and other derived tables) when required.

DML Data Manipulation Language which supports the manipulation or processing of database objects.

Domain A named set of values, with a common meaning, from which one or more attributes draw their actual values.

Domain of discourse The context in which information is used by a group or individuals.

Domain ontology A domain ontology is an ontology encoding the semantics of a specific logical application area (⇨ ontology).

Entity An entity represents a thing that has meaning in a given domain of discourse and about which there is a need to record data.

Entity–relationship modeling A representation of data and associations between them which is effective in displaying important elements of a conceptual data model.

Entity type A description of the properties common to a collection of entities.

Euclidean distance Used to measure the distance between two points in three-dimensional space.

Feature A characteristic of media data that can be extracted by a systematic process, also called a filter.

Feature extraction The use of one or more transformations of the input features to produce more expressive features.

Feature space A feature space is the space a feature would inhabit defined by its variables that can be used in queries by performing operations such as union, difference and set membership.

Feature vector	A feature vector represents a specific property of the image such as its color by a set of numbers which can be acquired for a sample image and matched to others in the database.
Foreign key	A column or columns in a table that reference specified candidate key column(s) in another table.
Frame	A frame is the term used for encapsulated network layer packets of the OSI reference model. A frame is also a single image in a video segment.
Function	A stored module that may accept one or more arguments and returns a value.
Fuzzy clustering	A procedure that assigns each input pattern a fractional degree of membership to each output cluster.
Grant	An SQL statement that lists the privileges on a table, view or persistent stored module.
Hard clustering	Attaches a label to each pattern identifying its class.
Host language	A conventional programming language which is extended to allow DML statements to be embedded within it.
Identifier	An attribute or minimal collection of attributes of an entity type which serve to uniquely identify specific instances of entities within the entity type; the attributes have values which are unique to a specific entity within that type.
Image processing	This is the effective processing and analyzing of images in order to faithfully extract the information of use in manipulating and transforming the image.
Index	A data structure offering the means of associating a symbol in a collection with the location of every occurrence of the symbol in that collection.
Information	Knowledge exchanged among people, machines and processes that has meaning in some agreed context.
Information system	A computer system with the primary purpose of supporting the information requirements of its users.
Instance	An occurrence of a class in UML.
Integrity	Ensuring that the contents of a database are meaningful within the domain of discourse, that the content can be trusted to be consistent and not to be corrupt.
Logical data independence	Independence between logical and external schema so that changes to the logical schema do not require changes to the external schema.
Logical schema	The schema concerned with the logical properties, constraints and structure of data in a database which is independent of its actual storage or the way in which it is accessed by applications and user processes; each database has a single logical schema.

Lossless compression	A type of compression in which the resulting data can be decompressed in such a way that none of the original information is lost.
Lossy compression	A type of compression in which some information is lost by the process.
Mahalanobis distance	This is a variant of Euclidean distance used in clustering techniques to measure the distance (similarity) between clusters.
Medial axes	Exploited in a technique to enable an object to be represented as a simple geometrical shape that is defined by the shape of the original object.
Meta correlation	This describes the process when metadata about different kinds of media data (e.g. text and image) have to be correlated to provide a unified picture of the multimedia database.
Metadata	Data about data.
Multimedia data	A range of different types of media from text, usually in the form of documents, image, audio or video.
Nested table	The storage table contains each value for each nested table in a nested table column. Each value occupies one row in the storage table.
Normalizing data	This has two meanings: in database design it is the process of producing relational tables; in information retrieval it means adjusting all the data in a column to a standard distribution so that columns that contain large numeric values do not swamp columns which contain small values.
Object	An instance of a class defined in UML.
Object database	A database based on a model of data in which data is defined as objects and organized and manipulated within an object-oriented program.
Object row	A row in an object table.
Object table	A table produced from an object type definition.
Object type	The specification given to a user-defined type. Object types can contain other object types.
Object view	The definition of an object view is based on a query so that data stored in a relational table is formatted into an object instance.
Ontology	A set of semantic concepts of knowledge interconnected by patterns of association that are consistent with a set of knowledge representation rules.
Packet	This is a generic term used to describe a unit of data at any layer of the OSI reference model.
Pattern	A pattern is a single data item used by a clustering algorithm that represents a vector of measurements.
Persistent data	Data which exists independent of its associated application programs.

Physical data independence	Independence between logical and storage schema so that changes to the storage schema do not require changes to the logical schema.
Physical schema	⇨ storage schema.
Pixels	The individual elements in two-dimensional digital images are referred to as picture elements. Pixel is an abbreviation.
Port	A port is an abstraction to allow transport protocols such as UDP and TCP the capability of handling communications between multiple hosts. Also called a socket.
Precision	This is a measure of how well the engine performs in not returning irrelevant documents.
Project	An operation on a relational table that selects certain columns.
Protocol	A set of rules that govern a communication between entities.
Quality of service	Standard of service a node receives from a network which is usually "best-effort" on the internet in terms of delay and reliability.
Query	A means of specifying the criteria for searching a database.
Query language	A user-focused language intended to permit a user to directly enter statements to be executed by the DBMS.
Relational database	A database with a structure defined by relational theory; data appears to be stored in tables and is manipulated according to a set of well-defined operators.
Relationship	An association between entities that has meaning within a domain of discourse and which needs to be recorded.
Relevance feedback	This involves allowing media objects such as images or documents retrieved by the first stage of a query process as terms to form the next stage in the query.
Scalability	The ability of a database system to handle increasingly large quantities of data and/or users without significant redesign of the database technology.
Schema	A specification of all the properties of the data to be held in a database which is expressed independently of a specific DBMS and specific user processes.
Segment	Video segment is used for any contiguous portion of a clip. Segment is also the term that is used to describe the data that is transmitted and received at the transport level of the OSI model.
Semantics	The study of meaning.
Session	This is a collection of communication exchanges which together make up a single overall identifiable task.
Shot	Shots define the low-level syntactic building blocks of a video sequence. A shot may be defined as a sequence of frames captured by a single camera in a single continuous action in time and space.
Snapshot	A copy of one or more tables. Sometimes from a *master* site to a *remote* site. They may be refreshed periodically.

SQL   Structured Query Language; a standard relational database query language.

Storage schema   The schema which specifies the physical storage of data in a database and how access to that data is achieved, for example with indexing; each database has a single storage schema. (Note: some forms of distributed database may have more than one storage schema.)

Streaming   Streaming is a technique for transferring data so that it can be processed as a steady and continuous stream.

Table   Structural organization of relational theory; tables can be broken down into rows and columns.

Tablespace   A collection of one or more data files. All database objects in Oracle are stored in tablespaces, typically holding a single table.

Text database   A database in which the data is structured as written sentences, paragraphs, documents, etc. without additional imposed structure or encoding.

Transaction   A series of updates to a database which together represent a single consistent unit of work.

Trigger   A stored routine that is executed when a specific operation occurs on a specific table, for example an insert.

Universe of discourse   ⇨ domain of discourse.

User-defined data type A data type that is defined by the user that is a combination of other built-in types or user-defined types.

User process   A mechanism to allow a user to access a database – such as an application program or a database tool.

User view   The selection and appearance of data in a database as presented to a specific user. Alternative ways of displaying and examining subsets of data in a database.

Varray   In Oracle a repeating set of columns within an object column.

Voxel   An abbreviation for volume picture elements – individual elements in three-dimensional images corresponding to pixels.

View or view(ed) table A derived table with a stored definition.

References

Source Bibliography

Baddeley, A.D. (1999) *Essentials of Human Memory*, Psychological Press, Hove.

Baker, T. (2000) *A Grammar of Dublin Core*. GMD-German National Research Centre for Information Technology Scientific Library and Publication Services, Schloss Birlinghoven, Germany.

Blaha, M., Premerlani, W. (1997) *Object-Oriented Modeling and Design for Database Applications*, Prentice-Hall, Englewood Cliffs, NJ.

Bertino, E., Martino, L. (1993) *Object-Oriented Database Systems – Concepts and Architectures*, Addison-Wesley, Reading, MA.

Bobak, A.R. (1996) *Distributed and Multi-Database Systems*, Artech House.

Boll, A., Klas, W., Seth, A. (1998) *Multimedia Data Management*. http.//www.informatik.uni-ulm.dc/dbis/mmbook/ChapterOne/ChapterOne.ps. *Using metadata to integrate and apply digital media*, pp. 1–24.

Britton, C., Doake, J. (2000) *Object-Oriented Systems Development*, McGraw-Hill.

Bunge, M.A. (1979) *Treatise on Basic Philosophy*, Vols 3 and 4, Reidel, Dordrecht, The Netherlands.

Burleson, D.K. (1994) *Managing Distributed Databases*, Wiley-QED.

Chang, B., Scardina, M., Karun, K., Kiritzov, S., Macky, I., Ramakrishnan, N.L. (2000) *Oracle XML Handbook*.

Chang, S.K. (ed.) (1996) *Intelligent Image Databases*, World Scientific, Singapore.

Chatfield, C., Collins, A.J. (1995) Multivariate distributions. In *Introduction to Multivariate Analysis*, Chapman and Hall, London, pp. 19–33.

Chen, C. (1999) *Information Visualisation and Virtual Environments*, Springer.

Cichoki, A., Unbenhauen, R. (1993) *Neural Networks for Optimisation and Signal Processing*, Wiley, New York.

CODASYL Database Task Group Report (1971) ACM, New York, April 1971.

Connolly, T., Begg, C., Strachan, A. (1997) *Database Systems*, 2nd edition, Addison-Wesley.

Crowcroft, J., Handley, M., Wakeman, I. (1999) *Internetworking Multimedia*, Morgan Kaufmann, San Francisco, CA.

Date, C.J. (2000) *An Introduction to Database Systems*, 7th edition, Addison-Wesley.

Date, C.J., with Darwen, H. (1997) *A Guide to the SQL Standard*, 4th edition, Addison-Wesley.

Date, C.J., Darwen, H. (1998) *Foundation for Object/Relational Databases: The Third Manifesto*, Addison-Wesley.

Dobie, M., Tansley, R., Joyce, D., Weal, M., Lewis, P., Hall, W. (1999) MAVIS 2: A New Approach to Content and Concept Based Navigation in Proceedings of the IEE Colloquium on Multimedia Databases and MPEG-7. Institution of Electrical Engineers. 99(056), January, pp. 9/1–9/5.

Dye, C. (1999) *Oracle Distributed Systems*, O'Reilly.

Edwards, J., Orfali, R. (1999) *3-Tier Client/Server at Work*, Wiley.

Elmagarmid, A., Jiang, H., Helal, A., Joshi, A., Ahmed, M. (1997) *Video Database Systems – Issues, Products and Applications*. Kluwer Academic Publishers.

Elmagarmid, A., Rusinekiewicz, Sheth, A., (1998) *Management of Heterogeneous and Autonomous Database Systems*, Morgan Kaufmann, San Francisco, CA.

Embley, D.W. (1998) *Object Database Development: Concepts and Principles*, Addison-Wesley Longman.

Fluckiger, F. (1995) *Understanding Networked Multimedia*, Prentice-Hall, London.

Furht, B. (1998) *Multimedia Technologies and Applications for the 21st Century*, Kluwer Academic Publishers.

Goldfarb, C., Prescod, P. (2001) *The XML Handbook*, 4th edition, Prentice Hall PTR.

Gong, Y. (1997) *Intelligent Image Databases*, Kluwer, Dordrecht.

Gupta, A., Santini, S., Jain, R. (1997) *In Search of Information Media Communications of the ACM*, 40(12) 35–42.

Heinckiens, P.M. (1998) *Building Scalable Database Applications. Object-Oriented Design, Architectures and Implementations*, Addison-Wesley.

Hoffman, D.D. (1998) *Visual Intelligence*, Norton, New York.

Howard, P., Hailstone, R., Versant, J. (1996) *Distributed and Multi-Database Systems*, Artech House.

Jacobsen, I. (1992) *Object-Oriented Software Engineering*, Addison-Wesley.

Jain, A.K., Dubes, R.C. (1988) *Algorithms for Clustering Data*, Prentice-Hall Advanced Reference Series, Prentice-Hall, Inc. New York.

Khoshafian, S., Brad Baker, A. (1995) *Multi-Media and Imaging Databases*, Morgan Kauffman.

Lewis, J. (2001) *Practical Oracle8i. Building Efficient Databases*, Addison-Wesley.

Lewis, P., Davis, H., Griffiths, S., Hall, W., Wilkins, R. (1996) Media-based Navigation with Generic Links, in *Proceedings of the Seventh ACM Conference on Hypertext*, New York, 215–223.

Linthicum, D. (2001) *B2B Application Integration*, Addison-Wesley.

Loney, K., Kock, G. (2000) *Oracle8i. The Complete Reference*, Oracle Press, Osbourne/McGraw-Hill.

Masunga, Y., Spaccapietra, S. (2000) *Advances in Multimedia and Databases for the New Century: A Swiss/Japanese Perspective*, World Scientific, Singapore.

McCullough-Dieter, C. with Prem, J., Chandak, R., Chandak, P. (1998) *Oracle8 Bible*, IDG Books Worldwide.

Naiburg, E.J., Maksimchuk, R.A. (2001) *UML for Database Design*, Addison-Wesley.

Ozsu, M.T., Valderiez (1999) *Principles of Distributed Database Systems*, 2nd edition, Prentice-Hall, Englewood Cliffs, NJ.

Perry, B., Chang, S.-K., Dinsmore, J., Doermann, D., Rosenfield, A., Stevens, S. (1999) *Content-Based Access to Multimedia Information*, Kluwer, Dordrecht.

Preece, J., Rogers, Y., Sharp, H. (2002) *Interaction Design*, Wiley.

Robb, R.A. (2000) *Biomedical Imaging, Visualization and Analysis*, Wiley-Liss.

Schaübe, P. (1997) *Multimedia Information Retrieval: Content-Based Information Retrieval from Large Text and Audio Databases*, Kluwer International Series in Engineering.

Serain, D., Craig, I. (1999) *Middleware*, Springer, Berlin and Heidelberg.

Smith, A. (1997) *Human Computer Factors*, McGraw-Hill, Maidenhead.

Stevens, P., Pooley, R. (2000) *Using UML*, Addison-Wesley.

Stonebraker, M., with Moore, D. (1998) *Object-Relational Dbms: Tracking the Next Great Wave*, Morgan Kaufmann, San Francisco, CA.

Stricker, M., Orengo, M. (1995) Similarity of Color Images, in *Storage and Retrieval for Image and Video Databases III* (Niblack, W.R. and Jain, R.C., eds) Proc. SPIE 2420 pp. 381–392.

Subrahmanian, V.S. (1997) *Principles of Multimedia Database Management Systems*, Morgan Kaufmann, San Francisco, CA.

Van Rijsbergen, C. (1979) *Information Retrieval*, London: Butterworths.

Van Rijsbergen, C. (ed.) (1998) *Information Retrieval: Uncertainty and Logics*, Kluwer, Dordrecht.

Vince, J. (1995) *Virtual Reality Systems*, ACM SIGGRAPH Series, Addison-Wesley.

Wijegunaratne, I., Fernandez, G. (1998) *Distributed Application Development*, Springer, Berlin and Heidelberg.

Won, K. (ed.) (1994) *Modern Database Systems: The Object Model, Interoperability and Beyond*, Addison-Wesley.

Research Papers

Adjei, O.N. (1996) The use of the Radon transforms and neural networks in image recognition. PhD thesis, Cranfield University.

Atkinson, M. (1990) The object oriented database system manifesto. In Proc. 1st Int. Conf. on Deductive and Object-Oriented Databases, Elsevier.

Atkinson, R.C., Shiffrin, R.M. (1968) Human memory a proposed system and its control processes. In *The Psychology of Learning and Motivation: Advances and Theory*, (eds K.W. Spence and J.T. Spence), Vol. 2, Academic Press, New York.

Bertino, E., Catania, B., Chiesa, L. (1998) Definition and analysis of index organizations for object-oriented database systems. *Information Systems*, **23**(2), 65–108.

Blackburn, C., Dunckley, L. (1995) The applications of Voronoi tessellations in the development of 3D stochastic models to represent tumour growth. *Zeitschrift für Angewandt Mathematik und Mechanik*, Journal no. 4.

Blum, H. (1967) A transformation for extracting new descriptors of shape in *Models for the perception of speech and visual forms*. W. Wathen-Dunn (editor), MIT Press pp. 362–380.

Borland, P., Ingwerson, P. (1997) The development of a method for the evaluation of interactive information retrieval systems. *Journal of Documentation*, **53**(3), 225–250.

Carson, C.S., *et al.* (1997) Region-based image querying. In *Proceedings of IEEE Workshop on Content-Based Access of Image and Video Libraries*, San Juan, Puerto Rico, pp. 42–49.

Corridoni, J.M., *et al.* (1998) Image retrieval by color semantics with incomplete knowledge. *Journal of the American Society for Information Science*, **49**(3), 267–282.

Cranefield, S. (2001) Networked knowledge representation and exchange using UML and RDF. *Journal of Digital Information*, **1**(8).

Damashek, M. (1995) Gauging similarity with n-grams: language-independent categorization of text. *Science*, **267**(5199), 843–848.

Darmont, J., Gruenwald, L. (1996) A comparison study of object-oriented database clustering techniques. *Information Sciences*, **94**(1–4), 55–86.

Darwen, H., Date, C.J. (2000) Temporal database systems. In *Advanced Database Technology and Design* (eds M. Piattini and O. Diaz), Artech House, Boston, MA.

Deutsch, D. (1995) Objects and SQL: strange relations? In SIGMOD'95, ACM, p. 466.

Dickinson, S., *et al.* (1998) Viewpoint-invariant indexing for content-based image retrieval. In *IEEE International Workshop on Content-Based Access of Image and Video Databases (CAIVD'98)*, Bombay, India, pp. 20–30.

Dumais, S.T. (1991) Improving the retrieval of information from external sources. *Behavior Research Methods, Instruments and Computers*, **23**, 229–236.

Eakins, J.P., Graham, M.E. (1999) Content-based image retrieval. Report to JISC Technology Applications Programme.

Fagin, R. (1981) A normal form for relational databases that is based on domains and keys. Transactions in Database Systems, **6**(3) September.

Formica, A., Groger, H.D., Missikoff, M. (1999) An efficient method for checking object-oriented database schema correctness. *ACM Tans. on Database Systems*, **23**(3), 333–369.

Fuhr, N., Van Rijsbergen, C.J., Smeaton, A.F., (eds) (1997) *Evaluation of Multimedia Information Retrieval*, Dagstuhl Seminar Report 175, Schloss Dagstuhl, April 1997.

Gong, Y. (1997) *Intelligent Image Databases*, Kluwer, Dordrecht.

Gupta, A., Santini, S., Jain, R. (1997) In search of information media. *Communications of the ACM*, **40**(12), 35–42.

Hines, M.L. (1998) Conceptual object-oriented database: a theoretical model. *Information Sciences*, **105**(1–4), 31–68.

Hobbs, J., Appelt, D., Bear, J., Israel, D., Kameyama, M., Stickel, M., Tyson, M. (1996) Fastus: a cascading finite-state transducer for extracting information from natural language text. In Finite State Devices for Natural Language Processing.

Iren, S., Amer, P.D., Conrad, P.T. (1999) The transport layer: tutorial and survey. *ACM Computing Surveys*, **31**(4), 361–394.

Jain, A.K., Murty, M.N., Flynn, P.J. (1999) Data clustering: a review. *ACM Computer Surveys*, **31**(3), 265–297.

Jin, J.S., Kurniawati, R., Xu, G. (1996) A scheme for intelligent image retrieval in multimedia databases. *Journal of Visual Communication and Image Representation*, **7**(4), 369–377.

Kato, T. and Kurita, T. (1990) Visual interaction with the Electronic Art Gallery. In *Database and Expert Systems Applications: Proceedings on an International Conference*, 234–240.

Kolasinski, E.M. (1995) Simulator sickness in virtual environments. Technical Report 1027, US Army Research Institute for the Behavioral and Social Sciences, Alexandria, VA.

Kornatzky, Y., Shoval, P. (1995) Conceptual design of object-oriented database schemas using the binary-relationship model. *Data and Knowledge Engineering*, **14**(3), 265–288.

Kubala, F., Colbath, S., Liu, D., Srivastava, A., Makhoul, J. (2000) Integrated technologies for indexing spoken language. *Communications of the ACM*, **43**(2), 49–55.

Letsche, T.A., Berry, M.W. (1997) Large-scale information retrieval and latent semantic indexing. *Information Science*, **100**, 105–137.

Lienhart, R., Pfeiffer, S., Effelsberg, W. (1997) Video abstracting. *Communications of the ACM*, **40**(12), 55–63.

Lindsay, P.H., Norman, D.A. (1977) *Human Information Processing: An introduction to Psychology*, 2nd edition, Academic Press, New York.

Liu, F., Picard, R.W. (1996) Periodicity, directionality and randomness: World features for image modelling and retrieval. *IEEE Transactions on Pattern Analysis and Machine Intelligence*, **18**(7), 722–733.

Manjunath, B.S., Ma, W.Y. (1996) Texture features for browsing and retrieval of large image data. *IEEE Transactions on Pattern Analysis and Machine Intelligence*, **18**, 837–842.

McAuliffe, M.J., Eberley, D.F., Daniel, S., Chaney, E.L., Pizer, S.M. (1996) Scale-space boundary evolution initialised by cores. *Visualization in Biomedical Computing*, Journal no. 1131, 173–182.

McKeown, D.W., Saiedian, H. (1997) Triggers for object-oriented database systems. *Journal of Object-Oriented Programming*, **10**(2), 15–21.

Miller, G.A. (1956) The magic number seven, plus or minus two: some limits on our capacity to process information. *Psychological Review*, **63**(2), 81–97.

Norman, D.A. (1986), Cognitive engineering. In *User Centered Systems Design: New Perspectives on Human–Computer Interaction* (eds D.A. Norman and S.W. Draper). Lawrence Erlbaum Associates, Hillsdale, New Jersey.

Parr, G., Curran, K. (2000) A paradigm shift in the distribution of multimedia. *Communications of the ACM*, **43**(6), 103–109.

Pejtersen, A.M. (1996) Empirical work place evaluation of complex systems. In Proc. 1st Int. Conf. on Applied Ergonomics (ICAE'96), Istanbul, Turkey, May 1996, pp. 21–24.

Permerani, W.J., Blaha, M.R., Rumbaugh, J.E., Varwig, T.A. (1990) An object oriented relational database. *Communications of the ACM*, **33**(11), 99–109.

Peters, R.J., Ozsu, M.T. (1997) An axiomatic model of dynamic schema evolution in objectbase systems. *ACM Tansactions on Database Systems*, **22**(1), 75–114.

Rasmussen, J., Pejtersen, A.M., Goodstein, L.P. (1994) *Cognitive Systems Engineering*, Wiley, New York.

Ravela, S., Manmatha, R. (1998) Retrieving images by appearance. In *Proc. IEEE Int. Conf. on Computer Vision (IICV98)*, Bombay, India, pp. 608–613.

Sanderson, P., Pipingas, A., Danieli, F., Silberstein, R. (1999) Neural imaging and dynamic display design: What can we learn? In Proc. 43rd Annual Meet. of the Human Factors and Ergonomics Society, Houston, TX, 27 September – 1 October.

Saracevic, T. (1975) Relevance: a review and a framework for the thinking on the notion in information science. *Journal of the American Society of Information Science*, **26**, 321–343.

Savnik, I., Tari, Z., Mohoric, T. (1999) QAL: a query algebra of complex objects. *Data and Knowledge Engineering*, **30**(1), pp. 57–94.

Seiter, L.M., Palsberg, J., Lieberherr, K.J. (1996) Evolution of object behaviour using context relations. In SIGSOFT'96, ACM, pp. 46–57.

Seshadri, P. (1998) Enhanced abstract data types in object-relational databases. *VLDB Journal*, **7**(3), pp. 130–140.

Shaw, E.A.G. (1974) The external ear. In *Handbook of Sensory Physiology* (eds W.D. Keidel and W.D. Neff), Springer, New York.

Stricker, M., Dimai, A. (1996) Color indexing with weak spatial constraints. In *Storage and Retrieval for Image and Video Databases IV*, (eds I.K. Sethi and R.C. Jain), *Proceedings of SPIE*, **2670**, 29–40.

Srihari, R.K. (1995) Automatic indexing and content-based retrieval of captioned images. *IEEE Computer*, **28**(9), 49–56.

Swain, M.J., Ballard, D.H. (1991) Color indexing. *International Journal of Computer Vision*, **7**(1), 11–32.

Tamura, H., *et al.* (1978) Textural features corresponding to visual perception. *IEEE Transactions on Systems, Man and Cybernetics*, **8**(6), 460–472.

Tari, Z., Stokes, J., Spaccapietra, S. (1997) Object normal forms and dependency constraints for object-oriented schemata. *ACM Tansactions on Database Systems*, **22**(4), 513–569.

Tootell, R.B.H., Dale, A.M., Sereno, M.I., Malach, R. (1996) New images from human visual cortex. *Trends in Neuroscience*, **19**(11), 481–489.

Venters, C.C., Cooper, M. (2000) *Content-Based Image Retrieval*. Technical report JTAP-054, JSIC Technology Application Program.

Wactlar, H., Kanade, T., Smith, M., Stevens, S. (1996) Intelligent access to digital video: Infomedia project. *IEEE Computer*, Journal no. 4, Volume 2.

Waltz, T.J., Yen, D., Lee, S. (1995) Object-oriented database systems: an implementation plan. *Industrial Management and Data Systems*. **95**(6), 8–17.

Witter, D.I, Berry, M.W. (1998) Downdating the latent semantic indexing model for conceptual information retrieval. *Computer Journal*, **41**(8), 589–601.

Yeo, B.-L., Yeung, M.M. (1997) Retrieving and visualizing video. *Communications of the ACM*. **40**(12), 43–54.

Websites

Brain map movies can be found at http://cogsci.ucsd.edu/~sereno/movies.html

The International Organisation for Standardisation is at http://www.iso.ch

The World Wide Web Consortium is at http://www.w3.org

Index